Consolidated Dismissal, Redundancy and Employee Consultation Legislation

Consolidated Dismissal, Redundancy and Employee Consultation Legislation

Edited by
Dr. Gavin Barrett

CLARUS
PRESS

Published by
Clarus Press Ltd,
Griffith Campus,
South Circular Road,
Dublin 8.

Typeset by
Datapage International Limited,
18 Docklands Innovation Park,
East Wall Road,
Dublin 3.

Printed by
MPG Books Ltd
Victoria Square, Bodmin, Cornwall.

ISBN
10 Digit No.
1-905536-05-4

13 Digit No.
978-1-905536-05-4

PREFACE

The aim of this book has been to present all those with an interest in Irish employment law with a user-friendly, up-to-date and consolidated version of the very considerable volume of statute law relating to redundancy, dismissal and employee consultation law in Ireland, in addition to a consolidated collection of the important statutory instruments in this field. The initial work on this volume was done several years ago during a much earlier period of research. Of the more recent work, much was carried out as one aspect of the editor's work while a Government of Ireland Research Fellow in 2005. The financial support of the Irish Research Council for the Humanities and the Social Sciences during this period is gratefully acknowledged. So too is the assistance in obtaining this support which was provided by Professor Paul O'Connor, Dean of the School of Law, University College Dublin and my colleague Anthony Kerr, BL, who has been for many years an outstanding contributor of published work in the field of Irish employment law.

Encouragement and advice was provided in abundance by my wife Madeleine, and invaluable help and advice was also provided by Dr. Max Barrett, Head of Legal and Compliance at Rabobank Ireland. Thanks should also be expressed to David McCartney of Clarus Press for his support and expert assistance in getting this project finished. Frequent visits into their father's study and occasional drawings on the original copies of statutes were provided by two wonderful children, Marie-Hélène and Stéphane, and much encouragement also came from Conor, Della and Michael Barrett. Gabhaim buíochas libh go léir, although, needless to say, responsibility for any errors rests with myself.

This book is dedicated to my son Sébastien, my goddaughter and niece Maria and my nephew Mikhalis, all of whom made their own appearances in this world shortly before this introduction was written.

Dr. Gavin Barrett, BL
School of Law,
University College Dublin
November, 2006.

A NOTE ON THIS BOOK AND HOW TO USE IT

This book is divided into two parts. In the first part, which occupies pages 1 to 450, are to be found all statutes relating to dismissal, redundancy and employee consultation, together with those few statutory instruments which carry out the important task of implementing the requirements of Community directives into the Community legal order.[1] Because of the relevance of doctrines such as direct effect, indirect effect and state liability, where statutes or statutory instruments in this volume implement European Community directives, the consolidated text of the relevant directive has also been included in this volume, directly after the domestic measure transposing it.

For ease of reference, all of the foregoing instruments are reproduced in chronological order except for the European Community directives, which, since they are most likely to be consulted in connection with the statute or statutory instrument implementing them in the domestic legal order, are reproduced (themselves in consolidated form) after the relevant implementing legislation rather than in chronological order.

The second part of the book, which occupies pages 451 to 529, contains other statutory instruments which it is felt may be of relevance. The approach to the question of which statutory instruments to include has had to be a somewhat selective one, in the sense that only the texts of those statutory instruments which it is felt will be of use to practitioners have been included here (although *all* statutory instruments which have not been revoked or rendered obsolete are referred to in footnotes to the statutory provisions which authorised their adoption). Thus the full texts of statutory instruments which merely *e.g.*, set the date of commencement of legislation, or vary the level of a fine referred to in a section of primary legislation are not reproduced, since doing this seems unlikely to be of much practical value to any reader.

For ease of reference, chronologically-ordered and alphabetically-ordered contents pages have been provided in addition to a contents page ordered according to subject matter.

Finally, a few miscellaneous matters merit mention. In general, no attempt has been made to correct errors in the drafting of statutes or statutory instruments in the writing of this work, even where such errors are obvious, the rationale here being that it is the objective of a work such as this to show the law as it is, not as it should be.[2] On the rare occasions where errors which could have practical implications have been detected in statutory provisions, the general such errors are brought to the reader's attention by means of the insertion of an appropriate comment contained in a footnote.

In this book, wherever legislation has been amended, the amendment has been inserted in the text of the amended legislation and a footnote has been inserted indicating this fact. To avoid pointless repetition, the text of the amendment inserted or

[1] Five of these are included in total: the Protection of Employment Order 1996 (S.I. No. 370 of 1996), the European Communities (Transnational Information and Consultation of Employees Act, 1996) (Amendment) Regulations, 1999 (S.I. No. 386 of 1999), the European Communities (Protection of Employment) Regulations, 2000 (S.I. No. 488 of 2000), the European Communities (Protection of Employees on Transfer of Undertakings) Regulations 2003 (S.I. No. 131 of 2003) and the European Communities (Protection of Employees (Employers' Insolvency)) Regulations 2005 (S.I. No. 630 of 2005).

[2] *Cf.* however the approach adopted in relation to s. 9(2) of the Protection of Employment Act, 1977, the amendment of which has given rise to particular difficulties.

substituted in the amended statute is not reproduced in the amending statute (where that is to be found in this book). Rather, a clear indication of what the amendment has done is provided there (*i.e.*, the fact that it repealed, amended or substituted another provision and what provision it affected in this way).

The use of square parentheses ('[' and ']') in the text has been kept to a minimum and they have been deployed only in somewhat unusual situations, such as where a provision which says one thing is legally required to be read as if it said something else, without however having been amended. Footnotes explaining the use of such parenthesis are provided wherever they are deployed.

For the purposes of ensuring internal consistency within this book, all references throughout this text to individual enactments appear as originally punctuated in the enactment itself. The reader's attention is however drawn to s. 14(3) of the Interpretation Act 2005, according to which in citing (*a*) an Act by its short title, or (*b*) any other enactment by its citation (if any), a comma immediately before a reference to a year and a comma immediately after such a reference that is not required for the purpose of punctuation *may* be omitted.

The day-to-day administration of claims in this area of the law has been undergoing something of a revolution because of the impact of the internet, with much time now capable of being saved by the use of online resources. The reader is referred to the website of the Department of Enterprise, Trade and Employment (http://www.entemp.ie/) in which a broad array of downloadable forms (see for example, in this regard http://www.entemp.ie/forms/index.htm#insolvency) and information is to be found. The Department's website is also a useful (although not comprehensive) place of recourse for those seeking the texts of more recent statutory instruments, since the normal online government location in which such statutory instruments are to be found (http://www.irishstatutebook.ie) is over a year out of date at the time of writing, providing as it does the text of no statutory instrument adopted later than July 2005. Finally, the Employment Appeals Tribunal now has its own website which provides, *inter alia*, downloadable claim forms (http://www.eatribunal.ie/en/homepage.aspx). As yet, the step has not been taken of putting all rulings of the EAT on its website, an innovation which in the view of this writer would not alone be appropriate but is long overdue in an era of supposed governmental openness, particularly given the need to maximise understanding of, and access to Irish employment law.

This book is up to date to 1 October, 2006 although the inclusion of some provisions which come into effect shortly after that point has been possible.

Gavin Barrett

Consolidated Dismissal, Redundancy and Employee Consultation Legislation

Contents*

Statutes, Community Directives and Statutory Instruments Implementing Community Directives

* The contents are listed here in the order in which they appear in this book (viz., chronologically, subject to the caveats that (a) the most significant group of instruments appears first, and thus a division has been made between, on the one hand, statutes, Community directives and statutory instruments implementing Community directives, and, on the other hand, other relevant statutory instruments; and that (b) since Community Directives are most likely to be consulted in connection with the statute or statutory instrument implementing them in the domestic legal order, such Directives are listed immediately after such legislation rather than in chronological order).

Statutory Instruments (Other than those which Implement European Community Directives)

Consolidated Dismissal, Redundancy and Employee Consultation Legislation

Contents of This Volume Listed Alphabetically

Consolidated Dismissal, Redundancy and Employee Consultation Legislation

Contents of This Volume Listed According to Subject Matter *

---

* Within each subject category in this list, statutes and those statutory instruments which implement European Community directives are listed first, followed by any other statutory instruments, followed by Community directives.

Statutes,
Statutory Instruments Implementing European Community Directives
and
European Community Directives

REDUNDANCY PAYMENTS ACT, 1967

Number 21 *of* 1967

ARRANGEMENT OF SECTIONS

PART I

PRELIMINARY AND GENERAL

PART II

REDUNDANCY PAYMENT

PART III

REDUNDANCY FUND

PART IV

MISCELLANEOUS PROVISIONS

Number 21 *of* 1967

REDUNDANCY PAYMENTS ACT, 1967

AN ACT TO PROVIDE FOR THE MAKING BY EMPLOYERS OF PAYMENTS TO EMPLOYEES IN RESPECT OF REDUNDANCY, TO ESTABLISH A REDUNDANCY FUND AND TO REQUIRE EMPLOYERS AND EMPLOYEES TO PAY CONTRIBUTIONS TOWARDS THAT FUND, TO PROVIDE FOR PAYMENTS TO BE MADE OUT OF THAT FUND TO EMPLOYERS AND EMPLOYEES, TO PROVIDE FINANCIAL ASSISTANCE TO CERTAIN UNEMPLOYED PERSONS CHANGING RESIDENCE, AND TO PROVIDE FOR OTHER MATTERS (INCLUDING OFFENCES) CONNECTED WITH THE MATTERS AFORESAID. [18*th December*, 1967.]

BE IT ENACTED BY THE OIREACHTAS AS FOLLOWS:—

PART I

PRELIMINARY AND GENERAL

1. —This Act may be cited as the Redundancy Payments Act, 1967.[1] Short title.

---

[1] Note that the Redundancy Payments Act, 1967, the Redundancy Payments Act, 1971, the Redundancy Payments Act, 1973, the Redundancy Payments Act, 1979, s. 12 of the Protection of Employees (Employers' Insolvency) Act, 1984, ss. 26, 27 and 29 of the Social Welfare Act, 1990, s. 39 (other than sub-s. (2)) of the Social Welfare Act, 1991 (although apparently by oversight no mention is made of s. 39 of the 1991 Act in any subsequent statute included in this list), the Protection of Employees (Part-Time Work) Act, 2001 (insofar as it relates to the foregoing legislation, apart from s. 39 of the 1991 Act) and the Redundancy Payments Act 2003 may be cited together as the Redundancy Payments Acts 1967 to 2003.
See in this regard, s. 20(2) of the Redundancy Payments Act, 1971, s. 2(2) of the Redundancy Payments Act, 1973, s. 21(2) of the Redundancy

Interpretation. **2.** —(1) In this Act—

1952, No. 11. "the Act of 1952" means the Social Welfare Act, 1952;

"adopting parent" [2] means an employee who is an employed adopting mother, an adopting father or sole male adopter within the meaning of *section 2 (1) of the Adoptive Leave Act, 1995*

"business" includes a trade, industry, profession or undertaking, or any activity carried on by a person or body of persons, whether corporate or unincorporate, or by a public or local authority or a Department of State, and the performance of its functions by a public or local authority or a Department of State;

"contract of employment" [3] means—

(*a*) a contract of service or apprenticeship, and

(*b*) any other contract whereby an individual agrees with another person, who is carrying on the business of an employment agency within the meaning of the Employment Agency Act 1971 and is acting in the course of that business, to do or perform personally any work or service for a third person (whether or not the third person is a party to the contract),

whether the contract is express or implied and, if express, whether it is oral or in writing and references to 'contract' shall be construed accordingly;

"date of dismissal", [4] in relation to an employee, means—

(*a*) where his contract of employment is terminated by notice given by his employer, the date on which that notice expires,

---

Payments Act, 1979, s. 18(2) of the Protection of Employees (Employers' Insolvency) Act, 1984, s. 1(4) of the Social Welfare Act, 1990, s. 1(3) of the Social Welfare Act, 1991, s. 1(4) of the Protection of Employees (Part-Time Work) Act, 2001 and s. 17(3) of the Redundancy Payments Act 2003.

[2] This definition was inserted by s. 27 of the Adoptive Leave Act, 1995.

[3] This definition was inserted by s. 3(a) of the Redundancy Payments Act 2003.

[4] Note however, s. 7(2) of the Minimum Notice and Terms of Employment Act, 1973, which provides as follows:

"In any case where an employee accepts payment in lieu of notice, the date of termination of that person's employment shall, for the purposes

(*b*) where his contract of employment is terminated without notice, whether by the employer or by the employee, the date on which the termination takes effect, and

(*c*) where he is employed under a contract for a fixed term, and that term expires without the contract being renewed, the date on which that term expires,

and cognate phrases shall be construed accordingly;

---

of the Act of 1967, be deemed to be the date on which notice, if given, would have expired."

Note also s. 40(2) of the Maternity Protection Act, 1994, which provides as follows:

"For the purposes of the Redundancy Payments Acts, 1967 to 1991, an employee to whom this section applies [*Editor's note: this refers to an employee who is entitled to return to work from an absence due to protective leave under the 1994 Act, but who is not permitted to do so by her employer*] who is also an employee to whom those Acts apply shall be deemed to have been dismissed by reason of redundancy, the date of dismissal being deemed to be the expected date of return."

Note also s. 29 of the Adoptive Leave Act, 1995, which provides as follows.

"(1) This section applies to an adopting parent within the meaning of section 2 of the [Redundancy Payments Act 1967] who, having complied with *section 20* [*Editor's note: s. 20 of the 1995 Act governs notification of intention to return to work after a period of adoptive or additional adoptive leave*] is entitled to return to work but is not permitted to do so by her employer, the successor or an associated employer.

(2) For the purposes of the Act of 1967, an adopting parent shall be deemed to have been dismissed by reason of redundancy, the date of dismissal being deemed to be the date specified in the relevant notification under *section 20 (1)* [*Editor's note: this will be the date on which the adopting parent expects to return to work*]."

Note also s. 16A(4) of the Parental Leave Act, 1998, as inserted by s. 11 of the Parental Leave (Amendment) Act 2006, which provides as follows:

"An employee who is entitled to return to work in the employment concerned in accordance with section 15 [*Editor's note: s. 15 governs entitlement to return to work on the expiration of a period of parental leave*] but is not permitted by his or her employer to do so—

... (*b*) shall be deemed for the purposes of the Redundancy Payments Acts 1967 to 2003, to have had his or her contract of employment with his or her employer terminated on the date aforesaid. [*Editor's note: 'the date aforesaid' refers to the date on which he or she was entitled to return to work*]."

Note also s. 16(4) of the Carer's Leave Act, 2001,

"employee" [5] means a person of 16 years and upwards who has entered into or works under (or, where the employment has ceased, entered into or worked under) a contract of employment and references, in relation to an employer, to an employee shall be construed as references to an employee employed by that employer and, for the purposes of this Act, a person holding office under, or in the service of, the State (including a civil servant within the meaning of the Civil Service Regulation Act 1956) shall be deemed to be an employee employed by the State or Government, as the case may be, and an officer or servant of a local authority, a harbour authority, the Eastern Regional Health Authority, the Northern Area Health Board, the East Coast Area Health Board or the South-Western Area Health Board, a health board or vocational education committee shall be deemed to be an employee employed by the authority, health board or vocational education committee, as the case may be; [6]

"An employee who is entitled to return to work in the employment concerned in accordance with *section 14* [*Editor's note: s. 14 governs entitlement to return to work on the termination of carer's leave*] but is not permitted by his or her employer to do so—

... (b) shall be deemed for the purposes of the Redundancy Payments Acts, 1967 to 1991, to have had his or her contract of employment with his or her employer terminated on the date aforesaid."

[5] This definition was inserted by s. 3(b) of the Redundancy Payments Act 2003, and substitutes for the original definition.

[6] Note that under s. 58 of the Health Act 2004, certain specified bodies including health boards, the Eastern Regional Health Authority and the Area Health Boards were dissolved. Under s. 59 of the same Act, the functions that were the functions of such specified bodies under or in connection with the Redundancy Payments Acts 1967 to 2003 were transferred to the Health Service Executive established under s. 6 of the 2004 Act. Note also that under s. 62(3) of the 2004 Act all rights and liabilities of these specified bodies arising by virtue of any contract or commitment (express or implied) entered into by that body were transferred to the Health Service Executive and that under s. 63 of the 2004 Act, it was provided that every contract, agreement or arrangement made between a specified body and any other person (*a*) continued in force, (*b*) was to be read and have effect as if the name of the Health Service Executive were substituted in the contract, agreement or arrangement for that of the specified body, and (*c*) was enforceable by and against the Health Service Executive.

(Text deleted) [6a]

["An Foras Áiseanna Saothair"] [7] means the service known by that title and operated under the control of the Minister;

"employer" [8] means, in relation to an employee, the person with whom the employee has entered into or for whom the employee works under (or, where the employment has ceased, entered into or worked under) a contract of employment, subject to the qualification that the person who under a contract of employment referred to in paragraph (*b*) of the definition of 'contract of employment' is liable to pay the wages of the individual concerned in respect of the work or service concerned shall be deemed to be the individual's employer;

"lay-off" has the meaning assigned to it by section 11 (1);

"local authority" means a county council, a city council or a town council for the purposes of the Local Government Act 2001;[9]

"lump sum" has the meaning assigned to it by section 19;

[6a] The definition of "employee's redundancy contribution" was deleted by s. 17 of the Redundancy Payments Act, 1979. The definition of "employer's redundancy contribution" was deleted by s. 39(1) of the Social Welfare Act, 1991.

[7] This provision originally referred to "the Employment Service", for which s. 19(1) of the Redundancy Payments Act, 1971 subsequently substituted "the National Manpower Service". By virtue of s. 18(4) of the Labour Services Act, 1987, references made to the Manpower Service in any Act of the Oireachtas (or in any instrument made under an Act of the Oireachtas) before the establishment under the 1987 Act of An Foras Áiseanna Saothair are now to be construed as references to An Foras Áiseanna Saothair.

[8] This definition was inserted by s. 3(c) of the Redundancy Payments Act 2003 in purported substitution for the then existing definition of 'employer' in s. 2(1). Prior to the coming into force of the 2003 Act, however, s. 2(1) of the 1967 Act contained no definition of 'employer', although attached to and forming part of the then definition of 'employee' was a clause stating that ' "employer" and reference to employment [should] be construed accordingly'.

[9] This definition was inserted by s. 3(d) of the Redundancy Payments Act 2003.

"the Minister" means [the Minister for Enterprise, Trade and Employment];[10]

"prescribed" means prescribed by regulations made by the Minister under this Act;

"rebate" has the meaning assigned to it by section 29;

"redundancy payment" has the meaning, assigned to it by section 7;

"short-time" [11] has the meaning assigned to it by section 11 (2) or section 11 (3) (as the case may be);

"sickness" or "illness" includes being incapable of work within the meaning of the Act of 1952;

"the Social Insurance Fund" [12] means the Social Insurance Fund established under section 39 of the Social Welfare Act,

---

[10] The text of the Act originally referred to the Minister for Labour. However, under Article 4(1) of the Labour (Transfer of Departmental Administration and Ministerial Functions) Order, 1993 (S.I. No. 18 of 1993), it was provided that the functions vested in the Minister for Labour by or under certain Acts (including this Act) be transferred to the Minister for Industry and Commerce. In Article 4(2) of the same Order, it was provided that references to the Minister for Labour contained in any such Act or instrument thereunder and relating to any functions transferred by Article 4 should, on and after the commencement of the Order, be construed as references to the Minister for Industry and Commerce. In Article 4 of the Industry and Commerce (Alteration of Name of Department and Title of Minister) Order, 1993 (S.I. No. 19 of 1993), which was adopted on the same day as S.I. No. 18 of 1993, it was provided that references in any enactment to the Minister for Industry and Commerce should be construed as references to the Minister for Enterprise and Employment. More recently, Article 4 of the Enterprise and Employment (Alteration of Name of Department and Title of Minister) Order, 1997 (S.I. No. 305 of 1997) has provided that references in any enactment to the Minister for Enterprise and Employment are to be construed as references to the Minister for Enterprise, Trade and Employment. It should be noted that the powers and duties which are conferred on the Minister for Enterprise, Trade and Employment by or under the Redundancy Payments Acts have been delegated by statutory instrument to the present Minister of State at the Department of Enterprise, Trade and Employment. (See now the Enterprise, Trade and Employment (Delegation of Ministerial Functions) Order 2004 (S.I. No. 809 of 2004).)

[11] The words after '11(2)' were inserted by s. 19(1) of the Redundancy Payments Act, 1971.

[12] This definition was inserted in its original form by s. 26(a) of the Social Welfare Act, 1990.

1952, and continued in being under [section 9 of the Social Welfare Consolidation Act 2005];

"special redundancy scheme" has the meaning assigned to it by section 47;

"the Tribunal" has the meaning assigned to it by section 39 (1);

"week", in relation to an employee whose remuneration is calculated weekly by a week ending on a day other than Saturday, means a week ending on that other day and, in relation to any other employee, means a week ending on Saturday, and "weekly" shall be construed accordingly;

"weekly payment" has the meaning assigned to it by section 30.

(2) In this Act a reference to a Part, section or schedule is to a Part or section of, or schedule to, this Act unless it is indicated that reference to some other enactment is intended.

(3) In this Act a reference to a subsection, paragraph, subparagraph or other division is to the subsection, paragraph, subparagraph or other division of the provision (including a schedule) in which the reference occurs, unless it is indicated that reference to another provision is intended.

(4) For the purposes of the operation of this Act in relation to an employee whose remuneration is payable to him by a person other than his employer, reference in this Act to an employer

---

Note that the reference at the end of this definition was originally to section 122 of the Social Welfare (Consolidation) Act, 1981, which was subsequently repealed by s. 300 of the Social Welfare (Consolidation) Act, 1993. The effect of s. 361(b) of the Social Welfare Consolidation Act 2005, however, appears to be that references to provisions of a repealed enactment such as that originally found at the end of the above definition are now to be read as references to the corresponding provisions of the 2005 Act. Even if this is not the effect of s. 361(b), the matter will in any case come within the more general provisions of s. 26 (2) of the Interpretation Act 2005, according to which, where an enactment is repealed and reenacted, with or without modification, by another enactment, a reference in any other enactment to the former enactment shall, with respect to a subsequent transaction, matter or thing, be read as a reference to the provisions of the new enactment relating to the same subject-matter as that of the former enactment. The appropriate reference has therefore been substituted in the text above.

shall be construed as reference to the person by whom the remuneration is payable.

Commencement.

3. —This Act shall come into operation on such day as the Minister appoints by order.[13]

Classes of persons to which this Act applies.

4. —(1) Subject to this section and to section 47 this Act shall apply to employees employed in employment which is insurable for all benefits under [the Social Welfare Acts] [14] and to

---

[13] In the Redundancy Payments Act, 1967 (Appointed Day) Order, 1967 (S.I. No. 302 of 1967), the Minister for Labour appointed 1 January, 1968 to be the day on which this Act came into operation.

[14] The text of s. 4(1) originally referred to the Social Welfare Acts, 1952 to 1966. The Social Welfare Acts 1952 to 1966 were repealed by s. 310 of the Social Welfare (Consolidation) Act, 1981, and their rules governing insurability replaced by provisions in the 1981 Act. The 1981 Act itself was in turn almost entirely repealed by s. 300 of the Social Welfare (Consolidation) Act, 1993, and the 1981 Act's provisions on insurability replaced by provisions in the 1993 Act. Subsequently, the 1993 Act was itself in turn repealed in its entirety by s. 360 of the Social Welfare Consolidation Act 2005. Once again, the 2005 Act entirely replaced the statutory rules governing insurability. These rules have since been amended by the Social Welfare Act 2005.

Under s. 26 (2) of the Interpretation Act 2005, where an enactment is repealed and reenacted, with or without modification, by another enactment, a reference in any other enactment to the former enactment shall, with respect to a subsequent transaction, matter or thing, be read as a reference to the provisions of the new enactment relating to the same subject-matter as that of the former enactment. The appropriate reference has therefore been substituted in the text above. (Note that under s. 3(8) of the Social Welfare Consolidation Act 2005, references in any other enactment to the "Social Welfare Acts" are now to mean "this Act and every enactment which is to be read together with it as one." Note also that under s. 14(2) of the Social Welfare Act 2005, the Social Welfare Acts and the Social Welfare Act 2005 (other than section 13 thereof) are to be read together as one. Finally, under s. 1(2) of Social Welfare Law Reform and Pensions Act 2006, the Social Welfare Acts and sections 1 to 37 of that Act are also to be read together as one).

Although detailed examination of the concept of insurable employment would be beyond the scope of the present work, it may be noted that s. 2 of the Social Welfare Consolidation Act 2005 now defines 'insurable employment' as meaning employment such that a person, over the age of 16 years and under pensionable age, employed in that employment would be an employed contributor within the meaning of that Act. The meaning to be attributed to the concept of an employed contributor and further rules governing employed contributors are to be found in Chapter 2 of the 2005 Act.

employees who were so employed in such employment in the period of four years ending on the date of termination of employment.[15]

(2) This Act shall apply to an employee employed in employment which would be insurable for all benefits under [the Social Welfare Acts] but for the fact that the employment concerned is an excepted employment by virtue of [paragraph 2, 4 or 5 of Part II of Schedule 1 to the Social Welfare Consolidation Act 2005].[16]

(3) (*a*) For the purpose of the application of this Act to an employee who is employed in a private household this Act (other than section 20) shall apply as if the

---

Note that under s. 8 of the Protection of Employees (Part-Time Work) Act, 2001, the Redundancy Payments Acts, 1967 to 1990 are to apply to a part-time employee (meaning, under s. 7(1) of that Act, an employee whose normal hours of work are less than the normal hours of work of an employee who is a comparable employee in relation to him or her) in the same manner (and subject to the like exceptions not inconsistent with s. 8) as they apply (other than by virtue of the 2001 Act) to an employee to whom the Redundancy Payments Acts, 1967 to 1990 relate. (Note also the broad definition given to "employee" by s. 3(1) of the Protection of Employees (Part-Time Work) Act, 2001, and finally, note that under s. 17(3) of the Redundancy Payments Act 2003, the Redundancy Payments Acts 1967 to 2003 are to be construed together as one).

[15] The word "four" was substituted for "two" in this subsection by s. 19(1) of the Redundancy Payments Act, 1971.

[16] This subsection was substituted in its entirety by s. 4 of the Redundancy Payments Act 2003 and in its original form (as substituted in 2003) made reference to the Social Welfare (Consolidation) Act, 1993 (which has since been repealed by s. 360 of the Social Welfare Consolidation Act, 2005) and to certain specific provisions of the First Schedule thereto. The effect of s. 361(b) of the 2005 Act, however, appears to be that references to provisions of a repealed enactment such as that originally found in the above definition are now to be read as references to the corresponding provisions of the 2005 Act. Even if this is not the effect of s. 361(b), s. 4(2) of the 1967 Act will in any case come within the more general provisions of s. 26 (2) of the Interpretation Act 2005, according to which, where an enactment is repealed and reenacted, with or without modification, by another enactment, a reference in any other enactment to the former enactment shall, with respect to a subsequent transaction, matter or thing, be read as a reference to the provisions of the new enactment relating to the same subject-matter as that of the former enactment. The appropriate references have therefore been substituted in the text above.

household were a business and the maintenance of the household were the carrying on of that business by the employer.

(*b*) This Act shall not apply to any person in respect of employment where the employer is the father, mother, grandfather, grandmother, stepfather, stepmother, son, daughter, grandson, granddaughter, stepson, stepdaughter, brother, sister, halfbrother or halfsister of the employee, where the employee is a member of the employer's household and the employment is related to a private dwelling house or a farm in or on which both the employer and the employee reside.

(*c*) In deducing any relationship for the purposes of paragraph (b)— [17]

(i) a person adopted under the Adoption Acts, 1952 and 1964,[18] shall be considered the legitimate offspring of the adopter or adopters;

(ii) subject to clause (i) of this paragraph, an illegitimate person shall be considered the legitimate offspring of his mother and reputed father;

(iii) a person in *loco parentis* to another shall be considered the parent of that other.

(4) The Minister may by order declare that this Act shall not apply to a class or classes of persons specified in the order and from the commencement of the order this Act shall not apply to that class or those classes.

(5) Notwithstanding subsection (2), the Minister may by order declare that this Act shall apply to a specified class of worker and from the commencement of the order this Act shall apply to that class.

---

[17] All of paragraph (c) was inserted by s. 19(1) of the Redundancy Payments Act, 1971.

[18] Note that the Adoption Act, 1952, the Adoption Act, 1964, the Adoption Act, 1974, the Adoption Act, 1976, the Adoption Act, 1988, the Adoption Act, 1991 and the Adoption Act, 1998 are now required to be construed together as one Act, under s. 18(2) of the Adoption Act, 1998.

(6) The Minister may by order amend or revoke an order under this section.

5. —(1) Whenever an order is proposed to be made under section 4 (4), 4 (5), 4 (6), 19 (3), 28 (3), 30 (3) or 47 or Section 17 of the Redundancy Payments Act, 1971, a draft of the proposed order shall be laid before each House of the Oireachtas and the order shall not be made until a resolution approving of the draft has been passed by each such House.[19]

Laying of regulations and certain draft orders before Houses of Oireachtas.

(2) Every regulation made under this Act shall be laid before each House of the Oireachtas as soon as may be after it is made and, if a resolution annulling the regulation is passed by either such House within the next twenty-one days on which that House has sat after the regulation is laid before it, the regulation shall be annulled accordingly, but without prejudice to the validity of anything previously done thereunder.

PART II

Redundancy Payment

6. —In this Part—

Definitons for Part II.

"cease" means cease either temporarily or permanently and from whatever cause;

"lock-out" means the closing of a place of employment, or the suspension of work, or the refusal by an employer to continue to employ any number of persons employed by him in consequence of a dispute, done with a view to compelling those persons, or to aid another employer in compelling persons employed by him, to accept terms or conditions of or affecting employment;

"notice of intention to claim" has the meaning assigned to it by section 12;

---

[19] The words "or Section 17 of the Redundancy Payments Act, 1971" were inserted by s. 19(1) of the Redundancy Payments Act, 1971. A reference in the original list of provisions in the sub-section to the now-deleted s. 28(3) of the 1967 Act (which related to employers' and employees' weekly redundancy contributions) was deleted by s. 39(1) of the Social Welfare Act, 1991.

"redundancy certificate" has the meaning assigned to it by section 18;

"strike" means the cessation of work by a body of persons employed acting in combination, or a concerted refusal or a refusal under a common understanding of any number of persons employed to continue to work for an employer in consequence of a dispute, done as a means of compelling their employer or any person or body of persons employed, or to aid other employees in compelling their employer or any person or body of persons employed, to accept or not to accept terms or conditions of or affecting employment.

General right to redundancy payment.

7. —(1) An employee, if he is dismissed by his employer by reason of redundancy or is laid off or kept on short-time for the minimum period, shall, subject to this Act, be entitled to the payment of moneys which shall be known (and are in this Act referred to) as redundancy payment provided—

(*a*) he has been employed for the requisite period, and

(*b*) he was an employed contributor in employment which was insurable for all benefits under [the Social Welfare Acts], [20] immediately before the date of the

[20] In its original form, s. 7(1)(b) made reference to the Social Welfare Acts, 1952 to 1966. The Social Welfare Acts, 1952 to 1966 were repealed by s. 310 of the Social Welfare (Consolidation) Act, 1981, and their rules governing insurability replaced by provisions in the 1981 Act. The 1981 Act was in turn almost entirely repealed by s. 300 of the Social Welfare (Consolidation) Act, 1993, and the 1981 Act's provisions on insurability replaced by provisions in the 1993 Act. Subsequently, the 1993 Act was in turn repealed in its entirety by s. 360 of the Social Welfare Consolidation Act 2005. Once again, the 2005 Act entirely replaced the statutory rules governing insurability. These rules were almost immediately amended by the Social Welfare Act 2005.
Under s. 26 (2) of the Interpretation Act 2005, where an enactment is repealed and reenacted, with or without modification, by another enactment, a reference in any other enactment to the former enactment shall, with respect to a subsequent transaction, matter or thing, be read as a reference to the provisions of the new enactment relating to the same subject-matter as that of the former enactment. The appropriate reference has therefore been substituted in the text above. (Note that under s. 3(8) of the Social Welfare Consolidation Act 2005, references in any other enactment to the "Social Welfare Acts" are now to mean "this Act and every enactment which is to be read together with it as one." Note also that under

termination of his employment, or had ceased to be ordinarily employed in employment which was so insurable in the period of four years [21] ending on that date.

(2) For the purposes of subsection (1), an employee who is dismissed shall be taken to he dismissed by reason of redundancy if for one or more reasons not related to the employee concerned [22] the dismissal is attributable wholly or mainly to—

(*a*) the fact that his employer has ceased, or intends to cease, to carry on the business for the purposes of which the employee was employed by him, or has ceased or intends to cease, to carry on that business in the place where the employee was so employed, or

(*b*) the fact that the requirements of that business for employees to carry out work of a particular kind in the place where he was so employed have ceased or diminished or are expected to cease or diminish, or [23]

(*c*) the fact that his employer has decided to carry on the business with fewer or no employees, whether by requiring the work for which the employee had been employed (or had been doing before his dismissal) to be done by other employees or otherwise, or [24]

(*d*) the fact that his employer has decided that the work for which the employee had been employed (or had been doing before his dismissal) should henceforward be done in a different manner for which the employee is not sufficiently qualified or trained, or [25]

---

s. 14(2) of the Social Welfare Act 2005, the Social Welfare Acts and the Social Welfare Act 2005 (other than section 13 thereof) are to be read together as one. Finally, under s. 1(2) of Social Welfare Law Reform and Pensions Act, 2006, the Social Welfare Acts and sections 1 to 37 of that Act are also to be read together as one).

[21] This was originally two years until amended by s. 19(1) of the Redundancy Payments Act, 1971.

[22] The words "for one or more reasons not related to the employee concerned" were inserted by s. 5 of the Redundancy Payments Act 2003.

[23] Section 7(2)(b) was substituted by s. 4 of the Redundancy Payments Act, 1971.

[24] Section 7(2)(c) was inserted by s. 4 of the Redundancy Payments Act, 1971.

[25] Section 7(2)(d) was inserted by s. 4 of the Redundancy Payments Act, 1971.

(*e*) the fact that his employer has decided that the work for which the employee had been employed (or had been doing before his dismissal) should henceforward be done by a person who is also capable of doing other work for which the employee is not sufficiently qualified or trained.[26]

(3) For the purposes of subsection (1), an employee shall be taken as having been laid off or kept on short-time for the minimum period if he has been laid off or kept on short-time for a period of four or more consecutive weeks, or for a period of six or more weeks which are not consecutive but which fall within a period of thirteen consecutive weeks.

(4) Notwithstanding any other provision of this Act, where an employee who has been serving a period of apprenticeship training with an employer under an apprenticeship agreement is dismissed within one month after the end of that period, that employee shall not, by reason of that dismissal, be entitled to redundancy payment.

(4A) In ascertaining, for the purposes of subsection (2) (*c*), whether an employer has decided to carry on a business with fewer or no employees, account shall not be taken of the following members of the employer's family—

father, mother, stepfather, stepmother, son, daughter, adopted child, grandson, granddaughter, stepson, stepdaughter, brother, sister, halfbrother, halfsister.[27]

(5) In this section "requisite period" means a period of 104 weeks' continuous employment [28] (within the meaning of Schedule 3) of the employee by the employer who dismissed him, laid him off or kept him on short-time, but excluding any period of employment with that employer before the employee had attained the age of 16 years.

Qualification of general right under section 7.

8. —(1) Notwithstanding anything in section 7, where an employee who has been dismissed by reason of redundancy or

---

[26] Section 7(2)(e) was inserted by s. 4 of the Redundancy Payments Act, 1971.
[27] Sub-s. (4A) was inserted by s. 4 of the Redundancy Payments Act, 1971.
[28] This was originally 208 weeks' continuous employment until amended by s. 19(1) of the Redundancy Payments Act, 1971.

laid off has, during the period of the four years immediately preceding the date of dismissal or the lay-off, been laid off for an average annual period of more than twelve weeks, the following provisions shall have effect:

(*a*) that employee shall not become entitled to redundancy payment by reason of dismissal or lay-off until a period equal to the average annual period of lay-off over the said four-year period in relation to that employee has elapsed after the date of dismissal or lay-off;

(*b*) if, before the termination of the period required to elapse under paragraph (*a*), that employee resumes work with the same employer, that employee shall not be entitled to redundancy payment in relation to that dismissal or lay-off;

(*c*) if, before the termination of the period required to elapse under paragraph (*a*), the employer offers to reemploy that employee and that employee unreasonably refuses the offer, he shall not be entitled to redundancy payment in relation to that dismissal or lay-off.

(2) In a case where this section applies, the period of four weeks first referred to in section 12 [29] or the period of thirteen weeks referred to in that section shall not commence until the expiration of the period (referred to in subsection (1) (*a*)) equal to the appropriate average annual period of lay-off.

Dismissal by employer.

9. —(1) For the purposes of this Part an employee shall, subject to this Part, be taken to be dismissed by his employer if but only if— [30]

---

[29] This provision originally referred to s. 12(2), but the substitution of all of the original s. 12 of the 1967 Act rendered necessary this amendment which was effected by s. 19(1) of the 1971 Act.

[30] Note however, s. 7(2) of the Minimum Notice and Terms of Employment Act, 1973, which provides as follows:

"In any case where an employee accepts payment in lieu of notice, the date of termination of that person's employment shall, for the purposes of the Act of 1967, be deemed to be the date on which notice, if given, would have expired."

(*a*) the contract under which he is employed by the employer is terminated by the employer, whether by or without notice, or

(*b*) where, under the contract under which the employee is employed by the employer the employee is employed for a fixed term or for a specified purpose (being a purpose of such a kind that the duration of the contract was limited but was, at the time of its making, incapable of precise ascertainment), that

---

Note also s. 40(2) of the Maternity Protection Act, 1994, which provides as follows:

"For the purposes of the Redundancy Payments Acts, 1967 to 1991, an employee to whom this section applies [*Editor's note: this refers to an employee who is entitled to return to work from an absence due to protective leave under the 1994 Act, but who is not permitted to do so by her employer*] who is also an employee to whom those Acts apply shall be deemed to have been dismissed by reason of redundancy, the date of dismissal being deemed to be the expected date of return."

Note also s. 29 of the Adoptive Leave Act, 1995, which provides as follows:

"(1) This section applies to an adopting parent within the meaning of section 2 of the [Redundancy Payments Act 1967] who, having complied with *section 20* [*Editor's note: s. 20 of the 1995 Act governs notification of intention to return to work after a period of adoptive or additional adoptive leave*] is entitled to return to work but is not permitted to do so by her employer, the successor or an associated employer.

(2) For the purposes of the Act of 1967, an adopting parent shall be deemed to have been dismissed by reason of redundancy, the date of dismissal being deemed to be the date specified in the relevant notification under *section 20 (1)* [*Editor's note: this will be the date on which the adopting parent expects to return to work*]."

Note also s. 16A(4) of the Parental Leave Act, 1998, as inserted by s. 11 of the Parental Leave (Amendment) Act 2006, which provides as follows:

"An employee who is entitled to return to work in the employment concerned in accordance with section 15 [*Editor's note: s. 15 governs entitlement to return to work on the expiration of a period of parental leave*] but is not permitted by his or her employer to do so—

... (*b*) shall be deemed for the purposes of the Redundancy Payments Acts 1967 to 2003, to have had his or her contract of employment with his or her employer terminated on the date aforesaid. [*Editor's note: 'the date aforesaid' refers to the date on which he or she was entitled to return to work*]."

Note also s. 16(4) of the Carer's Leave Act, 2001,

"An employee who is entitled to return to work in the employment concerned in accordance with *section 14* [*Editor's note: s. 14 governs*

term expires or that purpose ceases without being renewed under the same or similar contract, or [31]

(*c*) the employee terminates the contract under which he is employed by the employer [32] in circumstances (not falling within subsection (5)) such that he is entitled so to terminate it by reason of the employees conduct.

(2) An employee shall not be taken for the purposes of this Part to be dismissed by his employer if his contract of employment is renewed, or he is re-engaged by the same employer under a new contract of employment, and—

(*a*) in a case where the provisions of the contract as renewed or of the new contract as to the capacity and place in which he is employed, and as to the other terms and conditions of his employment, do not differ from the corresponding provisions of the previous contract, the renewal or re-engagement takes effect immediately on the ending of his employment under the previous contract, or

(*b*) in any other case, the renewal or re-engagement is in pursuance of an offer in writing made by his employer before the ending of his employment under the previous contract, and takes effect either immediately on

---

entitlement to return to work on the termination of carer's leave] but is not permitted by his or her employer to do so—

... (b) shall be deemed for the purposes of the Redundancy Payments Acts, 1967 to 1991, to have had his or her contract of employment with his or her employer terminated on the date aforesaid."

At an early point, the Oireachtas has provided for exceptions to s. 9(1). Hence, under s. 11(4) of the Transport (Miscellaneous Provisions) Act, 1971, it was provided that where by virtue of that section, an officer or servant of the County Donegal Railways Joint Committee became an officer or servant of Córas Iompair Éireann, he should be deemed not to have been dismissed by reason of redundancy within the meaning of that Act. More generally, note in particular the provisions of s. 20 of the 1967 Act relating to changes of ownership of businesses and those of the European Communities (Protection of Employees on Transfer of Undertakings) Regulations 2003 (S.I. No. 131 of 2003).

[31] Paragraph (b) was substituted by s. 6 of the Redundancy Payments Act 2003.

[32] The words "without notice" were deleted here by s. 19(1) of the 1971 Act.

the ending of that employment or after an interval of not more than four weeks thereafter.

(3) (*a*) An employee shall not be taken for the purposes of this Part as having been dismissed by his employer if—

(i) he is re-engaged by another employer (hereinafter referred to as the new employer) immediately on the termination of his previous employment,

(ii) the re-engagement takes place with the agreement of the employee, the previous employer and the new employer,

(iii) before the commencement of the period of employment with the new employer the employee receives a statement in writing on behalf of the previous employer and the new employer which—

(A) sets out the terms and conditions of the employee's contract of employment with the new employer,

(B) specifies that the employee's period of service with the previous employer will, for the purposes of this Act, be regarded by the new employer as service with the new employer,

(C) contains particulars of the service mentioned in clause (B), and

(D) the employee notifies in writing the new employer that the employee accepts the statement required by this subparagraph.

(*b*) Where in accordance with this subsection an employee is re-engaged by the new employer, the service of that employee with the previous employer [33] shall for the purposes of this Act be deemed to be service with the new employer.

---

[33] The words "with the previous employer" were substituted for the original (erroneous) wording here by s. 19(1) of the Redundancy Payments Acts, 1971.

(4) For the purposes of the application of subsection (2) to a contract under which the employment ends on a Friday, Saturday or Sunday—

(*a*) the renewal or re-engagement shall be treated as taking effect immediately on the ending of the employment under the previous contract if it takes effect on or before the next Monday after that Friday, Saturday or Sunday, and

(*b*) the interval of four weeks mentioned in subsection (2) (*b*) shall be calculated as if the employment had ended on that Monday.

(5) When an employee terminates his contract of employment without notice, being entitled to do so by reason of a lock-out by his employer, subsection (1) (*c*) shall not apply to that termination.

(6) Where by virtue of subsection (2) an employee is treated as not having been dismissed by reason of a renewal or re-engagement taking effect after an interval, then, in determining for the purposes of section 7 (1) whether he has been continuously employed for the requisite period the period of that interval shall count as a period of employment.

(7) In determining for the purposes of this Act whether at a particular time before the commencement of this Act an employee was dismissed by his employer, the appropriate provisions of this section shall apply as if the matter to be decided occurred after such commencement.

10. —(1) This section shall have effect where

Employee anticipating expiry of employer's notice.

(*a*) an employer gives notice to an employee to terminate his contract of employment, and

(*b*) at a time within the obligatory period of that notice, the employee gives notice in writing to the employer to terminate the contract of employment on a date earlier than the date on which the employer's notice is due to expire.

(2) Subject to subsection (3), in the circumstances specified in subsection (1) the employee shall, for the purposes of this

Part, be taken to he dismissed by his employer, and the date of dismissal in relation to that dismissal shall be the date on which the employee's notice expires.

(3) If, before the employee's notice is due to expire, the employer gives him notice in writing—

(*a*) requiring him to withdraw his notice terminating the contract of employment as mentioned in subsection (1) (*b*) and to continue in the employment until the date on which the employer's notice expires, and

(*b*) stating that, unless he does so, the employer will contest any liability to pay to him a redundancy payment in respect of the termination of his contract of employment,

but the employee unreasonably refuses to comply with the requirements of that notice, the employee shall not be entitled to a redundancy payment by virtue of subsection (2).

(3A) Where an employer agrees in writing with an employee to alter the date of dismissal mentioned in a notice under subsection (1) (*a*) given by him to that employee so as to ensure that the employee's notice under subsection (1) (*b*) will be within the obligatory period in relation to the notice under subsection (1) (*a*), the employee's entitlement to redundancy payment shall be unaffected and the employee shall, for the purposes of this Part, be taken to be dismissed by his employer, the date of dismissal in relation to that dismissal being the date on which the employee's notice expires.[34]

(4) In this section—

(*a*) if the actual period of the employer's notice (that is to say, the period beginning at the time when the notice is given and ending at the time when it expires) is equal to the minimum period which (whether by virtue of any enactment or other) is required to be given by the employer to terminate the contract of employment, "the obligatory period", in relation to that notice, means the actual period of the notice;

---

[34] Sub-s. 3A was inserted by s. 9 of the Redundancy Payments Act, 1979.

(*b*) in any other case,

"the obligatory period", in relation to an employer's notice, means that period which, being equal to the minimum period referred to in paragraph (*a*), expires at the time when the employer's notice expires.

11. —(1) Where [35] an employee's employment ceases by reason of his employer's being unable to provide the work for which the employee was employed to do, and— Lay-off and short time.

(*a*) it is reasonable in the circumstances for that employer to believe that the cessation of employment will not be permanent, and

(*b*) the employer gives notice to that effect to the employee prior to the cessation,

that cessation of employment shall be regarded for the purposes of this Act as lay-off.

(2) Where— [36]

(*a*) for any week an employee's remuneration is less than one half of his normal weekly remuneration or his hours of work are reduced to less than one-half of his normal weekly hours,

(*b*) the reduction in remuneration or hours of work is caused by a diminution either in the work provided for the employee by his employer or in other work of a kind which under his contract the employee is employed to do.

(*c*) it is reasonable in the circumstances for the employer to believe that the diminution in work will not be permanent and he gives notice to that effect to the employee prior to the reduction in remuneration or hours of work,

the employee shall, for the purposes of this Part, be taken to be kept on short-time for that week.

---

[35] The words "after the commencement of this Act" were deleted here by s. 19(1) of the Redundancy Payments Act, 1971.

[36] Sub s. 2 was substituted by s. 10 of the Redundancy Payments Act, 1979.

Right to redundancy payment by reason of lay-off or short-time.

12. —(1) An employee shall not be entitled to redundancy payment by reason of having been laid off or kept on short-time unless— [37]

(*a*) he has been laid off or kept on short-time for four or more consecutive weeks or, within a period of thirteen weeks, for a series of six or more weeks of which not more than three were consecutive, and

(*b*) after the expiry of the relevant period of lay-off or short-time mentioned in paragraph (*a*) and not later than four weeks after the cessation of the lay-off or short-time, he gives to his employer notice (in this Part referred to as a notice of intention to claim) in writing of his intention to claim redundancy payment in respect of lay-off or short-time.

(2) Where, after the expiry of the relevant period of lay-off or short-time mentioned in subsection (1) (*a*) and not later than four weeks after the cessation of the lay-off or short time, an employee to whom that subsection applies, in lieu of giving to his employer a notice of intention to claim, terminates his contract of employment either by giving him the notice thereby required or, if none is so required, by giving him not less than one week's notice in writing of intention to terminate the contract, the notice so given shall, for the purposes of this Part and of Schedule 2, be deemed to be a notice of intention to claim given in writing to the employer by the employee on the date on which the notice is actually given.

Right of employer to give counter-notice.

13. —(1) Subject to subsection (2), an employee shall not be entitled to redundancy payment in pursuance of a notice of intention to claim if, on the date of service of that notice, it was reasonably to be expected that the employee (if he continued to be employed by the same employer) would, not later than four weeks after that date, enter upon a period of employment of not less than thirteen weeks during which he would not be laid off or kept on short-time for any week.

(2) Subsection (1) shall not apply unless, within seven days after the service of the notice of intention to claim, the

[37] Section 12 was substituted in its entirety by s. 11 of the Redundancy Payments Act, 1971.

employer gives to the employee notice (in this Part referred to as a counter-notice) in writing that he will contest any liability to pay to him a redundancy payment in pursuance of the notice of intention to claim.

(3) If, in a case where an employee gives notice of intention to claim and the employer gives a counter-notice, the employee continues or has continued, during the next four weeks after the date of service of the notice of intention to claim, to be employed by the same employer, and he is or has been laid off or kept on short-time for each of those weeks it shall be conclusively presumed that the condition specified in subsection (1) was not fulfilled.

(4) For the purposes of section 12 [38] and for the purposes of subsection (3)—

(*a*) it is immaterial whether a series of weeks (whether it is four weeks, or four or more weeks, or six or more weeks) consists wholly of weeks for which the employee is laid off or wholly of weeks for which he is kept on short-time or partly of the one and partly of the other;

(*b*) no account shall be taken of any week for which an employee is laid off or kept on short-time where the lay-off or short-time is wholly or mainly attributable to a strike or a lock-out, whether the strike or lock-out is in the trade or industry in which the employee is employed or not and whether it is in the State or elsewhere.

Disentitlement to redundancy payment because of dismissal for misconduct.

14. —(1) Subject to subsection (2), an employee who has been dismissed shall not be entitled to redundancy payment if his employer, being entitled to terminate that employee's contract of employment without notice by reason of the employee's conduct, terminates the contract because of the employee's conduct—

(*a*) without notice,

[38] This provision originally referred to s. 12(2), but the substitution of all of the original s. 12 of the 1967 Act by s.11 of the Redundancy Payments Act, 1971 rendered necessary this amendment which was effected by s. 19(1) of the 1971 Act.

(*b*) by giving shorter notice than that which, in the absence of such conduct, the employer would be required to give to terminate the contract, or

(*c*) by giving notice (other than such notice as is mentioned in subparagraph (b)) which includes, or is accompanied by, a statement in writing that the employer would, by reason of such conduct, be entitled to terminate the contract without notice.

(2) When an employee who has received the notice required by section 17 takes part, before the date of dismissal, in a strike and his employer by reason of such participation, terminates the contract of employment with the employee in a manner mentioned in subsection (1), that subsection shall not apply to such termination.

(3) Where an employee who has given notice to terminate his contract of employment by reason of lay-off or short-time takes part, before the expiry of the notice, in a strike and, by reason of such participation, is dismissed, subsection (1) shall not apply.

Disentitlement to redundancy payment for refusal to accept alternative employment.

15. —(1) An employee [39] shall not be entitled to a redundancy payment if— [40]

(*a*) his employer has offered to renew that employee's contract of employment or to re-engage him under a new contract of employment,

(*b*) the provisions of the contract as renewed, or of the new contract, as to the capacity and place in which he would be employed and as to the other terms and conditions of his employment would not differ from the corresponding provisions of the contract in force immediately before the termination of his contract, [41]

---

[39] The words "who has received the notice required by section 17" were deleted from here by s. 19(1) of the Redundancy Payments Act, 1971.

[40] The words "in the period of two weeks ending on the date of dismissal" were deleted from here by s. 19(1) of the Redundancy Payments Act, 1971.

[41] The last four words were substituted for "his dismissal" by s. 19(1) of the Redundancy Payments Act, 1971.

(*c*) the renewal or re-engagement would take effect on or before the date of the termination of his contract, [42] and

(*d*) he has unreasonably refused the offer.

(2) An employee [43] shall not be entitled to a redundancy payment if [44]—

(*a*) his employer has made to him in writing an offer to renew the employee's contract of employment or to re-engage him under a new contract of employment,

(*b*) the provisions of the contract as renewed, or of the new contract, as to the capacity and place in which he would be employed and as to the other terms and conditions of his employment would differ wholly or in part from the corresponding provisions of his contract in force immediately before the termination of his contract,[45]

(*c*) the offer constitutes an offer of suitable employment in relation to the employee,

(*d*) the renewal or re-engagement would take effect not later than four weeks after the date of the termination of his contract, [46] and

(*e*) he has unreasonably refused the offer.

(2A) Where an employee who has been offered suitable employment and has carried out, for a period of not more than four weeks, the duties of that employment, refuses the offer, the temporary acceptance of that employment shall not solely constitute an unreasonable refusal for the purposes of this section.[47]

---

[42] The last four words were substituted for "dismissal" by s. 19(1) of the Redundancy Payments Act, 1971.

[43] The words "who has received the notice required by section 17" were deleted from here by s. 19(1) of the Redundancy Payments Act, 1971.

[44] The words "in the period of two weeks ending on the date of dismissal" were deleted from here by s. 19(1) of the Redundancy Payments Act, 1971.

[45] The last four words were substituted for "his dismissal" by s. 19(1) of the Redundancy Payments Act, 1971.

[46] The last four words were substituted for "dismissal" by s. 19(1) of the Redundancy Payments Act, 1971.

[47] Sub-s. 2A was inserted by s. 19(1) of the Redundancy Payments Act, 1971.

(2B) Where—

(*a*) an employee's remuneration is reduced substantially but not to less than one-half of his normal weekly remuneration, or his hours of work are reduced substantially but not to less than one-half of his normal weekly hours, and

(*b*) the employee temporarily accepts the reduction in remuneration or hours of work and indicates his acceptance to his employer, such a temporary acceptance for a period not exceeding 52 weeks shall not be taken to be an acceptance by the employee of an offer of suitable employment in relation to him.[48]

(3) Where a person who is entitled to a weekly payment has unreasonably refused suitable employment offered or approved by [An Foras Áiseanna Saothair], that person shall be disqualified from receiving any further weekly payments.[49]

Associated companies.

16. —(1) Where the employer is a company, any reference in this Part to re-engagement by the employer shall be construed as a reference to re-engagement by that company or by an associated company, and any reference in this Part to an offer made by the employer shall be construed as including a reference to an offer made by an associated company.

(2) Subsection (1) shall not affect the operation of section 20 in a case where the previous owner and new owner (as defined by that section) are associated companies; and where that section applies, subsection (1) shall not apply.

(3) Where an employee is dismissed by his employer, and the employer is a company (in this subsection referred to as the

---

[48] Sub-s. 2B was inserted by s. 11 of the Redundancy Payments Act, 1979.

[49] Sub-s. 3 was entirely substituted by s. 19(1) of the Redundancy Payments Act, 1971, and its reference to the Employment Service altered to a reference to the National Manpower Service. By virtue of s. 18(4) of the Labour Services Act, 1987, references made to the Manpower Service in any Act of the Oireachtas (or in any instrument made under an Act of the Oireachtas) before the establishment under the 1987 Act of An Foras Áiseanna Saothair are now to be construed as references to An Foras Áiseanna Saothair. Note also that the last four words of the subsection were substituted for the words "a weekly payment for a period not exceeding six weeks" by s. 17 of the Redundancy Payments Act, 1979.

employing company) which has one or more associated companies, then if—

(*a*) none of the conditions specified in section 7 (2) is fulfilled, but [50]

(*b*) one or other of those conditions would be fulfilled if the business of the employing company and the business of the associated company (or, if more than one, each of the associated companies) were treated as together constituting one business,

that condition shall for the purposes of this Part be taken to be fulfilled in relation to the dismissal of the employee.

(4) For the purposes of this section two companies shall be taken to be associated companies if one is a subsidiary of the other, or both are subsidiaries of a third company, and "associated company" shall be construed accordingly.

(5) in this section

"company" includes any body corporate;

"subsidiary" has the same meaning as, by virtue of section 155 of the Companies Act, 1963, it has for the purposes of that Act. 1963, No. 33.

Notice of proposed dismissal for redundancy.

17. —(1) An employer who proposes to dismiss by reason of redundancy an employee who has not less than 104 weeks [51] service with that employer shall, not later than two weeks before the date of dismissal, give to the employee notice in writing of the proposed dismissal.[52]

(2) The Minister may make regulations for giving effect to this section and, without prejudice to the generality of the foregoing, regulations under this section may relate to all or any of the following matters— [53]

---

[50] The words of s. 16(3)(a) were substituted by s. 19(1) of the Redundancy Payments Act, 1971 in consequence of the redefinition of redundancy effected by other amendments carried out by the 1971 Act.

[51] The last two words are a substitution for "four years" effected by s. 19(1) of the Redundancy Payments Act, 1971.

[52] The words "and send to the Minister a copy of that notice" were deleted by s. 7 of the Redundancy Payments Act 2003.

[53] See now the Redundancy (Notice of Dismissal) Regulations, 1991 (S.I. No. 348 of 1991). Note that s. 17(2), in its original form, had a Paragraph (c),

(*a*) the particulars to be stated in the notice,

(*b*) the method of service of the notice.

(2A) A notice under this section, a redundancy certificate and a claim for a rebate under section 36 may be combined in one document.[54]

(3) An employer who fails to comply with this section or who furnishes false information in a notice under this section shall be guilty of an offence and shall be liable on summary conviction to a fine not exceeding €3,000.[55]

Redundancy certificate.

18. — (1) When an employer dismisses by reason of redundancy an employee who has not less than 104 weeks' continuous employment, he shall give to the employee not later than the date of the dismissal a certificate (in this Part referred to as a redundancy certificate).[56]

(2) Whenever an employee who has not less than 104 weeks' continuous employment gives notice of intention to claim in accordance with section 12, his employer shall, subject to section 13, give him, not later than seven days after the service of the notice of intention to claim, a redundancy certificate.[57]

(3) The Minister may make regulations for giving effect to this section and, without prejudice to the generality of the foregoing, may prescribe the particulars to be stated on a redundancy certificate.[58]

(4) An employer who fails to comply with this section or who furnishes false information in a redundancy certificate shall

---

which referred to "the furnishing to the Minister of a copy of the notice and the time for furnishing such a copy." This Paragraph was deleted by s. 7 of the Redundancy Payments Act 2003.

[54] Sub-s. 2A was inserted by s. 7 of the Redundancy Payments Act 2003.

[55] This amount was substituted by s. 13 of the Redundancy Payments Act 2003.

[56] Sub-s. 1 was substituted by s. 19(1) of the Redundancy Payments Act, 1971, importing both the service requirement and the deadline for the giving of the redundancy certificate.

[57] Sub-s. 2 was substituted by s. 19(1) of the Redundancy Payments Act, 1971, importing the service requirement, the notice requirement and the deadline for the giving of the redundancy certificate.

[58] See now the Redundancy Certificate Regulations, 1991 (Statutory Instrument No. 347 of 1991).

be guilty of an offence and shall be liable on summary conviction to a fine not exceeding €3,000.[59]

19. —(1) Upon the dismissal by reason of redundancy of an employee who is entitled under this Part to redundancy payment, or where by virtue of section 12 an employee becomes entitled to redundancy payment, [60] his employer shall pay to him an amount which is referred to in this Act as the lump sum.

Payment of lump sum by employer.

(2) Schedule 3 shall apply in relation to the lump sum.

(3) The Minister may by order amend Schedule 3.

20. —(1) This section shall have effect where—

Change of ownership of business.

(*a*) a change occurs (whether by virtue of a sale or other disposition or by operation of law) in the ownership of a business for the purposes of which a person is employed, or of a part of such a business, and

(*b*) in connection with that change the person by whom the employee is employed immediately before the change occurs (in this section referred to as the previous owner) terminates the employee's contract of employment, whether by or without notice.

(2) If, by agreement with the employee, the person (in this section referred to as the new owner) who immediately after the change occurs is the owner of the business or of the part of the business in question as the case may be renews the employee's contract of employment (with the substitution of the new owner for the previous owner) or re-engages him under a new contract of employment, section 9 (2) shall have effect as if the renewal or re-engagement had been a renewal or re-engagement by the previous owner (without any substitution of the new owner for the previous owner).

(3) If the new owner offers to renew the employee's contract of employment (with the substitution of the new owner for the previous owner) or to re-engage him under a new contract of employment, but the employee refuses the offer, section 15 (1)

[59] This amount was substituted by s. 13 of the Redundancy Payments Act 2003 for the amount previously specified.

[60] This clause was substituted for the original version by s. 19(1) of the Redundancy Payments Act, 1971.

or section 15 (2) (as may be appropriate) shall have effect, subject to subsection (4) of this section, in relation to that offer and refusal as it would have had effect in relation to the like offer made by the previous owner and a refusal of that offer by the employee.

(4) For the purposes of the operation, in accordance with sub section (3) of this section, of section 15 (1) or 15 (2) in relation to an offer made by the new owner,—

(*a*) the offer shall not be treated as one whereby the provisions of the contract as renewed, or of the new contract, as the case may be, would differ from the corresponding provisions of the contract as in force immediately before the dismissal by reason only that the new owner would be substituted for the previous owner as the employer, and

(*b*) no account shall be taken of that substitution in determining whether the refusal of the offer was unreasonable.

(5) Subsections (1) to (4) shall have effect (subject to the necessary modifications) in relation to a case where—

(*a*) the person by whom a business, or part of a business, is owned immediately before a change is one of the persons by whom (whether as partners, trustees or otherwise) it is owned immediately after the change, or

(*b*) the persons by whom a business, or part of a business, is owned immediately before a change (whether as partners, trustees or otherwise) include the person by whom, or include one or more of the persons by whom, it is owned immediately after the change,

as those provisions have effect where the previous owner and the new owner are wholly different persons.

(5A) In a case mentioned in subsection (1) (*a*), the new owner shall be estopped from denying that an employee was in continuous employment (within the meaning of Schedule 3) unless, within 26 weeks of the change of ownership, he notifies the employee of his intention so to deny.[61]

---

[61] Sub-s. 5A was inserted by s. 5 of the Redundancy Payments Act, 1971.

(6) Nothing in this section shall be construed as requiring any variation of a contract of employment by agreement between the parties to be treated as constituting a termination of the contract.

21. —(1) Where, in accordance with any enactment or rule of law, any act on the part of an employer or any event affecting an employer (including, in the case of an individual, his death) operates so as to terminate a contract under which an employee is employed by him, that act or event shall for the purposes of this Act be treated as a termination of the contract by the employer, if apart from this subsection, it would not constitute a termination of the contract by him.

Implied or constructive termination of contract.

(2) Where—

(*a*) subsection (1) applies,

(*b*) the employee's contract of employment is not renewed, and

(*c*) he is not re-engaged under a new contract, as provided by section 9 (2),

he shall for the purposes of this Act be taken to be dismissed by reason of redundancy if the circumstances in which the contract is not renewed and he is not re-engaged (as provided by the said section 9 (2) are wholly or mainly attributable to a fact specified in section 7 (2).[62]

(3) For the purposes of subsection (2), section 7 (2) (*a*), in so far as it relates to the employer ceasing or intending to cease to carry on the business, shall be construed as if the reference to the employer included a reference to any person to whom, in consequence of the act or event in question, power to dispose of the business has passed.

(4) In this section reference to section 9 (2) includes reference to that section as applied by section 20 (2).

---

[62] The reference to s. 7(2) was substituted by s. 19(1) of the Redundancy Payments Act, 1971 in consequence of the redefinition of redundancy effected by other amendments carried out by the 1971 Act.

Application of this Part upon employer's or employee's death.

22. —(1) Part I of Schedule 2 shall have effect in relation to the death of an employer.

(2) Part 2 of Schedule 2 shall have effect in relation to the death of an employee.

Modification of right to redundancy payment where previous redundancy payment has been paid.

23. —(1) This section shall apply where—

(*a*) a lump sum is paid to an employee under section 19, whether in respect of dismissal, lay-off or short-time,

(*b*) the contract of employment under which he was employed (in this section referred to as the previous contract) is renewed, whether by the same or another employer, or he is re-engaged under a new contract of employment, whether by the same or another employer, and

(*c*) the circumstances of the renewal or re-engagement are such that, in determining for the purposes of section 7 (1) or Schedule 3 whether at any subsequent time he has been continuously employed for the requisite period, or for what period he has been continuously employed, the continuity of his period of employment would, apart from this section, be treated as not having been broken by the termination of the previous contract and the renewal or re-engagement.

(2) In determining for the purposes of section 7 (1) or section 19 in a case to which this section applies whether at any subsequent time an employee has been continuously employed for the requisite period, or for what period he has been continuously employed, the continuity of the period of employment shall be treated as having been broken at the date which was the date of dismissal in relation to the lump sum mentioned in subsection (1) (*a*), and any time before that date shall be disregarded.

(3) For the purposes of this section a lump sum shall be treated as having been paid if the whole of the payment has been paid to the employee by the employer or if the Minister has paid a sum to the employee in respect of the redundancy payment under section 32.

(4) This section shall not apply in any case to which section 19 of the Unfair Dismissals Act, 1977, applies.[63]

24. — [1] Notwithstanding any other provision of this Act, an employee shall not be entitled to a lump sum unless before the end of the period of 52 weeks [64] beginning on the date of dismissal or the date of termination of employment— Time-limit on claims for redundancy payment.

(*a*) the payment has been agreed and paid, or

(*b*) the employee has made a claim for the payment by notice in writing given to the employer, or

(*c*) a question as to the right of the employee to the payment, or as to the amount of the payment, has been referred to the Tribunal under section 39.

(2) Notwithstanding any provision of this Act, an employee shall not be entitled to a weekly payment unless he has become entitled to a lump sum.[65]

(2A) Where an employee who fails to make a claim for a lump sum within the period of 52 weeks mentioned in subsection (1) (as amended) makes such a claim before the end of the period of 104 weeks beginning on the date of dismissal or the date of termination of employment, the Tribunal, if it is satisfied that the employee would have been entitled to the lump sum and that the failure was due to a reasonable cause, may declare the employee to be entitled to the lump sum and the employee shall thereupon become so entitled.[66]

(3) Notwithstanding subsection (2A), where an employee establishes to the satisfaction of the Tribunal—

[63] Sub-s. 4 was inserted by s. 17 of the Redundancy Payments Act, 1979. Section 19 of the Unfair Dismissals Act, 1977 provides that where an employee is re-instated or re-engaged in pursuance of a determination or order under the 1977 Act, any payments made under the Redundancy Payments Acts shall be repaid.

[64] Substituted for "thirty weeks" by s. 12(2) of the Redundancy Payments Act, 1971. The renumbering of this sub-section is implied by the insertion of the later sub-sections rather than having been formally effected.

[65] Inserted by s. 12(1) of the Redundancy Payments Act, 1971.

[66] Inserted by s. 12(2) of the Redundancy Payments Act, 1971.

(*a*) that failure to make a claim for a lump sum before the end of the period of 104 weeks mentioned in that subsection was caused by his ignorance of the identity of his employer or employers or by his ignorance of a change of employer involving his dismissal and engagement under a contract with another employer, and

(*b*) that such ignorance arose out of or was contributed to by a breach of a statutory duty to give the employee either notice of his proposed dismissal or a redundancy certificate,

the period of 104 weeks shall commence from such date as the Tribunal at its discretion considers reasonable having regard to all the circumstances.[67]

Employment wholly or partly abroad.

25. —(1) An employee shall not be entitled to redundancy payment if on the date of dismissal he is outside the State, unless under his contract of employment he ordinarily worked in the State.

(2) Notwithstanding subsection (1), an employee [68] who under his contract of employment ordinarily works outside the State shall not be entitled to redundancy payment unless, immediately before he commenced to work outside the State, the employee was insurable for all benefits under [the Social Welfare Acts] or would have been insurable for all such benefits but for the fact that the employment concerned was an excepted employment by virtue of [paragraph 2, 4 or 5 of Part II of Schedule 1 to that Act] and the employee [69] was in the employment of the employer concerned and unless—

---

[67] Inserted by s. 13 of the Redundancy Payments Act, 1979.

[68] The foregoing words were substituted for "An employee" by s. 19(1) of the Redundancy Payments Act, 1971.

[69] The words from "the employee was insurable" to the words "and the employee" were substituted for the words "he was domiciled in the State and" by s. 8 of the Redundancy Payments Act 2003. In their original form, these newly-inserted words made reference to provisions of the Social Welfare (Consolidation) Act, 1993 which have since been repealed by s. 360 of the Social Welfare Consolidation Act 2005. The effect of s. 361(b) of the 2005 Act, however, appears to be that references to provisions of a repealed enactment such as those originally found in the text above are now to be read as references to the corresponding provisions of the 2005 Act. Even if this is not the effect of s. 361(b), s. 25(2) of the 1967 Act will in any case come within the more general provisions of s. 26 (2) of the Interpretation

(*a*) he was in the State in accordance with the instructions of his employer on the date of dismissal, or

(*b*) he had not been afforded a reasonable opportunity by his employer of being in the State on that date.

(2A) An employee who under a contract of employment has worked outside the State and was working in the State for at least two years immediately prior to the date of termination of the employment concerned shall be entitled to redundancy payment in respect of all his employment with the employer concerned.[70]

(3) In computing, for the purposes of this Act, for what period of service a person was in continuous employment, any period of service in the employment of the employer concerned while the employee was outside the State shall be deemed to have been service in the employment of that employer within the State.

(4) Where an employee who has worked for his employer outside the State becomes entitled to redundancy payment under this Act, the employer in making any lump sum payment due to the employee under section 19 shall be entitled to deduct from that payment any redundancy payment to which that employee may have been entitled under a statutory scheme relating to redundancy in the State in which he was working.

PART III

REDUNDANCY FUND[70a]

26. *(Deleted by s. 29 of the Social Welfare Act, 1990)* Establishment of the Redundancy Fund.

Act 2005, according to which, where an enactment is repealed and reenacted, with or without modification, by another enactment, a reference in any other enactment to the former enactment shall, with respect to a subsequent transaction, matter or thing, be read as a reference to the provisions of the new enactment relating to the same subject-matter as that of the former enactment. The appropriate references have therefore been substituted in the text above.

[70] Inserted by s. 8 of the Redundancy Payments Act 2003.

[70a] The title of Part III of the 1967 Act has not been replaced but is obsolete, with the functions originally ascribed to the Redundancy Fund by the 1967

Employers' redundancy contributions to be paid into Social Insurance Fund.[71]

27. —All moneys received by the Minister under this Act shall be paid into the Social Insurance Fund and all payments made pursuant to this Act shall be made out of that Fund.[72]

Amount of weekly contribution to Redundancy Fund.

28. *(Deleted by s. 39(1) of the Social Welfare Act, 1991)*

Rebates to employers from the Redundancy Fund.[73]

29. —(1) Subject to this Part, the Minister shall make from the Social Insurance Fund [74] a payment to an employer of such sum (in this Part referred to as a rebate) as is equivalent in amount to 60 per cent of each lump sum paid by that employer under section 19.

(2) Notwithstanding subsection (1), whenever an employer fails to comply with any provision of section 17, the Minister may at his discretion reduce the amount of the rebate payable in respect of the lump sum paid under section 19 to that

---

Act now carried out by the Social Insurance Fund. (See in particular s. 27 of the 1967 Act (below) as substituted by s. 39(1) of the Social Welfare Act, 1991.)

[71] The side-note to s. 27 was inserted in substitution of the original side-note by s. 26 of the Social Welfare Act, 1990 (which also substituted the entirety of the text of s. 27 of the 1967 Act. The new side-note was not deleted, but was rendered misleading by virtue of the second substitution of the entirety of the text of s. 27 of the 1967 Act by s. 39(1) of the Social Welfare Act, 1991.

[72] Section 27 was substituted by s. 39(1) of the Social Welfare Act, 1991. See now regarding the financing of payments made out of the Social Insurance Fund under, *inter alia*, the Redundancy Payments Acts, s. 6 of the Social Welfare Consolidation Act 2005 (replacing s. 6 of the Social Welfare (Consolidation) Act, 1993 which was repealed by s. 360 of the 2005 Act).

[73] The side-note to s. 29 has never been amended but its reference to the "Redundancy Fund" has been rendered obsolete by the substitution of the words "Social Insurance Fund" in the text of s. 29(1) by s. 26 of the Social Welfare Act, 1990.

[74] Section 29 was substituted in its entirety by s. 6 of the Redundancy Payments Act, 1979. The words "Social Insurance Fund" were substituted by s. 26 of the Social Welfare Act, 1990.

employer, but the amount of rebate when so reduced shall not be less than 40 per cent of the lump sum.

(3) The Minister may by regulation, made with the consent of the Minister for Finance, vary a rate of rebate specified in this section.

30. *(This section ceased to have effect under s. 8 of the Redundancy Payments Act, 1979.)* Weekly payments to employees from Redundancy Fund.

31. *(This section ceased to have effect under s. 8 of the Redundancy Payments Act, 1979.)* Regulations as to entitlement to weekly payment and to allowance under Industrial Training Act, 1967.

Other payments to employees from Redundancy Fund.[76]

32. —(1) When an employee claims that an employer is liable to pay to him a lump sum under section 19 and that— [75]

(*a*) the employee has taken all reasonable steps (other than legal proceedings) to obtain the payment of the lump sum from the employer and the employer has refused or failed to pay it or has paid part of it and has refused or failed to pay the balance, or [77]

(*b*) the employer is insolvent and the whole or part of the lump sum remains unpaid, or

(*c*) the employer has died and neither probate of his will has, nor letters of administration in respect of his estate have, been granted, and the whole or part of the lump sum remains unpaid,

---

[75] Note that s. 32 was substituted in its entirety by 14 of the Redundancy Payments Act, 1971.

[76] The side-notes to s. 32 have never been amended but the reference to the "Redundancy Fund" has been rendered obsolete by the substitution of the words "Social Insurance Fund" in the text of s. 32 by s. 26 of the Social Welfare Act, 1990.

[77] The word "or" was added by s. 17 of the Redundancy Payments Act, 1979.

the employee may apply to the Minister for a payment under this section.

(2) If on an application under this section the Minister is satisfied that an employee is entitled to a lump sum under section 19 which remains unpaid either in whole or in part, the Minister shall pay to the employee out of the Social Insurance Fund [78] so much of the lump sum as remains unpaid.

(3) Upon the payment by the Minister of a payment under this section all rights and remedies of the employee with respect to the lump sum concerned or, if the Minister has paid part of it, with respect to that part, shall thereupon stand transferred to and become vested in the Minister and any moneys recovered by the Minister by virtue of this subsection shall be paid into the Social Insurance Fund.[79]

(4) Where, in a case falling within subsection (1) (*a*), the Minister makes a payment to an employee under subsection (2), the Minister shall claim from the employer a sum equal to the amount of the payment made by the Minister under subsection (2) less the amount of the rebate that would have been payable to the employer from the Social Insurance Fund [80] under section 29 if the employer had paid the lump sum to the employee, save that, where it appears to the Minister that the refusal or failure of the employer was without reasonable excuse, the Minister may either withhold any rebate to which the employer would otherwise have been entitled or reduce the amount of that rebate to such extent as the Minister thinks appropriate, and in either such case the amount of the Minister's claim against the employer under this subsection may be increased accordingly.

(5) Where, in a case falling within subsection (1) (*b*), the Minister makes a payment to an employee under subsection (2), the Minister shall be entitled to claim in the bankruptcy,

---

[78] The words "Social Insurance Fund" were substituted for the previous wording by s. 26 of the Social Welfare Act, 1990.

[79] The words "Social Insurance Fund" were substituted for the previous wording by s. 26 of the Social Welfare Act, 1990.

[80] The words "Social Insurance Fund" were substituted for the previous wording by s. 26 of the Social Welfare Act, 1990.

arrangement, administration of the insolvent estate or winding up (as the case may be) in respect of, and only in respect of, a sum equal to the amount of the payment made by the Minister under subsection (2) less the amount of the rebate that would have been payable to the employer from the Social Insurance Fund [81] under section 29 if the employer had paid the lump sum to the employee.

(6) Where, in a case falling within subsection (1) (*c*), the Minister makes a payment to an employee under subsection (2), the Minister shall be entitled to claim from the deceased employer's estate in respect of, and only in respect of, a sum equal to the amount of the payment made by the Minister under subsection (2) less the amount of the rebate that would have been payable to the deceased employer's estate from the Social Insurance Fund [82] under section 29 if the employee had been paid the lump sum from the estate of the deceased employer.

(7) For the purpose of this section an employer shall be deemed to be insolvent if—

(*a*) the employer has been adjudicated bankrupt, has filed a petition for arrangement or has executed a deed of arrangement (within the meaning of section 4 of the Deeds of Arrangement Act, 1887), 1887, c. 57.

(*b*) the employer has died and his estate, being insolvent, is being administered in accordance with the rules set out in Part I of the First Schedule to the Succession Act, 1965, or 1965, No. 27.

(*c*) the employer is a company, and the company is insolvent and being wound up.

33. *(Deleted by s. 39(1) of the Social Welfare Act, 1991)* Regulations as to payment of contributions 1879, c. 58

[81] The words "Social Insurance Fund" were substituted for the previous wording by s. 26 of the Social Welfare Act, 1990.

[82] The words "Social Insurance Fund" were substituted for the previous wording by s. 26 of the Social Welfare Act, 1990.

Preparation and issue of redundancy stamps, etc.

1890, c. 21
1891, c. 38
1891, c. 39
1908, c. 48

34. *(Repealed by s. 19 of the Redundancy Payments Act, 1979)*

Persons employed by more than one employer, etc.

35. —(1) In relation to persons who—

(*a*) are employed by more than one employer in any week, or

(*b*) work under the general control or management of some person other than their immediate employer,

and in relation to any other cases for which it appears to the Minister that special provision is needed, regulations may provide that for the purposes of this Act the prescribed person shall be treated as their employer.[83]

(2) Regulations made relating to persons mentioned in subsection (1) (*b*) may provide for adjusting the rights between them of the person prescribed as the employer, the immediate employer and the persons employed.

Regulations for Part III.

36. —(1) The Minister may make regulations for giving effect to this Part.[84]

(2) Without prejudice to the generality of subsection (1), regulations under this section may make provision in relation to all or any of the following matters:

---

[83] See now in this regard the Redundancy Payments (Dublin Port Dockers) Regulations, 1971 (S.I. No. 301 of 1971), the Redundancy Payments (Dublin Port Dockers) Regulations, 1973 (S.I. No. 42 of 1973), the Redundancy Payments (Dundalk Port Dockers) Regulations, 1973 (S.I. No. 95 of 1973), the Redundancy Payments (Galway Port Dockers) Regulations, 1973 (S.I. No. 261 of 1973), the Redundancy Payments (Limerick Port Dockers) Regulations, 1974 (S.I. No. 59 of 1974), the Redundancy Payments (Waterford Port Dockers) Regulations, 1975 (S.I. No. 73 of 1975) and the Redundancy Payments (Cork Port Dockers) Regulations, 1987 (S.I. No. 211 of 1987).

[84] See now the Redundancy (Rebates) Regulations, 1990 (S.I. No. 122 of 1990).

(*a*) requiring an employer entitled to a rebate to make a claim therefor and prescribing the time within which such a claim is to be made;

(*b*) requiring an employer who has made a claim for a rebate to produce such evidence and other information as may be prescribed and to produce for examination on behalf of the Minister such documents as may he prescribed and are in that employer's custody or under his control;

(*c*) requiring, in connection with an application made to the Minister under section 32, the employer concerned to produce for examination on behalf of the Minister such documents as may be prescribed and are in the employer's custody or under his control;

(*d*) *(Repealed by s. 19 of the Redundancy Payments Act, 1979)* [85]

(*e*) prescribing the method, time and place for the making of weekly payments.

(3) A person who fails to comply with a regulation under subsection (2) (*b*) or (2) (*c*) or who, in relation to a regulation requiring information, furnishes false information shall be guilty of an offence and shall be liable on summary conviction to a fine not exceeding €3,000.[86]

PART IV

MISCELLANEOUS PROVISIONS

37. —The Minister may appoint [87] such and so many persons as he thinks proper to be deciding officers for the purposes of this Act, and every person so appointed shall hold office as a deciding officer during the pleasure of the Minister. Deciding officers.

[85] The repealed provision referred to procedural requirements to be met by an employee making a claim for a weekly payment.

[86] This sum was substituted for the amount previously specified by s. 13 of the Redundancy Payments Act 2003.

[87] The words "from his officers" were deleted here by s. 19(1) of the Redundancy Payments Acts, 1971.

Decisions by deciding officers.

38. —(1) Subject to this Act and in accordance with any relevant regulations, every question arising—

(*a*) in relation to a claim for a weekly payment,

(*b*) as to whether a person is disqualified for a weekly payment,

(*c*) as to the period of any disqualification for a weekly payment,

(*d*) *(Deleted by s. 39(1) of the Social Welfare Act, 1991)* [88]

(*e*) as to who is the employer of an employee, or

(*f*) on any such other matter relating to this Act as may be prescribed,

shall be decided by a deciding officer.

(2) A reference in this section to a question arising in relation to a claim for a weekly payment includes a reference to a question whether a weekly payment is or is not payable.

Redundancy Appeals Tribunal and appeals and references thereto.[90]

39. —(1) There shall be a Tribunal (which shall be known as the [Employment Appeals Tribunal] [89] and is in this section hereinafter referred to as the Tribunal) to determine the appeals provided for in this section.

(2) The Tribunal shall consist of the following members—

(*a*) a chairman who before his appointment shall have had not less than 7 years' experience as a practising barrister or practising solicitor, [91]

---

[88] This referred to the questions as to whether and at what rate a redundancy contribution should be payable by an employer.

[89] Section 39(1) originally referred to the Redundancy Appeals Tribunal. However, s. 18 of the Unfair Dismissals Act, 1977 provided that this Tribunal should be known as the Employment Appeals Tribunal and that references in the Redundancy Payments Act, 1967 and any other Act of the Oireachtas and any instrument made under any Act of the Oireachtas to the Redundancy Appeals Tribunal should be construed as references to the Employment Appeals Tribunal.

[90] This side note has never been amended but has been rendered misleading by the amendment of s. 39(1) which now refers to the Employment Appeals Tribunal, rather than to the Redundancy Appeals Tribunal.

[91] Section 39(2)(a) was substituted by s. 7 of the Redundancy Payments Act, 1971, replacing the original requirement that a chairman be a practising barrister or solicitor of at least 7 years' standing.

(*b*) not more than 5 vice-chairmen, [92]

(*c*) not less than 12 and not more than 30 ordinary members.[93]

(3) The members of the Tribunal shall be appointed by the Minister and shall be eligible for re-appointment.

(3A) Notwithstanding subsection (2), whenever the Minister is of the opinion that for the speedy despatch of the business of the Tribunal it is expedient that there should be added further vice-chairmen or further ordinary members (or both further vice-chairmen and further ordinary members), he may make such additional appointments, and the reference in subsection (4) shall include a reference to this subsection.[94]

(4) The appointments pursuant to subsection (3) of the ordinary members of the Tribunal shall be made—

(*a*) as to one-half of those members, being persons nominated for that purpose by an organisation representative of trade unions of workers, and

(*b*) as to the other half of those members, from among persons nominated for that purpose by a body or bodies representative of employers.

(5) The term of office of a member of the Tribunal shall be such period as is specified by the Minister when appointing such member.

---

[92] The limit of five was substituted by s. 17 of the Redundancy Payments Act, 1979. The original limit was three. The words "who, before their appointment, shall each have had not less than 5 years' experience as a practising barrister or practising solicitor" are to be inserted in s. 39(2)(b) of the 1967 Act by s. 9 of the Redundancy Payments Act 2003, but at the time of writing no order has yet been made by the Minister for Enterprise, Trade and Employment under s. 17(2) of the Redundancy Payment Act 2003, determining the date of the coming into operation of s. 9.

[93] The original provision was for not more than 12 ordinary members. S. 7 of the Redundancy Payments Act, 1971 changed this to not less than 12 and not more than 24. The present parameters were substituted by s. 17 of the Redundancy Payments Act, 1979.

[94] Section 39(3A) was inserted by s. 17 of the Redundancy Payments Act, 1979.

(6) (*a*) A member of the Tribunal may, by letter addressed to the Minister, resign his membership.

(*b*) A member of the Tribunal may be removed from office by the Minister.

(7) (*a*) Whenever a vacancy occurs in the membership of the Tribunal and is caused by the resignation, removal from office or death of an ordinary member mentioned in subsection (4) (*a*), the vacancy shall be filled by the Minister by appointment in the manner specified in that subsection.

(*b*) Whenever a vacancy occurs in the membership of the Tribunal and is caused by the resignation, removal from office or death of an ordinary member mentioned in subsection (4) (*b*), the vacancy shall be filled by the Minister by appointment in the manner specified in that subsection.

(8) In the case of a member of the Tribunal filling a vacancy caused by the resignation, removal from office or death of a member before the completion of the term of office of the last-mentioned member, the member filling that vacancy shall hold office for the remainder of the term of office of the person who so resigned, died or was so removed from office.

(9) A vice-chairman of the Tribunal shall act as chairman thereof when so required by the chairman or the Minister and when so acting shall have all the powers of the chairman.

(10) A member of the Tribunal shall be paid such remuneration (if any) and allowances as may be determined by the Minister with the consent of the Minister for Finance.

(11) Whenever the chairman of the Tribunal is of opinion that, for the speedy dispatch of the business of the Tribunal, it is expedient that the Tribunal should act by divisions, he may direct accordingly and, until he revokes his direction, the Tribunal shall be grouped as so directed.

(12) Each division of the Tribunal shall consist of either the chairman or a vice-chairman of the Tribunal, an ordinary member of the Tribunal mentioned in subsection (4) (*a*) and an ordinary member of the Tribunal mentioned in subsection (4) (*b*).

(13) The Minister may, with the consent of the Minister for Finance, appoint such officers and servants of the Tribunal as he considers necessary to assist the Tribunal in the performance of its functions, and such officers and servants shall hold office on such terms and receive such remuneration as the Minister for Finance determines.

(14) The decision of the Tribunal on any question referred to it under this section shall be final and conclusive, save that any person dissatisfied with the decision may appeal therefrom to the High Court on a question of law.

(15) Any employer who is dissatisfied with a decision given by the Minister in relation to a rebate or with any decision given by a deciding officer in relation to any question specified in section 38 (1) (*e*) or 38 (1) (*f*), [95] or any employee who is dissatisfied with a decision given by a deciding officer under section 38 or with any decision of an employer under this Act may appeal to the Tribunal against the decision; [96] provided however, that the Tribunal shall not be competent to decide whether or not an employee is or was at the material time in employment which is or was insurable for all benefits under the Social Welfare Acts.[97]

(16) A deciding officer may if he so thinks proper, instead of deciding it himself, refer in the prescribed manner to the

[95] A reference to s. 38(1)(*d*) was deleted here by s. 39(1) of the Social Welfare Act, 1991, which also deleted s. 38(1)(*d*) itself from the 1967 Act.

[96] The eight words to be found in the text before the footnote were substituted by s. 17 of the Redundancy Payments Act, 1979 replacing the somewhat more cumbersome original formulation which required the giving of notice of appeal to the Minister in a prescribed manner, and the question being 'referred' to the Tribunal.

[97] The text of s. 39(15) originally referred to "the Social Welfare Acts, 1952 to 1966", until this was altered by s. 39(1) of the Social Welfare Act, 1991 to a reference to the "Social Welfare Acts" *simpliciter*. Under s. 3(8) of the Social Welfare Consolidation Act 2005, references in any other enactment to the "Social Welfare Acts" are now to mean "this Act and every enactment which is to be read together with it as one." Under s. 14(2) of the Social Welfare Act 2005, the Social Welfare Acts and the Social Welfare Act 2005 (other than section 13 thereof) are to be read together as one. Under s. 1(2) of Social Welfare Law Reform and Pensions Act 2006, the Social Welfare Acts and sections 1 to 37 of that Act are to be read together as one.

Tribunal for a decision thereon any question which falls to be decided by him under section 38.

(17) (*a*) The Tribunal shall, on the hearing of any matter referred to it under this section, have power to take evidence on oath and for that purpose may cause to be administered oaths to persons attending as witnesses at such hearing.

(*b*) Any person who, upon examination on oath authorised under this subsection, wilfully and corruptly gives false evidence or wilfully and corruptly swears anything which is false, being convicted thereof, shall be liable to the penalties for wilful and corrupt perjury.

(*c*) The Tribunal may, by giving notice in that behalf in writing to any person, require such person to attend at such time and place as is specified in the notice to give evidence in relation to any matter referred to the Tribunal under this section or to produce any documents in his possession, custody or control which relate to any such matter.

(*d*) A notice under paragraph (*c*) may be given either by delivering it to the person to whom it relates or by sending it by post in a prepaid registered letter addressed to such person at the address at which he ordinarily resides.

(*e*) A person to whom a notice under paragraph (*c*) has been given and who refuses or wilfully neglects to attend in accordance with the notice or who, having so attended, refuses to give evidence or refuses or wilfully fails to produce any document to which the notice relates shall be guilty of an offence and shall be liable on summary conviction thereof to a fine not exceeding [€190.46].[98]

---

[98] The amount of £150, the equivalent in punts of the above amount, was substituted by s. 17 of the Redundancy Payments Act, 1979. Under Article 14 of Council Regulation (EC) No 974/98 of 3 May 1998 on the introduction of the euro (read in conjunction with Article 1 of the same instrument), references made in legislative and statutory provisions

(18) The Tribunal shall submit an annual report to the Minister which shall be published.

(19) The Minister may make regulations giving effect to this section and such regulations may, in particular but without prejudice to the generality of the foregoing, provide for all or any of the following matters—[99]

(*a*) the procedure to be followed regarding the submission of appeals to the Tribunal,

(*b*) the times and places of hearings by the Tribunal,

(*c*) the representation of parties attending hearings by the Tribunal,

(*d*) procedure regarding the hearing of appeals by the Tribunal,

(*e*) publication and notification of decisions of the Tribunal,

(*f*) notices relating to appeals or hearings by the Tribunal,

(*g*) the award by the Tribunal of costs and expenses and the payment of such awards,

(*h*) an official seal of the Tribunal,

(*i*) for treating the Minister as a party to any proceedings before the Tribunal where he would not otherwise be a party to them and entitling him to appear and be heard accordingly.

Reference and appeal to the High Court.

40. —(1) Where any question, other than a question specified in section 38 (1) (*a*), 38 (1) (*b*) or 38 (1) (*c*), is referred to the

---

existing on 31 December 2001 to units of Irish currency as they existed before the start of the third stage of economic and monetary union are to be read as references to the euro unit according to the respective conversion rates (with the rounding rules laid down in Regulation (EC) No 1103/97 of 17 June 1997 on certain provisions relating to the introduction of the euro applying).

[99] See now the Redundancy (Redundancy Appeals Tribunal) Regulations, 1968 (S.I. No. 24 of 1968), the Minimum Notice and Terms of Employment (Reference of Disputes) Regulations, 1973 (S.I. No. 243 of 1973) and the Redundancy (Employment Appeals Tribunal) Regulations, 1979 (S.I. No. 114 of 1979).

Tribunal, the Minister may, on the request of the Tribunal, refer the question for the decision of the High Court.[100]

(2) Where the Minister refers a question for the decision of the High Court under this section, or where a person appeals to the High Court under section 39 (14), the court may, at its discretion, order the payment by the Minister from the Social Insurance Fund [101] of the costs (in whole or in part as so ordered) when taxed of a party involved.

(3) Where the Minister refers a question for the decision of the High Court under this section, he may be represented as a party in that court at the hearing of the question.

Revision of decisions.

41. —(1) A deciding officer may, at any time and from time to time, revise any decision of a deciding officer, if it appears to him that the decision was erroneous in the light of new evidence or of new facts which have been brought to his notice since the date on which it was given or by reason of some mistake having been made with respect to the law or the facts, or if it appears to him in a case where a weekly payment has been payable that there has been any relevant change of circumstances since the decision was given, and the provisions of this Act as to appeals shall apply to such revised decision in the same manner as they apply to an original decision.

(2) Subsection (1) shall not apply to a decision relating to a matter which is on appeal or reference under section 39 unless the revised decision would be in favour of a claimant for a weekly payment.

(3) A revised decision given by a deciding officer shall take effect as follows:—

(*a*) where redundancy payment will, by virtue of the revised decision, be disallowed or reduced and the revised decision is given owing to the original

[100] Section 40 was substituted in its entirety by s. 9 of the Redundancy Payments Act, 1971, importing the provisions regarding costs and representation and removing a provision providing for appeal to the High Court on any question of law on the part of any person dissatisfied with a decision within the scope of this section decided by the Tribunal.

[101] The words "Social Insurance Fund" were substituted by s. 26 of the Social Welfare Act, 1990.

decision having been given, or having continued in effect, by reason of any statement or representation (whether written or oral) which was to the knowledge of the person making it false or misleading in a material respect or by reason of the wilful concealment of any material fact, it shall take effect as from the date on which the original decision took effect, but, in a case in which the redundancy payment is by way of periodical payment, the original decision may, in the discretion of the deciding officer continue to apply to any period covered by such original decision to which such false or misleading statement or representation or such wilful concealment of any material fact does not relate;

(*b*) in any other case, it shall take effect as from the date considered appropriate by the deciding officer, but any payment already made at the date of the revision shall not be affected.

(4) Regulations may provide for the treating of any redundancy payment paid to an employee under a decision of a deciding officer, which it is subsequently decided was not payable, as paid on account of any other redundancy payment which it is decided was payable to that employee or for the repayment of any such payment and the recovery thereof by deduction or otherwise.[102]

(5) Reference in this section to revision includes reference to revision consisting of a reversal.

42. —(1) There shall be included among the debts which, under section 285 of the Companies Act, 1963, [103] are, in the distribution of the assets of a company being wound up, to be paid in priority to all other debts, all contributions [104] payable

Provisions relating to winding up and bankruptcy.

[102] See now the Redundancy (Repayment and Recovery of Payments) Regulations, 1968 (S.I. No. 5 of 1968).

[103] Section 285 of the Companies Act, 1963 has been amended by section 10 of the Companies (Amendment) Act, 1982 and also by s. 134 of the Companies Act, 1990 but these amendments have not been reflected in any change to the manner in which s. 285 is referred to here.

[104] Words (relating to employers' redundancy contributions) were deleted here by s. 39(1) of the Social Welfare Act, 1991 (which amalgamated such contributions with employers' social insurance contributions).

1963, No. 33. by the company under this Act during the twelve months before the commencement of the winding up or the winding-up order and any lump sum (or portion of a lump sum) payable under this Act by such a company, and the said section 285 shall have effect accordingly, and formal proof of the debts to which priority is given under this subsection shall not be required except in cases where it may otherwise be provided by rules made under the Companies Act, 1963.[105]

(2) Subsection (1) shall not apply where a company is wound up voluntarily merely for the purposes of reconstruction or of amalgamation with another company.

1889, c. 60 [106] (3) There shall be included among the debts which, under [section 81(1) of the Bankruptcy Act, 1988] [107], are, in the distribution of the property of a bankrupt or arranging debtor, to be paid in priority to all other debts, all contributions [108] payable under this Act by the bankrupt or arranging debtor during the twelve months before the date of the order of adjudication in the case of a bankrupt or the filing of the petition for arrangement in the case of an arranging debtor and any lump sum (or portion of a lump sum) payable under this Act by a bankrupt or arranging debtor, and the said section [81(1)] [109] shall have effect accordingly, and formal proof of the debts to which priority is given under this subsection shall not be

[105] Section 42(1) was substituted by s. 14 of the Redundancy Payments Act, 1979.

[106] This reference, in the side-note to s. 42, to the Preferential Payments in Bankruptcy (Ireland) Act, 1889 has not been deleted but is now obsolete by virtue of the provision in s. 81(1) of the Bankruptcy Act, 1988 that references to s. 4 of the Preferential Payments in Bankruptcy (Ireland) Act, 1889 of the kind originally found in s. 42(3) of the 1967 Act should be construed as references to s. 81(1) of the 1988 Act.

[107] The text of the Act originally referred to s. 4 of the Preferential Payments in Bankruptcy (Ireland) Act, 1889. However, the Preferential Payments in Bankruptcy (Ireland) Act, 1889 was repealed by s. 6 of the Bankruptcy Act, 1988 and under s. 81(1) of the Bankruptcy Act, 1988, any reference to s. 4 of the 1889 Act of the kind which was to be found here is to be construed as a reference to s. 81(1) of the 1988 Act.

[108] Words (relating to employers' redundancy contributions) were deleted here by s. 39(1) of the Social Welfare Act, 1991 (which amalgamated such contributions with employers' social insurance contributions).

[109] See previous footnote.

required except in cases where it may otherwise be provided by general orders made under the Preferential Payments in Bankruptcy (Ireland) Act, 1889.[110]

(4) Every assignment of or charge on, and every agreement to assign or charge, a weekly payment shall be void and on the bankruptcy of any person entitled to a weekly payment the weekly payment shall not pass to the official assignee in bankruptcy or any trustee or other person acting on account of the creditors.

(5) Nothing in [section 57 of the Bankruptcy Act, 1988], [112] or in section 286 of the Companies Act, 1963, shall apply to any redundancy payments made by an employer. 1872, c. 58.[111]

Recovery of sums due to Social Insurance Fund.[113]

43. —All moneys due to the Social Insurance Fund under this Act shall be recoverable as debts due to the State and, without prejudice to any other remedy, may be recovered by the Minster as a debt under statute in any court of competent jurisdiction.[114]

---

[110] Section 42(3) was substituted by s. 14 of the Redundancy Payments Act, 1979.

[111] The reference, in the side-note to s. 42(5), to the Bankruptcy (Ireland) Amendment Act, 1872, has not been deleted but is now obsolete by virtue of the repeal of the entirety of the Bankruptcy (Ireland) Amendment Act, 1872 by s. 6 of the Bankruptcy Act, 1988 and the requirement by s. 26(2) of the Interpretation Act 2005 that the reference in s. 42(5) of the 1967 Act be construed as a reference to s. 57 of the Bankruptcy Act, 1988.

[112] The first statutory provision referred to in s. 42(5) was originally s. 53 of the Bankruptcy (Ireland) Amendment Act, 1872. However, the entirety of the Bankruptcy (Ireland) Amendment Act, 1872 was repealed by s. 6 of the Bankruptcy Act, 1988. Under s. 26 (2) of the Interpretation Act 2005, where an enactment is repealed and reenacted, with or without modification, by another enactment, a reference in any other enactment to the former enactment shall, with respect to a subsequent transaction, matter or thing, be read as a reference to the provisions of the new enactment relating to the same subject-matter as that of the former enactment. The provisions of s. 53 of the Bankruptcy (Ireland) Amendment Act, 1872 were reenacted and built upon by s. 57 of the Bankruptcy Act, 1988. The text of s. 42(5) of the 1967 Act has therefore been modified accordingly.

[113] This side-note was inserted in substitution of the original side-note by s. 26 of the Social Welfare Act, 1990.

[114] Section 43 was substituted by s. 26 of the Social Welfare Act, 1990 to take account of the dissolution of the Redundancy and Employers' Insolvency Fund by that Act.

Application of section 52 of the Act of 1952.[115]

44. — [Sections 251 and 252 of the Social Welfare Consolidation Act 2005 (other than subsection (6) of section 251 and subsection (8) of section 252] shall apply in relation to benefits under this Act as it applies to benefits and other payments under the [Social Welfare Consolidation Act, 2005].[116]

Application of section 53 of

45. —[Section 272 of the Social Welfare Consolidation Act, 2005] [117] shall apply in relation to offences under this Act

---

[115] The reference, in the side-note to s. 44, to s. 52 of the Social Welfare Act, 1952, has not been deleted but is now obsolete by virtue of the developments described in the next footnote.

[116] This version of s. 44 replaced the original version by virtue of s. 39(1) of the Social Welfare Act, 1991 and initially (in its newly-substituted state) its first words made reference to "Section 115 (other than subsections (3) and (5) thereof) of the Social Welfare (Consolidation) Act, 1981" (replacing the earlier reference to s. 52 (other than subsections (4) and (6) thereof) of the Social Welfare Act, 1952). The effect of s. 361(b) of the Social Welfare Consolidation Act 2005, however, appears to be that references to provisions of a repealed enactment such as that originally found in s. 44 (as inserted in the 1967 Act by the 1991 Act) are now to be read as references to the corresponding provisions of the 2005 Act. Even if this is not the effect of s. 361(b), the matter will in any case come within the more general provisions of s. 26 (2) of the Interpretation Act 2005, according to which, where an enactment is repealed and reenacted, with or without modification, by another enactment, a reference in any other enactment to the former enactment shall, with respect to a subsequent transaction, matter or thing, be read as a reference to the provisions of the new enactment relating to the same subject-matter as that of the former enactment. The appropriate references have therefore been substituted in the text above. (In this regard, it may be noted that s. 115 of the Social Welfare (Consolidation) Act, 1981 was repealed by s. 30 of the Social Welfare Act, 1993, s. 27 of the Social Welfare Act 1993 inserting instead new ss. 294H and 294I into the 1981 Act. Section 300 of the Social Welfare (Consolidation) Act, 1993, in turn, repealed, *inter alia,* ss. 294H and 294I of the 1981 Act and ss. 213 and 214 of the Social Welfare (Consolidation) Act, 1993 were enacted to take their place. Most recently, s. 360 of the Social Welfare Consolidation Act 2005 repealed, *inter alia*, ss. 213 and 214 of the 1993 Act and ss. 251 and 252 of the 2005 Act were enacted to take their place).

[117] The text of the Act originally referred to s. 53 of the Social Welfare Act, 1952, but s. 53 was repealed by s. 310 of the Social Welfare (Consolidation) Act, 1981 and replaced by s. 116 of the same Act. Section 300 of the Social Welfare (Consolidation) Act, 1993 subsequently repealed, *inter alia*, s. 116 of the 1981 Act with s. 224 of the 1993 Act being enacted to replace it. Most recently, s. 360 of the Social Welfare

or under regulations thereunder as it applies to offences under the Act of [2005] or to offences under regulations thereunder, save that in the said application reference in the said section [272] to the [Minister for Social and Family Affairs] [119] shall be construed as reference to the Minister.

the Act of 1952. [118]

46. —(1) The Minister may, for the purpose of promoting national economic policy, make with the consent of the

Aid to unemployed persons changing residence. [120]

Consolidation Act 2005 repealed, *inter alia*, s. 224 of the 1993 Act, and s. 272 of the 2005 Act was enacted to take its place. The effect of s. 361(b) of the Social Welfare Consolidation Act 2005, however, appears to be that references to provisions of a repealed enactment such as that originally found in s. 45 of the 1967 Act are now to be read as references to the corresponding provisions of the 2005 Act. Even if this is not the effect of s. 361(b), the matter will in any case come within the more general provisions of s. 26 (2) of the Interpretation Act 2005, according to which, where an enactment is repealed and reenacted, with or without modification, by another enactment, a reference in any other enactment to the former enactment shall, with respect to a subsequent transaction, matter or thing, be read as a reference to the provisions of the new enactment relating to the same subject-matter as that of the former enactment. The appropriate reference has therefore been substituted in the text above.

[118] This reference, in the side-note to s. 45, to s. 53 of the Social Welfare Act, 1952 has not been deleted but is now obsolete by virtue of the developments described in the first footnote to the text of s. 45.

[119] The original text of this provision referred to the Minister for Social Welfare. However, under Article 3 of the Social Welfare (Alteration of Name of Department and Title of Minister) Order, 1997 (S.I. No. 307 of 1997), the title of the Minister for Social Welfare was altered to that of the Minister for Social, Community and Family Affairs, with Article 4 of the same Order providing that in any enactment, references to the Minister for Social Welfare should be construed as references to the Minister for Social, Community and Family Affairs. In Article 3 of the Social, Community and Family Affairs (Alteration of Name of Department and Title of Minister) Order 2002 (S.I. No. 310 of 2002), the Minister's designation was altered again to that of the Minister for Social and Family Affairs. In Article 4 of the same Order, it was provided that in any enactment or any instrument made under an enactment, references to the Minister for Social, Community and Family Affairs should be construed as references to the Minister for Social and Family Affairs.

[120] This reference, in the side-note to s. 46, to "unemployed persons" has not been amended but has been superseded thanks to the elimination of the original reference to such persons in s. 46(1) by virtue of the substitution of that subsection by s. 18 of the Redundancy Payments Act, 1971.

Minister for Finance regulations providing for financial assistance out of moneys provided by the Oireachtas— [121]

(*a*) to persons who are obliged to change their normal place of residence in order to take up employment offered or approved by [An Foras Áiseanna Saothair] [122], or

(*b*) to enable persons to travel for selection for training at approved training centres or to undertake courses of training at such centres.

(2) Without prejudice to the generality of subsection (1), regulations under this section—

(*a*) may provide for the payment or recoupment, in whole or in part, of the costs of transport (including the transport of household effects) arising out of a change of residence and for allowances in respect of lodgings, and

(*b*) may impose conditions, time limits and financial limits in respect of any moneys payable under the regulations.

(3) Notwithstanding anything contained in section 4, regulations under this section may apply to workers belonging to a class excluded from this Act by the said section 4.

Special redundancy schemes for employees excluded from Act.

47. —(1) The Minister may, in respect of a class of employee excluded from this Act by section 4 or by an order made thereunder, and after consultation with representatives of

---

[121] See now the Redundancy (Resettlement Assistance) (Revocation) Regulations, 1982 (S.I. No. 251 of 1982).

[122] Section 46(1) was entirely substituted by s. 18 of the Redundancy Payments Act, 1971, with the aim of expanding the categories of persons who could benefit under such regulations, and its reference to the Employment Service altered to a reference to the National Manpower Service. By virtue of s. 18(4) of the Labour Services Act, 1987, references made to the Manpower Service in any Act of the Oireachtas (or in any instrument made under an Act of the Oireachtas) before the establishment under the 1987 Act of An Foras Áiseanna Saothair are now to be construed as references to An Foras Áiseanna Saothair.

employers interested in the form of work normally carried on by employees of that class and with representatives of employees so interested, prepare and cause to be carried out a scheme (in this Act referred to as a special redundancy scheme) providing in accordance with the terms of the special redundancy scheme for redundancy payment to employees of that class.

(2) Whenever the Minister has prepared a special redundancy scheme he shall, as soon as he thinks fit after such preparation, make an order providing for the carrying into effect on a specified date of that special redundancy scheme, and from that date that scheme shall be so carried into effect.

48. —(1) Section 9 of the Transport Act, 1964, shall not apply to a person who, after the commencement of this Act, becomes an officer or servant of the Board unless such person was, or, but for a casual interruption of his employment, would have been, an officer or servant of the Board at such commencement and continues to be an officer or servant of the Board except for casual interruptions of employment.

Provision for officers and servants of Córas Iompair Éireann and Óstlanna Iompair Éireann Teoranta.

1964, No. 30.

(2) Where, before the commencement of this Act, a person is in receipt of compensation under section 9 of the Transport Act, 1964, subsection (1) shall not operate to diminish his right to such compensation.

(3) Where a person, on or after the commencement of this Act, becomes entitled to compensation under section 9 (4) of the Transport Act, 1964, in consequence of the termination of his employment with the Board or with the Company, he shall, notwithstanding any other provision of this Act, stand disqualified, as on and from the date of such entitlement, for redundancy payment in respect of such employment and all contributions under this Act paid in respect of that person as an employee of the Board or of the Company shall be refunded to the person who paid such contributions.

(4) In this section—

"the Board" means Córas Iompair Éireann;

"the Company" means Óstlanna Iompair Éireann Teoranta.

Power to modify or wind-up existing schemes and arrangements for the provision of superannuation and redundancy payments.

49. —Any scheme or arrangement for the provision of pensions, compensation for redundancy or other benefits (including any scheme or arrangement established or provided by or under, or having statutory force by virtue of, any enactment and any scheme evidenced only by one or more policies of insurance) may be modified, or wound up, in connection with the establishment under this Act of a scheme for the provision of redundancy payments by agreement between the parties concerned in the scheme or arrangement.

Application of Probation of Offenders Act, 1907.[123]

1907, c. 17.

50. *(Deleted by s. 39(1) of the Social Welfare Act, 1991)*

Voidance of purported exclusion of provisions of this Act.

51. —Any provision in an agreement (whether a contract of employment or not) shall be void in so far as it purports to exclude or limit the operation of any provision of this Act.

Offences by bodies corporate.

52. —Where an offence under this Act committed by a body corporate is proved to have been committed with the consent or connivance of, or to be attributable to any neglect on the part of, any director, manager, secretary or other officer of the body corporate or any person who was purporting to act in any such capacity, he as well as the body corporate shall be guilty of that offence and shall be liable to be proceeded against and punished accordingly.

Provisions regarding notices.

53. —(1) Any notice which under this Act is required or authorised to be given by an employer to an employee may be given by being delivered to the employee, or left for him at his usual or last-known place of residence, or sent by post addressed to him at that place.

(2) Any notice which under this Act is required or authorised to be given by an employee to an employer may be given either by the employee himself or by a person authorised by him to

[123] Both references to the Probation of Offenders Act, 1907 in the side-notes to s. 50 have of course been rendered obsolete by the deletion of s. 50 by s. 39(1) of the Social Welfare Act, 1991.

act on his behalf, and, whether given by or on behalf of the employee,—

(*a*) may be given by being delivered to the employer, or sent by post addressed to him at the place where the employee is or was employed by him, or

(*b*) if arrangements in that behalf have been made by the employer, may be given by being delivered to a person designated by the employer in pursuance of the arrangements, or left for such a person at a place so designated, or sent by post to such a person at a place so designated.

(3) In this section reference to the delivery of a notice shall, in relation to a notice not required by this Act to be in writing, be construed as including a reference to the oral communication of the notice.

(4) Any notice which, in accordance with this section, is left for a person at a place referred to in this section shall, unless the contrary is proved, be presumed to have been received by him on the day on which it was left there.

(5) Nothing in subsection (1) or (2) shall be construed as affecting the capacity of an employer to act by a servant or agent for the purposes of any provision (including either of those subsections) of this Act.

Certificate of decision by deciding officer.

54. —A document purporting to be a certificate of a decision made pursuant to this Act or regulations by a deciding officer and to be signed by him shall be *prima facie* evidence of the making of the said decision, and of the terms thereof, without proof of the signature of such officer or of his official capacity.

Power to remove difficulties.

55. —(1) If in any respect any difficulty arises in bringing into operation this Act or any amendment or repeal effected by this Act, the Minister may by order do anything which appears to be necessary or expedient for bringing this Act into operation, and any such order may modify a provision of this Act so far as may appear necessary or expedient for carrying the order into effect.[124]

[124] One such order was made: the Redundancy Payments Act (Authorised Officers) Order, 1968 (S.I. No. 106 of 1968).

(2) Every order made by the Minister under this section shall be laid before each House of the Oireachtas as soon as may be after it is made, and if a resolution is passed by either House of the Oireachtas within the next twenty-one days on which that House has sat after the order is laid before it annulling such order, the order shall be annulled accordingly, but without prejudice to the validity of anything previously done under the order.

(3) No order may be made under this section after the expiration of one year after the commencement of this Act.

Expenses of Minister.

56. —(1) Any expenses incurred by the Minister or any other Minister in carrying this Act into effect shall, to such extent as may be sanctioned by the Minister for Finance, be paid out of moneys provided by the Oireachtas.

(2) There shall be paid to the Minister for Finance out of the Social Insurance Fund, [125] at such times and in such manner as the Minister for Finance may direct, such sums as the Minister may estimate, on such basis as may be agreed upon between him and the Minister for Finance, to be the part of the said expenses of the Minister or any other Minister in carrying into effect section 39 and section 40 [126], and any sums so paid shall be appropriated in aid of moneys provided by the Oireachtas for carrying this Act into effect.

(3) In estimating expenses for the purposes of subsection (2), there shall be included such amount as, in the opinion of the Minister for Finance, represents the amount of the accruing liability in respect of any superannuation or other retiring allowances, lump sums or gratuities accruing in respect of the employment of any officer or other person for the purposes of this Act.

Regulations regarding keeping of records, furnishing of information

57. —For the purpose of ensuring the effective operation of this Act, the Minister may make regulations providing for the keeping of records and the furnishing of information by employers and for the inspection by authorised officers of the

---

[125] The words "Social Insurance Fund" were substituted by s. 26 of the Social Welfare Act, 1990.

[126] The last three words were inserted by s. 19(1) of the Redundancy Payments Act, 1971.

Minister of records or other documents in the custody or under the control of employers.[127] and inspection of records.

Regulations providing for offences.

58. —The Minister may by regulations provide for offences consisting of contraventions of or failure to comply with a provision of this Act or of contraventions of or failure to comply with regulations under this Act and for the recovery on summary conviction of such offences of fines not exceeding specified amounts not exceeding [€63.49] [128], together with, in the case of continuing offences, further such fines in respect of each of the days on which the offences are continued.[129]

SCHEDULE 1

Section 30.

(Contents omitted) [130]

SCHEDULE 2

Section 22.

PART I

DEATH OF EMPLOYER OR OF EMPLOYEE

1. This Part shall have effect in relation to an employee where his employer (in this Part referred to as the deceased employer) dies.

---

[127] See now the Redundancy (Inspection of Records) Regulations, 1968 (S.I. No. 12 of 1968).

[128] The amount of £50, the equivalent in punts of the above amount, was substituted by s. 17 of the Redundancy Payments Act, 1979. Under Article 14 of Council Regulation (EC) No 974/98 of 3 May 1998 on the introduction of the euro (read in conjunction with Article 1 of the same instrument), references made in legislative and statutory provisions existing on 31 December 2001 to units of Irish currency as they existed before the start of the third stage of economic and monetary union are to be read as references to the euro unit according to the respective conversion rates (with the rounding rules laid down in Regulation (EC) No 1103/97 of 17 June 1997 on certain provisions relating to the introduction of the euro applying).

[129] See now the Redundancy (Inspection of Records) Regulations, 1979 (S.I. No. 115 of 1979), the Redundancy Certificate Regulations, 1991 (S.I. No. 347 of 1991) and the Redundancy (Notice of Dismissal) Regulations, 1991 (S.I. No. 348 of 1991).

[130] This Schedule applied, under s. 30 of the Act, to weekly payments from the Redundancy Fund. Since entitlement to weekly payments was terminated

2. Section 20 shall not apply to any change whereby the ownership of the business, for the purposes of which the employee was employed by the deceased employer, passes to a personal representative of the deceased employer.

3. Where, by virtue of section 21, the death of the deceased employer is to be treated for the purposes of this Act as a termination by him of the contract of employment, the employee shall nevertheless not be treated for those purposes as having been dismissed by the deceased employer if—

(*a*) his contract of employment is renewed by a personal representative of the deceased employer, or he is re-engaged under a new contract of employment by such a personal representative, and

(*b*) the renewal or re-engagement takes effect not later than eight weeks after the death of the deceased employer.

4. Where, by reason of the death of the deceased employer, the employee is treated for the purposes of this Act as having been dismissed by him, he shall not be entitled to a redundancy payment in respect of that dismissal if—

(*a*) a personal representative of the deceased employer has made to him an offer in writing to renew his contract of employment or to re-engage him under a new contract,

(*b*) in accordance with the particulars specified in that offer the renewal or re-engagement would take effect not later than eight weeks after the death of the deceased employer,

(*c*) either—

(i) the provisions of the contract as renewed, or of the new contract, as to the capacity and place in which he would be employed and as to the other terms and conditions of his employment would not differ from the corresponding provisions of

---

under s. 8 of the Redundancy Payments Act, 1979 (which deleted s. 30 of this Act) the contents of the Schedule are obsolete and have therefore been omitted.

the contract in force immediately before the death, or

(ii) if, notwithstanding that in accordance with the particulars specified in that offer the provisions mentioned in subparagraph (i) would differ (wholly or in part) from the corresponding provisions of the contract in force immediately before the death, the offer constitutes an offer of suitable employment in relation the employee,

and

(*d*) the employee has unreasonably refused that offer.

5. For the purposes of paragraph 4—

(*a*) an offer shall not be treated as one whereby the provisions of the contract as renewed, or of the new contract, would differ from the corresponding provisions of the contract in force immediately before the death of the deceased employer by reason only that the personal representative would be substituted as the employer for the deceased employer, and

(*b*) account shall not be taken of that substitution indetermining whether the refusal of the offer was unreasonable.

6. Where by virtue of section 21 the death of the deceased employer is to be treated as a termination by him of the contract of employment, any reference in section 21 (2) to section 9 (2) shall be construed as including a reference to paragraph 3 of this Schedule.

7. Where the employee has before the death of the deceased employer been laid off or kept on short-time for one or more than one week, but has not given to the deceased employer notice of intention to claim, then if after the death of the deemed employer—

(*a*) his contract of employment is renewed, or he is re-engaged under a new contract, as mentioned in paragraph 3 (*a*) or 3 (*b*) of this Schedule, and

(*b*) after the renewal or re-engagement, he is laid off or kept on short-time for one or more weeks by the personal representative of the deceased employer, sections 12 and 13 shall apply as if the week in which the deceased employer died and the first week of the employee's employment by the personal representative were consecutive weeks, and any reference in those sections to four weeks or thirteen weeks shall be construed accordingly.

8. Paragraph 9 or (as the case may be) paragraph 10 shall have effect where the employee has given to the deceased employer notice of intention to claim, and—

(*a*) the deceased employer has died before the end of the next four weeks after the service of that notice, and

(*b*) the employee has not terminated the contract of employment by notice expiring before the death of the deceased employer.

9. If in the circumstances specified in paragraph 8 the employee's contract of employment is not renewed by a personal representative of the deceased employer before the end of the next four weeks after the service of the notice of intention to claim, and he is not re-engaged under a new contract by such a personal representative before the end of those four weeks, sections 12 (1) and 12 (2) and section 13 (4) shall apply as if—

(*a*) the deceased employer had not died, and

(*b*) the employee had terminated the contract of employment by a week's notice (or, if under the contract he is required to give more than a week's notice to terminate the contract, he had terminated it by the notice which he is so required to give) expiring at the end of those four weeks,

but sections 13 (1) to 13 (3) shall not apply.

10. (1) This paragraph shall have effect where, in the circumstances specified in paragraph 8, the employee's contract of employment is renewed by a personal representative of the deceased employer before the end of the next four weeks after the service of the notice of intention to claim, or he is re-engaged under a new contract by such a personal representative before the end of those four weeks, and—

(*a*) he was laid off or kept on short-time by the deceased employer for one or more of those weeks, and (*b*) he is laid off or kept on short-time by the personal representative for the week, or for the next two or more weeks, following the renewal or re-engagement.

(2) Where the conditions specified in subparagraph (1) are fulfilled, sections 12 and 13 shall apply as if all the weeks for which the employee was laid off or kept on short-time as mentioned in the said subparagraph (1) were consecutive weeks during which he was employed (but laid off or kept on short-time) by the same employer.

11. In paragraphs 7 to 10 "week" and "notice of intention to claim" have the meanings respectively assigned to them by sections 2 and 12.

12. Where by virtue of paragraph 3 the employee is treated as not having been dismissed by reason of a renewal or re-engagement taking effect after the death of the deceased employer, then, in determining, for the purposes of section 7, whether he has been continuously employed for the requisite period, the interval between the death and the date on which the renewal or re-engagement takes effect shall count as a period of employment with the personal representative of the deceased employer, if, apart from this paragraph, it would not count for that purpose as such a period of employment.

13. For the purposes of the application, in accordance with section 4 (3), of any provisions of this Act to an employee who was employed in a private household, any reference to a personal representative in this Part shall be construed as including a reference to any person to whom, otherwise than in pursuance of a sale or other disposition for valuable consideration, the management of the household has passed in consequence of the death of the deceased employer.

14. Subject to the preceding provisions of this Part, in relation to an employer who has died—

(*a*) any reference in this Act to the doing of anything by, or in relation to, an employer shall be construed as including a reference to the doing of that thing by, or in relation to, any personal representative of the deceased employer, and (*b*) any reference in this Act to a thing required or authorised to be done by, or in relation to, an employer shall be construed as including a reference to anything which, in accordance with any provision of this Act as modified by this Part (including subparagraph (*a*)), is required or authorised to be done by, or in relation to, any personal representative of his.

15. Where by virtue of any provision of this Act, as modified by this Part, a personal representative of the deceased employer is liable to pay a redundancy payment, or part of redundancy payment, and that liability had not accrued before the death of the deceased employer, it shall be treated for all purposes as if it were a liability of the deceased employer which had accrued immediately before his death.

Part II

16. Where an employer has given notice to an employee to terminate his contract of employment and before that notice expires the employee dies, Part II of this Act shall apply as if the contract had been duly terminated by the employer by notice expiring on the date of the employee's death.

17. Where an employer before the termination of an employee's contract of employment [131] has offered to renew his contract of employment, or to re-engage him under a new contract, then if—

(*a*) the employee dies without having either accepted or refused the offer, and

(*b*) the offer has not been withdrawn before his death,

section 15 (1) or 15 (2) (as the case may be) shall apply as if for "the employee has unreasonably refused" there were

[131] The words "before the termination of an employee's contract of employment" were substituted into paragraph 17 by s. 19(1) of the Redundancy Payments Act, 1971, replacing the original requirement that the employer have given notice of termination to the employee.

substituted "it would have been unreasonable on the part of the employee to refuse".

18. (1) Where, in the circumstances specified in sections 10 (1) (*a*) and 10 (1) (*b*), the employee dies before the notice given by him under section 10 (1) (*b*) is due to expire and before the employer has given him notice under section 10 (3), section 10 (3) and section 10 (4) shall apply as if the employer had given him such notice and he had complied with it.

(2) Where, in the circumstances specified in sections 10 (1) (*a*) and 10 (1) (*b*), the employee dies before his notice given under section 10 (1) (*b*) is due to expire but after the employer has given him notice under section 10 (3), sections 10 (3) and 10 (4) shall apply as if the circumstances were that the employee had not died and had complied with the last-mentioned notice.

19. (1) *(Deleted by s. 19(1) of the Redundancy Payments Act, 1971)* [132]

(2) Where an employee, who has given notice of intention to claim, dies within seven days after the service of that notice, and before the employer has given a counter-notice, the provisions of sections 12 and 13 shall apply as if the employer had given a counter-notice within those seven days.

(3) In this paragraph "notice of intention to claim" and "counter-notice" have the meanings respectively assigned to them by sections 12 and 13.

20. *(Deleted by s. 19(1) of the Redundancy Payments Act, 1971)* [133]

21. Subject to the preceding provisions of this Part, in relation to an employee who has died—

(*a*) any reference in this Act to the doing of anything by, or in relation to, an employee shall be construed as

---

[132] This provision related to s. 12 of the 1967 Act, and was deleted by s. 19(1) of the Redundancy Payments Act, 1971 in consequence of the substitution of s. 12 of the 1967 Act by s. 11 of the 1971 Act.

[133] This provision related to the making of a claim by a personal representative of a deceased employee who died before the end of the period of 30 weeks beginning on the date of dismissal or termination of employment.

including a reference to the doing of that thing by, or in relation to, any personal representative of the deceased employee, and

(*b*) any reference in this Act to a thing required or authorised to be done by, or in relation to, an employee shall be construed as including a reference to anything which, in accordance with any provision of this Act as modified by this Part (including subparagraph (*a*)), is required or authorised to be done by, or in relation to, any personal representative of his.

22. Any right to a redundancy payment which had not accrued before the employee's death shall devolve on his personal representative.

23. In relation to any case where, under any provision contained in Part II of this Act as modified by the preceding provisions of this Part, the Tribunal has power to determine that an employer shall be liable to pay to a personal representative of a deceased employee either—

(*a*) the whole of a redundancy payment to which he would have been entitled apart from another provision therein mentioned, or

(*b*) such part of such a redundancy payment as the Tribunal thinks fit,

any reference in paragraph 22 to a right to a redundancy payment shall be construed as including a reference to any right to receive the whole or part of a redundancy payment if the Tribunal determines that the employer shall be liable to pay it.

Section 19.

SCHEDULE 3

Amount Of Lump Sum

1. (1) The amount of the lump sum shall be equivalent to the aggregate of the following:

(*a*) the product of two weeks of the employee's normal weekly remuneration and the number of years of continuous employment from the date on which the employee attained the age of 16 years with the employer by whom the employee was employed on the date of dismissal or by whom the employee was employed when the employee gave notice of intention to claim under section 12, and

(*b*) a sum equivalent to the employee's normal weekly remuneration.

(2) In calculating the amount of the lump sum, the amount per annum to be taken into account shall be that obtaining under section 4(2) of the Redundancy Payments Act 1979 at the time the employee is declared redundant.[134]

2. If the total amount of reckonable service is not an exact number of years, the "excess" days shall be credited as a proportion of a year.[135]

3. (*a*) For the purpose of ascertaining, for the purposes of paragraph 1, the number of years of continuous employment, the number of weeks in the period of continuous employment shall be ascertained in accordance with this Schedule and the result shall be divided by 52.

(*b*) In ascertaining the number of weeks in the period of continuous employment, a week which under this Schedule is not allowable as reckonable service shall be disregarded. [136]

Continuous Employment

4. For the purposes of this Schedule employment shall be taken to be continuous unless terminated by dismissal or by the employee's voluntarily leaving the employment, but for the purposes of this paragraph 'dismissal' does not include a dismissal within the meaning of the Unfair Dismissals Act,

---

[134] Paragraph 1 of Schedule 3 was substituted in its entirety by s. 11 of the Redundancy Payments Act 2003. By virtue of Article 2 of the Redundancy Payments (Lump Sum) Regulations 2004 (S.I. No. 695 of 2004), the amount obtaining under s. 4(2) of the Redundancy Payments Act, 1979 is €31,200.

[135] Paragraph 2 was substituted by s. 11 of the Redundancy Payments Act 2003.

[136] Paragraph 3 was substituted in its entirety by s. 11 of the Redundancy Payments Act 2003.

1977, and in respect of which redress has been awarded under section 7 (1) (a) or 7 (1) (b) of that Act.[137]

4A. Notwithstanding anything in paragraph 4 (and anything in clause (b) of the definition of "date of dismissal" in section (2), the period of notice due to an employee under section 4 (2) (a) of the Minimum Notice and Terms of Employment Act, 1973, but not given by the employer, shall, where the Tribunal so orders, be allowed as continuous service for redundancy purposes where, but for the failure of the employer to comply with the provisions of that Act, the employee would have qualified for redundancy payment.[138]

5. Where an employee's period of service has been interrupted by any one of the following— [139]

(*a*) any period by reason of—

(i) sickness,

(ii) lay-off,

(iii) holidays,

(iv) service by the employee in the Reserve Defence Forces of the State,

(v) any cause (other than the voluntary leaving of the employment concerned by the employee) not mentioned in clauses (i) to (iv) but authorised by the employer,

(*b*) a period during which, in accordance with the *Adoptive Leave Acts 1995* and *2005*, an adopting parent was absent from work while on adoptive leave or additional adoptive leave or while attending certain pre-adoption classes or meetings,[140]

---

[137] All of the text after the words "leaving the employment" was inserted by s. 17 of the Redundancy Payments Act, 1979.

[138] Para. 4A was inserted by s. 17 of the Redundancy Payments Act, 1979.

[139] Paragraph 5 of Schedule 3 was substituted in its entirety by s. 12 of the Redundancy Payments Act 2003.

[140] Subparagraph 5(b) of Schedule 3 of the 1967 Act was substituted in its entirety by s. 28 of the Adoptive Leave Act, 1995 (as substituted by s. 20 of the Adoptive Leave Act 2005).

(*c*) a period during which an employee was absent from work— [141]

(i) while on protective leave or natal care absence, within the meaning of Part IV of the Maternity Protection Act 1994 or to attend ante-natal classes in accordance with section 15A (inserted by *section 8* of the *Maternity Protection (Amendment) Act 2004)*, or for breastfeeding in accordance with section 15B (inserted by *section 9* of the *Maternity Protection (Amendment) Act 2004)*, of the first-mentioned Act,

(ii) while on parental leave or *force majeure* leave, or

(iii) while on carer's leave within the meaning of the Carer's Leave Act 2001,

(*d*) any period during which an employee was absent from work because of a lock-out by the employer or because the employee was participating in a strike, whether such absence occurred before or after the commencement of this Act,

continuity of employment shall not be broken by such interruption whether or not notice of termination of the contract of employment has been given.

(5A) If an employee is dismissed by reason of redundancy before attaining the period of 104 weeks referred to in Section 7(5) (as amended) of the Principal Act and resumes employment with the same employer within 26 weeks, his employment shall be taken to be continuous.[142]

6. Where a trade or business or an undertaking (whether or not it be an undertaking established by or under an Act of the Oireachtas), or part of a trade or business or of such an

---

[141] Sub-paragraph (c) was substituted by s. 24 of the Maternity Protection (Amendment) Act 2004.

[142] Paragraph 5A was inserted in the form shown above by s. 19(1) of the Redundancy Payments Act, 1971. The reference to 'the Principal Act' should be understood as a reference to 'this Act' since, under s. 1 of the 1971 Act, 'the Principal Act' means the Redundancy Payments Act, 1967.

undertaking, was or is transferred from one person to another, the period of employment of an employee in the trade, business or undertaking (or in the part of the trade, business or undertaking) at the time of the transfer shall count as a period of employment with the transferee, and the transfer shall not break the continuity of the period of employment.[143]

RECKONABLE SERVICE

7. For the purposes of this Schedule, a week falling within a period of continuous employment and during which (or during any part of which) the employee concerned either was actually at work, or was absent therefrom by reason of sickness, a dismissal within the meaning of the Unfair Dismissals Act, 1977, and in respect of which redress has been awarded under section 7 (1) (a) or 7 (1) (b) of that Act, [144] holidays or any other arrangement with his employer shall, subject to paragraph 8, be allowable as reckonable service.

8. During, and only during, the 3 year period ending with the date of termination of employment, none of the following absences shall be allowable as reckonable service— [145]

(*a*) absence in excess of 52 consecutive weeks by reason of an occupational accident or disease within the meaning of [the Social Welfare Consolidation Act 2005],

[143] Paragraph 6 was substituted by s. 19(1) of the Redundancy Payments Act, 1971. This provision should be read in conjunction with the European Communities (Protection of Employees on Transfer of Undertakings) Regulations 2003, implementing Council Directive 2001/23/EC of 12 March 2001 on the approximation of the laws of the Member States relating to the safeguarding of employees' rights in the event of transfers of undertakings, businesses or parts of undertakings or businesses. (Official Journal of the European Communities 22.3.2001 L 82/16).

[144] The foregoing clauses concerning dismissals within the meaning of the 1977 Act were inserted by s. 17 of the Redundancy Payments Act, 1979.

[145] Para. 8 was substituted by s. 12 of the Redundancy Payments Act 2003, and *inter alia,* limited the period in respect of which such absences would not be allowable as reckonable service. The reference in the side-note to '1966, No. 16.', although not deleted, is consequently obsolete and has been omitted here. Sub-para (a) (as inserted by the 2003 Act) originally referred to the Social Welfare (Consolidation) Act, 1993, which has since been repealed by s. 360 of the Social Welfare Consolidation Act 2005. The

(*b*) absence in excess of 26 consecutive weeks by reason of any illness not referred to in subparagraph (*a*),

(*c*) absence by reason of lay-off by the employer.

8A. The following absences shall be allowable as reckonable service: [146]

(*a*) a period during which, in accordance with the *Adoptive Leave Acts 1995* and *2005*, an adopting parent was absent from work while on adoptive leave or additional adoptive leave or while attending certain pre-adoption classes or meetings, [146a]

(*b*) a period during which an employee was absent from work—[146b]

(i) While on protective leave or natal care absence, within the meaning of Part IV of the Maternity Protection Act 1994 or to attend ante-natal classes in accordance with section 15A (inserted by *section 8* of the *Maternity Protection (Amendment) Act 2004*), or for breastfeeding in accordance with section 15B (inserted by *section 9* of the *Maternity Protection (Amendment) Act 2004*), of the first-mentioned Act,

(ii) while on parental leave of *force majeure* leave, or

---

effect of s. 361(b) of the Social Welfare Consolidation Act 2005, however, appears to be that references to provisions of a repealed enactment such as that originally found in sub-para (a) (as inserted by the 2003 Act) are now to be read as references to the corresponding provisions of the 2005 Act. Even if this is not the effect of s. 361(b), the matter will in any case come within the more general provisions of s. 26 (2) of the Interpretation Act 2005, according to which, where an enactment is repealed and reenacted, with or without modification, by another enactment, a reference in any other enactment to the former enactment shall, with respect to a subsequent transaction, matter or thing, be read as a reference to the provisions of the new enactment relating to the same subject-matter as that of the former enactment. The text above has been altered accordingly.

[146] Para. 8A was inserted by s. 12 of the Redundancy Payments Act 2003.

[146a] Subparagraph 8A(a) of Schedule 3 of the 1967 Act was substituted in its entirety by s.28 of the Adoptive Leave Act, 1995 (as substituted by s. 20 of the Adoptive Leave Act 2005).

[146b] Subparagraph 8A(b) of schedule 3 of the 1967 Act was substituted in its entirety by s. 24 of the Maternity Protection (Amendment) Act 2004.

(iii) while on carer's leave under the Carer's Leave Act 2001,

(*c*) any absences not mentioned in paragraphs (*a*) or (*b*) but authorised by the employer.[147]

9. Absence from work by reason of a strike in the business or industry in which the employee concerned is employed and which occurred before the commencement of this Act shall be allowable as reckonable service.

10. During, and only during, the 3 year period ending with the date of termination of employment, absence from work by reason of a strike in the business or industry in which the employee concerned is employed shall not be allowable as reckonable service.[148]

11. Absence from work by reason of a lock-out shall be allowable as reckonable service.

12. Absence from work by reason of a strike or lock-out in a business or industry other than that in which the employee concerned, is employed shall be allowable as reckonable service if it occurred before the commencement of this Act.

Normal Weekly Remuneration

13. For the purposes of this Schedule, in the case of an employee who is paid wholly by an hourly time rate or by a fixed wage or salary, and in the case of any other employee whose remuneration does not vary in relation to the amount of work done by him, his normal weekly remuneration shall be taken to be his earnings (including any regular bonus or allowance which does not vary in relation to the amount of work done and any payment in kind) [149] for his normal weekly working hours as at the date on which he was declared redundant, together

[147] Removing the limit of 13 weeks in a period of 52 weeks which formerly applied in respect of such absences by virtue of the original Paragraph 8(c) of Schedule 3, which has since been substituted.

[148] Para. 10 was substituted by s. 12 of the Redundancy Payments Act 2003, limiting the period in respect of which such absences would not be allowable as reckonable service.

[149] The words "and any payment in kind" were inserted by s. 19(1) of the Redundancy Payments Act, 1971.

with, in the case of an employee who is normally expected to work overtime, [150] his average weekly overtime earnings as determined in accordance with paragraph 14.

14. For the purpose of paragraph 13 the average weekly overtime earnings shall be determined by ascertaining the total amount of overtime earnings of the employee concerned in the period of 26 weeks which ended 13 weeks before the date on which the employee was declared redundant and dividing that amount by 26.

15. For the purpose of paragraph 14 any week during which the employee concerned did not work shall be disregarded and the most recent week before the 26-week period mentioned in paragraph 14 shall be taken into account instead of the week during which the employee did not work.

16. (i) In the case of an employee who is paid wholly or partly by piece rates, bonuses or commissions (being piece-rates, bonuses or commissions related directly to his output) and in the case of any other employee whose remuneration varies in relation to the amount of work done by him, his normal weekly remuneration shall be taken to be the amount as calculated in accordance with subparagraph (ii).

(ii) For the purposes of subparagraph (i) normal weekly remuneration shall be calculated by dividing the remuneration to be taken into account in accordance with subparagraph (iii) by the number of hours ascertained in accordance with subparagraph (vi) and multiplying the resulting hourly rate by the normal weekly working hours of the employee concerned at the date on which he was declared redundant.

(iii) The remuneration to be taken into account for the purposes of subparagraph (ii) shall be the total remuneration paid to the employee concerned for all the hours worked in the period of 26 weeks which ended 13 weeks before the date on which the employee was declared redundant, adjusted in respect of any

---

[150] The words "an employee who is normally expected to work overtime" were substituted by s. 19(1) of the Redundancy Payments Act, 1971.

variations in the rates of pay which became operative during the period of 13 weeks ending on the date on which the employee was declared redundant.

(iv) For the purposes of subparagraph (iii), weeks worked with different employers may be taken into account if the change of employer did not affect the employee's continuous employment as provided by paragraphs 4 to 6.

(v) For the purposes of subparagraph (iii), any week during which the employee did not work shall be disregarded and the most recent week before the 26-week period mentioned in subparagraph (iii) shall be taken into account instead of the week during which the employee did not work.

(vi) The number of hours to be taken into account for the purposes of subparagraph (ii) shall be the total number of hours worked in the period of 26 weeks mentioned in subparagraph (iii).

17. Where an employee receives additional remuneration for working more than a fixed number of hours, that fixed number of hours shall, for the purposes of paragraphs 13 and 16 (ii), be taken to be his normal weekly working hours, unless by his contract of employment he is required to work for more than that fixed number of hours, and in the last mentioned case the higher number of hours required by the contract shall be taken to be his normal weekly working hours.

18. Where in a particular week an employee qualifies for a payment of a bonus, pay allowance or commission which relates to more than the work done in that week, the appropriate portion of the payment may be taken into account under paragraphs 13 and 16 (iii).

19. An employee who is normally employed on a shift cycle and whose remuneration varies in relation to the particular shift he works, and an employee whose remuneration for his normal number of working hours varies in relation to the day of the week or the times of the day or night over which those hours are spread, shall be taken to be each an employee who is paid wholly or partly by piece-rates.

20. For the purposes of this Schedule, in the case of an employee who has no normal working hours, his normal weekly remuneration shall be taken to be the average weekly remuneration, including any bonus, pay allowance or commission, received by the employee concerned over the period of 52 weeks during which he was actually working immediately prior to the date on which he was declared redundant.

21. The date on which an employee is declared redundant shall for the purposes of this Schedule be taken to be the date on which a notice of proposed dismissal was given to the employee in accordance with section 17 or, where a redundancy payment is claimed in accordance with section 12, the first day of the series of weeks of lay-off or short-time referred to in section 7 (3).

22. Where under this Schedule account is to be taken of remuneration or other payments for a period which does not coincide with the periods for which the remuneration or other payments are calculated, part of the remuneration or other payments shall be duly apportioned in such manner as may be just.

23. For the purposes of paragraphs 13 and 16, account shall not be taken of any sums paid to an employee by way of recoupment of expenses necessarily incurred by him in the proper discharge of the duties of his employment.

MISCELLANEOUS

24. In this Schedule—

(Text deleted) [151]

"strike" and "lock-out" have the meanings respectively assigned to them by section 6.

---

[151] The definition of "overtime premium" formerly to be found here was deleted by s. 19(1) of the Redundancy Payments Act, 1971.

REDUNDANCY PAYMENTS ACT, 1971

Number 20 *of* 1971

ARRANGEMENT OF SECTIONS

Section

Number 20 *of* 1971

REDUNDANCY PAYMENTS ACT, 1971

AN ACT TO AMEND AND EXTEND THE REDUNDANCY PAYMENTS ACT, 1967, AND TO PROVIDE FOR OTHER MATTERS CONNECTED WITH THE MATTERS AFORESAID. [27*th July*, 1971.]

BE IT ENACTED BY THE OIREACHTAS AS FOLLOWS:

1. —In this Act "the Principal Act" means the Redundancy Payments Act, 1967.

Definition.
1967, No. 21.

2. —In relation to an employee whose employment is terminated by reason of redundancy on or after the commencement of this Act, any provision of the Principal Act or this Act which affects or relates to the preservation of continuity of the employee's employment shall apply to periods of employment before the 1st day of January, 1968, as they apply to such periods after that date.

Extension of application of certain provisions of Acts.

3. —Notwithstanding section 4 (1) of the Principal Act, that Act shall, with effect from the 6th day of April, 1980, not apply to a person who on the date of termination of his employment had attained the age which on that date is the pensionable age within the meaning of the [Social Welfare Consolidation Act, 2005].[2]

Provisions relating to persons who attain the age of 70 years.[1]

---

[1] The side-note to s. 3, although not deleted, has been rendered obsolete by the developments described in the footnote to the text of s. 3.

[2] Section 3 was substituted by s. 5 of the Redundancy Payments Act, 1979, replacing the original exclusion of any 'person who on the date of the termination of his employment had attained the age of 70 years'. The text of s. 3 (*i.e.,* as substituted by the 1979 Act) initially referred to the Social Welfare Act, 1952, but the 1952 Act was subsequently repealed by s. 310 of the Social Welfare (Consolidation) Act, 1981 and a provision defining what constituted pensionable age put in s. 2(1) of the 1981 Act. S. 2(1) of

Amendment of section 7 of Principal Act.

4. *(Substitution of s. 7(2)(b) of the Redundancy Payments Act, 1967 including addition of new paras. (c), (d) and (e))*

(Insertion of s. 7(4A) of the Redundancy Payments Act, 1967)

Amendment of section 20 of Principal Act.

5. *(Insertion of s. 20(5A) in the Redundancy Payments Act, 1967)*

Application of section 20 of Principal Act.

6.—(1) Where—

(i) a change relating to the control or management of a business (or part thereof) for the purposes of which a person is employed occurs, but a change in the ownership of the business (or part thereof) does not occur,

(ii) section 20 of the Principal Act would have applied to that change if it were a change in the ownership of that business (or part thereof), and

---

the 1981 Act was then in turn repealed by s. 300 of the Social Welfare (Consolidation) Act, 1993, and a definition provided of what constituted pensionable age in s. 2(1) of the Social Welfare (Consolidation) Act, 1993. Most recently, s. 2(1) of the Social Welfare (Consolidation) Act, 1993, *inter alia,* has been repealed by s. 360 of the Social Welfare Consolidation Act 2005, with "pensionable age" now being defined by s. 2(1) of the Social Welfare Consolidation Act 2005 as meaning the age of 66 years. The effect of s. 361(b) of the Social Welfare Consolidation Act 2005 appears to be that references to provisions of a repealed enactment such as that originally found in s. 3 of the Redundancy Payments Act 1971 are now to be read as references to the corresponding provisions of the 2005 Act. Even if this is not the effect of s. 361(b), the matter will in any case come within the more general provisions of s. 26 (2) of the Interpretation Act 2005, according to which, where an enactment is repealed and reenacted, with or without modification, by another enactment, a reference in any other enactment to the former enactment shall, with respect to a subsequent transaction, matter or thing, be read as a reference to the provisions of the new enactment relating to the same subject-matter as that of the former enactment.
The text above has been altered accordingly. Note that the original side-note to s. 3 of the 1971 Act, which referred to "Provisions relating to persons who attain age of 70 years", although never repealed, was rendered obsolete by the substitution of s. 3 of the 1971 Act in 1979 and has been omitted here.

(iii) an employee of the previous owner accepts, before, on or within four weeks of the termination of his contract of employment with the previous owner, an offer by the new owner of employment in the same place of employment and on terms which are either the same as, or not materially less advantageous to the employee than, his existing terms of employment,

the said section 20 shall apply to that change as if a change of ownership of that business (or part thereof) had occurred.

(2) In this section "previous owner" and "new owner" mean, respectively, the persons who would have been the previous owner and the new owner within the meaning of the said section 20 if a change of ownership of a business (or part thereof) had occurred.

Amendment of section 39 of Principal Act.

7. *(Substitution of s. 39(2)(a) of the Redundancy Payments Act, 1967)*

(Substitution of s. 39(2)(c) of the Redundancy Payments Act, 1967) [3]

Redundancy payment to certain employees dismissed before commencement of Act.

8. —(1) Where an employee who was dismissed before the commencement of this Act was not entitled to redundancy payment under the Principal Act in respect of the dismissal solely because the requirements of the business carried on by his employer for employees to carry out work of a particular kind, or to carry out such work in the place where the employee had been so employed, had not ceased or diminished or were not expected to cease or diminish, the Minister may, at his discretion and notwithstanding the Principal Act, pay to that employee out of the Redundancy Fund [4] a sum equal in amount to the sum to which he would have been entitled under the Principal Act if the said requirements had ceased or diminished or were expected to cease or diminish.

---

[3] This amendment has now been superseded by the subsequent further substitution of s. 39(2)(c) by s. 17 of the Redundancy Payments Act, 1979.

[4] This Fund was dissolved under Part VI of the Social Welfare Act, 1990, and moneys standing to its credit transferred to the Social Insurance Fund. Section 8 was not amended to take account of this, however, probably reflecting what in practice was the transitional nature of its relevance.

(2) In relation to the amendments of the Principal Act referred to in section 19 (2), the Minister may, in respect of a dismissal or a termination of employment in the period beginning on the 22nd day of January, 1971 and ending on the commencement of this section and notwithstanding the Principal Act, pay to an employee out of the Redundancy Fund any moneys to which the employee may become entitled by virtue of the said section 19 (2).

Reference and appeal to the High Court.

9. *(Substitution of s. 40 of the Redundancy Payments Act, 1967)*

Presumptions by Tribunal.

10. —For the purposes of a reference to the Tribunal—

(*a*) a person's employment during any period shall, unless the contrary is proved, be presumed to have been continuous;

(*b*) an employee who has been dismissed by his employer shall, unless the contrary is proved, be presumed to have been so dismissed by reason of redundancy;

(*c*) the Tribunal shall, after consultation with any person or body charged by statute with the fixing or determination of minimum wages or rates of pay, or the registration of employment agreements under the Industrial Relations Act, 1946, or the national minimum hourly rate of pay declared by order under the National Minimum Wage Act 2000 [5] have regard to any such minimum as is appropriate or relevant.

Right to redundancy payment by reason of lay-off or short-time.

11. *(Substitution of s. 12 of the Redundancy Payments Act, 1967)*

Time-limit on claims for redundancy payment.

12. —(1) *(Insertion of s. 24(2) of the Redundancy Payments Act, 1967)*

[5] The words "or the national minimum hourly rate of pay declared by order under the National Minimum Wage Act 2000" were inserted by s. 14 of the Redundancy Payments Act 2003.

(2) *(Substitution in s. 24 of the Redundancy Payments Act, 1967)*

(Insertion of s. 24(2A) of the Redundancy Payments Act, 1967)

13. *(Substitution of s. 29 of the Redundancy Payments Act, 1967)* [6] Rebates to employers from Redundancy Fund.

14. *(Substitution of s. 32 of the Redundancy Payments Act, 1967)* Other payments to employees from Redundancy Fund.

Provisions relating to special redundancy schemes.

15. —(1) Any dispute arising under a special redundancy scheme may be referred by a party to the scheme to the Tribunal and shall be deemed to be a question referred under section 39 of the Principal Act to the Tribunal for a decision on the question.

(2) For the purpose of providing moneys for making payments which under this Act are to be made out of a fund established under a special redundancy scheme, there shall be paid into that fund—

(*a*) as may be provided in that scheme, contributions by employers, and

(*b*) advances as provided for in subsections (3) and (4).[7]

(3) The Minister for Finance may from time to time, on the recommendation of the Minister, advance to any fund established under a special redundancy scheme moneys to enable payments required under the scheme to be made out of the fund, and any advances under this subsection shall be made out of the Central Fund or the growing produce thereof and shall be on such terms as to interest and repayment as the Minister for Finance may determine.

---

[6] This amendment has now been superseded, since s. 6 of the Redundancy Payments Act, 1979 has since substituted s. 29 of the Redundancy Payments Act, 1967 in its entirety once again.

[7] Sub-s. 2 was substituted in its entirety by s. 15 of the Redundancy Payments Act, 1979, eliminating the previous mention both of weekly contributions and of contributions by employees.

(4) The Minister may, with the consent of the Minister for Finance, from time to time authorise the transfer of moneys from the Social Insurance Fund to any fund established under a special redundancy scheme, and any moneys transferred under this subsection shall be repayable to the Social Insurance Fund on such terms (including terms as to interest) as the Minister for Finance may determine.[8]

(5) (*a*) A fund established under a special redundancy scheme shall comprise a current account, to be managed and controlled by the Minister, and an investment account, to be managed and controlled by the Minister for Finance.

(*b*) Save where otherwise specifically provided, sums payable into a fund established under a special redundancy scheme shall be paid into the current account of that fund and sums payable out of that fund shall be paid out of that account.

(*c*) Moneys standing to the credit of the current account of a fund established under a special redundancy scheme and not required to meet current expenditure shall be transferred to the investment account of that fund.

(*d*) Whenever the moneys in the current account of a fund established under a special redundancy scheme are insufficient to meet the liabilities of that account there shall be transferred to that account from the investment account of that fund such sums as may be necessary for the purpose of discharging those liabilities.

(*e*) Subject to paragraph (*d*), moneys standing to the credit of the investment account of a fund established under a special redundancy scheme shall be invested by the Minister for Finance, and income arising from any such investment shall be paid into that account.

---

[8] Sub-s. 4 was substituted by s. 27 of the Social Welfare Act, 1990, with the purpose of changing the Fund referred to in the sub-section to the Social Insurance Fund.

(*f*) An investment pursuant to paragraph (*e*) may be in any securities in which trustees are for the time being by law empowered to invest trust funds or in any of the stocks, funds and securities as are for the time being authorised by law as investments for the Post Office Savings Bank funds.

(*g*) The accounts of a fund established under a special redundancy scheme shall be prepared in such form, in such manner and at such times as the Minister for Finance may direct and the Comptroller and Auditor General shall examine and certify every such account and a copy thereof, together with the report thereon of the Comptroller and Auditor General, shall be laid before each House of the Oireachtas.

Offences relating to payments under Principal Act.

16.—(1) A person who fraudulently claims a weekly payment, fraudulently applies to the Minister for a payment under section 32 of the Principal Act or fraudulently makes a claim for a rebate, shall be guilty of an offence and shall be liable on summary conviction to a fine not exceeding [€380.92].[9]

(2) A person who aids, abets, counsels or procures another person to commit an offence under subsection (1) of this section shall be guilty of an offence and shall be liable on summary conviction to a fine not exceeding [€380.92].[10]

[9] The amount of £300, the equivalent in punts of the above amount, was substituted by s. 18 of the Redundancy Payments Act, 1979. Under Article 14 of Council Regulation (EC) No 974/98 of 3 May 1998 on the introduction of the euro (read in conjunction with Article 1 of the same instrument), references made in legislative and statutory provisions existing on 31 December 2001 to units of Irish currency as they existed before the start of the third stage of economic and monetary union are to be read as references to the euro unit according to the respective conversion rates (with the rounding rules laid down in Regulation (EC) No 1103/97 of 17 June 1997 on certain provisions relating to the introduction of the euro applying).

[10] The amount of £300, the equivalent in punts of the above amount, was substituted by s. 18 of the Redundancy Payments Act, 1979. See, regarding the effect of Article 14 of Council Regulation (EC) No 974/98 of 3 May 1998 on the introduction of the euro (read in conjunction with Article 1 of the same instrument), the previous footnote.

(3) Notwithstanding any provision in any Act specifying the period within which summary proceedings may be commenced, proceedings in respect of an offence under this section may be commenced at any time within the period of three months from the date on which evidence, sufficient in the opinion of the Minister to justify a prosecution for the offence, comes to his knowledge, or within the period of twelve months after the commission of the offence, whichever period last expires.

Reciprocal arrangements.

17.—(1) The Minister may make such orders as may be necessary to carry out any reciprocal or other arrangements, made with the proper authority under any other Government, in respect of matters relating to redundancy payments, and may by any such order make such adaptations of and modifications in the Principal Act as he considers necessary.

(2) The Minister may by order amend or revoke an order under this section.

Aid to persons changing residence or undergoing certain training.

18. *(Substitution of s. 46(1) of the Redundancy Payments Act, 1967)*

Miscellaneous amendments of Principal Act.

19. —(1) Each provision of the Principal Act mentioned in column (1) of the Schedule to this Act is hereby amended in the manner stated in column (2) of that Schedule opposite the mention of that provision in column (1).

(2) Notwithstanding section 20 (3), this section, in so far as it relates to the first amendment of section 4 of the Principal Act, the first amendment of section 7 of that Act, the fifth amendment of Schedule 1 of that Act and the fourth amendment of Schedule 3 of that Act, shall be deemed to have come into operation on the 22nd day of January, 1971.

Short title, construction, collective citation and commencement.

20. —(1) This Act may be cited as the Redundancy Payments Act, 1971.

(2) The Principal Act and this Act shall be construed as one Act and may be cited together as the Redundancy Payments Acts, 1967 and 1971.[11]

(3) This Act shall come into operation on such day as the Minister appoints by order.[12]

SCHEDULE

Section 19.

MISCELLANEOUS AMENDMENTS OF THE PRINCIPAL ACT

Provision Amended (1)	Nature of Amendment (2)
Section 2.	*(Substitution in s. 2(1) of the Redundancy Payments Act, 1967)* *(Insertion in s. 2(2) of the Redundancy Payments Act, 1967)*
Section 4.	*(Substitution in s. 4(1) of the Redundancy Payments Act, 1967)*

[11] Note that the Redundancy Payments Act, 1967, the Redundancy Payments Act, 1971, the Redundancy Payments Act, 1973, the Redundancy Payments Act, 1979, s. 12 of the Protection of Employees (Employers' Insolvency) Act, 1984, ss. 26, 27 and 29 of the Social Welfare Act, 1990, s. 39 (other than sub-s. (2)) of the Social Welfare Act, 1991 (although apparently by oversight no mention is made of s. 39 of the 1991 Act in any subsequent statute included in this list), the Protection of Employees (Part-Time Work) Act, 2001 (insofar as it relates to the foregoing legislation, apart from s. 39 of the 1991 Act) and the Redundancy Payments Act 2003 may be cited together as the Redundancy Payments Acts 1967 to 2003.
See in this regard, in addition to s. 20(2) of the Redundancy Payments Act, 1971, s. 2(2) of the Redundancy Payments Act, 1973, s. 21(2) of the Redundancy Payments Act, 1979, s. 18(2) of the Protection of Employees (Employers' Insolvency) Act, 1984, s. 1(4) of the Social Welfare Act, 1990, s. 1(3) of the Social Welfare Act, 1991, s. 1(4) of the Protection of Employees (Part-Time Work) Act, 2001 and s. 17(3) of the Redundancy Payments Act 2003.

[12] In the Redundancy Payments Act, 1971 (Commencement) Order, 1971 (S.I. No. 230 of 1971), the Minister for Labour appointed 1 September, 1971 to be the day on which this Act came into operation.

Provision Amended (1)	Nature of Amendment (2)
	(Insertion of s. 4(3)(c) in the Redundancy Payments Act, 1967)
Section 5.	*(Insertion in s. 5(1) of the Redundancy Payments Act, 1967)*
Section 7.	*(Substitution in s. 7(1)(b) of the Redundancy Payments Act, 1967)* *(Substitution in s. 7(5) of the Redundancy Payments Act, 1967)*
Section 8.	*(Substitution in s. 8(2) of the Redundancy Payments Act, 1967)*
Section 9.	*(Deletion in s. 9(1) (c) of the Redundancy Payments Act, 1967)* *(Substitution in s. 8(3)(b) of the Redundancy Payments Act, 1967)*
Section 11.	*(Deletion in s. 11(1) of the Redundancy Payments Act, 1967)* *(Insertion of s. 11(3) of the Redundancy Payments Act, 1967)* [13]
Section 13.	*(Substitution in s. 13(4) of the Redundancy Payments Act, 1967)*
Section 15.	*(Deletions in s. 15(1) and s. 15(2) of the Redundancy Payments Act, 1967)* *(Substitutions in s. 15(1)(b), s. 15(2)(b), s. 15(1)(c) and s. 15(2)(d) of the Redundancy Payments Act, 1967)* *(Insertion of s. 15(2A) of the Redundancy Payments Act, 1967)*

[13] This amendment has now been superseded, since s. 10 of the Redundancy Payments Act, 1979 substituted ss. 11(2) and 11(3) of the Redundancy Payments Act, 1967 in their entirety.

Provision Amended (1)	Nature of Amendment (2)
	(Substitution of s. 15(3) of the Redundancy Payments Act, 1967)
Section 16.	*(Substitution in s. 16(3)(a) of the Redundancy Payments Act, 1967)*
Section 17.	*(Substitution in s. 17(1) of the Redundancy Payments Act, 1967)*
Section 18.	*(Substitution of s. 18(2) of the Redundancy Payments Act, 1967)*
Section 19.	*(Substitution in s. 19(1) of the Redundancy Payments Act, 1967)*
Section 21.	*(Substitution in s. 21(2) of the Redundancy Payments Act, 1967)*
Section 25.	*(Substitution in s. 25(2) of the Redundancy Payments Act, 1967)*
Section 30.	*(Substitution in s. 30(1) of the Redundancy Payments Act, 1967)* [14]
Section 37.	*(Deletion in s. 37 of the Redundancy Payments Act, 1967)*
Section 56.	*(Insertion in s. 56(2) of the Redundancy Payments Act, 1967)*
Schedule 1.	*(Substitution of paras. 2, 4 and 5 of Schedule 1 to the Redundancy Payments Act, 1967)* [15]

[14] This amendment has now been superseded, as s. 8 of the Redundancy Payments Act, 1979 has since provided that s. 30 of the 1967 Act should cease to have effect.

[15] These amendments have now been superseded, as s. 8 of the Redundancy Payments Act, 1979 has since provided that s. 30 of the 1967 Act should cease to have effect, rendering Schedule 1 of the 1967 Act obsolete.

Provision Amended (1)	Nature of Amendment (2)
	(Insertion in para. 6 of Schedule 1 to the Redundancy Payments Act, 1967) [16] *(Substitution of para. 7 of Schedule 1 to the Redundancy Payments Act, 1967)* [17] *(Two substitutions in para. 9 of Schedule 1 to the Redundancy Payments Act, 1967)* [18] *(Insertion in para. 14 of Schedule 1 to the Redundancy Payments Act, 1967)* [19] *(Insertion of para. 15 of Schedule 1 to the Redundancy Payments Act, 1967)* [20]
Schedule 2.	*(Substitution in para. 17 of Schedule 2 to the Redundancy Payments Act, 1967)*
	(Deletion of para. 19(1) of Schedule 2 to the Redundancy Payments Act, 1967) *(Deletion of para. 20 of Schedule 2 to the Redundancy Payments Act, 1967)*

[16] This amendment has now been superseded, as s. 8 of the Redundancy Payments Act, 1979 has since provided that s. 30 of the 1967 Act should cease to have effect, rendering Schedule 1 of the 1967 Act obsolete.

[17] This amendment has now been superseded, as s. 8 of the Redundancy Payments Act, 1979 has since provided that s. 30 of the 1967 Act should cease to have effect, rendering Schedule 1 of the 1967 Act obsolete.

[18] These amendments have now been superseded, as s. 8 of the Redundancy Payments Act, 1979 has since provided that s. 30 of the 1967 Act should cease to have effect, rendering Schedule 1 of the 1967 Act obsolete.

[19] This amendment has now been superseded, as s. 8 of the Redundancy Payments Act, 1979 has since provided that s. 30 of the 1967 Act should cease to have effect, rendering Schedule 1 of the 1967 Act obsolete.

[20] This amendment has now been superseded, as s. 8 of the Redundancy Payments Act, 1979 has since provided that s. 30 of the 1967 Act should cease to have effect, rendering Schedule 1 of the 1967 Act obsolete.

Provision Amended (1)	Nature of Amendment (2)
Schedule 3.	*(Insertion in paras. 1(a) and (b) of Schedule 3 to the Redundancy Payments Act, 1967)* [21]
	(Deletion in para. 1(b) of Schedule 3 to the Redundancy Payments Act, 1967) [22]
	(Insertion of para. 1(c) of Schedule 3 to the Redundancy Payments Act, 1967) [23]
	(Deletion of para. 2 of Schedule 3 to the Redundancy Payments Act, 1967) [24]
	(Substitution in para. 5(1) of Schedule 3 to the Redundancy Payments Act, 1967) [25]
	(Insertion in para. 5(1)(a) of Schedule 3 to the Redundancy Payments Act, 1967) [26]
	(Insertion of para. 5(1)(ai) of Schedule 3 to the Redundancy Payments Act, 1967) [27]

---

[21] This amendment has now been superseded as a result of the substitution of Paragraph 1 of Schedule 3 to the 1967 Act by s. 11 of the Redundancy Payments Act 2003.

[22] This amendment has now been superseded as a result of the substitution of Paragraph 1 of Schedule 3 to the 1967 Act by s. 11 of the Redundancy Payments Act 2003.

[23] This amendment has now been superseded as a result of the substitution of Paragraph 1 of Schedule 3 to the 1967 Act by s. 11 of the Redundancy Payments Act 2003.

[24] This amendment has been superseded as a result of the substitution of Paragraph 2 of Schedule 3 to the 1967 Act by s. 11 of the Redundancy Payments Act 2003.

[25] This amendment has been superseded as a result of the substitution of Paragraph 5 of Schedule 3 to the 1967 Act by s. 12 of the Redundancy Payments Act 2003.

[26] This amendment has been superseded as a result of the substitution of Paragraph 5 of Schedule 3 to the 1967 Act by s. 12 of the Redundancy Payments Act 2003.

[27] This amendment has been superseded as a result of the substitution of Paragraph 5 of Schedule 3 to the 1967 Act by s. 12 of the Redundancy Payments Act 2003.

Provision Amended (1)	Nature of Amendment (2)
	(Deletion of para. 5 (1)(b)(iii) of Schedule 3 to the Redundancy Payments Act, 1967) [28]
	(Substitution in para. 5(1) of Schedule 3 to the Redundancy Payments Act, 1967) [29]
	(Insertion of para. 5A of Schedule 3 to the Redundancy Payments Act, 1967)
	(Substitution of para. 6 of Schedule 3 to the Redundancy Payments Act, 1967)
	(Insertion in para. 13 of Schedule 3 to the Redundancy Payments Act, 1967)
	(Substitution in para. 13 of Schedule 3 to the Redundancy Payments Act, 1967)
	(Deletion in para. 24 of Schedule 3 to the Redundancy Payments Act, 1967)

[28] This amendment has been superseded as a result of the substitution of Paragraph 5 of Schedule 3 to the 1967 Act by s. 12 of the Redundancy Payments Act 2003.

[29] This amendment has been superseded as a result of the substitution of Paragraph 5 of Schedule 3 to the 1967 Act by s. 12 of the Redundancy Payments Act 2003.

MINIMUM NOTICE AND TERMS OF EMPLOYMENT ACT, 1973

Number 4 *of* 1973

ARRANGEMENT OF SECTIONS

Section

FIRST SCHEDULE

COMPUTATION OF CONTINUOUS SERVICE

SECOND SCHEDULE

RIGHTS OF EMPLOYEE DURING PERIOD OF NOTICE

Number 4 *of* 1973

MINIMUM NOTICE AND TERMS OF EMPLOYMENT ACT, 1973

AN ACT TO REQUIRE A MINIMUM PERIOD OF NOTICE TO TERMINATE THE EMPLOYMENT OF THOSE WHO HAVE BEEN EMPLOYED FOR A QUALIFYING PERIOD, TO PROVIDE FOR MATTERS CONNECTED WITH THE GIVING OF NOTICE, AND TO REQUIRE EMPLOYERS TO GIVE WRITTEN PARTICULARS OF THE TERMS OF EMPLOYMENT, AND TO PROVIDE FOR OTHER MATTERS CONNECTED WITH THE MATTERS AFORESAID. [*9th May,* 1973]

BE IT ENACTED BY THE OIREACHTAS AS FOLLOWS:

1. —In this Act— Interpretation.

"the Act of 1967" means the Redundancy Payments Act, 1967;

'civil servant' has the same meaning as in the Civil Service Regulation Act 1956; [1]

'Department' has the same meaning as in the Public Service Management Act 1997; [1a]

"employee" means an individual who has entered into or works under a contract with an employer, whether the contract be for manual labour, clerical work or otherwise, whether it be expressed or implied, oral or in writing, and whether it be a contract of service or of apprenticeship or otherwise, and cognate expressions shall be construed accordingly;

---

[1] This definition was inserted by s. 24 of the Civil Service Regulation (Amendment) Act 2005.

[1a] This definition was inserted by s. 24 of the Civil Service Regulation (Amendment) Act 2005.

"lay-off" has the meaning assigned to it by the Act of 1967;

1967, No. 21. "lock-out" has the meaning assigned to it by Part II of the Act of 1967;

"Minister" [1b] means the [Minister for Enterprise, Trade and Employment];

"prescribed" means prescribed by regulations made by the Minister under this Act;

'Scheduled Office' has the same meaning as it has in the Civil Service Regulation Act 1956; [2]

"short-time" has the meaning assigned to it by the Act of 1967;

[1b] The text of the Act originally referred to the Minister for Labour. However, under Article 4(1) of the Labour (Transfer of Departmental Administration and Ministerial Functions) Order, 1993 (S.I. No. 18 of 1993), it was provided that the functions vested in the Minister for Labour by or under certain Acts (including this Act) be transferred to the Minister for Industry and Commerce. Under Article 4(2) of the same Order, it was provided that references to the Minister for Labour contained in any such Act or instrument thereunder and relating to any functions transferred by Article 4 should, on and after the commencement of the Order, be construed as references to the Minister for Industry and Commerce. Under Article 4 of the Industry and Commerce (Alteration of Name of Department and Title of Minister) Order, 1993 (S.I. No. 19 of 1993), which was adopted on the same day as S.I. No. 18 of 1993, it was provided that references in any enactment to the Minister for Industry and Commerce should be construed as references to the Minister for Enterprise and Employment. More recently, Article 4 of the Enterprise and Employment (Alteration of Name of Department and Title of Minister) Order, 1997 (S.I. No. 305 of 1997) has provided that references in any enactment to the Minister for Enterprise and Employment are to be construed as references to the Minister for Enterprise, Trade and Employment. It should be noted that the powers and duties which are conferred on the Minister for Enterprise, Trade and Employment by or under the Minimum Notice and Terms of Employment Acts have been delegated by statutory instrument to the present Minister of State at the Department of Enterprise, Trade and Employment. (See now the Enterprise, Trade and Employment (Delegation of Ministerial Functions) Order 2004 (S.I. No. 809 of 2004).)

[2] This definition was inserted by s. 24 of the Civil Service Regulation (Amendment) Act 2005.

"strike" has the meaning assigned to it by Part II of the Act of 1967;

"the Tribunal" means the Tribunal established under the Act of 1967;

"week" means any period of seven consecutive days;

"year" means any period of fifty-two weeks.

Application of Act to civil servants.

1A. —(1) For the purposes of this Act, a reference to an 'employee' shall be construed as including a civil servant who holds office in the Civil Service of the Government or in the Civil Service of the State.[2a]

(2) Subject to subsection (4), for the purposes of this Act, as respects a civil servant, a reference in this Act to an 'employer' shall be construed as including the State, a Minister of the Government, a Department or a Scheduled Office in which the civil servant concerned holds office.

(3) As respects a civil servant, for the purposes of this Act, 'contract of employment' means such arrangements as are made by the Minister for Finance under section 17 of the Civil Service Regulation Act 1956, together with such further terms and conditions of service which apply to the civil servant concerned, made in respect of a particular Department or Scheduled Office which extend or alter the arrangements under the said section 17.

(4) Nothing in this section shall be construed as affecting the status of a civil servant as an officer.

(5) For the purposes of this section and the First Schedule—

(*a*) 'Department' includes such bodies or organisations (whether established by or under statute, or otherwise) other than a Scheduled Office, for which the Minister having charge of the Department concerned is responsible, and

(*b*) 'Scheduled Office' includes such bodies or organisations (whether established by or under statute or otherwise)

[2a] The entirety of s. 1A was inserted in the form shown above by s. 25 of the Civil Service Regulation (Amendment) Act 2005.

for which the Minister of the Government having charge of the Scheduled Office is responsible.

Commencement.

2. —This Act shall come into operation on such day as the Minister appoints by order.[2b]

Non-application of Act.

3. —(1) This Act shall not apply to—

(*a*) employment of an employee who is normally expected to work for the same employer for less than eighteen hours in a week,[3]

(*b*) employment by an employer of an employee who is the father, mother, grandfather, grandmother, stepfather, stepmother, son, daughter, grandson, granddaughter, stepson, stepdaughter, brother, sister, halfbrother or halfsister of the employer and who is a member of the employer's household and whose place of employment is a private dwellinghouse or a farm in or on which both the employee and the employer reside,

1956, No. 45.

(*c*) *(Deleted by s. 26 of the Civil Service Regulation (Amendment) Act 2005)*

(*d*) employment as a member of the Permanent Defence Forces (other than a temporary member of the Army Nursing Service),

(*e*) employment as a member of the Garda Síochána, and

(*f*) employment under an employment agreement pursuant to Part II or Part IV of the Merchant Shipping Act, 1894.

1894, c. 60.

(2) The Minister may by order declare that any provision of this Act shall not apply to a class or classes of employment specified in the order and from the commencement of the order this Act shall not apply to that class or those classes.

[2b] In the Minimum Notice and Terms of Employment Act, 1973 Commencement) Order, 1973 (S.I. No. 242 of 1973), the Minister for Labour appointed 1 September, 1973 to be the day on which this Act came into operation.

[3] The word "eighteen" was substituted here for the original "twenty-one" by s. 13 of the Protection of Employees (Employers' Insolvency) Act, 1984.

(3) Notwithstanding subsection (1) or (2) of this section, the Minister may by order declare that any provision of this Act shall apply to a class or classes of employment specified in the order and from the commencement of the order this Act shall apply to that class or those classes.

(4) An order made by the Minister under this section may include such transitional and other supplemental and incidental provisions as appear to the Minister to be necessary or expedient.

(5) The Minister may by order amend or revoke an order made under this section, including this subsection.

4. —(1) An employer shall, in order to terminate the contract of employment of an employee who has been in his continuous service for a period of thirteen weeks or more, give to that employee a minimum period of notice calculated in accordance with the provisions of subsection (2) of this section. Minimum period of notice.

(2) The minimum notice to be given by an employer to terminate the contract of employment of his employee shall be—

(*a*) if the employee has been in the continuous service of his employer for less than two years, one week,

---

Note, however, that under s. 8 of the Protection of Employees (Part-Time Work) Act, 2001, the Minimum Notice and Terms of Employment Acts, 1973 and 1984 are to apply to a part-time employee (meaning, under s. 7(1) of that Act, an employee whose normal hours of work are less than the normal hours of work of an employee who is a comparable employee in relation to him or her) in the same manner (and subject to the like exceptions not inconsistent with s. 8) as they apply (other than by virtue of the 2001 Act) to an employee to whom the Minimum Notice and Terms of Employment Acts, 1973 and 1984 relate. (Note also the broad definition given to "employee" by s. 3(1) of the Protection of Employees (Part-Time Work) Act, 2001. Note finally that the Minimum Notice and Terms of Employment Act, 1973, s. 13 of the Protection of Employees (Employers' Insolvency) Act, 1984, the Protection of Employees (Part-Time Work) Act, 2001 (insofar as it relates to the foregoing legislation) and Part 7 of the Civil Service Regulation (Amendment) Act 2005 may be cited together as the Minimum Notice and Terms of Employment Acts 1973 to 2005 and are required to be construed together as one.
(See s. 18(3) of the Protection of Employees (Employers' Insolvency) Act, 1984, s. 1(2) of the Protection of Employees (Part-Time Work) Act, 2001, and s. 1(4) of the Civil Service Regulation (Amendment) Act 2005.)

(*b*) if the employee has been in the continuous service of his employer for two years or more, but less than five years, two weeks,

(*c*) if the employee has been in the continuous service of his employer for five years or more, but less than ten years, four weeks,

(*d*) if the employee has been in the continuous service of his employer for ten years or more, but less than fifteen years, six weeks,

(*e*) if the employee has been in the continuous service of his employer for fifteen years or more, eight weeks.

(3) The provisions of the First Schedule to this Act shall apply for the purposes of ascertaining the period of service of an employee and whether that service has been continuous.[4]

---

[4] Note however s. 40(3) of the Maternity Protection Act, 1994, which provides as follows:

> "For the purposes of the Minimum Notice and Terms of Employment Act, 1973, the contract of employment of an employee to whom this section applies [*i.e.* an employee who is entitled to return to work from an absence due to protective leave under the 1994 Act, but who is not permitted to do so by her employer] who is also an employee to whom that Act applies shall be deemed to have been terminated on the expected date of return."

Note also s. 30 of the Adoptive Leave Act, 1995, under which, for the purposes of the Minimum Notice and Terms of Employment Acts, 1973 to 1991, the contract of employment of an adopting parent who (a) is entitled to return to work from adoptive or additional adoptive leave (having complied with s. 20 (1) of the 1995 Act [*i.e.*, caused his or her employer to have been given the required notice in writing of the adopting parent's intention to return to work, and of the date on which he or she expects to return to work]) but is not permitted to do so by his or her employer, the successor or an associated employer; and who (b) is an employee to whom the Minimum Notice and Terms of Employment Acts, 1973 to 1991 apply, shall be deemed to have been terminated on the date specified in the relevant notification under s. 20(1) of the 1995 Act. Note further that although the 1995 Act refers to the Minimum Notice and Terms of Employment Acts, 1973 to 1991, this designation is now obsolete: instead, the Minimum Notice and Terms of Employment Act, 1973, s. 13 of the Protection of Employees (Employers' Insolvency) Act, 1984, the Protection of Employees (Part-Time Work) Act, 2001 (insofar as it relates to the foregoing legislation) and Part 7 of the Civil Service Regulation

(4) The Minister may by order vary the minimum period of notice specified in subsection (2) of this section.

(5) Any provision in a contract of employment, whether made before or after the commencement of this Act, which provides for a period of notice which is less than the period of notice specified in subsection (2) of this section, shall have effect as if that contract provided for a period of notice in accordance with this section.

(6) The Minister may by order amend or revoke an order under this section including this subsection.

Rights of employee during period of notice.

5. —(1) The provisions of the Second Schedule to this Act shall have effect in relation to the liability of an employer during the period of notice required by this Act to be given—

(*a*) by an employer to terminate the contract of employment of an employee who has been in his continuous service for thirteen weeks or more, and

(*b*) by an employee who has been in such continuous service to terminate his contract of employment with that employer.

(Amendment) Act 2005 may be cited together as the Minimum Notice and Terms of Employment Acts 1973 to 2005. (See s. 18(3) of the Protection of Employees (Employers' Insolvency) Act, 1984, s. 1(2) of the Protection of Employees (Part-Time Work) Act, 2001 and s. 1(4) of the Civil Service Regulation (Amendment) Act 2005.)

Note also s. 25(3) of the Parental Leave Act, 1998, which provides as follows:

"An employee who is entitled to return to work in the employment concerned in accordance with *section 15* [*i.e.*, to return to work on the expiration of a period of parental leave] but is not permitted by his or her employer to do so—

…(*c*) shall be deemed for the purposes of the Minimum Notice and Terms of Employment Acts, 1973 to 1991, to have had his or her contract of employment with his or her employer terminated on the date aforesaid."

Note also s. 16(4) of the Carer's Leave Act, 2001:

"An employee who is entitled to return to work in the employment concerned in accordance with *section 14* [*i.e.*, to return to work on the termination of carer's leave] but is not permitted by his or her employer to do so—

…(*a*) shall be deemed to have been dismissed on the date on which he or she was entitled to so return to work…"

(2) This section shall not apply in any case where an employee gives notice to terminate his contract of employment in response to a notice of lay-off or short-time given by his employer.

(3) Any provision in a contract which purports to exclude or limit the obligation imposed on an employer by this section shall be void.

Right of employer to notice.

6. —An employer shall, subject to the right of an employee to give counter-notice under section 10 of the Act of 1967 or to give notice of intention to claim redundancy payment in respect of lay-off or short-time under section 12 of that Act, be entitled to not less than one week's notice from an employee who has been in his continuous employment for thirteen weeks or more of that employee's intention to terminate his contract of employment.

Right to waive notice.

7. —(1) Nothing in this Act shall operate to prevent an employee or an employer from waiving his right to notice on any occasion or from accepting payment in lieu of notice.[5]

---

[5] Section 41(13) of the National Minimum Wage Act, 2000 provides as follows:

"A payment in lieu of notice to an employee in accordance with the Minimum Notice and Terms of Employment Acts, 1973 to 1991, shall not have regard to any exemption under this section and the payment in lieu of notice shall be made to the employee as if the employee had been paid the national minimum hourly rate of pay to which he or she was otherwise entitled under this Act, for the period of the exemption."

The exemption referred to relates to the power which the Labour Court enjoys under s. 41 of the National Minimum Wage Act, 2000 to exempt an employer in financial difficulty from the obligation to pay an employee or employees an hourly rate of pay that on average is not less than the national minimum hourly rate of pay.

As regards this obligation, note more generally the provision in s. 14 of the National Minimum Wage Act, 2000 that subject to certain exceptions an employee who has attained the age of 18 years is to be remunerated in respect of his or her working hours in any pay reference period, at an hourly rate of pay that on average is not less than the national minimum hourly rate of pay, with employees who have not attained that age to be remunerated in respect of his or her working hours in any pay reference period, at an hourly rate of pay that on average is not less than 70 per cent of the national minimum hourly rate of pay.

Note finally that although s. 41(13) of the National Minimum Wage Act, 2000 refers to the Minimum Notice and Terms of Employment Acts, 1973 to 1991, it is now the case that the Minimum Notice and Terms of Employment

(2) In any case where an employee accepts payment in lieu of notice, the date of termination of that person's employment shall, for the purposes of the Act of 1967, be deemed to be the date on which notice, if given, would have expired.

Right to terminate contract of employment without notice.

8. —Nothing in this Act shall affect the right of any employer or employee to terminate a contract of employment without notice because of misconduct by the other party.

Written statement of terms of employment.

9. —*(Repealed by s. 13 of the Terms of Employment (Information) Act, 1994)*

Failure of employer to furnish statement.

10. —*(Repealed by s. 13 of the Terms of Employment (Information) Act, 1994)*

Reference of disputes to Tribunal.

11. —(1) Any dispute arising on any matter under this Act (other than a dispute arising on any matter under section 9 of this Act) shall be referred in the prescribed manner to the Tribunal.[6]

Act, 1973, s. 13 of the Protection of Employees (Employers' Insolvency) Act, 1984, the Protection of Employees (Part-Time Work) Act, 2001 (insofar as it relates to the foregoing legislation) and Part 7 of the Civil Service Regulation (Amendment) Act 2005 may be cited together as the Minimum Notice and Terms of Employment Acts 1973 to 2005 and are required to be construed together as one. (See in this regard s. 18(3) of the Protection of Employees (Employers' Insolvency) Act, 1984, s. 1(2) of the Protection of Employees (Part-Time Work) Act, 2001, and s. 1(4) of the Civil Service Regulation (Amendment) Act 2005.)

[6] See now the Minimum Notice and Terms of Employment (Reference of Disputes) Regulations, 1973 (S.I. No. 243 of 1973). Note also in this regard the provisions of s. 32(2) of the Adoptive Leave Act, 1995, which provides as follows:

"Any dispute other than—

(*a*) *(not relevant)*

(*b*) *(not relevant)*

(*c*) a dispute under section 11 of the Minimum Notice and Terms of Employment Act, 1973, as extended by *section 30, (i.e., of the 1995 Act, which makes provision for the application of the Act in the situation of an adopting parent being denied their entitlement to return to work having taken adoptive or additional adoptive leave)*

between an adopting parent and the relevant employer, relating to the adopting parent's entitlements under this Act (or to any matter arising out of or related to such entitlements), may be referred by either party to the dispute to a rights commissioner."

(2) The decision of the Tribunal on any matter referred to it under this section shall be final and conclusive, save that any person dissatisfied with the decision may appeal therefrom to the High Court on a question of law.

(3) The Minister may, on the request of the Tribunal, refer any question of law for the decision of the High Court.

Rights of employee on default of employer.

12. —(1) If an employer—

(*a*) fails to give to an employee the notice required by section 4 (2) of this Act, or

(*b*) fails to comply with the provisions of section 5 of this Act in relation to the rights of the employee during the period of notice,

the employee may refer the matter to the Tribunal for arbitration and the Tribunal may award to the employee compensation for any loss sustained by him by reason of the default of the employer.

(2) The amount of any compensation awarded by the Tribunal under subsection (1) of this section shall be recoverable by the employee from his employer as a simple contract debt in a court of competent jurisdiction.

(3) Proceedings for the recovery of any sum due by way of compensation awarded by the Tribunal under subsection (1) of this section may be instituted and maintained on behalf of the employee by the Minister or by that employee's trade union.

Under s. 32(1) of the 1995 Act, this provision does not apply to members of the Defence Forces.

Note also the provisions of s. 18(2) of the Parental Leave Act, 1998, which provides as follows:

"Any dispute or difference between an employee and his or her employer relating to the entitlements of the employee under this Act (or to any matter arising out of or related to those entitlements or otherwise arising under this Act) other than a dispute or difference—

(*a*) *(not relevant)*

(*b*) *(not relevant)*

(*c*) a dispute to which section 11 of the Minimum Notice and Terms of Employment Act, 1973, applies,

may be referred by either of those parties to a rights commissioner…"

Under s. 18(1) of the 1998 Act, this provision does not apply to members of the Defence Forces.

13.—(1) There shall be included among the debts which, under section 285 of the Companies Act, 1963 [7], are, in the distribution of the assets of a company being wound up, to be paid in priority to all other debts, all compensation payable under section 12 of this Act by the Company to an employee, and that Act shall have effect accordingly, and formal proof of the debts to which priority is given under this subsection shall not be required except in cases where it may otherwise be provided by rules made under that Act.

Provisions relating to winding up and bankruptcy.

1963, No. 33

(2) There shall be included among the debts which, under [section 81(1) of the Bankruptcy Act, 1988] [9], are in the distribution of the property of a bankrupt or arranging debtor, to be paid in priority to all other debts, all compensation payable under section 12 of this Act by the bankrupt or arranging debtor, as the case may be, to an employee, and that Act shall have effect accordingly, and formal proof of the debts to which priority is given under this subsection shall not be required except in cases where it may otherwise be provided by general orders made under the said Act.

1889, c. 60.[8]

14.—The Minister may make regulations in relation to any matter referred to in this Act as prescribed.[10]

Regulations.

15.—Whenever an order is proposed to be made under section 3, 4, or 9 of this Act, a draft of the proposed order shall

Laying of Regulations

[7] Section 285 of the Companies Act, 1963 has been amended by section 10 of the Companies (Amendment) Act, 1982 and also by s. 134 of the Companies Act, 1990 but these amendments have not been reflected in any change to the manner in which s. 285 is referred to here.

[8] The reference, in the side-note to s. 13(2), to the Preferential Payments in Bankruptcy (Ireland) Act, 1889, has not been deleted but is now obsolete by virtue of the repeal of the Preferential Payments in Bankruptcy (Ireland) Act, 1889 by s. 6 of the Bankruptcy Act, 1988 and by virtue of the requirement under s. 81(1) of the Bankruptcy Act, 1988 that any reference to s. 4 of the 1889 Act of the kind found in s. 13(2) is to be construed as a reference to s. 81(1) of the 1988 Act.

[9] The text of the Act originally referred to s. 4 of the Preferential Payments in Bankruptcy (Ireland) Act, 1889. However, the Preferential Payments in Bankruptcy (Ireland) Act, 1889 was repealed by s. 6 of the Bankruptcy Act, 1988 and under s. 81(1) of the Bankruptcy Act, 1988, any reference to s. 4 of the 1889 Act of the kind found in s. 13(2) is to be construed as a reference to s. 81(1) of the 1988 Act.

[10] See now the Minimum Notice and Terms of Employment (Reference of Disputes) Regulations, 1973 (S.I. No. 243 of 1973).

and certain draft orders before Houses of Oireachtas.

be laid before each House of the Oireachtas and the order shall not be made until a resolution approving of the draft has been passed by both Houses of the Oireachtas.

(2) Every regulation made under this Act shall be laid before each House of the Oireachtas as soon as may be after it is made and, if a resolution annulling the regulation is passed by either such House within the next twenty-one days on which that House has sat after the regulation is laid before it, the regulation shall be annulled accordingly but without prejudice to the validity of anything previously done thereunder.

Expenses of Minister.

16.—Any expenses incurred by the Minister in the administration of this Act shall, to such extent as may be sanctioned by the Minister for Finance, be paid out of moneys provided by the Oireachtas.

Short title.

17. —This Act may be cited as the Minimum Notice and Terms of Employment Act, 1973.[11]

FIRST SCHEDULE [12]

Section 4.

Computation of Continuous Service

Continuity of Service

1. The service of an employee in his employment shall be deemed to be continuous unless that service is terminated by—

[11] Note that the Minimum Notice and Terms of Employment Act, 1973, s. 13 of the Protection of Employees (Employers' Insolvency) Act, 1984, the Protection of Employees (Part-Time Work) Act, 2001 (insofar as it relates to the foregoing legislation) and Part 7 of the Civil Service Regulation (Amendment) Act 2005 may be cited together as the Minimum Notice and Terms of Employment Acts 1973 to 2005 and are required to be construed together as one. (See s. 18(3) of the Protection of Employees (Employers' Insolvency) Act, 1984, s. 1(2) of the Protection of Employees (Part-Time Work) Act, 2001, and s. 1(4) of the Civil Service Regulation (Amendment) Act 2005.)

[12] Note that this Schedule has by now been used to calculate continuous service under a number of different statutes. See in this regard, s. 2(4) of the Unfair Dismissals Act, 1977, s. 2(3) of the Terms of Employment (Information) Act, 1994, s. 7(6) of the Carer's Leave Act, 2001, s. 9(5) of the Protection of Employees (Fixed-Term) Work Act 2003.

(*a*) the dismissal of the employee by his employer, or

(*b*) the employee voluntarily leaving his employment.

2. A lock-out shall not amount to a dismissal of the employee by his employer.

3. A lay-off shall not amount to the termination by an employer of his employee's service.

4. A strike by an employee shall not amount to that employee's voluntarily leaving his employment.

5. An employee who claims and receives redundancy payment in respect of lay-off or short time shall be deemed to have voluntarily left his employment.[13]

6. The continuous service of an employee in his employment shall not be broken by the dismissal of the employee by his employer followed by the immediate re-employment of the employee.

7. Where the whole or part of a trade, business or undertaking was or is transferred to another person either before or after the passing of this Act, the service of an employee before the transfer in the trade, business or undertaking, or the part thereof so transferred—

(*a*) shall be reckoned as part of the service of the employee with the transferee, and

(*b*) the transfer shall not operate to break the continuity of the service of the employee,

unless the employee received and retained redundancy payment from the transferor at the time of and by reason of the transfer.[14]

---

[13] Para. 5 of the First Schedule was substituted by s. 20 of the Unfair Dismissals Act, 1977. Under the original para. 5, the mere giving by an employee of notice of intention to claim redundancy payment in respect of lay-off or short-time sufficed for that employee to be deemed to have voluntarily left his employment.

[14] Paragraph 7 of the First Schedule, originally substituted in its entirety by s. 20 of the Unfair Dismissals Act, 1977 (and thereby made applicable to transfers of parts of trades, businesses or undertakings) was substituted

Computable Service

8. Any week in which an employee is not normally expected to work for at least eighteen hours [15] or more will not count in computing a period of service.

9. If an employee is absent from his employment by reason of service in the Reserve Defence Force, such period of absence shall count as a period of service.

10. If an employee is absent from his employment for not more than twenty-six weeks between consecutive periods of employment because of—

(*a*) a lay-off,

(*b*) sickness or injury, or

(*c*) by agreement with his employer,

such period shall count as a period of service.

11. If, in any week or part of a week, an employee is absent from his employment because he was taking part in a strike in

---

again in its entirety by s. 15 of the Unfair Dismissals (Amendment) Act, 1993 (importing the final two lines of para. 7).

[15] The word "eighteen" was substituted here for the original "twenty-one" by s. 13 of the Protection of Employees (Employers' Insolvency) Act, 1984. Note, however, that under s. 8 of the Protection of Employees (Part-Time Work) Act, 2001, the Minimum Notice and Terms of Employment Acts, 1973 and 1984 are to apply to a part-time employee (meaning, under s. 7(1) of that Act, an employee whose normal hours of work are less than the normal hours of work of an employee who is a comparable employee in relation to him or her) in the same manner (and subject to the like exceptions not inconsistent with s. 8) as they apply (other than by virtue of the 2001 Act) to an employee to whom the Minimum Notice and Terms of Employment Acts, 1973 and 1984 relate. Note also that the Minimum Notice and Terms of Employment Act, 1973, s. 13 of the Protection of Employees (Employers' Insolvency) Act, 1984, the Protection of Employees (Part-Time Work) Act, 2001 (insofar as it relates to the foregoing legislation) and Part 7 of the Civil Service Regulation (Amendment) Act 2005 may now be cited together as the Minimum Notice and Terms of Employment Acts 1973 to 2005 and are required to be construed together as one. (See s. 18(3) of the Protection of Employees (Employers' Insolvency) Act, 1984, s. 1(2) of the Protection of Employees (Part-Time Work) Act, 2001, and s. 1(4) of the Civil Service Regulation (Amendment) Act 2005.)

relation to the trade or business in which he is employed, that week shall not count as a period of service.

12. If, in any week or part of a week, an employee was, for the whole or any part of the week, absent from work because of a lock-out by his employer, that week shall count as a period of service.

13. If, in any week or part of a week, an employee is absent from his employment by reason of a strike or lock-out in a trade or business other than that in which he is employed, that week shall count as a period of service.

14. For the avoidance of doubt, a civil servant shall be considered as having given continuous service, notwithstanding the fact that the civil servant may have served in more than one Department or Scheduled Office provided that the service would otherwise, by virtue of the provisions of this Schedule, be considered to be continuous.[15a]

SECOND SCHEDULE

Rights of Employee During Period of Notice

Section 5.

1. Subject to the provisions of this Schedule, an employee shall, during the period of notice, be paid by his employer in accordance with the terms of his contract of employment and shall have the same rights to sick pay or holidays with pay as he would have if notice of termination of his contract of employment had not been given.

Employments for which there are normal working hours

2. (*a*) (i) An employee shall be paid by his employer in respect of any time during his normal working hours when he is ready and willing to work but no work is provided for him by his employer.

(ii) In this subparagraph "normal working hours" in the case of an employee who is normally

[15a] Paragraph 14 of the First Schedule was inserted (in indented format) by s. 24 of the Civil Service Regulation (Amendment) Act 2005.

expected to work overtime, include the hours during which such overtime is usually worked.

(*b*) In any case where an employee's pay is not wholly calculated by reference to time, the pay which his employer is bound to pay him under subparagraph (*a*) shall be calculated by reference to the average rate of pay earned by the employee in respect of any time worked during the thirteen weeks next preceding the giving of notice.

Employments for which there are no normal working hours

3. Subject to paragraph 4 of this Schedule, an employer shall pay to an employee, if there are no normal working hours for that employee under the contract of employment in force in the period of notice, in respect of each week in the period of notice, a sum not less than the average weekly earnings of the employee in the thirteen weeks next preceding the giving of notice.

4. An employer shall not be liable to pay to his employee any sum under paragraph 3 of this Schedule unless the employee is ready and willing to do work of a reasonable nature and amount to earn remuneration at the rate mentioned in the said paragraph 3.

REDUNDANCY PAYMENTS ACT, 1973

Number 11 *of* 1973

ARRANGEMENT OF SECTIONS

Section

Number 11 *of* 1973

REDUNDANCY PAYMENTS ACT, 1973

AN ACT TO AMEND AND EXTEND THE REDUNDANCY PAYMENTS ACTS, 1967 AND 1971. [28*th June*, 1973]

BE IT ENACTED BY THE OIREACHTAS AS FOLLOWS:

1. *(Insertion of s. 28(3A) of the Redundancy Payments Act, 1967)* [1]

Amendment of section 28 of Redundancy Payments Act, 1967.

1967, No. 21.

1952, No. 11.

1973, No. 10.

2. —(1) This Act may be cited as the Redundancy Payments Act, 1973.

Short title, collective citation and commencement.

(2) The Redundancy Payments Acts, 1967 and 1971, and this Act may be cited together as the Redundancy Payments Acts, 1967 to 1973.[2]

---

[1] This insertion of s. 28(3A) of the 1967 Act (which exempted employed contributors in receipt of certain benefits, pensions and allowances under social welfare legislation from having to pay redundancy contributions) was superseded by the substitution of s. 28 of the 1967 Act by s. 3 of the Redundancy Payments Act, 1979, and further superseded by the subsequent deletion of all of s. 28 of the 1967 Act (which concerned redundancy contributions) by s. 39(1) of the Social Welfare Act, 1991.

[2] Note that the Redundancy Payments Act, 1967, the Redundancy Payments Act, 1971, the Redundancy Payments Act, 1973, the Redundancy Payments Act, 1979, s. 12 of the Protection of Employees (Employers' Insolvency) Act, 1984, ss. 26, 27 and 29 of the Social Welfare Act, 1990, s. 39

(3) This Act shall come into operation on such day as the Minister appoints by order.[3]

(other than sub-s. (2)) of the Social Welfare Act, 1991 (although apparently by oversight no mention is made of s. 39 of the 1991 Act in any subsequent statute included in this list), the Protection of Employees (Part-Time Work) Act, 2001 (insofar as it relates to the foregoing legislation, apart from s. 39 of the 1991 Act) and the Redundancy Payments Act 2003 may be cited together as the Redundancy Payments Acts 1967 to 2003.
See in this regard, in addition to s. 2(2) of the Redundancy Payments Act, 1973, s. 20(2) of the Redundancy Payments Act, 1971, s. 21(2) of the Redundancy Payments Act, 1979, s. 18(2) of the Protection of Employees (Employers' Insolvency) Act, 1984, s. 1(4) of the Social Welfare Act, 1990, s. 1(3) of the Social Welfare Act, 1991, s. 1(4) of the Protection of Employees (Part-Time Work) Act, 2001 and s. 17(3) of the Redundancy Payments Act 2003.

[3] In the Redundancy Payments Act, 1973 (Commencement) Order, 1973 (S.I. No. 175 of 1973), the Minister for Labour appointed 2 July, 1973 to be the day on which this Act came into operation.

PROTECTION OF EMPLOYMENT ACT, 1977

Number 7 *of* 1977

ARRANGEMENT OF SECTIONS

PART I

PRELIMINARY AND GENERAL

Section

PART II

CONSULTATION AND NOTIFICATION

PART III

COMMENCEMENT OF COLLECTIVE REDUNDANCIES

PART IV

MISCELLANEOUS

ACTS REFERRED TO

Merchant Shipping Act, 1984	1894, c. 60.
Trade Union Act, 1941	1941, No. 22.
Local Government Act, 1941	1941, No. 23.
Industrial Relations Act, 1969	1969, No. 14.
Trade Union Act, 1971	1971, No. 33.
Minimum Notice and Terms of Employment Act, 1973	1973, No. 4.

Number 7 *of* 1977

PROTECTION OF EMPLOYMENT ACT, 1977

AN ACT TO PROVIDE FOR THE IMPLEMENTATION OF THE DIRECTIVE OF THE COUNCIL OF THE EUROPEAN COMMUNITIES DONE AT BRUSSELS ON THE 17TH DAY OF FEBRUARY, 1975, REGARDING THE APPROXIMATION OF THE LAWS OF MEMBER STATES OF THOSE COMMUNITIES RELATING TO COLLECTIVE REDUNDANCIES, AND TO PROVIDE FOR OTHER MATTERS RELATING TO THAT MATTER [1] [*5th April*, 1977]

BE IT ENACTED BY THE OIREACHTAS AS FOLLOWS:

PART I

PRELIMINARY AND GENERAL

1. —(1) This Act may be cited as the Protection of Employment Act, 1977. Short title and commencement.

(2) This Act shall come into operation on such day as may be appointed by order of the Minister.[2]

2. —(1) In this Act— Interpretation.

---

[1] Note that the Directive referred to in the text above — Directive 75/129/EEC of 17 February 1975 on the approximation of the laws of the Member States relating to collective redundancies — was repealed by Article 8 of Council Directive 98/59/EC of 20 July 1998 on the approximation of the laws of the Member States relating to collective redundancies. The text of Directive 98/59/EC, which replaced the (amended) text of the 1975 Directive is reproduced in this volume.

[2] In the Protection of Employment Act, 1977 (Commencement) Order, 1977 (S.I. No. 139 of 1977) the Minister for Labour appointed 10 May, 1977 to be the day on which the 1977 Act came into operation.

"authorised officer" means a person appointed by the Minister to be an authorised officer for the purposes of this Act;

"contract of employment" [3] means:

(*a*) a contract of service or of apprenticeship, and

(*b*) any other contract whereby an individual agrees with another person, who is carrying on the business of an employment agency within the meaning of the Employment Agency Act 1971 (No. 27 of 1971), and is acting in the course of that business, to do or perform personally any work or service for a third person (whether or not the third person is a party to the contract),

whether the contact is express or implied and, if express, whether it is oral or in writing;

"employee" means a person who has entered into or works under (or, in the case of a contract which has been terminated, worked under) a contract of employment with an employer, whether the contract is for manual labour, clerical work or otherwise, is express or implied, oral or in writing,; [4]

"employees' representatives" [5], in relation to employees who are affected, or are likely to be affected, by proposed collective

[3] This definition of "contract of employment" was substituted by Article 4 of the Protection of Employment Order, 1996 (S.I. No. 370 of 1996) importing everything found in the present definition after the word "apprenticeship".

[4] The words "and 'employer' and references to employment shall be construed accordingly" were deleted from this definition by Article 4 of the Protection of Employment Order, 1996 (S.I. No. 370 of 1996). The comma before the semi-colon was retained in error. Note the definition of "employer" which was inserted into the 1977 Act by the same Article of the 1996 Order and is to be seen in the text below.

[5] This definition was substituted by Regulation 3 of the European Communities (Protection of Employment) Regulations, 2000 (S.I. No. 488 of 2000), retrenching on the much broader earlier definition of "employees' representatives"—itself substituted into the Act by Article 4 of the Protection of Employment Order, 1996 (S.I. No. 370 of 1996)—as 'a trade union or staff association or a person or persons chosen by the employees likely to be affected by the proposed redundancies to represent them.' Prior to the coming into force of the 1996 Order, the notion of "employees' representatives" had been extremely narrow, being confined to officials

redundancies (whether by being selected for redundancy or otherwise), means—

(*a*) a trade union, staff association or excepted body with which it has been the practice of the employer to conduct collective bargaining negotiations, or

(*b*) in the absence of such a trade union, staff association or excepted body, a person or persons chosen (under an arrangement put in place by the employer) by such employees from amongst their number to represent them in negotiations with the employer;

"employer" [6] means the person with whom the employee has entered into or for whom the employee works under (or, where the employment has ceased, entered into or worked under) a contract of employment, subject to the qualification that the person who, under a contract of employment referred to in paragraph (b) of the definition of "contract of employment", is liable to pay the remuneration of the individual concerned in respect of the work or service concerned shall be deemed to be the individual's employer;

"excepted body" [7] has the meaning assigned to it by section 6(3) of the Trade Union Act, 1941 (No. 22 of 1941), as amended;

"the Minister" [8] means the [Minister for Enterprise, Trade and Employment];

(including shop stewards) of a trade union or of a staff association with which it had been the practice of the employer to conduct collective bargaining negotiations.

[6] This definition was inserted by Article 4 of the Protection of Employment Order, 1996 (S.I. No. 370 of 1996).

[7] This definition was inserted by Regulation 3 of the European Communities (Protection of Employment) Regulations, 2000 (S.I. No. 488 of 2000).

[8] The text of the Act originally referred to the Minister for Labour. However, under Article 4(1) of the Labour (Transfer of Departmental Administration and Ministerial Functions) Order, 1993 (S.I. No. 18 of 1993), it was provided that the functions vested in the Minister for Labour by or under certain Acts (including this Act) be transferred to the Minister for Industry and Commerce. In Article 4(2) of the same Order, it was provided that references to the Minister for Labour contained in any such Act or instrument thereunder and relating to any functions transferred by Article 4 should, on and after the commencement of the Order, be construed as references to

"prescribed" means prescribed by regulations under this Act;

"staff association" means a body of persons all the members of which are employed by the same employer and which carries on negotiations for the fixing of the wages or other conditions of employment of its own members only;

"trade union" means a trade union which is the holder of a negotiation licence granted under the Trade Union Acts, 1941 and 1971.

(2) In this Act a reference to a section is to a section of this Act unless it is indicated that reference to some other enactment is intended.

(3) In this Act a reference to a subsection is to the subsection of the section in which the reference occurs unless it is indicated that reference to some other section is intended.

Regulations and orders.

3.—(1) The Minister may make regulations for the purpose of giving effect to this Act.

(2) (*a*) The Minister may by order amend any provision of this Act so as to comply with any international obligations relating to collective redundancies that the State has decided to assume.[9]

---

the Minister for Industry and Commerce. In Article 4 of the Industry and Commerce (Alteration of Name of Department and Title of Minister) Order, 1993 (S.I. No. 19 of 1993), which was adopted on the same day as S.I. No. 18 of 1993, it was provided that references in any enactment to the Minister for Industry and Commerce should be construed as references to the Minister for Enterprise and Employment. More recently, Article 4 of the Enterprise and Employment (Alteration of Name of Department and Title of Minister) Order, 1997 (S.I. No. 305 of 1997) has provided that references in any enactment to the Minister for Enterprise and Employment are to be construed as references to the Minister for Enterprise, Trade and Employment. It should be noted that the powers and duties which are conferred on the Minister for Enterprise, Trade and Employment by or under the Protection of Employment Act, 1977 have been delegated by statutory instrument to the present Minister of State at the Department of Enterprise, Trade and Employment. (See now the Enterprise, Trade and Employment (Delegation of Ministerial Functions) Order 2004 (S.I. No. 809 of 2004).)

[9] The Protection of Employment Order, 1996 (S.I. No. 370 of 1996), which is included in this volume, was adopted under s. 3(2) of the 1977 Act.

(*b*) The Minister may by order amend or revoke an order under this section.

(3) Regulations under this section may contain such incidental, supplementary and consequential provisions as appear to the Minister to be necessary for the purposes of the regulations.

4. —(1) Every order and regulation under this Act (other than an order under section 3, section 6 or section 7 (3)) shall be laid before each House of the Oireachtas as soon as possible after it is made and, if a resolution annulling the order or regulation is passed by either House within the next 21 days on which that House has sat after the order or regulation is laid before it, the order or regulation shall be annulled accordingly, but without prejudice to the validity of anything previously done under it.

Laying of orders and regulations before Houses of Oireachtas.

(2) Where an order is proposed to be made under section 3, section 6 or section 7 (3), a draft of the order shall be laid before both Houses of the Oireachtas and the order shall not be made until a resolution approving of the draft has been passed by each House.

5. —The expenses incurred in the administration of this Act shall, to such extent as may be sanctioned by the Minister for Finance, be paid out of moneys provided by the Oireachtas.

Expenses.

6. —(1) For the purpose of this Act, "collective redundancies" means dismissals effected by an employer for one or more reasons not related to the individual concerned where in any period of 30 consecutive days the number of such dismissals is — [10]

Meaning of collective redundancies.

(a) at least 5 in an establishment normally employing more than 20 and less than 50 employees,

(b) at least 10 in an establishment normally employing at least 50 but less than 100 employees,

(c) at least ten per cent. of the number of employees in an establishment normally employing at least 100 but less than 300 employees, and

[10] S. 6 was replaced in its entirety by Article 5 of the Protection of Employment Order, 1996 (S.I. No. 370 of 1996). The new s. 6 decoupled the meaning of 'collective redundancies' for the purposes of the 1977 Act from the concept of redundancy deployed under the Redundancy Payments Acts, and removed the consequently now superfluous definition of 'business' found in the original version of s. 6. It also redefined the concept of an 'establishment'.

(d) at least 30 in an establishment normally employing 300 or more employees.

(2) For the purpose of calculating the number of redundancies where the number of dismissals is at least 10 in an establishment normally employing more than 20 and less than 100 employees, terminations of a contract of employment which occur to the individual workers concerned shall be assimilated to redundancies provided there are at least 5 redundancies.

(3) In this section "establishment" means an employer or a company or a subsidiary company or a company within a group of companies which can independently effect redundancies.

Application and non-application of Act.

7. —(1) Subject to subsection (2), this Act applies to all persons in employment on or after the commencement of this Act in an establishment normally employing more than 20 persons.

(2) This Act does not apply to—

(*a*) dismissals of employees engaged under a contract of employment for a fixed term or for a specified purpose (being a purpose of such a kind that the duration of the contract was limited but was, at the time of its making, incapable of precise ascertainment) where the dismissals occurred only because of the expiry of the term or the cesser of the purpose,

(*b*) a person employed by or under the State other than persons standing designated for the time being under section 17 of the Industrial Relations Act, 1969.

(*c*) officers of a body which is a local authority within the meaning of the Local Government Act, 1941,

(*d*) employment under an employment agreement pursuant to Part II or IV of the Merchant Shipping Act, 1894,

(Text deleted) [11]

---

[11] Para. (e) of s. 7(2) was deleted by Article 6 of the Protection of Employment Order, 1996 (S.I. No. 370 of 1996). Previously, it had ensured that the Act did not apply to employees in an establishment in which the business carried on was being terminated following bankruptcy or winding-up proceedings or for any other reason as a result of a decision of a court of competent jurisdiction.

(3) (*a*) The Minister may by order declare that this Act shall not apply to a class of employees specified in the order and from the commencement of the order this Act shall not apply to that class.

(*b*) The Minister may by order declare that this Act shall apply to a specified class of employee and from the commencement of the order this Act shall apply to that class.

(*c*) The Minister may by order amend or revoke an order under this subsection.

(4) Where a notice of dismissal by reason of redundancy which was given before the commencement of this Act expires after such commencement, sections 9, 10, 12 and 14 shall not apply to the dismissal concerned, but such a notice shall be in accordance with the Minimum Notice and Terms of Employment Act, 1973, and with the relevant contract of employment.

(5) In this section "establishment" has the same meaning as in section 6.

Calculation of normal number of employees.

8. —For the purposes of this Act, the number of employees normally employed in an establishment (within the meaning of section 6) shall be taken to be the average of the number so employed in each of the 12 months preceding the date on which the first dismissal takes effect.

PART II

CONSULTATION AND NOTIFICATION

Obligation on employer to consult employees' representatives.

9. —(1) Where an employer proposes to create collective redundancies he shall, with a view to reaching an agreement, initiate consultations with employees' representatives.[12]

(2) Consultations under this section shall include the following matters—

(*a*) the possibility of avoiding the proposed redundancies, reducing the number of employees affected by them

[12] The words "representing the employees affected by the proposed redundancies" were deleted here by Article 7 of the Protection of Employment Order, 1996 (S.I. No. 370 of 1996).

or **mitigating their consequences** [13] **by recourse to accompanying social measures aimed, *inter alia*, at aid for redeploying or retraining employees made redundant,**[14]

(*b*) the basis on which it will be decided which particular employees will be made redundant.

(3) Consultations under this section shall be initiated at the earliest opportunity and in any event at least 30 days before the first dismissal takes effect.

Obligation on employer to supply certain information.

10. —(1) For the purpose of consultations under section 9, the employer concerned shall supply the employees' representatives with all relevant information relating to the proposed redundancies.

(2) Without prejudice to the generality of subsection (1), information supplied under this section shall include the following, of which details shall be given in writing—

[13] The word "consequences" was substituted for the word "circumstances" by Article 4 of the European Communities (Protection of Employment) Regulations, 2000 (S.I. No. 488 of 2000). See however the following footnote.

[14] The highlighted wording of s. 9(2)(a) shown here indicates merely the *intended* result of two poorly executed attempts at amendment of s. 9(2)(a). Article 8 of the Protection of Employment Order, 1996 (S.I. No. 370 of 1996) provided that the original s. 9(2)(a) of the Protection of Employment Act, 1977 be amended by the substitution for the words "otherwise mitigating their circumstances" originally found in s. 9(2)(a) of almost all of the more extensive wording seen above from the word 'mitigating' onwards. The difficulty is that the original s. 9(2)(a) did not contain the words "otherwise mitigating their circumstances", but rather only the words "otherwise mitigating their consequences". Article 8 of the Protection of Employment Order, 1996 also contained a second error in that the wording it purported to substituted into s. 9(2)(a) was itself flawed, containing another reference to 'circumstances' where the word 'consequences' should have been employed. This second error was corrected by Regulation 4 of the European Communities (Protection of Employment) Regulations, 2000 (S.I. No. 488 of 2000), but the original, more serious error (which may have rendered the original amendment invalid) was not. A purposive construction of this amendment process would result in the overlooking of this error too. Some difficulty, however, may stem from the fact that violation of s. 9(2)(a) is intended to result in the possibility of criminal prosecution under s. 11 of the 1977 Act. It is an established principle that penal statutes are to be construed strictly (see in this regard J. Bell and G. Engle, *Cross on Statutory Interpretation* (third edition,

(*a*) the reasons for the proposed redundancies,

(*b*) the number, and descriptions or categories, of employees whom it is proposed to make redundant,

(*c*) the number of employees, and description or categories, normally employed,[15]

(*d*) the period during which it is proposed to effect the proposed redundancies.

(*e*) the criteria proposed for the selection of the workers to be made redundant, and[16]

(*f*) the method for calculating any redundancy payments other than those methods set out in the Redundancy Payment Acts, 1967 to 1991, or any other relevant enactment for the time being in force or, subject thereto, in practice. [17]

(3) An employer shall as soon as possible supply the Minister with copies of all information supplied in writing under subsection (2).

Application of sections 9 and 10.[17a]

10A. —Sections 9 and 10 shall apply to an employer irrespective of whether the decision regarding collective redundancies is being taken by the employer or by an undertaking which controls the employer and it shall not be a defence on the part of the employer that the necessary information had not been provided

---

Butterworths, London, 1995) at pp. 172 to 175). The effectiveness of the purported amendment in 1996 of s. 9(2)(a) from its original form into a more onerous version thus seems somewhat uncertain. At any rate, it is submitted that this minor saga demonstrates the desirability of significant amendments of Acts of the Oireachtas being themselves carried out by an Act of the Oireachtas, with all the scrutiny which this involves, rather than by statutory instrument.

[15] Section 10(2)(c) was substituted by Article 9 of the Protection of Employment Order, 1996 (S.I. No. 370 of 1996), the substantive effect of this being the addition of the requirement to supply information as to the description or categories of employees normally employed.

[16] Section 10(2)(e) was inserted by Article 9 of the Protection of Employment Order, 1996 (S.I. No. 370 of 1996).

[17] Section 10(2)(f) was inserted by Article 9 of the Protection of Employment Order, 1996 (S.I. No. 370 of 1996). Note that the Redundancy Payments Acts, 1967 to 2003 are required to be construed together as one, by virtue of s. 17(3) of the Redundancy Payments Act 2003.

[17a] This side-note was inserted by Article 10 of the Protection of Employment Order, 1996 (S.I. No. 370 of 1996).

to the employer by a controlling party, or parties, which took the decision leading to the collective redundancies.[18]

Penalty for contravention of section 9 or 10.

11. —An employer who fails to initiate consultations under section 9 or fails to comply with section 10 shall be guilty of an offence and shall be liable on summary conviction to a fine not exceeding [€1,904.61].[19]

Obligation on employer to notify Minister of proposed redundancies.

12. —(1) Where an employer proposes to create collective redundancies, he shall notify the Minister in writing of his proposals at the earliest opportunity and in any event at least 30 days before the first dismissal takes effect.

(2) The Minister may prescribe the particulars to be specified in a notification under this section.[20]

(3) A copy of a notification under this section shall be supplied as soon as possible by the employer affected to the employees' representatives affected who may forward to the Minister in writing any observations they have relating to the notification.

(4) In the case of collective redundancies arising from the employer's business being terminated following bankruptcy or winding up proceedings or for any other reason as a result of a decision of a court of competent jurisdiction the person responsible for the affairs of the business need comply with subsection (1) only if the Minister so requests.[21]

---

[18] Section 10A was inserted by Article 10 of the Protection of Employment Order, 1996 (S.I. No. 370 of 1996).

[19] The amount of £1,500, the equivalent in punts of the above amount, was substituted by Regulation 5 of the European Communities (Protection of Employment) Regulations, 2000 (S.I. No. 488 of 2000). In Article 14 of Council Regulation (EC) No 974/98 of 3 May 1998 on the introduction of the euro (read in conjunction with Article 1 of the same instrument), references made in legislative and statutory provisions existing on 31 December 2001 to units of Irish currency as they existed before the start of the third stage of economic and monetary union are to be read as references to the euro unit according to the respective conversion rates (with the rounding rules laid down in Regulation (EC) No 1103/97 of 17 June 1997 on certain provisions relating to the introduction of the euro applying).

[20] See now the Protection of Employment Act, 1977 (Notification of Proposed Collective Redundancies) Regulations, 1977 (S.I. No. 140 of 1977).

[21] Section 12(4) was inserted by Article 11 of the Protection of Employment Order, 1996 (S.I. No. 370 of 1996).

13. —An employer who contravenes section 12 shall be guilty of an offence and shall be liable on summary conviction to a fine not exceeding [€1,904.61].[22]

Penalty for contravention of section 12.

PART III

COMMENCEMENT OF COLLECTIVE REDUNDANCIES

14. —(1) Collective redundancies shall not take effect before the expiry of the period of 30 days beginning on the date of the relevant notification under section 12.

Collective redundancies not to take effect for 30 days.

(2) Where collective redundancies are effected by an employer before the expiry of the 30-day period mentioned in subsection (1) the employer shall be guilty of an offence and shall be liable on conviction on indictment to a fine not exceeding €12,500.[23]

(3) Subsections (1) and (2) shall not apply in the case of collective redundancies arising from the employer's business being terminated following bankruptcy or winding up proceedings or for any other reason as a result of a decision of a court of competent jurisdiction.[24]

15. —(1) For the purpose of seeking solutions to the problems caused by the proposed redundancies, the employer concerned

Further consultations with Minister.

---

[22] The amount of £1,500, the equivalent in punts of the above amount, was substituted by Regulation 5 of the European Communities (Protection of Employment) Regulations, 2000 (S.I. No. 488 of 2000). Under Article 14 of Council Regulation (EC) No 974/98 of 3 May 1998 on the introduction of the euro (read in conjunction with Article 1 of the same instrument), references made in legislative and statutory provisions existing on 31 December 2001 to units of Irish currency as they existed before the start of the third stage of economic and monetary union are to be read as references to the euro unit according to the respective conversion rates (with the rounding rules laid down in Regulation (EC) No 1103/97 of 17 June 1997 on certain provisions relating to the introduction of the euro applying).

[23] The figure of €12,500 was inserted by s. 21 of the Protection of Employees (Part-Time Work) Act, 2001, replacing the original figure of £3,000 (equivalent to €3,809.21) — in other words, more than tripling the maximum size of the fine which could be imposed under s. 14.

[24] Section 14(3) was inserted by Article 12 of the Protection of Employment Order, 1996 (S.I. No. 370 of 1996).

shall, at the Minister's request, enter into consultations with him or an authorised officer.

(2) For the purpose of consultations under this section, an employer shall supply the Minister or an authorised officer with such information relating to the proposed redundancies as the Minister or the officer may reasonably require.

Saver for employees' rights to notice, etc.

16. —Nothing in this Act shall affect the right of any employee to a period of notice of dismissal or to any other entitlement under any other Act or under his contract of employment.

Provisions relating to authorised officers.

17. —(1) An authorised officer may—

(*a*) enter at all reasonable times any premises or place where he has reasonable grounds for supposing that any employee is employed,

(*b*) there make any examination or enquiry necessary for ascertaining whether this Act has been or is being complied with,

(*c*) require an employer or his representative to produce any records which the employer is required by this Act to keep, and inspect and take copies of entries in the records.

(*d*) examine with regard to any matters under this Act any person whom he has reasonable cause to believe to be or to have been an employer or employee and require him to answer any questions (other than questions tending to incriminate him) which the officer may put relating to those matters and to sign a declaration of the truth of the answers.

(2) The powers conferred on an authorised officer by subsection (1) (a) shall not be exercisable in respect of a private dwelling house unless the Minister (or an officer of the Minister appointed by the Minister for the purpose) certifies that he has reasonable grounds for believing that an offence under this section in relation to an employee employed in the house has been committed by the employer, and the authorised officer in applying for admission to the house produces the certificate.

(3) Any person who—

(*a*) obstructs or impedes an authorised officer in the exercise of any power conferred by this section,

(*b*) refuses to produce any record which an authorised officer lawfully requires him to produce,

(*c*) produces, or causes to be produced or knowingly allows to be produced, to an authorised officer any record which is false in any material respect knowing it to be false,

(*d*) prevents or attempts to prevent any person from appearing before or being questioned by an authorised officer, or

(*e*) wilfully fails or refuses to comply with any lawful requirement of an authorised officer under subsection (1) (*d*)

shall be guilty of an offence and shall be liable on summary conviction to a fine not exceeding [€1,904.61].[25]

(4) An authorised officer shall be furnished with a certificate of his appointment and, on applying for admission to any premises or place, shall, if so required, produce the certificate to the occupier and to any person being examined by him.

PART IV

MISCELLANEOUS

18. —(1) An employer shall keep such records as may be necessary to enable the Minister or an authorised officer to ascertain whether or not the provisions of this Act are being and have been complied with. Records to be kept by employers.

[25] The amount of £1,500, the equivalent in punts of the above amount, was substituted by Regulation 5 of the European Communities (Protection of Employment) Regulations, 2000 (S.I. No. 488 of 2000). Under Article 14 of Council Regulation (EC) No 974/98 of 3 May 1998 on the introduction of the euro (read in conjunction with Article 1 of the same instrument), references made in legislative and statutory provisions existing on 31 December 2001 to units of Irish currency as they existed before the start of the third stage of economic and monetary union are to be read as references to the euro unit according to the respective conversion rates (with the rounding rules laid down in Regulation (EC) No 1103/97 of 17 June 1997 on certain provisions relating to the introduction of the euro applying).

(2) Records kept under this section shall be retained by an employer for a period of not less than three years from the date on which they were made.

(3) An employer who contravenes subsection (1) or (2) shall be guilty of an offence and shall be liable on summary conviction to a fine not exceeding [€1,904.61].[26]

(4) Where an employer fails to keep or retain records under this section the onus of proving that he has complied or is complying with this Act shall lie on him.

Certain provisions to be null and void.

19. —Any provision in any agreement (whether a contract of employment or otherwise) purporting to exclude or limit the operation of any provision of this Act shall be null and void.

Notices, etc. to Minister.

20. —Any notice or other document which is required or authorised by this Act to be given by an employer to the Minister shall be in writing and shall be sent by registered post addressed to the head office of the [Department of Enterprise, Trade and Employment] [27] or, where that is not practicable, shall be delivered to that office.

Proceedings under Act.

21. —(1) An offence under this Act may be prosecuted by the Minister.

(2) Proceedings for an offence under this Act may be commenced within one year from the date of the offence.

(3) Where an offence under this Act committed by a body corporate is proved to have been committed with the consent or connivance of, or to be attributable to any neglect on the

---

[26] The amount of £1,500, the equivalent in punts of the above amount, was substituted by Regulation 5 of the European Communities (Protection of Employment) Regulations, 2000 (S.I. No. 488 of 2000). Under Article 14 of Council Regulation (EC) No 974/98 of 3 May 1998 on the introduction of the euro (read in conjunction with Article 1 of the same instrument), references made in legislative and statutory provisions existing on 31 December 2001 to units of Irish currency as they existed before the start of the third stage of economic and monetary union are to be read as references to the euro unit according to the respective conversion rates (with the rounding rules laid down in Regulation (EC) No 1103/97 of 17 June 1997 on certain provisions relating to the introduction of the euro applying).

[27] The text of the Act originally referred to the Department of Labour. However, under Article 3(2) of the Labour (Transfer of Departmental

part of, any director, manager, secretary or other officer of the body corporate or any person who was purporting to act in any such capacity, he as well as the body corporate shall be guilty of that offence and shall be liable to be proceeded against and punished accordingly.

22. —Where an employer is convicted of an offence under section 11 or 14, he may plead in mitigation of the penalty for that offence that there were substantial reasons related to his business which made it impracticable for him to comply with the section under which the offence was committed. Mitigation of penalty for certain offences.

Administration and Ministerial Functions) Order, 1993 (S.I. No. 18 of 1993) certain references to the Department of Labour (including this one) were required be construed as references to the Department of Industry and Commerce. Under Article 4 of the Industry and Commerce (Alteration of Name of Department and Title of Minister) Order, 1993 (S.I. No. 19 of 1993), which was adopted on the same day, references in any enactment to the Department of Industry and Commerce were required to be construed as references to the Department of Enterprise and Employment. Finally, Article 4 of the Enterprise and Employment (Alteration of Name of Department and Title of Minister) Order, 1997 (S.I. No. 305 of 1997) has since provided that references in any enactment to the Department of Enterprise and Employment are to be construed as references to the Department of Enterprise, Trade and Employment.

UNFAIR DISMISSALS ACT, 1977

Number 10 *of* 1977

ARRANGEMENT OF SECTIONS

Section

Acts Referred To

Agriculture Act, 1931	1931, No. 8
Anti-Discrimination (Pay) Act, 1974	1974, No. 15
Companies Act, 1963	1963, No. 33
Defence Act, 1954	1954, No. 18
Industrial Relations Act, 1946	1946, No. 26
Industrial Relations Act, 1969	1969, No. 14
Industrial Training Act, 1967	1967, No. 5
Local Government Act, 1941	1941, No. 23
Minimum Notice and Terms of Employment Act, 1973	1973, No. 4
Preferential Payments in Bankruptcy (Ireland) Act, 1889	1889, c. 60
Redundancy Payments Act, 1967	1967, No. 21
Redundancy Payments Act, 1971	1971, No. 20
Vocational Education Act, 1930	1930, No. 29

Number 10 *of* 1977

UNFAIR DISMISSALS ACT, 1977

AN ACT TO PROVIDE FOR REDRESS FOR EMPLOYEES UNFAIRLY DISMISSED FROM THEIR EMPLOYMENT, TO PROVIDE FOR THE DETERMINATION OF CLAIMS FOR SUCH REDRESS BY RIGHTS COMMISSIONERS AND BY THE TRIBUNAL ESTABLISHED, FOR THE PURPOSE OF DETERMINING CERTAIN APPEALS, BY THE REDUNDANCY PAYMENTS ACT, 1967, TO PROVIDE THAT THAT TRIBUNAL SHALL BE KNOWN AS THE EMPLOYMENT APPEALS TRIBUNAL, TO MAKE PROVISION FOR OTHER MATTERS CONNECTED WITH THE MATTERS AFORESAID AND TO AMEND THE MINIMUM NOTICE AND TERMS OF EMPLOYMENT ACT, 1973. [*6th April*, 1977]

BE IT ENACTED BY THE OIREACHTAS AS FOLLOWS:

1.—[(1) [1]] In this Act— Definitions.

"adopting parent" [2] means an employee who is an employed adopting mother, an adopting father or sole male adopter within the meaning of *section 2 (1)* of the *Adoptive Leave Act, 1995*;

"contract of employment" means a contract of service or of apprenticeship, whether it is express or implied and (if it is express) whether it is oral or in writing;

"date of dismissal" [3] means—

---

[1] Notwithstanding the numbering shown above, no numbering for what is here termed sub-s. 1 has ever been expressly inserted in s. 1. However, the intention that such numbering be employed seems to be implicit from the insertion by s. 2 of the Unfair Dismissals (Amendment) Act, 1993 of a sub-s. 2 and a sub-s. 3 into s. 1 of the 1977 Act.

[2] This definition was inserted by s. 22 of the Adoptive Leave Act, 1995.

[3] Note also s. 40(4) of the Maternity Protection Act, 1994, which provides as follows:

"For the purposes of the [Unfair Dismissals Act, 1977]—

(*a*) where prior notice of the termination of the contract of employment is given and it complies with the provisions of that contract and of the Minimum

---

(*a*) an employee to whom this section applies [*Editor's note: the section applies an employee who is entitled to return to work from an absence due to protective leave under the 1994 Act, but who is not permitted to do so by her employer*] who is also an employee to whom that Act applies shall be deemed to have been dismissed on the expected date of return; and

(*b*) the dismissal shall be deemed to be an unfair dismissal unless, having regard to all the circumstances, there were substantial grounds justifying the dismissal."

Note also s. 26(2) of the Adoptive Leave Act, 1995, which provides as follows:

"For the purposes of the [Unfair Dismissals Act, 1977], an adopting parent [*Editor's note: this refers to an adopting parent within the meaning of s. 1 of the Unfair Dismissals Act, 1977 (as amended) and who is entitled to return to work but is not permitted to do so by his or her employer, the successor or an associated employe*r] shall be deemed to have been dismissed on the date specified in the relevant notification under *section 20 (1)* [*Editor's note: this refers to s. 20(1) of the 1995 Act, and refers to notification in writing of the adopting parent's intention to return to work and of the date on which he or she expects to return to work*], and the dismissal shall be deemed to be an unfair dismissal unless, having regard to all the circumstances, there were substantial grounds justifying the dismissal."

Note also s. 16A(4) of the Parental Leave Act, 1998, as inserted by s. 11 of the Parental Leave (Amendment) Act 2006, which provides as follows:

"An employee who is entitled to return to work in the employment concerned in accordance with section 15 [*Editor's note: s. 15 governs entitlement to return to work on the expiration of a period of parental leave*] but is not permitted by his or her employer to do so—

(*a*) shall be deemed to have been dismissed on the date on which he or she was entitled to so return to work and the dismissal shall be deemed, for the purposes of the Unfair Dismissals Acts 1977 to 2005, to have been an unfair dismissal unless, having regard to all the circumstances, there were substantial grounds justifying the dismissal..."

Note also s. 16(4) of the Carer's Leave Act, 2001,

"An employee who is entitled to return to work in the employment concerned in accordance with *section 14* [*Editor's note: s. 14 governs entitlement to return to work on the termination of carer's leave*] but is not permitted by his or her employer to do so—

(*a*) shall be deemed to have been dismissed on the date on which he or she was entitled to so return to work and the dismissal shall be deemed, for the purposes of the Unfair Dismissals Acts, 1977 to 1993, to have been an unfair dismissal unless, having regard to all the circumstances, there were substantial grounds justifying the dismissal..."

Finally, note that under s. 1(6) of the Protection of Employees (Part-Time Work) Act, 2001, insofar as the 2001 Act relates to the Unfair Dismissals Acts,

Notice and Terms of Employment Act, 1973, [4] the date on which that notice expires.

(*b*) where either prior notice of such termination is not given or the notice given does not comply with the provisions of the contract of employment or the Minimum Notice and Terms of Employment Act, 1973, [5] the date on which such a notice would have expired, if it had been given on the date of such termination and had been expressed to expire on the later of the following dates—

(i) the earliest date that would be in compliance with the provisions of the contract of employment,

(ii) the earliest date that would be in compliance with the provisions of the Minimum Notice and Terms of Employment Act, 1973,[6]

(*c*) where a contract of employment for a fixed term expires without its being renewed under the same contract or, in the case of a contract for a specified purpose (being a purpose of such a kind that the duration of the contract was limited, but was, at the time of its making, incapable of precise ascertainment), there is a cesser of the purpose, the date of the expiry or cesser,

"dismissal" [7], in relation to an employee, means—

1977 to 1993, those Acts and the 2001 Act are required to be construed together as one and may be cited together as the Unfair Dismissals Acts, 1977 to 2001, and that under s. 1(3) of the Civil Service Regulation (Amendment) Act 2005, the Unfair Dismissals Acts, 1977 to 2001 and Part 6 of the 2005 Act may be cited together as the Unfair Dismissals Acts 1977 to 2005 and are required to be construed together as one.

[4] Note that the Minimum Notice and Terms of Employment Act, 1973, s. 13 of the Protection of Employees (Employers' Insolvency) Act, 1984, the Protection of Employees (Part-Time Work) Act, 2001 (insofar as it relates to the foregoing legislation) and Part 7 of the Civil Service Regulation (Amendment) Act 2005 may now be cited together as the Minimum Notice and Terms of Employment Acts 1973 to 2005 and are required to be construed together as one. (See s. 18(3) of the Protection of Employees (Employers' Insolvency) Act, 1984, s. 1(2) of the Protection of Employees (Part-Time Work) Act, 2001, and s. 1(4) of the Civil Service Regulation (Amendment) Act 2005.)

[5] See previous footnote.

[6] See footnote 4 above.

[7] See footnote 3 above.

(*a*) the termination by his employer of the employee's contract of employment with the employer, whether prior notice of the termination was or was not given to the employee.

(*b*) the termination by the employee of his contract of employment with his employer, whether prior notice of the termination was or was not given to the employer, in circumstances in which, because of the conduct of the employer, the employee was or would have been entitled, or it was or would have been reasonable for the employee, to terminate the contract of employment without giving prior notice of the termination to the employer, or

(*c*) the expiration of a contract of employment for a fixed term without its being renewed under the same contract or, in the case of a contract for a specified purpose (being a purpose of such a kind that the duration of the contract was limited but was, at the time of its making, incapable of precise ascertainment), the cesser of the purpose;

"employee" means an individual who has entered into or works under (or, where the employment has ceased, worked under) a contract of employment and, in relation to redress for a dismissal under this Act, includes, in the case of the death of the employee concerned at any time following the dismissal, his personal representative.

"employer", in relation to an employee, means the person by whom the employee is (or, in a case where the employment has ceased, was) employed under a contract of employment and an individual in the service of a local authority for the purposes of the Local Government Act, 1941, shall be deemed to be employed by the local authority;

"industrial action" means lawful action taken by any number or body of employees acting in combination or under a common understanding, in consequence of a dispute, as a means of compelling their employers or any employee or body of employees, or to aid other employees in compelling their employer or any employee or body of employees, to accept or not to accept terms or conditions of or affecting employment;

"the Minister" means the Minister for [Enterprise, Trade and Employment];[8]

"redundancy" means any of the matters referred to in paragraphs (*a*) to (*e*) of section 7 (2) of the Redundancy Payments Act, 1967, as amended by the Redundancy Payments Act, 1971;

"statutory apprenticeship" means an apprenticeship in a designated industrial activity within the meaning of the Industrial Training Act, 1967, and includes any apprenticeship in a trade to which an order, rule or notice referred to in paragraph (*a*) or (*b*) of section 49 (1) of that Act applies;

"strike" means the cessation of work by any number or body of employees acting in combination or a concerted refusal or a refusal under a common understanding of any number of employees to continue to work for an employer, in consequence of a dispute, done as a means of compelling their employer or any employee or body of employees, or to aid other employees

---

[8] The text of the Act originally referred to the Minister for Labour. However, under Article 4(1) of the Labour (Transfer of Departmental Administration and Ministerial Functions) Order, 1993 (S.I. No. 18 of 1993), it was provided that the functions vested in the Minister for Labour by or under certain Acts (including this Act) be transferred to the Minister for Industry and Commerce. Under Article 4(2) of the same Order, it was provided that references to the Minister for Labour contained in any such Act or instrument thereunder and relating to any functions transferred by Article 4 should, on and after the commencement of the Order, be construed as references to the Minister for Industry and Commerce. Under Article 4 of the Industry and Commerce (Alteration of Name of Department and Title of Minister) Order, 1993 (S.I. No. 19 of 1993), which was adopted on the same day as S.I. No. 18 of 1993, it was provided that references in any enactment to the Minister for Industry and Commerce should be construed as references to the Minister for Enterprise and Employment. More recently, Article 4 of the Enterprise and Employment (Alteration of Name of Department and Title of Minister) Order, 1997 (S.I. No. 305 of 1997) has provided that references in any enactment to the Minister for Enterprise and Employment are to be construed as references to the Minister for Enterprise, Trade and Employment. It should be noted that the powers and duties which are conferred on the Minister for Enterprise, Trade and Employment by or under the Unfair Dismissals Acts have been delegated by statutory instrument to the present Minister of State at the Department of Enterprise, Trade and Employment. (See now the Enterprise, Trade and Employment (Delegation of Ministerial Functions) Order 2004 (S.I. No. 809 of 2004).)

in compelling their employer or any employee or body of employees, to accept or not to accept terms or conditions of or affecting employment;

"trade union" [9] means a trade union which is the holder of a negotiation licence under Part II of the Trade Union Act, 1941;

"the Tribunal" [10] means the Tribunal established by section 39 of the Redundancy Payments Act, 1967, and known, by virtue of section 18 of this Act, as the Employment Appeals Tribunal.

(2) Where on the date of an award to an employee of re-instatement under this Act—

(*a*) the terms or conditions on which are employed other employees of the same employer who occupy positions similar to that from which the employee was dismissed, or

(*b*) if there are no such employees, the terms or conditions on which are employed employees generally of the same employer,

are more favourable to the employees concerned than they were at the date of the dismissal, then, the references in sections 5 (4) and 7 (1) (*a*) of this Act to the terms and conditions on which an employee was employed immediately before his dismissal shall, in the case of the first-mentioned employee, be construed as references to terms and conditions corresponding to those on which the other employees concerned are employed on the date of the award.[11]

(3) In this Act a reference to any enactment shall, unless the context otherwise requires, be construed as a reference to that enactment as amended, adapted or extended by or under any subsequent enactment including this Act.[12]

---

[9] This definition was substituted by s. 2 of the Unfair Dismissals (Amendment) Act, 1993.

[10] This definition was substituted by s. 2 of the Unfair Dismissals (Amendment) Act, 1993.

[11] Section 1(2) was inserted in its entirety by s. 2 of the Unfair Dismissals (Amendment) Act, 1993.

[12] Section 1(3) was inserted by s. 2 of the Unfair Dismissals (Amendment) Act, 1993.

2.—(1) Except in so far as any provision of this Act otherwise provides [13] [t]his Act shall not apply in relation to any of the following persons: Exclusions.

(*a*) an employee (other then a person referred to in section 4 of this Act) who is dismissed, who, at the date of his dismissal, had less than one year's continuous service with the employer who dismissed him,[14]

(*b*) an employee who is dismissed and who, on or before the date of his dismissal, had reached the normal retiring age for employees of the same employer in similar employment or who on that date had not attained the age of 16 years,[15]

(*c*) a person who is employed by his spouse, father, mother, grandfather, grandmother, step-father, step-mother, son, daughter, grandson, granddaughter, step-son, step-daughter, brother, sister, half-brother or half-sister, is a member of his employer's household and whose place of employment is a private dwellinghouse or a farm in or on which both the employee and the employer reside,

(*d*) a person in employment as a member of the Defence Forces, the Judge Advocate-General, the chairman of the Army Pensions Board or the ordinary member thereof who is not an officer of the Medical Corps of the Defence Forces,

(*e*) a member of the Garda Síochána,

(*f*) a person (other than a person employed under a contract of employment) who is receiving a training allowance

---

[13] The words up to this point were inserted by s. 38(1) of the Maternity Protection Act, 1994. This amendment did not expressly remove the capital letter in the next word, but this change has to be implied, as the sentence would not otherwise make sense.

[14] The words 'and whose dismissal does not result wholly or mainly from the matters referred to in section 6 (2) (f) of this Act' were deleted here by s. 38(1) of the Maternity Protection Act, 1994.

[15] The words "or who on that date had not attained the age of 16 years" were substituted by s. 6(3)(*d*) of the Employment Equality Act 1998, by virtue of s. 6(3)(d) itself being substituted by s. 4 of the Equality Act 2004.

from or undergoing instruction by [An Foras Áiseanna Saothair] [16] or is receiving a training allowance from and undergoing instruction by that body,

(*g*) a person who is employed by [An Foras Áiseanna Saothair] [17] under a contract of apprenticeship,

(*h*) subject to the provisions of this subsection a person who was employed by or under the State who was dismissed by the Government,[17a]

(*i*) a manager for a local authority for the purposes of *section 144* of the *Local Government Act, 2001*,[18]

(*j*) officers of a vocational committee established by the Vocational Education Act 1930,[19]

(*k*) the chief executive officer of the Health Service Executive for the purposes of *section 17* of the *Health Act 2004*.[20]

(2) This Act shall not apply in relation to—

(*a*) dismissal where the employment was under a contract of employment for a fixed term made before the 16th day of September, 1976, and the dismissal consisted only of the expiry of the term without its being renewed under the same contract, or

(*b*) dismissal where the employment was under a contract of employment for a fixed term or for a specified purpose (being a purpose of such a kind that the

---

[16] The text of s. 2(1)(f) refers to An Chomhairle Oiliúna. However, under s. 18(1) of the Labour Services Act, 1987, An Chomhairle Oiliúna was dissolved and under s. 18(4) of the same Act, references in any Act of the Oireachtas or any instrument made under an Act of the Oireachtas dating from before this time to An Chomhairle Oiliúna have since then been required to be construed as references to An Foras Áiseanna Saothair.

[17] See previous footnote.

[17a] Section 2(1)(h) was substituted by s. 22 of the Civil Service Regulation (Amendment) Act 2005.

[18] Section 2(1)(i) was substituted s. 164 of the Local Government Act, 2001.

[19] S. 2(1)(j) was substituted by s. 75 of the Health Act 2004 (replacing the earlier substitution of the same subparagraph by s. 3 of the Unfair Dismissals (Amendment) Act, 1993).

[20] S. 2(1)(k) was inserted by s. 75 of the Health Act 2004.

duration of the contract was limited but was, at the time of its making, incapable of precise ascertainment) and the dismissal consisted only of the expiry of the term without its being renewed under the said contract or the cesser of the purpose and the contract is in writing, was signed by or on behalf of the employer and by the employee and provides that this Act shall not apply to a dismissal consisting only of the expiry or cesser aforesaid.

Provided that where, following dismissal consisting only of the expiry of the term of a contract of employment such as aforesaid ('the prior contract') without the term being renewed under the contract or the cesser of the purpose of the contract— [21]

(i) the employee concerned is re-employed by the employer concerned within 3 months of the dismissal under a contract of employment such as aforesaid made between the employer and the employee ('the subsequent contract') and the nature of the employment is the same as or similar to that of the employment under the prior contract,

(ii) the employee is dismissed from the employment,

(iii) the dismissal consisted only of the expiry of the term of the subsequent contract without the term being renewed under the contract or the cesser of the purpose of the contract, and

(iv) in the opinion of the rights commissioner, [22] the Tribunal or the Circuit Court, as the case may be, the entry by the employer into the subsequent contract was wholly or partly for

---

[21] This entire proviso from the word 'Provided' onward, and everything that follows it in s. 2(2) up to, but not including, paragraph (c), were inserted by s. 3 of the Unfair Dismissals (Amendment) Act, 1993.

[22] Note that under s. 35(1) of the Industrial Relations Act, 1990, rights commissioners operate as a service of the Labour Relations Commission and references to rights commissioners in the Unfair Dismissals Act, 1977 are to be taken to be references to rights commissioners so operating.

or was connected with the purpose of the avoidance of liability under this Act—

then—

(I) this Act shall, subject to the other provisions thereof, apply to the dismissal, and

(II) the term of the prior contract and of any antecedent contracts shall be added to that of the subsequent contract for the purpose of the ascertainment under this Act of the period of service of the employee with the employer and the period so ascertained shall be deemed for those purposes to be one of continuous service.

In this proviso 'antecedent contract', in relation to a prior contract, means—

(A) a contract of employment such as aforesaid the term of which expired not more than 3 months before the commencement of the prior contract, or

(B) each of a series of contracts the term of the last of which expired not more than 3 months before the commencement of that of the prior contract and the term of the other or of each of the other contracts in the series expired not more than 3 months before the commencement of that of the other, or the next, contract in the series,

being a contract or contracts made between the employer and the employee who were parties to the prior contract and the nature of the employment under which was the same as or similar to that of the employment under the prior contract.

(*c*) dismissal where the employee's employer at the commencement of the employment informs the employee in writing that the employment will terminate on the return to work with that employer of another employee who is absent from work while on protective leave or natal care absence, within the meaning of Part IV of the Maternity Protection Act 1994, or is absent from work attending ante-natal classes in accordance with section 15A (inserted by *section 8* of the *Maternity Protection (Amendment) Act 2004*), or for breast-feeding in accordance with section 15B (inserted by *section 9* of the *Maternity Protection (Amendment) Act 2004*), of the first-mentioned Act, and the dismissal of the first-mentioned employee duly occurs for the purpose of facilitating the return to work of that other employee.[23]

(*d*) dismissal where—[24]

(i) the employee's employer at the commencement of the employment informs the employee in writing that the employment will terminate on the return to work with that employer of an adopting parent who is absent from work in accordance with the *Adoptive Leave Acts 1995* and *2005* during a period of adoptive leave or additional adoptive leave or a period of time off from work while attending certain pre-adoption classes or meetings, and

(ii) the dismissal of the employee duly occurs for the purpose of facilitating the return to work of the adopting parent.

(*e*) dismissal where the employer at the commencement of the employment informs the employee in writing

---

[23] S. 2(2)(c) was substituted in its entirety by s. 23 of the Maternity Protection (Amendment) Act 2004 (for text which itself had been earlier inserted (in substitution for text originally inserted by s. 24 of the Maternity Protection of Employees Act, 1981) by s. 38(2) of the Maternity Protection Act, 1994 and amended by s. 23 of the Adoptive Leave Act, 1995). The full stop at the end of the subparagraph appears to be an error.

[24] This version of s. 2(2)(d) of the 1977 Act was substituted for the original version (which had been inserted by s. 23 of the Adoptive Leave Act, 1995 and amended by s. 27(1) of the Carer's Leave Act, 2001) by s. 23 of the Adoptive Leave Act, 1995 (as substituted by s. 18 of the Adoptive Leave Act 2005). The full stop at the end of the subparagraph appears to be an error.

that the employment will terminate on the return to work with that employer of an employee who is absent from work while on carer's leave under the *Carer's Leave Act, 2001,* and the dismissal of the employee duly occurs for the purpose of facilitating the return to work of the employee who has been on carer's leave.[25]

(3) (*a*) This Act shall not apply in relation to the dismissal of an employee who, under the relevant contract of employment, ordinarily worked outside the State unless—

(i) he was ordinarily resident in the State during the term of the contract, or

(ii) he was domiciled in the State during the term of the contract, and the employer—

(I) in case the employee was an individual, was ordinarily resident in the State, during the term of the contract, or

(II) in case the employer was a body corporate or an unincorporated body of persons, had its principal place of business in the State during the term of the contract.

(*b*) In this subsection "term of the contract" means the whole of the period from the time of the commencement of work under the contract to the time of the relevant dismissal.

(4) The First Schedule to the Minimum Notice and Terms of Employment Act, 1973, as amended by section 20 of this Act,[26] shall apply for the purpose of ascertaining for the

---

[25] Section 2(2)(e) was inserted by s. 27(1) of the Carer's Leave Act, 2001.

[26] Note, however, that under s. 8 of the Protection of Employees (Part-Time Work) Act, 2001, the Unfair Dismissals Acts, 1977 to 1993 are to apply to a part-time employee (meaning, under s. 7(1) of that Act, an employee whose normal hours of work are less than the normal hours of work of an employee who is a comparable employee in relation to him or her) in the same manner (and subject to the like exceptions not inconsistent with s. 8) as they apply (other than by virtue of the 2001 Act) to an employee to

purposes of this Act the period of service of an employee and whether that service has been continuous.

(5) Notwithstanding subsection (4) of this section, the dismissal (not being a dismissal referred to in the proviso (inserted by the *Unfair Dismissals (Amendment) Act, 1993*) to subsection (2) of this section) of an employee followed by his re-employment by the same employer not later than 26 weeks after the dismissal shall not operate to break the continuity of service of the employee with the employer if the dismissal was wholly or partly for or was connected with the purpose of the avoidance of liability under this Act.[27]

Application of Act to certain civil servants.

2A. —(1) For the purposes of this Act, as respects the dismissal of a person who prior to such dismissal was a civil servant a reference in this Act to an 'employee' shall be construed as including a civil servant who held office in the Civil Service of the Government or in the Civil Service of the State.[27a]

---

whom the Unfair Dismissals Acts, 1977 to 1993 relate. (Note also the broad definition given to "employee" by s. 3(1) of the Protection of Employees (Part-Time Work) Act, 2001 and note further that under s. 1(6) of the Protection of Employees (Part-Time Work) Act, 2001, insofar as the 2001 Act relates to the Unfair Dismissals Acts, 1977 to 1993, those Acts and the 2001 Act are required to be construed together as one and may be cited together as the Unfair Dismissals Acts, 1977 to 2001. Note further that under s. 1(3) of the Civil Service Regulation (Amendment) Act 2005, the Unfair Dismissals Acts, 1977 to 2001 and Part 6 of that Act may be cited together as the Unfair Dismissals Acts 1977 to 2005 and are required to be construed together as one.)

Finally, note also that under s. 11 (6) of the Protection of Employees (Employers' Insolvency) Act, 1984, the reference in section 2 (4) of the Unfair Dismissals Act, 1977 to the First Schedule to the Act of 1973 is to be construed as being a reference —

(*a*) in case an order under s.11 of the 1984 Act amending the First Schedule to the Act of 1973 is for the time being in force, to the First Schedule to the Act of 1973 as amended by s. 20 of the Unfair Dismissals Act, 1977, by s. 13 of the 1984 Act and by the order,

(*b*) in case no such order is so in force, to the First Schedule to the Act of 1973 as amended both by s. 20 of the Unfair Dismissals Act, 1977 and s. 13 of the 1984 Act.

[27] Section 2(5) was inserted by s. 3 of the Unfair Dismissals (Amendment) Act, 1993.

[27a] The entirety of s. 2A was inserted in the form shown in the text above by s. 22 of the Civil Service Regulation (Amendment) Act 2005.

(2) Subject to subsection (4), for the purposes of this Act, as respects the dismissal of a person who prior to such dismissal was a civil servant a reference in this Act to an 'employer' shall be construed as including the State, a Minister of the Government, a Department or a Scheduled Office (which term has the same meaning as it has in the Civil Service Regulation Act 1956) in which the civil servant concerned held office prior to the dismissal.

(3) As respects a civil servant to whom this Act applies, for the purposes of this Act, 'contract of employment' means such arrangements as are made by the Minister for Finance under section 17 of the Civil Service Regulation Act 1956, together with such further terms and conditions of service which apply to the civil servant concerned, made in respect of a particular Department or Scheduled Office which extend or alter the arrangements under the said section 17.

(4) For the purposes of this section and the First Schedule—

(*a*) 'Department' includes such bodies or organisations (whether established by or under statute, or otherwise) other than a Scheduled Office, for which the Minister having charge of the Department concerned is responsible, and

(*b*) 'Scheduled Office' includes such bodies or organisations (whether established by or under statute or otherwise) for which the Minister of the Government having charge of the Scheduled Office is responsible.

(5) Where, as respects a person who was dismissed as a civil servant, the dismissal is found to be an unfair dismissal, and the rights commissioner, the Tribunal or the Circuit Court, as the case may be, considers, pursuant to section 7, that it is appropriate that such person be re-engaged or re-instated, the right of re-instatement or re-engagement shall be construed to be a right to be re-instated or re-engaged, as the case may be, in the grade or rank held by that civil servant prior to his dismissal.

(6) Nothing in this section shall be construed as affecting the status of a civil servant as an officer.

3. — Except in so far as any provision of this Act otherwise provides [28]

Dismissal during probation or training.

(1) [t]his Act shall not apply in relation to the dismissal of an employee during a period starting with the commencement of the employment when he is on probation or undergoing training—

(*a*) if his contract of employment is in writing, the duration of the probation or training is 1 year or less and is specified in the contract, or

(*b*) if his contract of employment was made before the commencement of this Act and was not in writing and the duration of the probation or training is 1 year or less.

(2) [t]his Act shall not apply in relation to the dismissal of an employee during a period starting with the commencement of the employment when he is undergoing training for the purpose of becoming qualified or registered, as the case may be, as a nurse, pharmacist, health inspector, medical laboratory technician, occupational therapist, physiotherapist, speech therapist, radiographer or social worker.

4. —Except in so far as any provision of this Act otherwise provides [29] [t]his Act shall not apply in relation to the dismissal of a person who is or was employed under a statutory apprenticeship if the dismissal takes place within 6 months after the commencement of the apprenticeship or within 1 month after the completion of the apprenticeship.

Dismissal during apprenticeship.

---

[28] The words "Except in so far as any provision of this Act otherwise provides" were inserted by s. 38(3) of the Maternity Protection Act, 1994. The 1994 Act did not expressly effect the indicated changes in capitalisation indicated in the text here at the beginning of s. 3(1) and s. 3(2) but it has been assumed here to have implicitly done so, as otherwise, the amendment would lack grammatical sense.

[29] The words "Except in so far as any provision of this Act otherwise provides" were inserted by s. 38(3) of the Maternity Protection Act, 1994. The 1994 Act did not expressly effect the indicated change in capitalisation in the text immediately after the footnote but has been assumed here to have implicitly done so, as otherwise, the amendment would lack grammatical sense.

Dismissal by way of lock-out or for taking part in strike.

5.—(1) For the purposes of this Act (other than section 2 (4)), the lock-out of an employee shall be deemed to be a dismissal and the dismissal shall be deemed to be an unfair dismissal if, after the termination of the lock-out— [30]

(*a*) the employee was not permitted to resume his employment on terms and conditions at least as favourable to the employee as those specified in paragraph (*a*) or (*b*) of subsection (1) of section 7 of this Act, and

(*b*) one or more other employees in the same employment were so permitted.

(2) The dismissal of an employee for taking part in a strike or other industrial action shall be deemed for the purposes of this Act to be an unfair dismissal if—

(*a*) one or more employees of the same employer who took part in the strike or other industrial action were not dismissed for so taking part, or

(*b*) one or more of such employees who were dismissed for so taking part were subsequently permitted to resume their employment on terms and conditions at least as favourable to the employees as those specified in the said paragraph (*a*) or (*b*) and the employee was not.[31]

(3) The said section 7 shall be construed in relation to an unfair dismissal specified in subsection (1) or (2) of this section as if it contained a requirement that the terms or conditions on which the person the subject of the unfair dismissal is, if appropriate, to be re-instated under paragraph (*a*) of subsection (1) of that section or re-engaged under paragraph (*b*) of that subsection included a term that the re-instatement or re-engagement should be deemed to have commenced on such day as is agreed upon by the employer concerned and by or on behalf of the employees or, in the absence of such agreement, on the earliest date from which re-instatement or re-engagement,

---

[30] Section 5(1) was substituted in its entirety by s. 4 of the Unfair Dismissals (Amendment) Act 2003.

[31] Section 5(2) was substituted in its entirety by s. 4 of the Unfair Dismissals (Amendment) Act 2003.

as the case may be, was offered to a majority of the other employees of the same employer who were the subject of the lock-out concerned or took part in the strike or other industrial action concerned.[32]

(4) In this section a reference to an offer of re-instatement or re-engagement, in relation to an employee, is a reference to an offer (made either by the original employer or by a successor of that employer or by an associated employer) to re-instate that employee in the position which he held immediately before his dismissal on the terms and conditions on which he was employed immediately before his dismissal together with a term that the re-instatement shall be deemed to have commenced on the day of the dismissal, or to re-engage him, either in the position which he held immediately before his dismissal or in a different position which would be reasonably suitable for him, on such terms and conditions as are reasonable having regard to all the circumstances.

(5) In this section—

"lock-out" means an action which, in contemplation or furtherance of a trade dispute (within the meaning of the Industrial Relations Act, 1946 [33]), is taken by one or more employers, whether parties to the dispute or not, and which consists of the exclusion of one or more employees from one or more factories, offices or other places of work or of the suspension of work in one or more such places or of the collective, simultaneous or otherwise connected termination or suspension of employment of a group of employees;

"the original employer" means, in relation to the employee, the employer who dismissed the employee.

---

[32] Section 5(3) was substituted in its entirety by s. 4 of the Unfair Dismissals (Amendment) Act, 2003.

[33] Under s. 24(1) of the Industrial Relations Act, 1969, the 1969 Act is to be construed as one with the 1946 Act. Under s. 12(1) of the Industrial Relations Act, 1976, that Act is also to be construed as one with the 1946 Act. Under s. 2(1) of the Industrial Relations Act, 1990, the 1990 Act (other than Part II thereof) and the Industrial Relations Acts, 1946, 1969 and 1976 are to be construed together as one Act. Under s. 13(1) of the Industrial Relations (Amendment) Act, 2001, that Act and the previous Acts mentioned in this footnote may be cited together as the Industrial Relations Acts, 1946 to 2001, and shall be construed together as one.

Unfair dismissal.

6.—(1) Subject to the provisions of this section, the dismissal of an employee shall be deemed, for the purposes of this Act, to be an unfair dismissal unless, having regard to all the circumstances, there were substantial grounds justifying the dismissal.[34]

---

[34] Note further here s. 40(4) of the Maternity Protection Act, 1994, which provides as follows:

"For the purposes of the [Unfair Dismissals Act, 1977]—

(*a*) an employee to whom this section applies [*Editor's note: the section applies to an employee who is entitled to return to work from an absence due to protective leave under the 1994 Act, but who is not permitted to do so by her employer*] who is also an employee to whom that Act applies shall be deemed to have been dismissed on the expected date of return; and

(*b*) the dismissal shall be deemed to be an unfair dismissal unless, having regard to all the circumstances, there were substantial grounds justifying the dismissal."

Note also s. 26(2) of the Adoptive Leave Act, 1995, which provides as follows:

"For the purposes of the [Unfair Dismissals Act, 1977], an adopting parent [*Editor's note: this refers to an adopting parent within the meaning of s. 1 of the Unfair Dismissals Act, 1977 (as amended) and who is entitled to return to work but is not permitted to do so by his or her employer, the successor or an associated employer*] shall be deemed to have been dismissed on the date specified in the relevant notification under *section 20 (1)* [*Editor's note: this refers to s. 20(1) of the 1995 Act, and refers to notification in writing of the adopting parent's intention to return to work and of the date on which he or she expects to return to work*], and the dismissal shall be deemed to be an unfair dismissal unless, having regard to all the circumstances, there were substantial grounds justifying the dismissal."

Note also s. 16A(4) of the Parental Leave Act, 1998, as inserted by s. 11 of the Parental Leave (Amendment) Act 2006, which provides as follows:

"An employee who is entitled to return to work in the employment concerned in accordance with section 15 [*Editor's note: s. 15 governs entitlement to return to work on the expiration of a period of parental leave*] but is not permitted by his or her employer to do so—

(*a*) shall be deemed to have been dismissed on the date on which he or she was entitled to so return to work and the dismissal shall be deemed, for the purposes of the Unfair Dismissals Acts 1977 to 2005, to have been an unfair dismissal unless, having regard to all the circumstances, there were substantial grounds justifying the dismissal..."

Note also s. 16(4) of the Carer's Leave Act, 2001,

"An employee who is entitled to return to work in the employment concerned in accordance with *section 14* [*Editor's note: s. 14 governs entitlement to return to work on the termination of carer's leave*] but is not permitted by his or her employer to do so—

(2) Without prejudice to the generality of subsection (1) of this section, the dismissal of an employee shall be deemed, for the

---

(*a*) shall be deemed to have been dismissed on the date on which he or she was entitled to so return to work and the dismissal shall be deemed, for the purposes of the Unfair Dismissals Acts, 1977 to 1993, to have been an unfair dismissal unless, having regard to all the circumstances, there were substantial grounds justifying the dismissal..."

Note also s. 36 of the National Minimum Wage Act, 2000, which provides as follows.

"(1) An employer shall not cause or suffer any action prejudicial to an employee for the employee having—

(*a*) exercised or having proposed to exercise a right under this Act,

(*b*) in good faith opposed or proposed to oppose by lawful means an act which is unlawful under this Act, or

(*c*) become, or in future will or might become, entitled in accordance with this Act to remuneration at an hourly rate of pay that on average is not less than the national minimum rate of pay, or a particular percentage of that rate of pay.

(2) Dismissal of an employee in contravention of subsection (1) shall be deemed to be an unfair dismissal of the employee within the meaning and for the purposes of section 6(1) of the Unfair Dismissals Acts, 1977 to 1993 (but without prejudice to sections 2 to 5 of the Unfair Dismissals Act, 1977, except that it is not necessary for the employee to have at least one year's continuous service with the employer and that Act shall apply as if the Worker Protection (Regular Part-Time Employees) Act, 1991, were repealed in relation to the number of hours an employee is normally expected to work for the purposes of that Act) and those Acts, with the necessary modifications, shall apply accordingly."

(Note further in the context of the last-mentioned provision that s. 5 of the Protection of Employees (Part-Time Work) Act, 2001 repealed the Worker Protection (Regular Part-Time Employees) Act, 1991, thus rendering otiose the derogation in s. 36(2) of the National Minimum Wage Act, 2000 from the normal operation of the 1991 Act as regards the number of hours an employee is normally expected to work for the purposes of the 1991 Act. Finally, note that under s. 1(6) of the Protection of Employees (Part-Time Work) Act, 2001, insofar as the 2001 Act relates to the Unfair Dismissals Acts, 1977 to 1993, those Acts and the 2001 Act are required to be construed together as one and may be cited together as the Unfair Dismissals Acts, 1977 to 2001, and that under s. 1(3) of the Civil Service Regulation (Amendment) Act 2005, the Unfair Dismissals Acts, 1977 to 2001 and Part 6 of that Act may be cited together as the Unfair Dismissals Acts 1977 to 2005 and are required to be construed together as one.)

Note finally that under s. 27(2)(a) of the Safety, Health and Welfare at Work Act 2005, "penalisation" within the meaning of s. 27 of that Act, which, under

purposes of this Act, to be an unfair dismissal if it results wholly or mainly from one or more of the following:[34a]

(*a*) the employee's membership, or proposal that he or another person become a member, of, or his engaging in activities on behalf of, a trade union or excepted body under the Trade Union Acts, 1941 and 1971, where the times at which he engages in such activities are outside his hours of work or are times during his hours of work in which he is permitted pursuant to the contract of employment between him and his employer so to engage,

(*b*) the religious or political opinions of the employee,

(*c*) civil proceedings whether actual, threatened or proposed against the employer to which the employee is or will be a party or in which the employee was or is likely to be a witness,

(*d*) criminal proceedings against the employer, whether actual, threatened or proposed, in relation to which the employee has made, proposed or threatened to make a complaint or statement to the prosecuting authority or to any other authority connected with or involved in the prosecution of the proceedings or in which the employee was or is likely to be a witness,

---

s. 27(3) of that Act, is prohibited when done for specified reasons, includes suspension, lay-off or dismissal (including a dismissal within the meaning of the Unfair Dismissals Acts 1977 to 2001), or the threat of suspension, lay-off or dismissal. Furthermore, under s. 27(4) of the 2005 Act, the dismissal of an employee shall be deemed, for the purposes of the Unfair Dismissals Acts, to be an unfair dismissal if it results wholly or mainly from penalisation as referred to in s. 27(2)(a) of that Act.

[34a] Note that under s. 5(3) of the Standards in Public Office Act, 2001, where an employer dismisses an employee to whom the Unfair Dismissals Act, 1977, applies and the dismissal constitutes disciplinary action taken in contravention of s. 5(1) of the 2001 Act in relation to the employee, "the dismissal is a dismissal deemed for the purposes of [the 1977 Act], by virtue of section 6(2)(*f*) thereof, to be an unfair dismissal." The reference specifically to subsection (f) seems to be an error since even when the 2001 Act was adopted s. 6(2)(f) related to matters pertaining to maternity protection legislation.

(*dd*) the exercise or proposed exercise by the employee of the right to parental leave, *force majeure* leave under and in accordance with the Parental Leave Act, 1998, or carer's leave under and in accordance with the *Carer's Leave Act, 2001*,[35]

(*e*) the race, colour or sexual orientation of the employee,[36]

(*ee*) the age of the employee,[37]

(*eee*) the employee's membership of the travelling community,[38]

(*f*) the employee's pregnancy, attendance at ante-natal classes, giving birth or breastfeeding or any matters connected therewith,[39]

(*g*) the exercise or proposed exercise by the employee of the right under the Maternity Protection Act 1994 to any form of protective leave or natal care absence, within the meaning of Part IV of that Act, or to time off from work to attend ante-natal classes in accordance with section 15A (inserted by *section 8* of the *Maternity Protection* (*Amendment*) *Act 2004*), or to time off from work or a reduction of working hours for breastfeeding in accordance with section 15B (inserted by *section 9* of the *Maternity Protection* (*Amendment*) *Act 2004*), of the first-mentioned Act,[40]

---

[35] Section 6(2)(dd) was substituted by s. 27(2) of the Carer's Leave Act, 2001, having been originally inserted by s. 25(2) of the Parental Leave Act, 1998.

[36] Section 6(2)(e) was substituted by s. 5 of the Unfair Dismissals (Amendment) Act, 1993. The original s. 6(2)(e) referred only to the race or colour of the employee.

[37] Section 6(2)(ee) was inserted by s. 5 of the Unfair Dismissals (Amendment) Act, 1993.

[38] Section 6(2)(eee) was inserted by s. 5 of the Unfair Dismissals (Amendment) Act, 1993.

[39] This version of s. 6(2)(f) was substituted by s. 23 of the Maternity Protection (Amendment) Act 2004 in place of the earlier version (which had been substituted by s. 38(4) of the Maternity Protection Act, 1994).

[40] This version of s. 6(2)(g) was substituted by s. 23 of the Maternity Protection (Amendment) Act 2004 in place of the earlier version (which had been substituted by s. 38(4) of the Maternity Protection Act, 1994, having originally been inserted by s. 25 of the Maternity Protection of Employees Act 1981).

(*h*) the exercise or contemplated exercise by an adoptive parent of the parent's right under the *Adoptive Leave Acts 1995* and *2005* to adoptive leave or additional adoptive leave or a period of time off to attend certain pre-adoption classes or meetings.[41]

(2A) Sections 3 and 4 of this Act do not apply to a case falling within paragraph (*f*), (*g*) or (*h*) of subsection (2) of this section and, for the purposes of those paragraphs, 'employee' and 'adopting parent' include a person who would otherwise be excluded from this Act by paragraph (*a*), (*c*), (*f*) or (*g*) of section 2 (1) of this Act.[42]

(2B) Sections 3 and 4 do not apply to a case falling within subsection (2)(*dd*) and, for the purpose of that paragraph, 'employee' includes a person who would otherwise be excluded from this Act by paragraph (*a*), (*c*), (*f*) or (*g*) of section 2(1).[43]

(2C) Sections 3 and 4 do not apply to a case falling within subsection (2)(*dd*) and, for the purpose of that paragraph, 'employee' includes a person who would otherwise be excluded from this Act by paragraph (*a*), (*b*), (*c*), (*d*), (*e*), (*f*), (*g*), (*h*), (*i*) or (*j*) of section 2(1).[44]

(3) Without prejudice to the generality of subsection (1) of this section, if an employee was dismissed due to redundancy but the circumstances constituting the redundancy applied equally to one or more other employees in similar employment with the same employer who have not been dismissed, and either—

(*a*) the selection of that employee for dismissal resulted wholly or mainly from one or more of the matters specified in subsection (2) of this section or another matter that would not be a ground justifying dismissal, or

---

[41] This version of s. 6(2)(h) of the 1977 Act was substituted for the original version (which had been inserted by s. 24 of the Adoptive Leave Act, 1995) by s. 24 of the Adoptive Leave Act, 1995 (as substituted by s. 19 of the Adoptive Leave Act 2005).

[42] Originally inserted by s. 38(5) of the Maternity Protection Act, 1994, s. 6(2A) was substituted (and updated to take account of other amendments to the Act) by s. 25 of the Adoptive Leave Act, 1995.

[43] Section 6(2B) was inserted by s. 25(2) of the Parental Leave Act, 1998.

[44] Section 6(2C) was inserted by s. 27(2) of the Carer's Leave Act, 2001.

(*b*) he was selected for dismissal in contravention of a procedure (being a procedure that has been agreed upon by or on behalf of the employer and by the employee or a trade union, or an excepted body under the Trade Union Acts, 1941 and 1971, representing him or has been established by the custom and practice of the employment concerned) relating to redundancy and there were no special reasons justifying a departure from that procedure,

then the dismissal shall be deemed, for the purposes of this Act, to be an unfair dismissal.[45]

(4) Without prejudice to the generality of subsection (1) of this section, the dismissal of an employee shall be deemed, for the purposes of this Act, not to be an unfair dismissal, if it results wholly or mainly from one or more of the following:

(*a*) the capability, competence or qualifications of the employee for performing work of the kind which he was employed by the employer to do,

(*b*) the conduct of the employee,

(*c*) the redundancy of the employee, and

(*d*) the employee being unable to work or continue to work in the position which he held without contravention (by

---

[45] Note that under s. 16A(1) of the Parental Leave Act, 1998 (as inserted by s. 11 of the Parental Leave (Amendment) Act 2006), penalisation of an employee for proposing to exercise or having exercised his or her entitlement to parental leave or *force majeure* leave is prohibited. The relevance of this in the present context is that penalisation of the employee is expressly referred to in s. 16A(2)(b) of the 1998 Act (as inserted by s. 11 of the Parental Leave (Amendment) Act 2006) as including "unfair treatment of the employee, including selection for redundancy". Note further that although penalisation of an employee constituting a dismissal of the employee — referred to s. 16A (2)(a) of the 1998 Act (as inserted by s. 11 of the Parental Leave (Amendment) Act 2006) — results in the employee being confined to instituting proceedings under the Unfair Dismissals Acts in respect of that dismissal (with s. 16A(3) of the Parental Leave Act, 1998 (as inserted by s. 11 of the Parental Leave (Amendment) Act 2006) providing that such dismissal may *not* be referred to a rights commissioner under Part IV of the 1998 Act) no such restriction has been imposed in relation to a s. 16A(2)(b)-type penalisation of the employee *via* selection for redundancy. Thus proceedings under Part IV of the Parental Leave Act, 1998 are a possibility in this latter situation.

him or by his employer) of a duty or restriction imposed by or under any statute or instrument made under statute.

(5) (*a*) Without prejudice to the generality of subsection (1) of this section, the dismissal by the Minister for Defence of a civilian employed with the Defence Forces under section 30 (1) (*g*) of the Defence Act, 1954, shall be deemed for the purposes of this Act not to be an unfair dismissal if it is shown that the dismissal was for the purpose of safeguarding national security.

(*b*) A certificate purporting to be signed by the Minister for Defence and stating that a dismissal by the Minister for Defence of a civilian named in the certificate from employment with the Defence Forces under section 30 (1) (*g*) of the Defence Act, 1954, was for the purpose of safeguarding national security shall be evidence, for the purposes of this Act, of the facts stated in the certificate without further proof.

(6) In determining for the purposes of this Act whether the dismissal of an employee was an unfair dismissal or not, it shall be for the employer to show that the dismissal resulted wholly or mainly from one or more of the matters specified in subsection (4) of this section or that there were other substantial grounds justifying the dismissal.

(7) Without prejudice to the generality of subsection (1) of this section, in determining if a dismissal is an unfair dismissal, regard may be had, if the rights commissioner, the Tribunal or the Circuit Court, as the case may be, considers it appropriate to do so—

(*a*) to the reasonableness or otherwise of the conduct (whether by act or omission) of the employer in relation to the dismissal, and

(*b*) to the extent (if any) of the compliance or failure to comply by the employer, in relation to the employee, with the procedure referred to in section 14 (1) of this Act or with the provisions of any code of practice referred to in paragraph (d) (inserted by the *Unfair*

Dismissals (Amendment) Act, 1993) of section 7 (2) of this Act.[46]

7. —(1) Where an employee is dismissed and the dismissal is an unfair dismissal, the employee shall be entitled to redress consisting of whichever of the following the rights commissioner, the Tribunal or the Circuit Court, as the case may be, considers appropriate having regard to all the circumstances: [47]

Redress for unfair dismissal.

(*a*) re-instatement by the employer of the employee in the position which he held immediately before his dismissal on the terms and conditions on which he was employed immediately before his dismissal together with a term that the re-instatement shall be deemed to have commenced on the day of the dismissal, or

---

[46] Section 6(7) was substituted in its entirety by s. 5 of the Unfair Dismissals Amendment) Act, 1993.

[47] Note in this regard s. 20(3) of the Adoptive Leave Act, 1995, which provides as follows.

"In the absence of reasonable grounds, failure to give notice under [s. 20(1) of the 1995 Act (*i.e.*, notice in writing on the part of an adopting parent who has been on adoptive leave or additional adoptive leave of his or her intention to return to work and of the date on which he or she expects to return to work)] or the giving of it otherwise than in the time limits specified thereunder are matters that may be taken into account by a rights commissioner, the Tribunal or Circuit Court in determining the adopting parent's rights under the Act of 1977, this Act or any other relevant enactment so far as the remedies of reinstatement, re-engagement or compensation are concerned."

Note that s. 101(4) of the Employment Equality Act, 1998 provides as follows.

"An employee who has been dismissed shall not be entitled to seek redress (or to exercise, or continue to exercise, any other power) under Part VII of that Act if, as a result of the dismissal—...

(*b*) in the exercise of powers under the Unfair Dismissals Acts, 1977 to 1993, a rights commissioner has issued a recommendation in respect of the dismissal, or

(*c*) the Employment Appeals Tribunal has begun a hearing into the matter of the dismissal."

Note also that s. 101(5) of the 1998 Act provides as follows.

"If an employee who has been dismissed has referred the case of the dismissal to the Labour Court under *section 77* [of the 1998 Act] and either a settlement has been reached by mediation or the Labour Court has begun an investigation under *section 79* [of the 1998 Act] —...

(*b*) re-engagement by the employer of the employee either in the position which he held immediately before his dismissal or in a different position which would be reasonably suitable for him on such terms and conditions as are reasonable having regard to all the circumstances, or

---

(*b*) the employee shall not be entitled to seek redress (or to exercise, or continue to exercise, any other power) under the Unfair Dismissals Acts, 1977 to 1993, in respect of the dismissal."

Note also s. 4(3) of the Protections for Persons Reporting Child Abuse Act, 1998, which provides as follows:

"If a penalisation of an employee, in contravention of [s. 4(1) of the 1998 Act (which prohibits an employer from penalising an employee for having formed an opinion that a child has been or is being assaulted, ill-treated, neglected or sexually abused or that a child's health, development or welfare has been or is being avoidably impaired or neglected, and communicated that opinion, whether in writing or otherwise, to an appropriate person, if the employee has acted reasonably and in good faith in forming that opinion and communicating it to the appropriate person)], constitutes a dismissal of the employee within the meaning of the Unfair Dismissals Acts, 1977 to 1993, relief may not be granted to the employee in respect of that penalisation both under [s. 4 of the 1998 Act] and under those Acts."

Note also s. 16(3) of the Carer's Leave Act, 2001, which provides as follows:

"If a penalisation of an employee, in contravention of [s. 16(1) of the 2001 Act (which prohibits an employer from penalising an employee for proposing to exercise or having exercised his or her entitlement to carer's leave)], constitutes a dismissal of the employee...the employee may institute proceedings under the Unfair Dismissals Acts, 1977 to 1993, in respect of that dismissal and such dismissal may not be referred to a rights commissioner under *Part 4* [of the Carer's Leave Act, 2001]."

Note also s. 15(3) of the Protection of Employees (Part-Time Work) Act, 2001, which provides as follows:

"If a penalisation of an employee, in contravention of [subsection (1) of the 2001 Act (which prohibits an employer from penalising an employee for (a) invoking any right of the employee to be treated, in respect of the employee's conditions of employment, in the manner provided for by Part 2 of the 2001 Act, or (b) for having in good faith opposed by lawful means an act which is unlawful under the 2001 Act, or (c) for refusing to accede to a request by the employer to transfer from performing full-time work to performing part-time work, or vice versa or (d) for giving evidence in any proceedings under the 2001 Act or giving notice of his or her intention to do so or to do any of the other things referred to in (a), (b) or (c)], constitutes a dismissal of the employee within the meaning of the Unfair Dismissals Acts, 1977 to 1993, relief may not be granted to the employee in respect of that penalisation both under [Part 2 of the 2001 Act)] and under those Acts."

(*c*) (i) if the employee incurred any financial loss attributable to the dismissal, payment to him by the employer of such compensation in respect of the loss (not exceeding in amount 104 weeks remuneration in respect of the employment from which he was dismissed calculated in accordance with regulations under section 17 of this Act) as is just and equitable having regard to all the circumstances, or

---

Note also s. 18(1) of the Protection of Employees (Fixed-Term Work) Act 2003, which provides as follows:

"If penalisation of an employee, in contravention of [section 13(1) of the 2003 Act (which prohibits an employer from penalising an employee (*a*) for invoking any right of the employee to be treated, in respect of the employee's conditions of employment, in the manner provided for by Part 2 of the 2003 Act, (*b*) for having in good faith opposed by lawful means an act which is unlawful under the 2003 Act, (*c*) for giving evidence in any proceeding under the 2003 Act or for giving notice of his or her intention to do so or to do any other thing referred to in (a) or (b), or (*d*) by dismissing the employee from his or her employment if the dismissal is wholly or partly for or connected with the purpose of the avoidance of a fixed-term contract being deemed to be a contract of indefinite duration under section 9(3) of the 2003 Act)], constitutes a dismissal of the employee within the meaning of the Unfair Dismissals Acts, 1977 to 2001, relief may not be granted to the employee in respect of that penalisation both under [Part 3 of the 2003 Act] and under those Acts."

Note also s. 101(2) of the Employment Equality Act, 1998 (as substituted by s. 46(1) of the Equality Act 2004), which provides as follows:

"Where an individual has referred a case to the Director under [s. 77(1) of the 1998 Act (which (as substituted by s. 46(1) of the 2004 Act) provides that a person who claims (*a*) to have been discriminated against or subjected to victimisation, (*b*) to have been dismissed in circumstances amounting to discrimination or victimisation, (*c*) not to be receiving remuneration in accordance with an equal remuneration term, or (*d*) not to be receiving a benefit under an equality clause, in contravention of the 1998 Act, may seek redress by referring the case to the Director of the Equality Tribunal)] and either a settlement has been reached by mediation or the Director has begun an investigation under [section 79 of the 2004 Act], the individual—

(*a*) shall not be entitled to recover damages at common law in respect of the case, and

(*b*) if he or she was dismissed before so referring the case, shall not be entitled to seek redress (or to exercise, or continue to exercise, any other power) under the Unfair Dismissals Acts 1977 to 1993 in respect of the dismissal."

(ii) if the employee incurred no such financial loss, payment to the employee by the employer of such compensation (if any, but not exceeding in amount 4 weeks remuneration in respect of the employment from which he was dismissed calculated as aforesaid) as is just and equitable having regard to all the circumstances,

and the references in the foregoing paragraphs to an employer shall be construed, in a case where the ownership of the business of the employer changes after the dismissal, as references to the person who, by virtue of the change, becomes entitled to such ownership.[48]

Note also s. 16A(3) of the Parental Leave Act, 1998 (as inserted by s. 11 of the Parental Leave (Amendment) Act 2006), which provides as follows.

"If a penalisation of an employee, in contravention of subsection (1) [*Editor's note: subsection (1) of s. 16A of the 2006 Act prohibits penalisation by an employer of an employee for proposing to exercise or having exercised his or her entitlement to parental leave or force majeure leave*], constitutes a dismissal of the employee...the employee may institute proceedings under the Unfair Dismissals Acts 1977 to 2005 in respect of that dismissal and such dismissal may not be referred to a rights commissioner under Part IV [*Editor's note: this refers to Part IV of the Parental Leave Act, 1998*]."

Note that under s. 1(6) of the Protection of Employees (Part-Time Work) Act, 2001, insofar as the 2001 Act relates to the Unfair Dismissals Acts, 1977 to 1993, those Acts and the 2001 Act are required to be construed together as one and may be cited together as the Unfair Dismissals Acts, 1977 to 2001, and that under s. 1(3) of the Civil Service Regulation (Amendment) Act 2005, the Unfair Dismissals Acts, 1977 to 2001 and Part 6 of that Act may be cited together as the Unfair Dismissals Acts 1977 to 2005 and are required to be construed together as one.

Finally, note also s. 27(5) of the Safety, Health and Welfare at Work Act 2005, which provides that if penalisation of an employee, in contravention of s. 27(3) of that Act constitutes a dismissal of the employee within the meaning of the Unfair Dismissals Acts, relief may not be granted to the employee in respect of that penalisation both under this Part and under those Acts.

[48] The entirety of s. 7(1)(c) was substituted by s. 6 of the Unfair Dismissals (Amendment) Act, 1993, so as to permit payment of compensation to an unfairly dismissed employee even in the absence of financial loss and to make provision for where the ownership of the business of the employer changes after dismissal.

(2) Without prejudice to the generality of subsection (1) of this section in determining the amount of compensation payable under that subsection regard shall be had to—

(*a*) the extent (if any) to which the financial loss referred to in that subsection was attributable to an act, omission or conduct by or on behalf of the employer,

(*b*) the extent (if any) to which the said financial loss was attributable to an action, omission or conduct by or on behalf of the employee,

(*c*) the measures (if any) adopted by the employee or, as the case may be, his failure to adopt measures, to mitigate the loss aforesaid,[49]

(*d*) the extent (if any) of the compliance or failure to comply by the employer, in relation to the employee, with the procedure referred to in subsection (1) of section 14 of this Act or with the provisions of any code of practice relating to procedures regarding dismissal approved of by the Minister,[50]

(*e*) the extent (if any) of the compliance or failure to comply by the employer, in relation to the employee, with the said section 14, and [51]

(*f*) the extent (if any) to which the conduct of the employee (whether by act or omission) contributed to the dismissal.[52]

(2A) In calculating financial loss for the purposes of subsection (1), payments to the employee— [53]

---

[49] The word 'and' was deleted from the end of s. 7(2)(c) by s. 6 of the Unfair Dismissals (Amendment) Act, 1993.

[50] Section 7(2)(d) was substituted by s. 6 of the Unfair Dismissals (Amendment) Act, 1993, eliminating any mention of failure to comply with procedures or provisions of codes of practice by the employee.

[51] Section 7(2)(e) was inserted by s. 6 of the Unfair Dismissals (Amendment) Act, 1993.

[52] Section 7(2)(f) was inserted by s. 6 of the Unfair Dismissals (Amendment) Act, 1993.

[53] The entirety of s. 7(2A) as shown here was inserted by s. 6 of the Unfair Dismissals (Amendment) Act, 1993, with the sole difference that the text of the sub-section which has been parenthesised here referred (as originally

(*a*) under [the Social Welfare Acts], in respect of any period following the dismissal concerned, or

(*b*) under the Income Tax Acts arising by reason of the dismissal,

shall be disregarded.

(3) In this section—

"financial loss", in relation to the dismissal of an employee, includes any actual loss and any estimated prospective loss of income attributable to the dismissal and the value of any loss or diminution, attributable to the dismissal, of the rights of the employee under the Redundancy Payments Acts, 1967 to 1973,[54] or in relation to superannuation;

"remuneration" includes allowances in the nature of pay and benefits in lieu of or in addition to pay.

Determination of claims for unfair dismissal

8.—(1) A claim by an employee against an employer for redress under this Act for unfair dismissal may be brought by the employee before a rights commissioner [54a]

---

inserted) to "the Social Welfare Acts, 1981 to 1993", the bulk of which have been repealed in later enactments. Under s. 26 (2) of the Interpretation Act 2005, where an enactment is repealed and reenacted, with or without modification, by another enactment, a reference in any other enactment to the former enactment shall, with respect to a subsequent transaction, matter or thing, be read as a reference to the provisions of the new enactment relating to the same subject-matter as that of the former enactment. The text of the sub-section has been altered here accordingly. (Note that under s. 3(8) of the Social Welfare Consolidation Act 2005, references in any other enactment to the "Social Welfare Acts" are now to mean "this Act and every enactment which is to be read together with it as one." Note also that under s. 14(2) of the Social Welfare Act, 2005, the Social Welfare Acts and the Social Welfare Act, 2005 (other than section 13 thereof) are to be read together as one. Finally, under s. 1(2) of Social Welfare Law Reform and Pensions Act 2006, the Social Welfare Acts and sections 1 to 37 of that Act are also to be read together as one).

[54] The Redundancy Payments Acts now consist of the Redundancy Payments Acts, 1967 to 2003. (See s. 17(3) of the Redundancy Payments Act, 2003.) The text of s. 7(3), however, has not been amended to reflect this. Note however that the Redundancy Payments Acts, 1967 to 2003 are required to be construed together as one, by virtue of s. 17(3) of the Redundancy Payments Act, 2003.

[54a] Under s. 35(1) of the Industrial Relations Act, 1990, references in the Unfair Dismissals Act, 1977 to rights commissioners are to be taken to be

or the Tribunal and the commissioner or Tribunal shall hear the parties and any evidence relevant to the claim tendered by them and, in the case of a rights commissioner, shall make a recommendation in relation to the claim, and, in the case of the Tribunal, shall make a determination in relation to the claim.[55]

(1A) There shall be included in— [56]

---

references to rights commissioners operating as a service of the Labour Relations Commission established by s. 24 of the 1990 Act.

[55] Note in this regard the provisions of s. 32(2) of the Adoptive Leave Act, 1995, which provides as follows.

"Any dispute other than—

(*a*) a dispute relating to a dismissal, including a dismissal within the meaning of the Act of 1977 or, the termination of a contract of employment, or...

(*b*) *(not relevant)*

(*c*) *(not relevant)*

between an adopting parent and the relevant employer, relating to the adopting parent's entitlements under this Act (or to any matter arising out of or related to such entitlements), may be referred by either party to the dispute to a rights commissioner."

Under s. 32(1) of the 1995 Act, this provision does not apply to members of the Defence Forces.

Note also the provisions of s. 18(2) of the Parental Leave Act, 1998, which provides as follows.

"Any dispute or difference between an employee and his or her employer relating to the entitlements of the employee under this Act (or to any matter arising out of or related to those entitlements or otherwise arising under this Act) other than a dispute or difference—

(*a*) relating to a dismissal from employment, including a dismissal within the meaning of the Unfair Dismissals Acts, 1977 to 1993,

(*b*) *(not relevant)*

(*c*) *(not relevant)*

may be referred by either of those parties to a rights commissioner..."

Under s. 18(1) of the 1998 Act, this provision does not apply to members of the Defence Forces.

Finally, note that under s. 1(6) of the Protection of Employees (Part-Time Work) Act, 2001, insofar as the 2001 Act relates to the Unfair Dismissals Acts, 1977 to 1993, those Acts and the 2001 Act are required to be construed together as one and may be cited together as the Unfair Dismissals Acts, 1977 to 2001, and that under s. 1(3) of the Civil Service Regulation (Amendment) Act 2005, the Unfair Dismissals Acts, 1977 to 2001 and Part 6 of that Act may be cited together as the Unfair Dismissals Acts 1977 to 2005 and are required to be construed together as one.

[56] Section 8(1A) was inserted by s. 7 of the Unfair Dismissals (Amendment) Act, 1993.

(*a*) a recommendation of a rights commissioner under subsection (1) of this section,

(*b*) a determination of the Tribunal under the said subsection (1), and

(*c*) an order of the Circuit Court, under section 11 of the *Unfair Dismissals (Amendment) Act, 1993*,

under which specified redress under this Act is awarded to an employee a statement of the reasons why either of the other forms of redress specified in section 7 (1) of this Act was not awarded to the employee.

(2) A claim for redress under this Act shall be initiated by giving a notice in writing (containing such particulars (if any) as may be specified in regulations under section 17 of this Act made for the purposes of subsection (8) of this section) to a rights commissioner or the Tribunal, as the case may be— [57]

(*a*) within the period of 6 months beginning on the date of the relevant dismissal, or

(*b*) if the rights commissioner or the Tribunal, as the case may be, is satisfied that exceptional circumstances prevented the giving of the notice within the period aforesaid, then, within such period not exceeding 12 months from the date aforesaid as the rights commissioner or the Tribunal, as the case may be, considers reasonable,

and a copy of the notice shall be given by the rights commissioner or the Tribunal, as the case may be, to the employer concerned as soon as may be after the receipt of the notice by the rights commissioner or the Tribunal.

(3) A rights commissioner shall not hear a claim for redress under this Act if— [58]

---

[57] Section 8(2) was substituted in its entirety by s. 7 of the Unfair Dismissals (Amendment) Act, 1993, creating the possibility of the extension of the six month limitation period, and placing the onus of giving a copy of the notice on the rights commissioner or the Tribunal.

[58] Section 8(3) was substituted in its entirety by s. 7 of the Unfair Dismissals (Amendment) Act, 1993, introducing the 21 day limitation period.

(*a*) the Tribunal has made a determination in relation to the claim, or

(*b*) any party concerned notifies the rights commissioner in writing, within 21 days of the giving to the employer pursuant to subsection (2) of this section of the copy of the notice concerned referred to in that subsection and relating to the claim, that he objects to the claim being heard by a rights commissioner.

(4) (*a*) Where a recommendation of a rights commissioner in relation to a claim for redress under this Act has not been carried out by the employer concerned in accordance with its terms, the time for bringing an appeal against the recommendation has expired and no such appeal has been brought, the employee concerned may bring the claim before the Tribunal and the Tribunal shall, notwithstanding subsection (5) of this section, without hearing the employer concerned or any evidence (other than in relation to the matters aforesaid), make a determination to the like effect as the recommendation.[59]

(*b*) The bringing of a claim before the Tribunal by virtue of this subsection shall be effected by giving to the Tribunal a notice in writing containing such particulars (if any) as may be specified in regulations under section 17 of this Act made for the purposes of subsection (8) of this section.

(5) the Tribunal shall not hear a claim for redress under this Act (except by way of appeal from a recommendation of a rights commissioner)— [60]

---

[59] Section 8(4) was substituted in its entirety by s. 7 of the Unfair Dismissals (Amendment) Act, 1993, replacing with stricter provisions (contained in s. 8(4)(a)) the former stipulated consequence of failure on the part of an employer to carry out a recommendation of a rights commissioner (which was simply that the employee could bring the claim before the Tribunal).

[60] The words 'Subject to subsection (4) of this section,' which were originally the first words of s. 8(5) were deleted by s. 7 of the Unfair Dismissals (Amendment) Act, 1993. The amending provision failed to capitalise the new first word of the amended s. 8(5).

(*a*) if a rights commissioner has made a recommendation in relation to the claim, or

(*b*) unless, before the commencement of the hearing of the claim, one of the parties concerned notifies in writing— [61]

(i) in a case where the claim has been initiated before a rights commissioner, the rights commissioner, or

(ii) in any other case, the Tribunal,

that he objects to the claim being heard by a rights commissioner.

(6) Proceedings under this section before a rights commissioner shall be conducted otherwise than in public.

(7) A rights commissioner shall notify the Tribunal of any recommendation he makes under this section.

(8) Regulations under section 17 of this Act may provide for all or any of the following matters and for anything consequential thereon or incidental or ancillary thereto—

(*a*) the procedure to be followed regarding the bringing of claims under this section or appeals under section 9 of this Act before the Tribunal,

(*b*) the times and places of hearings by the Tribunal,

(*c*) the representation of parties attending hearings by the Tribunal.

(*d*) procedure regarding the hearing of such claims and appeals as aforesaid by the Tribunal,

(*e*) publication and notification of determinations of the Tribunal,

(*f*) the particulars to be contained in the notices referred to in subsections (2) and (4) of this section and section 9 of this Act,

[61] The entirety of s. 8(5)(b) was substituted by s. 7 of the Unfair Dismissals (Amendment) Act, 1993 rendering it both more carefully-crafted and more demanding on the objecting party.

(*g*) the award by the Tribunal of costs and expenses in relation to such claims and appeals as aforesaid and the payment thereof.

(9) Section 21 (2) of the Industrial Relations Act, 1946, shall apply in relation to all proceedings before the Tribunal as if the references in that section to the Labour Court were references to the Tribunal and subsection (17) of section 39 of the Redundancy Payments Act, 1967, shall apply in relation to proceedings before the Tribunal under this Act as it applies to matters referred to it under the said section 39 with the substitution in paragraph (*e*) of the said subsection (17) of 'a fine not exceeding [€1269.74]' for 'a fine not exceeding [€25.39]'.[62]

(10) (*a*) A dispute in relation to a dismissal as respects which a recommendation has been made by a rights commissioner under this Act or a hearing by the Tribunal under this Act has commenced shall not be referred,

---

[62] The words from 'with' onwards were inserted in s. 8(9) by s. 7 of the Unfair Dismissals (Amendment) Act, 1993. The amounts actually stipulated in s. 8(9) are, respectively, '£1,000' and 'twenty pounds', rather than €1269.74 and €25.39, but under Article 14 of Council Regulation (EC) No. 974/98 of 3 May 1998 on the introduction of the euro (read in conjunction with Article 1 of the same instrument), references made in legislative and statutory provisions existing on 31 December 2001 to units of Irish currency as they existed before the start of the third stage of economic and monetary union are to be read as references to the euro unit according to the respective conversion rates (with the rounding rules laid down in Regulation (EC) No. 1103/97 of 17 June 1997 on certain provisions relating to the introduction of the euro applying).
Note further that the amount of €190.46 (rather than €25.39) is the amount now stipulated in s. 39(17)(e) of the Redundancy Payments Act, 1967. This is because the amount of £150 (the equivalent in punts of €190.46) was substituted by s. 17 of the Redundancy Payments Act, 1979 for the original amount of £20 (the equivalent of €25.39), and, as already noted, under Article 14 of Council Regulation (EC) No. 974/98 of 3 May 1998 on the introduction of the euro (read in conjunction with Article 1 of the same instrument), references made in legislative and statutory provisions existing on 31 December 2001 to units of Irish currency as they existed before the start of the third stage of economic and monetary union are to be read as references to the euro unit according to the respective conversion rates (with the rounding rules laid down in Regulation (EC) No. 1103/97 of 17 June 1997 on certain provisions relating to the introduction of the euro applying).

under the Industrial Relations Acts, 1946 to 1990, [63] to a rights commissioner or the Labour Court.[64]

(*b*) Where, in relation to a dismissal, a recommendation has been made by a rights commissioner, or a hearing by the Labour Court under the said Acts has commenced, the employee concerned shall not be entitled to redress under this Act in respect of the dismissal.

(11) Where the dismissal of an employee is an unfair dismissal and a term or condition of the contract of employment concerned contravened any provision of or made under the Income Tax Acts or [the Social Welfare Acts], the employee shall, notwithstanding the contravention, be entitled to redress under this Act, in respect of the dismissal.[65]

(12) Where, in proceedings under this Act, it is shown that a term or condition of a contract of employment contravened any such provision as aforesaid, the rights commissioner, the

---

[63] The Industrial Relations Acts are now known as the Industrial Relations Acts 1946 to 2004 (see now s. 17(2) of the Industrial Relations (Miscellaneous Provisions) Act 2004) but s. 8(10)(a) has not been amended.

[64] The entirety of s. 8(10) was substituted by s. 7 of the Unfair Dismissals (Amendment) Act, 1993, clarifying it, extending the scope of the exclusionary content of what is now s. 8(10)(a) and introducing the exclusionary content of s. 8(10)(b).

[65] Section 8(11) was inserted by s. 7 of the Unfair Dismissals (Amendment) Act, 1993, with the difference that the words parenthesised here originally referred to "the Social Welfare Acts, 1981 to 1993". Most of the provisions of these enactments have subsequently been repealed in later enactments. Under s. 26 (2) of the Interpretation Act 2005, however, where an enactment is repealed and reenacted, with or without modification, by another enactment, a reference in any other enactment to the former enactment shall, with respect to a subsequent transaction, matter or thing, be read as a reference to the provisions of the new enactment relating to the same subject-matter as that of the former enactment. The text of the sub-section has been altered here accordingly. (Note that under s. 3(8) of the Social Welfare Consolidation Act 2005, references in any other enactment to the "Social Welfare Acts" are now to mean "this Act and every enactment which is to be read together with it as one." Note also that under s. 14(2) of the Social Welfare Act 2005, the Social Welfare Acts and the Social Welfare Act 2005 (other than section 13 thereof) are to be read together as one. Finally, under s. 1(2) of Social Welfare Law Reform and Pensions Act 2006, the Social Welfare Acts and sections 1 to 37 of that Act is also to be read together as one).

Tribunal or the Circuit Court, as the case may be, shall notify the Revenue Commissioners or the [Minister for Social and Family Affairs], [66] as may be appropriate, of the matter.[67]

9.—(1) A party concerned may appeal to the Tribunal from a recommendation of a rights commissioner in relation to a claim for redress under this Act and the Tribunal shall hear the parties and any evidence relevant to the appeal tendered by them and shall make a determination in relation to the appeal.

Appeal from recommendation of rights commissioner.

(2) An appeal under this section shall be initiated by a party by giving, within 6 weeks of the date on which the recommendation to which it relates was given to the parties concerned, a notice in writing (containing such particulars (if any) as may be specified in regulations under section 17 of this Act for the purposes of section 8 (8) thereof) to the Tribunal and stating the intention of the party concerned to appeal against the recommendation and a copy of the notice shall be given to the other party concerned by the Tribunal as soon as may be after the receipt by it of the notice.[68]

10. *(Repealed by s. 16 of the Unfair Dismissals (Amendment) Act, 1993)*

Proceedings in Circuit Court for redress under Act.

---

[66] The actual text of s. 8(12) refers to the Minister for Social Welfare. However, under Article 3 of the Social Welfare (Alteration of Name of Department and Title of Minister) Order, 1997 (S.I. No. 307 of 1997), the title of the Minister for Social Welfare was altered to that of the Minister for Social, Community and Family Affairs, with Article 4 of the same Order providing that in any enactment, references to the Minister for Social Welfare should be construed as references to the Minister for Social, Community and Family Affairs. Under Article 3 of the Social, Community and Family Affairs (Alteration of Name of Department and Title of Minister) Order, 2002 (S.I. No. 310 of 2002), the Minister's designation was altered again to that of the Minister for Social and Family Affairs. Under Article 4 of the same Order, it was provided that in any enactment or any instrument made under an enactment, references to the Minister for Social, Community and Family Affairs should be construed as references to the Minister for Social and Family Affairs.

[67] Section 8(12) was inserted by s. 7 of the Unfair Dismissals (Amendment) Act, 1993.

[68] The words 'by the Tribunal as soon as may be after the receipt by it of the notice' were substituted in s. 9(2) by s. 8 of the Unfair Dismissals (Amendment) Act, 1993 for the original 'within the said period of 6 weeks'.

Service of documents on bodies.

11. —Any summons or other document required to be served for the purpose or in the course of any proceedings under this Act on a body corporate or an unincorporated body of persons may be served by leaving it at or sending it by post to the registered office for the purpose of the Companies Act, 1963, of that body or, if there is no such office, by leaving it at or sending it by post to any place in the State at which that body conducts its business.

Provisions relating to winding up and bankruptcy.

12. —(1) There shall be included among the debts which, under section 285 of the Companies Act, 1963,[69] are, in the distribution of the assets of a company being wound up, to be paid in priority to all other debts, all compensation payable under this Act by the company to an employee, and that Act shall have effect accordingly, and formal proof of the debts to which priority is given under this subsection shall not be required except in cases where it may otherwise be provided by rules made under that Act.

(2) There shall be included among the debts which, under [section 81(1) of the Bankruptcy Act, 1988] [70], are, in the distribution of the property of a bankrupt or arranging debtor, to be paid in priority to all other debts, all compensation payable under this Act by the bankrupt or arranging debtor, as the case may be, to an employee, and that Act shall have effect accordingly, and formal proof of the debts to which priority is given under this subsection shall not be required except in cases where it may otherwise be provided by general orders made under the said Act.

Voidance of certain provisions in agreements.

13. —A provision in an agreement (whether a contract of employment or not and whether made before or after the

---

[69] Section 285 of the Companies Act, 1963 has been amended by section 10 of the Companies (Amendment) Act, 1982 and also by s. 134 of the Companies Act, 1990 but these amendments have not been reflected in any change to the manner in which s. 285 is referred to here.

[70] The text of the Act originally referred to s. 4 of the Preferential Payments in Bankruptcy (Ireland) Act, 1889. However, the Preferential Payments in Bankruptcy (Ireland) Act, 1889 was repealed by s. 6 of the Bankruptcy Act, 1988 and under s. 81(1) of the Bankruptcy Act, 1988, any reference to s. 4 of the 1889 Act of the kind which was to be found here is to be construed as a reference to s. 81(1) of the 1988 Act.

commencement of this Act) shall be void in so far as it purports to exclude or limit the application of, or is inconsistent with, any provision of this Act.

Notice to employees of procedure for, and grounds of, dismissal.

14. —(1) An employer shall, not later than 28 days after he enters into a contract of employment with an employee, give to the employee a notice in writing setting out the procedure which the employer will observe before and for the purpose of dismissing the employee.

(2) Where there is an alteration in the procedure referred to in subsection (1) of this section, the employer concerned shall, within 28 days after the alteration takes effect, give to any employee concerned a notice in writing setting out the procedure as so altered.

(3) The reference in subsection (1) of this section to a procedure is a reference to a procedure that has been agreed upon by or on behalf of the employer concerned and by the employee concerned or a trade union or an excepted body within the meaning of the Trade Union Act, 1941, representing him or has been established by the custom and practice of the employment concerned, and the references in subsection (2) of this section to an alteration in the said procedure are references to an alteration that has been agreed upon by the employer concerned or a person representing him and by the employee concerned or a trade union, or an excepted body, within the meaning aforesaid, representing him.[71]

(4) Where an employee is dismissed, the employer shall, if so requested, furnish to the employee within 14 days of the request, particulars in writing of the principal grounds for dismissal, but, in determining for the purposes of this Act whether, in accordance with the provisions of this Act, the dismissal was an unfair dismissal, there may be taken into account any other grounds which, subject to the provisions of

[71] Section 14(3) was substituted by s. 9 of the Unfair Dismissals (Amendment) Act, 1993, introducing the possibility of the relevant agreement having been reached with the employee rather than with a trade union or excepted body.

this Act and having regard to all the circumstances, are substantial grounds justifying the dismissal.[72]

Alternative remedies of employee.

15. —(1) Nothing in this Act, apart from this section, shall prejudice the right of a person to recover damages at common law for wrongful dismissal.

(2) Where a recommendation has been made by a rights commissioner in respect of a claim by an employee for redress under this Act or the hearing of a claim by the Tribunal has commenced, the employee shall not be entitled to recover damages at common law for wrongful dismissal in respect of the dismissal concerned.[73]

(3) Where the hearing by a court of proceedings for damages at common law for wrongful dismissal of an employee has commenced, the employee shall not be entitled to redress under this Act in respect of the dismissal to which the proceedings relate.[74]

(4) A person who accepts redress awarded under section 9 or 10 of the Anti-Discrimination (Pay) Act, 1974, in respect of any dismissal shall not be entitled to accept redress awarded under section 7 of this Act in respect of that dismissal and a person who accepts redress awarded under the said section 7 in respect of any dismissal shall not be entitled to accept redress awarded under the said section 9 or 10 in respect of that dismissal.[75]

---

[72] Section 14(4) was substituted by s. 9 of the Unfair Dismissals (Amendment) Act, 1993, introducing the clauses beginning with, respectively, 'in accordance with' and 'subject to'.

[73] Section 15(2) was substituted by s. 10 of the Unfair Dismissals (Amendment) Act, 1993. Under the original version of s. 15(2), the mere giving of notice in writing to a rights commissioner or the Tribunal under s. 8(2) in respect of a dismissal sufficed to disentitle the employee in the manner described.

[74] Section 15(3) was substituted by s. 10 of the Unfair Dismissals (Amendment) Act, 1993. The original version of s. 15(2), the mere giving of notice in writing to a rights commissioner or the Tribunal under s. 8(2) in respect of a dismissal sufficed to disentitle the employee in the manner described.

[75] Note that s. 5(1) of the Employment Equality Act, 1998 repealed the Anti-Discrimination (Pay) Act, 1974. The equivalent provision to s. 9 is now s. 98 of the Employment Equality Act, which however, is considerably broader in terms of the behaviour in respect of which it authorises redress

16. —(1) The Minister may by order amend section 2 (1) of this Act so as to extend the application of the Act to any class of employee specified in that section or part (defined in such manner and by reference to such matters as the Minister considers appropriate) of any such class.

Amendment of Act by order of Minister.

(2) The Minister may by order amend paragraph (*c*) of section 7 (1) of this Act so as to vary the maximum amount of compensation referred to in the said paragraph (*c*).

(3) The Minister may by order amend section 2 (2), 3 or 4 of this Act so as to vary—

(*a*) the application of this Act in relation to dismissals where the employment was under a contract of employment for a fixed term or a specified purpose,

(*b*) the periods of 1 year specified in the said section 3, or

(*c*) the periods of 6 months and 1 month specified in the said section 4 or either of them.

(4) The Minister may, by order, made with the consent of the Minister for Health, amend subsection (2) of section 3 of this Act so as to extend the application of the subsection to other employments connected with medicine or health.

(5) The Minister may by order amend any provision of this Act so as to comply with any international obligations in relation to dismissals that the State has decided to assume.

(6) An order under this section may contain such supplementary and ancillary provisions as the Minister considers necessary or expedient.

(7) The Minister may by order revoke or amend an order under this section including an order under this subsection.

---

than were ss. 9 and 10 of the Anti-Discrimination (Pay) Act, 1974. Under s. 26 (2) of the Interpretation Act 2005, however, where an enactment is repealed and reenacted, with or without modification, by another enactment, a reference in any other enactment to the former enactment shall, with respect to a subsequent transaction, matter or thing, be read as a reference to the provisions of the new enactment relating to the same subject-matter as that of the former enactment.

(8) Where an order is proposed to be made under this section, a draft thereof shall be laid before both Houses of the Oireachtas and the order shall not be made until a resolution approving of the draft has been passed by each such House.

Regulations.

17. —(1) The Minister may make regulations for the purposes of sections 7 (1) (*c*) and 8 (8) of this Act and for the purpose of enabling any other provisions of this Act to have full effect.[76]

(2) Regulations under this section may contain such incidental, supplementary and consequential provisions as appear to the Minister to be necessary for the purposes of the regulations.

(3) Every regulation made under this section shall be laid before each House of the Oireachtas as soon as may be after it is made, and if a resolution annulling the regulation is passed by either such House within the next 21 days on which that House has sat after the regulation is laid before it, the regulation shall be annulled accordingly, but without prejudice to the validity of anything previously done thereunder.

Employment Appeals Tribunal.

18. —The tribunal established by section 39 of the Redundancy Payments Act, 1967, shall be known as the Employment Appeals Tribunal and references in that Act and any other Act of the Oireachtas and any instrument made under any Act of the Oireachtas to the Redundancy Appeals Tribunal shall be construed as references to the Employment Appeals Tribunal.

Repayment of moneys paid under Redundancy Payments Acts, 1967 and 1973.[77]

19. —Where an employee is re-instated or re-engaged by an employer in pursuance of a determination or order under this Act in relation to the dismissal of the employee by the employer, any payments made under the Redundancy Payments Acts, 1967 and 1973,[78] in relation to the dismissal

[76] See now the Unfair Dismissals (Claims and Appeals) Regulations, 1977 (S.I. No. 286 of 1977) and the Unfair Dismissals (Calculation of Weekly Remuneration) Regulations, 1977 (S.I. No. 287 of 1977).

[77] The reference in this side-note to the Redundancy Payments Acts, 1967 *and* 1973 is erroneous. See in this regard the next footnote.

[78] This reference is erroneous and should more correctly be to the Redundancy Payments Acts, 1967 *to* 1973 (as is the reference in s. 7(3) above). The Redundancy Payments Acts now consist of the Redundancy

shall be repaid by the person to whom they were made to the person by whom they were made and may be recovered by the latter from the former as a simple contract debt in any court of competent jurisdiction and any moneys due and owing to any person under those Acts in relation to the dismissal shall cease to be due or owing.

20. —(*Substitution of paras. 5 and 7 of the First Schedule to the Minimum Notice and Terms of Employment Act, 1973)* [79]

Amendment of First Schedule to Minimum Notice and Terms of Employment Act, 1973.

21. —The expenses incurred by the Minister in the administration of this Act shall, to such extent as may be sanctioned by the Minister for Finance, be paid out of moneys provided by the Oireachtas.

Expenses.

22. —(1) This Act may be cited as the Unfair Dismissals Act, 1977.[80]

Short title and commencement.

(2) This Act shall come into operation on such day as the Minister may appoint by order.[81]

Payments Acts 1967 to 2003 (see s. 17(3) of the Redundancy Payments Act 2003) but the text of s. 19 has not been amended to reflect this. Note, however, that the Redundancy Payments Acts 1967 to 2003 are required to be construed together as one, by virtue of s. 17(3) of the Redundancy Payments Act 2003.

[79] Note that the substitution, effected by s. 20, of para. 7 of the First Schedule to the Minimum Notice and Terms of Employment Act, 1973 has now been superseded by the substitution of the same paragraph by s. 15 of the Unfair Dismissals (Amendment) Act, 1993.

[80] Note that the Unfair Dismissals Act, 1977, the Unfair Dismissals (Amendment) Act, 1993, the Protection of Employees (Part-Time Work) Act, 2001 (insofar as it relates to the foregoing legislation) and Part 6 of the Civil Service Regulation (Amendment) Act 2005 may be cited together as the Unfair Dismissals Acts 1977 to 2005 and are required to be construed together as one. (See s. 17(2) of the Unfair Dismissals (Amendment) Act, 1993, s. 1(6) of the Protection of Employees (Part-Time Work) Act, 2001 and s. 1(3) of the Civil Service Regulation (Amendment) Act 2005.)

[81] In the Unfair Dismissals Act, 1977 (Commencement) Order, 1977 (S.I. No. 138 of 1977), the Minister for Labour appointed 9 May, 1977 to be the day on which this Act came into operation.

REDUNDANCY PAYMENTS ACT, 1979

Number 7 *of* 1979

ARRANGEMENT OF SECTIONS

PART I

Section

ACTS REFERRED TO

Companies Act, 1963	1963, No. 33
Minimum Notice and Terms of Employment Act, 1973	1973, No. 4
Preferential Payments in Bankruptcy (Ireland) Act, 1889	1889, c. 60
Redundancy Payments Act, 1967	1967, No. 21
Redundancy Payments Act, 1971	1971 No. 20
Redundancy Payments Act, 1973	1973, No. 11
Redundancy Payments Acts, 1967 to 1973	
Social Welfare Act, 1952	1952, No. 11
Social Welfare Acts, 1952 to 1978	
Social Welfare (Amendment) Act, 1978	1978, No. 25
Unfair Dismissals Act, 1977	1977, No. 10

Number 7 *of* 1979

REDUNDANCY PAYMENTS ACT, 1979

AN ACT TO AMEND AND EXTEND THE REDUNDANCY PAYMENTS ACTS, 1967 TO 1973, AND TO PROVIDE FOR OTHER CONNECTED MATTERS. [20*th March*, 1979]

BE IT ENACTED BY THE OIREACHTAS AS FOLLOWS:

1. —In this Act— Definitions.

"the Act of 1971" means the Redundancy Payments Act, 1971;

"the Minister" [1] means the [Minister for Enterprise, Trade and Employment];

---

[1] The text of the Act originally referred to the Minister for Labour. However, under Article 4(1) of the Labour (Transfer of Departmental Administration and Ministerial Functions) Order, 1993 (S.I. No. 18 of 1993), it was provided that the functions vested in the Minister for Labour by or under certain Acts (including this Act) be transferred to the Minister for Industry and Commerce. In Article 4(2) of the same Order, it was provided that references to the Minister for Labour contained in any such Act or instrument thereunder and relating to any functions transferred by Article 4 should, on and after the commencement of the Order, be construed as references to the Minister for Industry and Commerce. In Article 4 of the Industry and Commerce (Alteration of Name of Department and Title of Minister) Order, 1993 (S.I. No. 19 of 1993), which was adopted on the same day as S.I. No. 18 of 1993, it was provided that references in any enactment to the Minister for Industry and Commerce should be construed as references to the Minister for Enterprise and Employment. More recently, Article 4 of the Enterprise and Employment (Alteration of Name of Department and Title of Minister) Order, 1997 (S.I. No. 305 of 1997) has provided that references in any enactment to the Minister for Enterprise and Employment are to be construed as references to the Minister for Enterprise, Trade and Employment. It should be noted that the powers and duties which are conferred on the Minister for Enterprise, Trade and Employment by or under the Redundancy Payments Acts have been delegated by statutory instrument to the present Minister of State at the Department of Enterprise,

"the Principal Act" means the Redundancy Payments Act, 1967.

Financing of Redundancy Fund

2. *(Substitution of s. 27(1) of the Redundancy Payments Act, 1967)* [2]

Contributions to Redundancy Fund

3. *(Substitution of s. 28 of the Redundancy Payments Act, 1967)* [3]

Provisions relating to lump sum under Principal Act, and consequential provisions.

4. *(Insertion of Paragraph 2 in Schedule 3 of the Redundancy Payments Act, 1967)* [4]

(2) The Minister may by regulations made with the consent of the Minister for Finance—

(*a*) vary the amount of [€31,200] [5] referred to in paragraph 2 of Schedule 3 of the Principal Act (inserted by this section), [6] and

(*b*) alter the method of calculation of a lump sum under the Principal Act.

(3) When making regulations under subsection (2) of this section, the Minister shall take into account any changes in the average earnings of workers in the transportable goods

---

Trade and Employment. (See now the Enterprise, Trade and Employment (Delegation of Ministerial Functions) Order 2004 (S.I. No. 809 of 2004).)

[2] This amendment was superseded when s. 39(1) of the Social Welfare Act, 1991 substituted the entirety of s. 27 of the Redundancy Payments Act, 1967. (See further in this regard the notes on that section of the 1967 Act).

[3] This amendment has now been superseded with the deletion by s. 39(1) of the Social Welfare Act, 1991 of s. 28 of the Redundancy Payments Act, 1967.

[4] This amendment has now been superseded as a result of the substitution of Paragraph 2 of Schedule 3 to the 1967 Act by s. 11 of the Redundancy Payments Act, 2003.

[5] The amount referred to in the actual text of s. 4(2)(a) is £5,000. By virtue of a series of provisions in statutory instruments, however, the most recent of which has been Article 2 of the Redundancy Payments (Lump Sum) Regulations 2004 (S.I. No. 695 of 2004), this amount has gradually been raised to its present level of €31,200.

[6] Note that since the coming into force of s. 11 of the Redundancy Payments Act 2003 (which occurred, under Article 3(1) of the Redundancy Payments Act 2003 (Commencement) Order 2005 (S.I. No. 77 of 2005), on 10 April, 2005), the new paragraph 2 of Schedule 3 of the 1967 Act makes no reference to any amount (this now being done by paragraph 1(2) of Schedule 3 of the 1967 Act). The result of this is that the Minister now appears to have been unintentionally deprived of the statutory power to vary the amount per annum to be taken into account in calculating the amount of the lump sum.

industries as recorded by the Central Statistics Office since the date by reference to which the sum specified in subsection (1) of this section was last determined.

(4) (*a*) Subject to paragraph (*b*) of this subsection, the Redundancy Payments (Weekly Payments and Lump Sum) Order, 1974 (S.I. No. 82 of 1974), and the Redundancy Payments (Weekly Payments) Order, 1976 (S.I. No. 126 of 1976), shall cease to have effect from the commencement of this section.

(*b*) Notwithstanding paragraph (*a*) of this subsection but subject to section 8 of this Act, an employee who at the commencement of this section is in receipt of weekly payments shall continue to receive such payments as if that paragraph were not enacted.

5. *(Substitution of s. 3 of the Redundancy Payments Act, 1971)*

Provisions relating to persons reaching qualifying age for old age pension.

6. *(Substitution of s. 29 of the Redundancy Payments Act, 1967)*

Rebates to employers from Redundancy Fund.

Employee's right to time off for certain purposes while under notice of dismissal for redundancy.

7. —(1) This section applies to an employee who has not less than 104 weeks' service with an employer and has been given notice of proposed dismissal by reason of redundancy.

(2) An employee to whom this section applies shall be entitled during the two weeks ending on the expiration of his notice of dismissal to be allowed by his employer reasonable time off during the employee's working hours in order to look for new employment or make arrangements for training for future employment.

(3) An employee who is allowed time off under this section shall be entitled to be paid remuneration by his employer for the period of absence at the appropriate hourly rate obtaining on the date of his notice of dismissal and to remuneration equal to this amount in a case where the employer unreasonably refuses time off under this section.

(4) The employer of an employee to whom this section applies may require the employee to furnish him with such evidence as he requests of arrangements made by the employee relating to effort to obtain new employment or training for future employment, and the employee shall furnish any evidence so requested if it is not prejudicial to the employee's interest.

(5) Any dispute arising under this section shall be deemed to be a decision referred to in section 39 (15) of the Principal Act, and any amount ordered by the Employment Appeals Tribunal to be paid by an employer to an employee shall be recoverable as a simple contract debt in a court of competent jurisdiction.

Termination of entitlement to weekly payments.

8. —*(Provision for ss. 30 and 31 of the Redundancy Payments Act, 1967 to cease to have effect,*[7] *and now-obsolete transitional provisions concerning this provision)*

Amendment of section 10 of Principal Act.

9. *(Insertion of s. 10(3A) in the Redundancy Payments Act, 1967)*

Amendment of section 11 of Principal Act.

10. *(Substitution of s. 11(2) and s. 11(3) of the Redundancy Payments Act, 1967)*

Amendment of section 15 of Principal Act.

11. *(Insertion of s. 15(2B) in the Redundancy Payments Act 1967)*

Application to certain cases of sections 10 and 11.

12. —Where—

(*a*) a dismissal (or termination of employment) occurred before the comFmencement of this section,

(*b*) the employee concerned would have been entitled to redundancy payment if section 10 or 11 of this Act had been in operation on the date of dismissal or termination of employment, and

(*c*) the employee concerned had appealed to the Tribunal before the 1st day of January, 1979, but a decision relating to that appeal had not been made before the commencement of this section,

the Tribunal shall, as soon as practicable after the commencement of this section, make a decision relating to that appeal as

[7] These provisions formerly provided for an entitlement to weekly payments on dismissal by reason of redundancy.

if sections 10 and 11 of this Act had been in operation on the date of dismissal or termination of employment.

13. *(Insertion of s. 24(3) of the Redundancy Payments Act, 1967)*

Amendment of section 24 of Principal Act.

14. *(Substitution of s. 42(1) and s. 42(3) of the Redundancy Payments Act, 1967)*

Amendment of section 42 of Principal Act.

15. *(Substitution of s. 15(2) of the Redundancy Payments Act, 1971)*

Amendment of section 15 of Act of 1971.

16. —(1) If in any respect any difficulty arises in bringing into operation this Act or any amendment or repeal effected by this Act, the Minister may by order do anything which appears to be necessary or expedient for bringing this Act into operation, and any such order may modify a provision of this Act so far as may appear necessary or expedient for carrying the order into effect.

Power to remove difficulties.

(2) Every order made by the Minister under this section shall be laid before each House of the Oireachtas as soon as may be after it is made, and if a resolution is passed by either House of the Oireachtas within the next 21 days on which that House has sat after the order is laid before it annulling such order, the order shall be annulled accordingly but without prejudice to the validity of anything previously done under the order.

(3) No order may be made under this section after the expiration of one year after the commencement of this section.

17. —Each provision of the Principal Act mentioned in column (1) of the Schedule to this Act is amended in the manner stated in column (2) of that Schedule opposite the mention of the provision in column (1).

Miscellaneous amendments of Principal Act.

18. *(Substitutions in s. 16(1) and s. 16(2) of the Redundancy Payments Act, 1971)*

Amendment of section 16 of Act of 1971.

19. Sections 34 and 36(2)(d) of the Principal Act are repealed.[8]

Repeals.

---

[8] These provisions made provision, respectively, for redundancy stamps and for regulations concerning the modalities of claiming a weekly redundancy payment.

Expenses.

20. —Any expenses incurred by the Minister or any other Minister of the Government in carrying this Act into effect shall, to such extent as may be sanctioned by the Minister for Finance, be paid out of moneys provided by the Oireachtas.

Short title, construction, collective citation and commencement.

21. —(1) This Act may be cited as the Redundancy Payments Act, 1979.

(2) The Redundancy Payments Acts, 1967 to 1973, and this Act shall be construed together as one Act and may be cited together as the Redundancy Payments Acts, 1967 to 1979.[9]

(3) This Act shall come into operation on such day or days as may be fixed by order or orders of the Minister, and different days may be so fixed for different provisions of this Act.[10]

---

[9] Note that the Redundancy Payments Act, 1967, the Redundancy Payments Act, 1971, the Redundancy Payments Act, 1973, the Redundancy Payments Act, 1979, s. 12 of the Protection of Employees (Employers' Insolvency) Act, 1984, ss. 26, 27 and 29 of the Social Welfare Act, 1990, s. 39 (other than sub-s. (2)) of the Social Welfare Act, 1991 (although apparently by oversight no mention is made of s. 39 of the 1991 Act in any subsequent statute included in this list), the Protection of Employees (Part-Time Work) Act, 2001 (insofar as it relates to the foregoing legislation, apart from s. 39 of the 1991 Act) and the Redundancy Payments Act 2003 may be cited together as the Redundancy Payments Acts 1967 to 2003.
See in this regard, in addition to s. 21(2) of the Redundancy Payments Act, 1979, s. 20(2) of the Redundancy Payments Act, 1971, s. 2(2) of the Redundancy Payments Act, 1973, s. 18(2) of the Protection of Employees (Employers' Insolvency) Act, 1984, s. 1(4) of the Social Welfare Act, 1990, s. 1(3) of the Social Welfare Act, 1991, s. 1(4) of the Protection of Employees (Part-Time Work) Act, 2001 and s. 17(3) of the Redundancy Payments Act 2003.

[10] In the Redundancy Payments Act, 1979 (Commencement) Order, 1979 (S.I. No. 95 of 1979), the Minister for Labour appointed 6 April, 1979 to be the day on which this Act came into operation.

SCHEDULE

Section 17.

MISCELLANEOUS AMENDMENTS OF PRINCIPAL ACT

Provision Amended (1)	Nature of Amendment (2)
Section 2 (1)	*(Substitution in s. 2(1) of the Redundancy Payments Act, 1967)*
Section 4 (2)	*(Substitution in s. 4(2) of the Redundancy Payments Act, 1967)* [11]
Section 15 (3)	*(Substitution in s. 15(3) of the Redundancy Payments Act, 1967)*
Section 17 (3)	*(Substitution in s. 17(3) of the Redundancy Payments Act, 1967)* [12]
Section 18 (4)	*(Substitution in s. 18(4) of the Redundancy Payments Act, 1967)* [13]
Section 23	*(Insertion in s. 23 of the Redundancy Payments Act, 1967)*
Section 32	*(Insertion in s. 32 of the Redundancy Payments Act, 1967)*
Section 33 (2)	*(Substitutions in s. 33(2) of the Redundancy Payments Act, 1967)* [14]
Section 36 (3)	*(Substitution in s. 36(3) of the Redundancy Payments Act, 1967)* [15]

[11] This amendment has now been superseded, since s. 4 of the Redundancy Payments Act 2003 substituted s. 4(2) of the Redundancy Payments Act, 1967 in its entirety.

[12] This substitution of text in s. 17(3) has now been superseded by the subsequent one effected by s. 13 of the Redundancy Payments Act 2003.

[13] This substitution of text in s. 18(4) has now been superseded by the subsequent one effected by s. 13 of the Redundancy Payments Act 2003.

[14] This amendment has now been superseded by the deletion of s. 33 of the 1967 Act by s. 39(1) of the Social Welfare Act, 1991.

[15] This substitution of text in s. 36(3) has now been superseded by the subsequent one effected by s. 13 of the Redundancy Payments Act 2003.

Provision Amended (1)	Nature of Amendment (2)
Section 39 (2)	*(Substitution of s. 39(2)(b) and s. 39(2)(c) of the Redundancy Payments Act, 1967)*
Section 39 (3)	*(Insertion of s. 39(3A) of the Redundancy Payments Act, 1967)*
Section 39 (15)	*(Substitution in s. 39(15) of the Redundancy Payments Act, 1967)*
Section 39 (17) (e)	*(Substitution in s. 39(17)(e) of the Redundancy Payments Act, 1967)*
Section 58	*(Substitution in s. 58 of the Redundancy Payments Act, 1967)*
Schedule 1	*(Substitution of Paragraphs 8 and 9 of Schedule 1 to the Redundancy Payments Act, 1967)* [16]
Schedule 3	*(Insertion in paragraph 4 of Schedule 3 of the Redundancy Payments Act, 1967)*
	(Insertion of paragraph 4A of Schedule 3 of the Redundancy Payments Act, 1967)
	(Insertion of paragraph 5(1)(d) of Schedule 3 of the Redundancy Payments Act, 1967) [17]
	(Insertion in paragraph 7 of Schedule 3 of the Redundancy Payments Act, 1967)

[16] With the efflux of time the effect of these amendments has been superseded, as s. 8 of the Redundancy Payments Act, 1979 provided that s. 30 of the 1967 Act should cease to have effect, rendering Schedule 1 of the 1967 Act obsolete once any then-existing entitlement to weekly redundancy payments expired.

[17] This amendment has since been superseded, most recently by the substitution by s. 12 of the Redundancy Payments Act 2003 of the entirety of para. 5 of Schedule 3 to the Redundancy Payments Act 2003.

PROTECTION OF EMPLOYEES (EMPLOYERS' INSOLVENCY) ACT, 1984

Number 21 *of* 1984

ARRANGEMENT OF SECTIONS

ACTS REFERRED TO

Deeds of Arrangement Act, 1887	1887, c. 57
Preferential Payments in Bankruptcy (Ireland) Act, 1889	1889, c. 60
Industrial Relations, Act, 1946	1946, No. 26
Companies Act, 1963	1963, No. 33
Redundancy Payments Act, 1967	1967, No. 21
Minimum Notice and Terms of Employment Act, 1973	1973, No. 4
Holidays (Employees) Act, 1973	1973, No. 25
Anti-Discrimination (Pay) Act, 1974	1974, No. 15
Unfair Dismissal Act, 1977	1977, No. 10
Employment Equality Act, 1977	1977, No. 16
Redundancy Payments Act, 1979	1979, No. 7
Social Welfare (Consolidation) Act, 1981	1981, No. 1
Social Welfare Acts, 1981 to 1984	

Number 21 *of* 1984

PROTECTION OF EMPLOYEES (EMPLOYERS' INSOLVENCY) ACT, 1984

AN ACT TO CONFER, ON THE INSOLVENCY OF EMPLOYERS, CERTAIN RIGHTS ON EMPLOYEES, TO AMEND CERTAIN ENACTMENTS RELATING TO THE RIGHTS OF EMPLOYEES AND TO PROVIDE FOR OTHER MATTERS (INCLUDING OFFENCES) CONNECTED WITH THE MATTERS AFORESAID. [30*th November*, 1984]

BE IT ENACTED BY THE OIREACHTAS AS FOLLOWS:

1. —(1) In this Act— Interpretation.

"the Act of 1967" means the Redundancy Payments Act, 1967;

'the Act of 1969' [1] means the Industrial Relations Act 1969;

"the Act of 1973" means the Minimum Notice and Terms of Employment Act, 1973;

"the Act of 1974" means the Anti-Discrimination (Pay) Act, 1974;

"the Act of 1977" means the Unfair Dismissals Act, 1977;

"the Act of 1981" means the Social Welfare (Consolidation) Act, 1981;

'the Act of 1990' [2] means the Industrial Relations Act 1990;

---

[1] This definition was inserted by Regulation 3 of the European Communities (Protection of Employees (Employers' Insolvency) Regulations 2005 (Statutory Instrument No. 630 of 2005).

[2] This definition was inserted by Regulation 3 of the European Communities (Protection of Employees (Employers' Insolvency) Regulations 2005 (Statutory Instrument No. 630 of 2005).

'the Act of 1991' [3] means the Payment of Wages Act 1991;

'the Act of 1994' [4] means the Terms of Employment (Information) Act 1994;

'the Act of 1996' [5] means the Protection of Young Persons (Employment) Act 1996;

'the Act of 1997' [6] means the Organisation of Working Time Act 1997;

'the Act of 1998' [7] means the Protections for Persons Reporting Child Abuse Act 1998;

'the Act of 2001' [8] means the Protection of Employees (Part-Time Work) Act 2001;

'the Act of 2002' [9] means the Competition Act 2002;

'the Act of 2003' [10] means the Protection of Employees (Fixed-Time Work) Act 2003;

---

[3] This definition was inserted by Regulation 3 of the European Communities (Protection of Employees (Employers' Insolvency) Regulations 2005 (Statutory Instrument No. 630 of 2005).

[4] This definition was inserted by Regulation 3 of the European Communities (Protection of Employees (Employers' Insolvency) Regulations 2005 (Statutory Instrument No. 630 of 2005).

[5] This definition was inserted by Regulation 3 of the European Communities (Protection of Employees (Employers' Insolvency)) Regulations 2005 (Statutory Instrument No. 630 of 2005).

[6] This definition was inserted by Regulation 3 of the European Communities (Protection of Employees (Employers' Insolvency)) Regulations 2005 (Statutory Instrument No. 630 of 2005).

[7] This definition was inserted by Regulation 3 of the European Communities (Protection of Employees (Employers' Insolvency)) Regulations 2005 (Statutory Instrument No. 630 of 2005).

[8] This definition was inserted by Regulation 3 of the European Communities (Protection of Employees (Employers' Insolvency)) Regulations 2005 (Statutory Instrument No. 630 of 2005).

[9] This definition was inserted by Regulation 3 of the European Communities (Protection of Employees (Employers' Insolvency) Regulations 2005 (Statutory Instrument No. 630 of 2005).

[10] This definition was inserted by Regulation 3 of the European Communities (Protection of Employees (Employers' Insolvency)) Regulations 2005 (Statutory Instrument No. 630 of 2005).

'the Act of 2004' [11] means the Industrial Relations (Miscellaneous Provisions) Act 2004;

'the Act of 2006' means the *Employment Permits Act* 2006; [11a]

"company" means, except when the context otherwise requires, a company within the meaning of section 2 of the Companies Act, 1963, or any other body corporate whether incorporated within or outside the State;

'competent authority' [12] means the authority referred to in Article 2(1) of Council Directive 80/987/EEC of 20 October 1980 [2] as amended by Article 1 (2) of Directive 2002/74/EC of the European Parliament and of the Council of 23 September 2002 [1];

---

[2] OJ No. L283, 28.10.1980, p. 23
[1] OJ No. L270, 8.10.2002, p. 10

"employee" means a person who has entered into or works under (or, in the case of a contract which has been terminated, worked under) a contract with an employer, whether the contract is for manual labour, clerical work or otherwise, is express or implied, oral or in writing, and whether it is a contract of service or apprenticeship or otherwise, and "employer" and any reference to employment shall be construed accordingly;

"holiday pay" means—

(*a*) pay in respect of a holiday actually taken; or

(*b*) any holiday pay which had accrued at the date of the termination of the employee's employment and which, had his employment with the employer continued until he became entitled to a holiday, would

---

[11] This definition was inserted by Regulation 3 of the European Communities (Protection of Employees (Employers' Insolvency)) Regulations 2005 (Statutory Instrument No. 630 of 2005).

[11a] This definition was inserted by Paragraph 6(1) of Schedule 2 to the Employment Permits Act 2006 (as given effect to by s. 26(4) of that Act).

[12] This definition was inserted by Regulation 3 of the European Communities (Protection of Employees (Employers' Insolvency)) Regulations 2005 (Statutory Instrument No. 630 of 2005).

under the employee's contract of employment in the ordinary course have become payable to him on becoming so entitled;

'Member State' [13] means a Member State of the European Union

"the Minister" means [the Minister for Enterprise, Trade and Employment][14];

"occupational pension scheme" means any scheme or arrangement which, forming part of a contract of employment, provides or is capable of providing, in relation to employees in any description of employment, benefits (in the form of pensions or otherwise) payable to or in respect of any such employees on the termination of their employment or on their death or retirement;

---

[13] This definition was inserted by Regulation 3 of the European Communities (Protection of Employees (Employers' Insolvency)) Regulations 2005 (Statutory Instrument No. 630 of 2005).

[14] The text of the Act originally referred to the Minister for Labour. However, under Article 4(1) of the Labour (Transfer of Departmental Administration and Ministerial Functions) Order, 1993 (S.I. No. 18 of 1993), it was provided that the functions vested in the Minister for Labour by or under certain Acts (including this Act) be transferred to the Minister for Industry and Commerce. Under Article 4(2) of the same Order, it was provided that references to the Minister for Labour contained in any such Act or instrument thereunder and relating to any functions transferred by Article 4 should, on and after the commencement of the Order, be construed as references to the Minister for Industry and Commerce. Under Article 4 of the Industry and Commerce (Alteration of Name of Department and Title of Minister) Order, 1993 (S.I. No. 19 of 1993), which was adopted on the same day as S.I. No. 18 of 1993, it was provided that references in any enactment to the Minister for Industry and Commerce should be construed as references to the Minister for Enterprise and Employment. More recently, Article 4 of the Enterprise and Employment (Alteration of Name of Department and Title of Minister) Order, 1997 (S.I. No. 305 of 1997) has provided that references in any enactment to the Minister for Enterprise and Employment are to be construed as references to the Minister for Enterprise, Trade and Employment. It should be noted that the powers and duties which are conferred on the Minister for Enterprise, Trade and Employment by or under the Protection of Employees (Employers' Insolvency) Acts have been delegated by statutory instrument to the present Minister of State at the Department of Enterprise, Trade and Employment. (See now the Enterprise, Trade and Employment (Delegation of Ministerial Functions) Order 2004 (S.I. No. 809 of 2004).)

"prescribed" means prescribed by regulations under this Act;

"relevant officer" means an executor, an administrator, the official assignee or a trustee in bankruptcy, a liquidator, a receiver or manager, a trustee under an arrangement between an employer and his creditors or under a trust deed for his creditors executed by an employer, or, where the employer is an undertaking which is insolvent under the laws, regulations and administrative procedures of another Member State in accordance with Article 2(1) of Council Directive 80/987/EEC of 20 October 1980 as amended by Article 1(2) of Directive 2002/74/EC of the European Parliament and of the Council of 23 September 2002 and the employees concerned are employed or habitually employed in the State, the person appointed by the appropriate competent authority to perform the functions of a relevant officer; [15]

"the Social Insurance Fund" [16] means the Social Insurance Fund established under section 39 of the Social Welfare Act, 1952, and continued in being under [section 9 of the Social Welfare Consolidation Act 2005];

---

[15] This definition was amended by Regulation 3 of the European Communities (Protection of Employees (Employers' Insolvency) Regulations 2005 (Statutory Instrument No. 630 of 2005), which deleted the word "or" which was to be found after the word "manager" in the original version of this definition, and by adding all of the words now found after the words "executed by an employer".

[16] This definition was inserted by s. 28 of the Social Welfare Act, 1990. Note that the reference at the end of this definition was originally to section 122 of the Social Welfare (Consolidation) Act, 1981, which was subsequently repealed by s. 300 of the Social Welfare (Consolidation) Act 1993. The effect of s. 361(b) of the Social Welfare Consolidation Act 2005, however, appears to be that references to provisions of a repealed enactment such as that originally found in the above definition are now to be read as references to the corresponding provisions of the 2005 Act. Even if this is not the effect of s. 361(b), the matter will in any case come within the more general provisions of s. 26 (2) of the Interpretation Act 2005, according to which, where an enactment is repealed and reenacted, with or without modification, by another enactment, a reference in any other enactment to the former enactment shall, with respect to a subsequent transaction, matter or thing, be read as a reference to the provisions of the new enactment relating to the same subject-matter as that of the former enactment. The appropriate reference has therefore been substituted in the text above.

"the Tribunal" means the Employment Appeals Tribunal.

(2) Any reference in this Act to the assets of an occupational pensions scheme is a reference to the funds or other property out of which the benefits provided by the scheme are payable from time to time, including the proceeds of any policy of insurance taken out, or contract entered into, for the purposes of the scheme.

(3) For the purposes of this Act, an employer shall be taken to be or, as may be appropriate, to have become insolvent if, but only if,

(*a*) he has been adjudicated bankrupt or has filed a petition for or has executed a deed of, arrangement (within the meaning of section 4 of the Deeds of Arrangement Act, 1887); or

(*b*) he has died and his estate, being insolvent, is being administered in accordance with the rules set out in Part I of the First Schedule to the Succession Act, 1965; or

(*c*) where the employer is a company, a winding up order is made or a resolution for voluntary winding up is passed with respect to it, or a receiver or manager of its undertaking is duly appointed, or possession is taken, by or on behalf of the holders of any debentures secured by any floating charge, of any property of the company comprised in or subject to the charge; [17] or

(*d*) he is an employer of a class or description specified in regulations under *section 4 (2)* of this Act which are for the time being in force and the circumstances specified in the regulations as regards employers of such class or description obtain in relation to him; or [18]

[17] The semicolon in s. 1(3)(c) was substituted in place of a comma by Regulation 3 of the European Communities (Protection of Employees (Employers' Insolvency) Regulations 2005 (Statutory Instrument No. 630 of 2005).

[18] The "; or" in s. 1(3)(d) was substituted in place of a full stop by Regulation 3 of the European Communities (Protection of Employees (Employers' Insolvency) Regulations 2005 (Statutory Instrument No. 630 of 2005).

(*e*) the employer is an undertaking which is insolvent under the laws, regulations and administrative procedures of another Member State in accordance with Article 2(1) of Council Directive 80/987/EEC of 20 October 1980 as amended by Article 1(2) of Directive 2002/74/EC of the European Parliament and of the Council of 23 September 2002 and the employees concerned are employed or habitually employed in the State.[19]

2. *(Repealed by s. 39(2) of the Social Welfare Act, 1991)* Redundancy and Employers' Insolvency Fund.

3. —Subject to section 11 of this Act, this Act applies to employees [20] employed in employment which is insurable for all benefits under [the Social Welfare Consolidation Act 2005] [21] or would be so insurable but for the fact that— Application of Act.

---

[19] Section 1(3)(e) was inserted by Regulation 3 of the European Communities (Protection of Employees (Employers' Insolvency) Regulations 2005 (Statutory Instrument No. 630 of 2005).

[20] Note that under s. 8 of the Protection of Employees (Part-Time Work) Act, 2001, the Protection of Employees (Employers' Insolvency) Acts, 1984 and 1990 are to apply to a part-time employee (meaning, under s. 7(1) of the 2001 Act, an employee whose normal hours of work are less than the normal hours of work of an employee who is a comparable employee in relation to him or her) in the same manner (and subject to the like exceptions not inconsistent with s. 8) as they apply (other than by virtue of the 2001 Act) to an employee to whom the Protection of Employees (Employers' Insolvency) Acts, 1984 and 1990 relate. (Note also the broad definition given to "employee" by s. 3(1) of the Protection of Employees (Part-Time Work) Act, 2001. Note in addition that under s. 1(3) of the Protection of Employees (Part-Time Work) Act, 2001, insofar as the 2001 Act relates to the Protection of Employees (Employers' Insolvency) Acts, 1984 and 1990, those Acts and the 2001 Act are required to be construed together as one and may be cited together as the Terms of Employment (Information) Acts, 1994 to 2001. Further, under s. 17(1) of the Industrial Relations (Miscellaneous Provisions) Act 2004, insofar as it relates to the Protection of Employees (Employers' Insolvency) Acts, 1984 to 2001, s. 15 of the 2004 Act, as well as s. 17(3) of the that Act and the Protection of Employees (Employers' Insolvency) Acts, 1984 to 2001 shall be construed together as one and may be cited together as the Protection of Employees (Employers' Insolvency) Acts 1984 to 2004.)

[21] The entirety of s. 3 was substituted by Regulation 4 of the European Communities (Protection of Employees (Employers' Insolvency))

(*a*) the employment concerned is an excepted employment by virtue of [paragraph 2, 4 or 5 of Part II of Schedule 1 to the Social Welfare Consolidation Act 2005] [22], or

(*b*) the employees concerned have attained the age of 66 years.

Regulations 2005 (Statutory Instrument No. 630 of 2005). It should be noted that the opening paragraph of the new version of s. 3 (as inserted by Regulation 4 of Statutory Instrument No. 630 of 2005) originally referred to the Social Welfare (Consolidation) Act, 1993, which has since been repealed in its entirety by s. 360 of the Social Welfare Consolidation Act, 2005. The effect of s. 361(b) of the Social Welfare Consolidation Act, 2005, however, appears to be that references to provisions of a repealed enactment such as that originally found here are now to be read as references to the corresponding provisions of the 2005 Act. The text of the opening paragraph of s. 3 of the 1984 Act has been altered accordingly. (Note in this regard the amendments to the rules concerning insurability in the Social Welfare Consolidation Act 2005 which have subsequently been effected by the Social Welfare Act 2005). Even if this is not the effect of s. 361(b) of the Social Welfare Consolidation Act 2005, the matter will in any case come within the more general provisions of s. 26 (2) of the Interpretation Act 2005, according to which, where an enactment is repealed and reenacted, with or without modification, by another enactment, a reference in any other enactment to the former enactment shall, with respect to a subsequent transaction, matter or thing, be read as a reference to the provisions of the new enactment relating to the same subject-matter as that of the former enactment.

Although further examination of the concept of insurable employment would be beyond the scope of the present work, it may be noted that s. 2 of the Social Welfare Consolidation Act 2005 now defines 'insurable employment' as meaning employment such that a person, over the age of 16 years and under pensionable age, employed in that employment would be an employed contributor within the meaning of that Act. The meaning to be attributed to the concept of an employed contributor and further rules governing employed contributors are to be found in Chapter 2 of the 2005 Act.

[22] Paragraph (a), in common with the rest of s. 3, was inserted in the 1984 Act by Regulation 4 of the European Communities (Protection of Employees (Employers' Insolvency)) Regulations 2005 (S.I. No. 630 of 2005). As originally inserted it made reference to provisions of the Social Welfare (Consolidation) Act, 1993, which have subsequently been repealed by s. 360 of the Social Welfare Consolidation Act 2005 (*viz.*, paragraphs 2, 4 and 5 of Part II of the First Schedule to the Social Welfare (Consolidation) Act, 1993). The effect of s. 361(b) of the Social Welfare Consolidation Act 2005, however, appears to be that references to

4. —(1) An employer who is for the purposes of this Act insolvent shall for such purposes be regarded as having become insolvent on— Insolvency for the purposes of Act.

(*a*) where the employer has been adjudicated bankrupt, the date of such adjudication,

(*b*) where the employer petitioned for arrangement, the date on which the petition is filed,

(*c*) where the employer executed a deed referred to in *section 1 (3) (a)* of this Act, the date of such execution,

(*d*) where the employer has died, the date of his death,

(*e*) where the employer is a company within the meaning of section 2 of the Companies Act, 1963—

(i) in case either a receiver is appointed on behalf of the holder of any debenture secured by a floating charge, or possession is taken by or on behalf of such a debenture holder of any property of the company comprised in or subject to the charge, the date of the appointment of the receiver or possession being taken as aforesaid, as may be appropriate, or

(ii) in any other case the date which, in relation to the company, is the relevant date within the meaning of section 285 of the Companies Act, 1963,[23]

---

provisions of a repealed enactment such as those originally found in s. 3(a) are now to be read as references to the corresponding provisions of the 2005 Act. Even if this is not the effect of s. 361(b), the matter will in any case come within the more general provisions of s. 26 (2) of the Interpretation Act 2005, according to which, where an enactment is repealed and reenacted, with or without modification, by another enactment, a reference in any other enactment to the former enactment shall, with respect to a subsequent transaction, matter or thing, be read as a reference to the provisions of the new enactment relating to the same subject-matter as that of the former enactment. The appropriate references have therefore been substituted in the text above.

[23] The word "and" was deleted from the end of s. 4(1)(e) by Regulation 5 of the European Communities (Protection of Employees (Employers' Insolvency)) Regulations 2005. It should also be noted that s. 285 of the

(*f*) where the employer is an employer of a class or description specified in regulations under *subsection (3)* of this section which are for the time being in force, the day on which under the regulations such an employer is for such purposes to be regarded as having become insolvent, and [24]

(*g*) where the employer is an undertaking which is insolvent under the laws, regulations and administrative procedures of another Member State in accordance with Article 2(1) of Council Directive 80/987/EEC of 20 October 1980 as amended by Article 1(2) of Directive 2002/74/EC of the European Parliament and of the Council of 23 September 2002 and the employees concerned are employed or habitually employed in the State, the date on which the insolvency was established under the laws, regulations and administrative procedures of that other Member State.[25]

(2) The Minister may by regulations specify the circumstances in which employers who are of a class or description specified in the regulations are, for the purposes of this Act, to be taken to be, or to have become, insolvent.

(3) The Minister may by regulations specify the day on which any employer who is of a class or description specified in the regulations and who is also an employer who for the purposes of this Act is insolvent, is to be regarded as having become so insolvent.[26]

Companies Act, 1963 has been amended by section 10 of the Companies (Amendment) Act, 1982 and also by s. 134 of the Companies Act, 1990 but these amendments have not been reflected in any change to the manner in which s. 285 is referred to here. Neither amendment, however, altered the definition of "relevant date" in s. 285 of the 1963 Act.

[24] Regulation 5 of the European Communities (Protection of Employees (Employers' Insolvency)) Regulations 2005 (S.I. No. 630 of 2005) replaced the words "having become insolvent." originally found at the end of s. 4(1)(f) with the words "having become insolvent, and"

[25] Section 4(1)(g) was inserted by Regulation 5 of the European Communities (Protection of Employees (Employers' Insolvency)) Regulations 2005 (S.I. No. 630 of 2005).

[26] See now the Protection of Employees (Employers' Insolvency) (Specification of Date) Regulations, 1985 (S.I. No. 232 of 1985) and the

5. —(1) Where—

Appointment in certain circumstances of persons to perform functions assigned by Act to relevant officers.

(*a*) by virtue of *section 1 (3) (d)* of this Act, an employer becomes insolvent for the purposes of this Act, or

(*b*) an employer otherwise becomes insolvent for such purposes and there is not for the time being in relation to the insolvency a relevant officer,

the Minister may appoint as regards such insolvency a person under this subsection.

(2) Where the Minister makes an appointment under this section the following provisions shall apply:

(*a*) the functions assigned by this Act to a relevant officer shall, as regards the employer concerned, be performed by, and only by, the person to whom the appointment relates, or, if through illness or because his appointment is revoked or for any other reason the person so appointed is unable to perform such functions, another person so appointed, and

(*b*) for so long as the appointment remains in force, each of the references to a relevant officer in *sections 6, 7* and *8* of this Act shall be construed as including a reference to the person to whom the appointment relates.

6. —(1) If, on an application made to him in the prescribed form [27] by or on behalf of an individual, the Minister is satisfied that—

Employees' rights on insolvency of employer.

(*a*) the person by or on whose behalf the application is made (which person is in this section subsequently referred to as "the applicant") is a person to whom this Act applies, and that he was employed by an employer who has become insolvent, and

(*b*) the date on which the employer became insolvent is a day not earlier than the 22nd day of October, 1983, and

---

Protection of Employees (Employers' Insolvency) (Specification of Date) Regulations, 1986 (S.I. No. 50 of 1986).

[27] See now the Protection of Employees (Employers' Insolvency) (Forms and Procedure) Regulations 2005 (S.I. No 682 of 2005).

(*c*) on the relevant date the applicant was entitled to be paid the whole or part of any debt to which this section applies,

the Minister shall, subject to this section, pay to or in respect of the applicant out of the Social Insurance Fund [28] the amount which, in the opinion of the Minister, is or was due to the applicant in respect of that debt.

(2) (*a*) Subject to *paragraph (b)* of this subsection, the following are debts to which this section applies—

(i) any arrears of normal weekly remuneration in respect of a period, or of periods in the aggregate, not exceeding eight weeks, and to which the applicant became entitled during the relevant period,[29]

(ii) any arrears due, in respect of a period or periods not exceeding eight weeks in all

---

[28] The words "Social Insurance Fund" were substituted for the words "Redundancy and Employers' Insolvency Fund" by s. 28 of the Social Welfare Act, 1990.

[29] Section 41(14) of the National Minimum Wage Act, 2000 provides as follows:

> "A payment from the Social Insurance Fund in accordance with section 6(2)(a)(i) of the Protection of Employees (Employers' Insolvency) Acts, 1984 to 1991, shall not have regard to any exemption under this section and any such payment shall be made to the employee as if the employee had been paid the national minimum hourly rate of pay to which he or she was otherwise entitled under this Act, for the period of the exemption."

The exemption referred to relates to the power which the Labour Court enjoys under s. 41 of the National Minimum Wage Act, 2000 to exempt an employer in financial difficulty from the obligation to pay an employee or employees an hourly rate of pay that on average is not less than the national minimum hourly rate of pay.

As regards this obligation, note more generally the provision in s. 14 of the National Minimum Wage Act, 2000 that subject to certain exceptions an employee who has attained the age of 18 years is to be remunerated in respect of his or her working hours in any pay reference period, at an hourly rate of pay that on average is not less than the national minimum hourly rate of pay, with employees who have not attained that age to be remunerated in respect of his or her working hours in any pay reference period, at an hourly rate of pay that on average is not less than 70 per cent of the national minimum hourly rate of pay.

under a scheme or arrangement which, forming part of an employee's contract of employment, provides or is capable of providing in relation to employees in any description of employment, payments payable to any such employees in respect of periods during which they are unable to fulfil their contract of employment due to ill health and to which the applicant became entitled during the relevant period,

(iii) at the election of the employee, either—[30]

(I) any amount which an employer is required to pay, by virtue of an award under section 12 of the Act of 1973 made not earlier than the commencement of the relevant period, either for the period of notice required by section 4 of the Act of 1973 or by reason of a failure by that employer to give the notice required by the said section 4, or

(II) any unpaid normal weekly remuneration certified by the relevant officer as being the amount of normal weekly remuneration due to the employee in lieu of the statutory notice prescribed in section 4 of the Act of 1973,

---

[30] Section 6(2)(a)(iii) of the Protection of Employees (Employers' Insolvency) Act, 1984 was substituted in its entirety by s. 15 of the Redundancy Payments Act 2003, giving the employee the option, for the first time, of electing whether the amount referred to in Clause I above or the amount referred to in Clause II above should constitute a debt to which s. 6 applied, instead of this debt being automatically constituted by the amount referred to in Clause I, as was the case prior to the substitution of s. 6(2)(a)(iii) by the 2003 Act. Note that in Article 3(1) of the Redundancy Payments Act 2003 (Commencement) Order 2003 (S.I. No. 194 of 2003), the Minister for Enterprise, Trade and Employment appointed 25 May, 2003 to be the day on which s. 15 of the 2003 Act came into operation. The amended form of s. 6(2)(a)(iii) thus applies only to circumstances where the relevant date defined by s. 6(9) of the Protection of Employees (Employers' Insolvency) Act, 1984 occurs on or after 25 May, 2003. (See, confirming this latter point, Article 3(2) of S.I. No. 194 of 2003).

(iv) any holiday pay in respect of a period or periods of holiday not exceeding eight weeks in all, and to which the applicant became entitled during the relevant period,

(v) any amount which an employer is required to pay by virtue of—[31]

(I) a determination under section 8 (1) or 9 (1) or an order under section 10 (2) of the 1977 Act, or

(II) a decision, determination or order under Part V of the Maternity Protection Act, 1994, Part IV of the Parental Leave Act, 1998, or Part 4 of the *Carer's Leave Act, 2001*,[32]

and made, in any case, not earlier than the commencement of the relevant period,

(vi) any amount to which a recommendation under section 8 (1) of the Act of 1977 relates, being a recommendation which was made not earlier than the commencement of the relevant period,

(vii) any amount which an employer is required to pay by virtue of an employment regulation order within the meaning of Part IV of the Industrial Relations Act, 1946, being an amount by reference to which proceedings have been instituted against the employer for an offence under section 45 (1) of that Act,

---

[31] Section 6(2)(a)(v) was substituted in its entirety by s. 41(2) of the Maternity Protection Act, 1994, the net effect of this substitution being the inclusion in the scope of the sub-paragraph of any amount which an employer might be required to pay by virtue of a decision, determination or order under Part V of that Act. The newly-inserted clause in which this was done, however – Clause II – was subsequently substituted by s. 26(2) of the Parental Leave Act, 1998, then substituted again by s. 30 of the Carer's Leave Act, 2001, each of these substitutions expanding its scope.

[32] See previous footnote. Note also that in s. 40 of the Adoptive Leave Act, 1995, it was provided that the references in s. 6(2)(a)(v) to a determination or order should be construed as including references to a decision, determination or order under Part V of the Adoptive Leave Act, 1995.

(viii) any amount—

(I) specified in a recommendation issued under section 7 (3) of the Act of 1974, or section 19 (3) of the Employment Equality Act, 1977,[33]

(II) which an employer is required to pay by virtue of a decision or determination of an appeal by the Labour Court under subsection (1) of section 8 of the Act of 1974 or subsection (2) of section 21 of the Employment Equality Act, 1977 or, where appropriate, a decision of the High Court given by virtue of either subsection (3) of the said section 8 or subsection (4) of the said section 21,[34] or

(III) which an employer is required to pay by virtue of a decision, determination or order of a court falling within *section 103(3)* of the *Employment Equality Act, 1998*,[35]

(ix) damages awarded under section 24 (3) (a) of the Employment Equality Act, 1977,[36]

(x) a fine imposed under section 8 (4) (*c*) (i) or paragraph (*a*) (inserted by section 30 of the Employment Equality Act, 1977) of section 9 (3) of the Act of 1974 or under section 25 (3) (*a*) (iii) or 26 (3) (*a*) (iii) of the Employment Equality Act, 1977,[37]

---

[33] Note however that s. 5(1) of the Employment Equality Act, 1998 repealed both the Anti-Discrimination (Pay) Act, 1974 and the Employment Equality Act, 1977.

[34] See previous footnote.

[35] Section 6(2)(a)(viii)(III) was inserted by s. 103(4) and 103(5) of the Employment Equality Act, 1998.

[36] Note however that s. 5(1) of the Employment Equality Act, 1998 repealed the Employment Equality Act, 1977.

[37] The word 'and' was deleted from the end of this sub-paragraph by s. 47 of the National Minimum Wage Act, 2000. Note also that s. 5(1) of the Employment Equality Act, 1998 repealed both the Anti-Discrimination (Pay) Act, 1974 and the Employment Equality Act, 1977.

(xi) compensation directed to be paid under section 10 (1) (*d*) (inserted by section 31 of the Employment Equality Act, 1977) or section 10 (3) (*a*) (inserted by the said section 31) of the Act of 1974 or under section 26 (1) (*d*) (iii) of the Employment Equality Act, 1977,[38]

(xii) any amount which an employer is required to pay by virtue of the *National Minimum Wage Act, 2000*, being an amount by reference to which proceedings have been instituted against the employer for an offence under *section 35* of the *National Minimum Wage Act, 2000*, and [39]

(xiii) any amount which an employer is required to pay by virtue of— [40]

(I) a decision of a rights commissioner under *section 26* of the *National Minimum Wage Act, 2000*, or

(II) a determination of the Labour Court under *section 29* of the *National Minimum Wage Act, 2000*,

and made, in any case, not earlier than the commencement of the relevant period,

(xiv) any amount which an employer is required to pay by virtue of a decision by way of order by a rights commissioner under section 6(2) of the Act of 1991 or a determination by the Employment Appeals Tribunal

---

[38] The comma at the end of this sub-paragraph was substituted by s. 47 of the National Minimum Wage Act, 2000. Note also that s. 5(1) of the Employment Equality Act, 1998 repealed both the Anti-Discrimination (Pay) Act, 1974 and the Employment Equality Act, 1977.

[39] Section 6(2)(a)(xii) was inserted by s. 47 of the National Minimum Wage Act, 2000.

[40] Section 6(2)(a)(xiii) was inserted by s. 47 of the National Minimum Wage Act, 2000. The comma at the end of the subsection was substituted for a full stop by Regulation 6 of the European Communities (Protection of Employees (Employers' Insolvency) Regulations 2005 (Statutory Instrument No. 630 of 2005).

under section 7(1) of the Act of 1991 and made, in any case, not earlier than the commencement of the relevant period, provided that a claim in respect of the amount to which the decision or determination refers has not been made under another provision of this section,[41]

(xv) any amount which an employer is required to pay by virtue of a recommendation by way of order by a rights commissioner under section 7(2)(d) of the Act of 1994 or a determination by the Employment Appeals Tribunal under section 8(1) or section 8(6)(a) of the Act of 1994 and made, in any case, not earlier than the commencement of the relevant period,[42]

(xvi) any amount which an employer is required to pay by virtue of a recommendation by a rights commissioner under section 18(2) of the Act of 1996 or a determination by the Employment Appeals Tribunal under subsection (1) or (6) of section 19 of the Act of 1996 and made, in any case, not earlier than the commencement of the relevant period,[43]

(xvii) any amount which an employer is required to pay by virtue of a decision by a rights commissioner under section 27(2) of the Act of 1997 or a determination by the Labour Court under subsection (1) or (8) of section 28 of the Act of 1997 and made, in any

---

[41] Section 6(2)(a)(xiv) was inserted by Regulation 6 of the European Communities (Protection of Employees (Employers' Insolvency)) Regulations 2005 (Statutory Instrument No. 630 of 2005).

[42] Section 6(2)(a)(xv) was inserted by Regulation 6 of the European Communities (Protection of Employees (Employers' Insolvency)) Regulations 2005 (Statutory Instrument No. 630 of 2005).

[43] Section 6(2)(a)(xvi) was inserted by Regulation 6 of the European Communities (Protection of Employees (Employers' Insolvency)) Regulations 2005 (Statutory Instrument No. 630 of 2005).

case, not earlier than the commencement of the relevant period,[44]

(xviii) any amount which an employer is required to pay by virtue of a decision by a rights commissioner under section 4(4) of the Act of 1998 or a determination by the Employment Appeals Tribunal under subsection (1) or (6)(a) of section 8 of the Act of 1994 as amended and extended by section 4(6)(b) of the Act of 1998 and made, in any case, not earlier than the commencement of the relevant period,[45]

(xix) any amount which an employer is required to pay by virtue of a decision by a rights commissioner under section 16(1) of the Act of 2001 or a determination by the Labour Court under subsection (1) or (8) of section 17 of the Act of 2001 and made, in any case, not earlier than the commencement of the relevant period,[46]

(xx) any amount which an employer is required to pay by virtue of a decision by a rights commissioner under section 14(1)(b) of the Act of 2003 or a determination by the Labour Court under subsection (1)(b) or (8) of section 15 of the Act of 2003 and made, in any case, not earlier than the commencement of the relevant period,[47]

(xxi) any amount which an employer is required to pay by virtue of a decision by a rights

---

[44] Section 6(2)(a)(xvii) was inserted by Regulation 6 of the European Communities (Protection of Employees (Employers' Insolvency)) Regulations 2005 (Statutory Instrument No. 630 of 2005).

[45] Section 6(2)(a)(xviii) was inserted by Regulation 6 of the European Communities (Protection of Employees (Employers' Insolvency)) Regulations 2005 (Statutory Instrument No. 630 of 2005).

[46] Section 6(2)(a)(xix) was inserted by Regulation 6 of the European Communities (Protection of Employees (Employers' Insolvency)) Regulations 2005 (Statutory Instrument No. 630 of 2005).

[47] Section 6(2)(a)(xx) was inserted by Regulation 6 of the European Communities (Protection of Employees (Employers' Insolvency)) Regulations 2005 (Statutory Instrument No. 630 of 2005).

commissioner under Regulation 6(1) of the European Communities (Protection of Employment) Regulations 2000 (S.I. No. 488 of 2000) or a determination by the Employment Appeals Tribunal under subsection (1) or (6)(a) of section 8 of the Act of 1994 as amended and extended by the same Regulations and made, in any case, not earlier than the commencement of the relevant period,[48]

(xxii) any amount which an employer is required to pay by virtue of a decision by a rights commissioner under Regulation 10(4)(b) of the European Communities (Protection of Employees on Transfer of Undertakings) Regulations 2003 (S.I. No. 131 of 2003) or a determination by the Employment Appeals Tribunal under regulation 11(1)(b) of the same regulations and made, in any case, not earlier than the commencement of the relevant period,[49]

(xxiii) any amount which an employer is required to pay by virtue of a decision by a rights commissioner under paragraph 4 of the Third Schedule to the Act of 2002 or a determination by the Employment Appeals Tribunal under subsection (1) or (6)(a) of section 8 of the Act of 1994 as amended and extended by paragraph 6(b) of the Third Schedule to the Act of 2002 and made, in any case, not earlier than the commencement of the relevant period,[50]

(xxiv) any amount which an employer is required to pay to an employee in respect of remuneration

---

[48] Section 6(2)(a)(xxi) was inserted by Regulation 6 of the European Communities (Protection of Employees (Employers' Insolvency)) Regulations 2005 (Statutory Instrument No. 630 of 2005).

[49] Section 6(2)(a)(xxii) was inserted by Regulation 6 of the European Communities (Protection of Employees (Employers' Insolvency)) Regulations 2005 (Statutory Instrument No. 630 of 2005).

[50] Section 6(2)(a)(xxiii) was inserted by Regulation 6 of the European Communities (Protection of Employees (Employers' Insolvency)) Regulations 2005 (Statutory Instrument No. 630 of 2005).

by virtue of a registered employment agreement within the meaning of Part III of the Industrial Relations Act 1946, being an amount by reference to which an order of the Labour Court has been made under section 32(1)(b) of that Act or section 10(1)(b) of the Act of 1969, or proceedings have been instituted under section 54(1) of the Act of 1990, [51]

(xxv) any amount which an employer is required to pay to an employee in respect of remuneration by virtue of a decision of a rights commissioner under subsection (4)(b) of section 9 of the Act of 2004 or a determination by the Labour Court under subsection (1)(b) of section 10 of the Act of 2004, and [52]

(xxvi) any amount which an employer is required to pay by virtue of a decision of a rights commissioner under paragraph 1(2)(*b*) of *Schedule 2* to the Act of 2006 or a determination by the Labour Court under paragraph 2(1) of that Schedule.[52a]

(*b*) Any amount, damages, fine or compensation referred to in *subparagraph (viii), (ix), (x), (xi), (xiv), (xv), (xvi), (xvii), (xviii), (xix), (xx), (xxi), (xxii), (xxiii), (xxiv),* (xxv) or (xxvi) [53] of *paragraph (a)* of this subsection shall be regarded as being a debt to which

---

[51] Section 6(2)(a)(xxiv) was inserted by Regulation 6 of the European Communities (Protection of Employees (Employers' Insolvency)) Regulations 2005 (Statutory Instrument No. 630 of 2005). The word "and" was deleted from the end of s. 6(2)(a)(xxiv) by Paragraph 6(2) of Schedule 2 to the Employment Permits Act 2006 (as given effect to by s. 26(4) of that Act).

[52] Section 6(2)(a)(xxv) was inserted by Regulation 6 of the European Communities (Protection of Employees (Employers' Insolvency)) Regulations 2005 (Statutory Instrument No. 630 of 2005). The word ", and" at the end of s. 6(2)(a)(xxv) was substituted by Paragraph 6(2) of Schedule 2 to the Employment Permits Act 2006 (as given effect to by s. 26(4) of that Act) for the full stop which was previously to be found there.

[52a] Section 6(2)(a)(xxvi) was inserted by Paragraph 6(2) of Schedule 2 to the Employment Permits Act 2006 (as given effect to by s. 26(4) of that Act).

[53] The contents of s. 6(2)(b) after "*(x)*" as far as the footnote marker were all originally substituted by Regulation 6 of the European Communities

this section applies if, and only if, the relevant recommendation, decision, determination, award or order was made during, or after the expiration of, the relevant period.

(*c*) A payment shall not be made under this section in respect of a debt referred to in subparagraph (xiv), (xv), (xvi), (xvii), (xviii), (xix), (xx), (xxi), (xxii), (xxiii), (xxv) or (xxvi) of paragraph (a) of this subsection until the period for making an appeal against—[54]

(i) the decision or recommendation, as appropriate, of the rights commissioner,

(ii) the determination of the Employment Appeals Tribunal or the Labour Court, as appropriate, has expired, or any such appeal made has been withdrawn or determined.

(3) Where—

(*a*) legal proceedings are instituted by or on behalf of an employee and on foot of all or any of the following—

(i) a claim for arrears described in *subparagraph (i)* or *(ii)* of subsection *(2)* of this section, [54a]

(ii) a claim for holiday pay described in *subparagraph (iv)* of the said *subsection (2)*, [54b]

(Protection of Employees (Employers' Insolvency) Regulations 2005 (Statutory Instrument No. 630 of 2005) in place of the original words "or *(xi)*". The contents of s. 6(2)(b) from what is now the final comma before the footnote marker as far as the footnote marker were then subsequently substituted in the form shown in the text above by Paragraph 6(2) of Schedule 2 to the Employment Permits Act 2006 (as given effect to by s. 26(4) of that Act).

[54] Section 6(2)(c) was inserted in its entirety by Regulation 6 of the European Communities (Protection of Employees (Employers' Insolvency) Regulations 2005 (Statutory Instrument No. 630 of 2005) except for that portion of it which reads ", (xxv) or (xxvi)", which was substituted for the original text by Paragraph 6(2) of Schedule 2 to the Employment Permits Act 2006 (as given effect to by s. 26(4) of that Act).

[54a] This reference is erroneous. There is neither a s. 6(2)(i) nor a s. 6(2)(ii) in this Act. There is, however, both a s. 6(2)(a)(i) and a s. 6(2)(a)(ii), to which these references are clearly meant to refer.

[54b] This reference is erroneous. There is no s. 6(2)(iv) in the 1984 Act. There is, however, a s. 6(2)(a)(iv) to which this reference is clearly meant to refer.

(iii) a claim for damages at common law for wrongful dismissal,

an award is made by the court in favour of the employee, and

(*b*) had the employee made an application under *subsection (1)* of this section in respect of any of the matters referred to in *subparagraph (i)*, *(ii)* or *(iii)* of *paragraph (a)* of this subsection he would have satisfied the requirements of *paragraphs (a)*, *(b)* and *(c)* of the said *subsection (1)*,

subject to subsection (4) (a) of this section, there shall be paid out of the Social Insurance Fund, [55] to or in respect of the employee, an amount equal to—

(i) the amount of the award, or

(ii) the maximum which would have been payable out of the said Fund by virtue of this Act had the employcc succcssfully sought redress under section 8 (1) or 9 (1) of the Act of 1977.

(4) (*a*) The amount payable to an employee in respect of any debt mentioned in *subsection (2)* or award mentioned in *subsection (3)* of this section shall, where the amount of that debt is or may be calculated by reference to the employee's remuneration, not exceed [€600] [56] in respect of any one week or, in respect of any period of less than a week, an amount bearing the same proportion to [€600] [57] as that period bears to the normal weekly working hours of the employee at the relevant date.

(*b*) An amount payable under this section in respect of a debt mentioned in *subsection (2) (a) (ii)* of this section as regards a particular period, shall not exceed the difference between the amount of any

---

[55] The words 'Social Insurance Fund' were substituted for the words 'Redundancy and Employers' Insolvency Fund' by s. 28 of the Social Welfare Act, 1990.

[56] The amount of €600 was inserted in each place in which it occurs in s. 4(a) (in substitution for the previous amount mentioned there) by Article 3 of the Protection of Employees (Employers' Insolvency)(Variation of Limit) Regulations 2004 (S.I. No. 696 of 2004).

[57] See previous footnote.

disability benefit or injury benefit payable under [the Social Welfare Consolidation Act 2005] [58] to the employee concerned as regards the period (together with, in either case, the amount of any pay-related benefit payable to such employee under [the Social Welfare Consolidation Act 2005] [59] as regards the period) and the amount of his normal weekly remuneration as regards the period.

(*c*) (i) A payment shall not be made under this section in respect of an amount which an employer is required to pay by virtue of a determination [60] having been made under section 8 (1) or 9 (1) of the Act of 1977, unless—

(I) if proceedings are instituted under [section 11 of the Unfair Dismissals (Amendment) Act, 1993], [61] the proceedings are withdrawn, or

---

[58] The text of s. 6(4)(b) originally referred here to 'the Act of 1981', meaning the Social Welfare (Consolidation) Act, 1981. However, all relevant provisions of the 1981 Act were repealed by s. 300 of the Social Welfare (Consolidation) Act, 1993 with equivalent new provisions being enacted in that legislation. The entirety of the 1993 Act was then subsequently repealed by s. 360 of the Social Welfare Consolidation Act 2005 with, again, equivalent new provisions being enacted in the 2005 Act. The effect of s. 361(b) of the Social Welfare Consolidation Act 2005, however, appears to be that references to provisions of a repealed enactment such as that originally found in s. 6(4)(b) of the 1984 Act are now to be read as references to the corresponding provisions of the 2005 Act. Even if this is not the effect of s. 361(b), the matter will in any case come within the more general provisions of s. 26 (2) of the Interpretation Act 2005, according to which, where an enactment is repealed and reenacted, with or without modification, by another enactment, a reference in any other enactment to the former enactment shall, with respect to a subsequent transaction, matter or thing, be read as a reference to the provisions of the new enactment relating to the same subject-matter as that of the former enactment. The appropriate reference has therefore been substituted in the text above.

[59] See previous footnote.

[60] Under s. 40 of the Adoptive Leave Act, 1995, the references in s. 6(4)(c)(i) to a determination are to be construed as including references to a decision or determination under Part V of the Adoptive Leave Act, 1995.

[61] Section 6(4)(c)(i)(I) originally referred to s. 10 of the Unfair Dismissals Act, 1977. Section 10 of the 1977 Act was repealed by s. 16 of the Unfair

(II) in case an appeal is brought under section 10 (4) of the Act of 1977 [62] from the determination,[63] the appeal has been either withdrawn or determined, or

(III) in case there is no such appeal, the time for bringing such an appeal has expired.

(ii) A payment shall not be made under this section in respect of an amount to which a recommendation under section 8 (1) of the Act of 1977 relates unless—

(I) in case an appeal from the recommendation is brought under section 9 (1) of the Act of 1977, the appeal is withdrawn, or

---

Dismissals (Amendment) Act, 1993. Its function is now carried out by s. 11 of the 1993 Act. Under s. 26 (2) of the Interpretation Act 2005, where an enactment is repealed and reenacted, with or without modification, by another enactment, a reference in any other enactment to the former enactment shall, with respect to a subsequent transaction, matter or thing, be read as a reference to the provisions of the new enactment relating to the same subject-matter as that of the former enactment. The appropriate reference has therefore been substituted in the text above.

[62] Section 6(4)(c)(i)(II) originally referred to s. 10 (4) of the Act of 1977. Section 10 of the Unfair Dismissals Act, 1977 was repealed by s. 16 of the Unfair Dismissals (Amendment) Act, 1993, however. The function of s. 10 (4) of the Act of 1977 is now carried out by s. 11(1) of the 1993 Act. Under s. 26 (2) of the Interpretation Act 2005, where an enactment is repealed and reenacted, with or without modification, by another enactment, a reference in any other enactment to the former enactment shall, with respect to a subsequent transaction, matter or thing, be read as a reference to the provisions of the new enactment relating to the same subject-matter as that of the former enactment. The appropriate reference has therefore been substituted in the text above. It is important to note further that under s. 40 of the Adoptive Leave Act, 1995, the reference in s. 6(4)(c)(i)(II) to section 10 (4) of the Act of 1977 is also required to be construed as including a reference to section 35 or 36, as may be appropriate, of the Adoptive Leave Act, 1995.

[63] Under s. 40 of the Adoptive Leave Act, 1995, the references in s. 6(4)(c)(i) to a determination are to be construed as including references to a decision or determination under Part V of the Adoptive Leave Act, 1995.

(II) in case there is no such appeal, the time for bringing such an appeal has expired.

(iii) A payment shall not be made under this section as regards a recommendation referred to in *subsection (2) (a) (viii) (I)* of this section unless—

(I) in case an appeal is brought under section 8 (1) (a) of the Anti-Discrimination (Pay) Act, 1974, or section 21 (1) of the Employment Equality Act, 1977, against the recommendation, the appeal is withdrawn,[64] or

(II) in case there is no such appeal, the time for bringing such an appeal has expired.[65]

(iv) a payment shall not be made under this section in respect of an amount to which a decision under Part V of the Maternity Protection Act, 1994, Part IV of the Parental Leave Act, 1998, or Part 4 of the *Carer's Leave Act, 2001*, relates unless— [66]

(I) in case an appeal from the decision to the Tribunal is brought under the Part in question, the appeal is withdrawn, or

(II) in case there is no such appeal, the time for bringing such an appeal has expired.

(v) a payment shall not be made under this section in respect of an amount to which a determination under Part V of the Maternity

---

[64] Note that the Anti-Discrimination (Pay) Act, 1974, and the Employment Equality Act, 1977 were repealed by s. 5(1) of the Employment Equality Act, 1998.

[65] See previous footnote.

[66] The entirety of s. 6(4)(c)(iv) was inserted by s. 41(3) of the Maternity Protection Act, 1994. Subsequently, the text of s. 6(4)(c)(iv) to this point—in other words, the text of s. 6(4)(c)(iv) other than clauses (I) and (II)—was substituted by s. 26(3) of the Parental Leave Act, 1998, then substituted again by s. 30 of the Carer's Leave Act, 2001, each of these substitutions expanding the range of decisions referred to.

Protection Act, 1994, Part IV of the Parental Leave Act, 1998, or Part 4 of the *Carer's Leave Act, 2001*, relates unless— [67]

(I) in case an appeal from the determination is brought to the High Court under the Part in question, the appeal is withdrawn, or

(II) in case there is no appeal, the time for bringing such an appeal has expired.

(vi) A payment shall not be made under this section in respect of an amount to which a decision or determination under any provision of the *Employment Equality Act, 1998*, applies unless— [68]

(I) in case an appeal from the decision or determination is brought under that Part, the appeal is withdrawn, or

(II) in case there is no such appeal, the time for bringing such an appeal has expired.

(vii) A payment shall not be made under this section in respect of an amount to which a decision of a rights commissioner under *section 26* of the *National Minimum Wage Act, 2000*, relates unless— [69]

(I) in case an appeal from the decision to the Labour Court is brought under *section 27* of that Act, the appeal is withdrawn, or

[67] The entirety of s. 6(4)(c)(v) was inserted by s. 41(3) of the Maternity Protection Act, 1994. Subsequently, the text of s. 6(4)(c)(v) to this point—in other words, the text of s. 6(4)(c)(v) other than clauses (I) and (II)—was substituted by s. 26(3) of the Parental Leave Act, 1998, then substituted again by s. 30 of the Carer's Leave Act, 2001, each of these substitutions expanding the range of determinations referred to.

[68] The entirety of s. 6(4)(c)(vi) was inserted by s. 103(4) and s. 103(6) of the Employment Equality Act, 1998.

[69] The entirety of s. 6(4)(c)(vii) was inserted by s. 47 of the National Minimum Wage Act, 2000. The comma preceding the word "relates" appears to have been put there in error.

(II) in case there is no such appeal, the time for bringing such an appeal has expired.

(viii) A payment shall not be made under this section in respect of an amount to which a determination under *section 29* of the *National Minimum Wage Act, 2000*, relates unless— [70]

(I) in case an appeal from the determination is brought to the High Court under *section 30* of that Act, the appeal is withdrawn, or

(II) in case there is no appeal, the time for bringing an appeal has expired.

(5) The provisions of subsections *(6)* and *(7)* of this section shall apply in a case where a relevant officer is either appointed or required to be appointed.

(6) Subject to *subsection (7)* of this section, the Minister shall not in a case which is a case referred to in *subsection (5)* of this section make any payment under this section in respect of any debt until he has received a statement in the prescribed form from the relevant officer of the amount of that debt which appears to have been owed to the employee on the relevant date and to remain unpaid; and the relevant officer shall, on a request being made in that behalf, by the Minister, provide him, as soon as is reasonably practicable, with such a statement.

(7) Where—

(*a*) a period of six months has elapsed since the application for a payment under this section was received by the Minister, but no such payment has been made,

(*b*) the Minister is satisfied that a payment under this section should be made, and

(*c*) it appears to the Minister that there is likely to be further delay before he receives a statement referred

[70] The entirety of s. 6(4)(c)(viii) was inserted by s. 47 of the National Minimum Wage Act, 2000.

to in *subsection (6)* of this section regarding the debt in question,

then, the Minister may, if the applicant so requests, or if the Minister thinks fit, without such a request, make a payment under this section notwithstanding the fact that no such statement has been received.

(8) Where an application is made to the Minister under this section and in relation to any or each of the debts to which the application relates, the Minister is satisfied that—

(*a*) there was an agreement between the applicant and the employer concerned that the whole or any part of the debt would be the subject of an application under this section, and

(*b*) when the agreement was made such employer had the means to pay such debt or the part thereof,

the Minister may either refuse the application or disallow it in so far as it relates to such debt or part.

(9) In this section—

"normal weekly remuneration" has the meaning assigned to it by Schedule 3 to the Act of 1967 for the purposes of that Schedule save that any reference in that Schedule to the date on which an employee was declared redundant may, where appropriate, be construed as including a reference to the relevant date;

"the relevant date" means—

(*a*) in relation to a debt which is an amount, damages, fine or compensation referred to in subparagraph *(iii)(I)*, [71] *(v)*, *(vi)*, *(viii)*, *(ix)*, (x), (xi), (xiii), (xiv), (xv), (xvi),

---

[71] The words "subparagraph (iii)(I)" were substituted by s. 15 of the Redundancy Payments Act 2003, in consequence of the changes effected by that section of the 2003 Act to s. 6(2)(a) of this Act. Note that in Article 3(1) of the Redundancy Payments Act 2003 (Commencement) Order 2003 (S.I. No. 194 of 2003), the Minister for Enterprise, Trade and Employment appointed 25 May, 2003 to be the day on which s. 15 of the 2003 Act came into operation. The amended form of s. 6(9)(a) thus applies only to circumstances where the relevant date defined by s. 6(9) of the Protection of Employees (Employers' Insolvency) Act, 1984 occurs on or after 25

(xvii), (xviii), (xix), (xx), (xxi), (xxii), (xxiii), (xxiv), (xxv) or (xxvi) of subsection (2)(*a*) [72] of this section, the date on which the relevant employer became insolvent or the date on which the relevant recommendation, decision, determination, award or order is made, whichever is the later,

(*aa*) in relation to a debt referred to in subparagraph (iii)(II), the date of termination of employment,[73]

(*b*) in relation to any other debt to which this section applies—

(i) in case the relevant applicant's employment is terminated as a result of the relevant employer's insolvency, the date on which such employer became insolvent, or the date of such termination, whichever such applicant shall as regards the debt nominate, or

---

May, 2003. (See, confirming this latter point, Article 3(2) of S.I. No. 194 of 2003).

[72] The words "(x), (xi), (xiii), (xiv), (xv), (xvi), (xvii), (xviii), (xix), (xx), (xxi), (xxii), (xxiii), (xxiv) or (xxv)" were substituted into s. 6(9) by Regulation 6 of the European Communities (Protection of Employees (Employers' Insolvency)) Regulations 2005 (S.I. No. 630 of 2005) for the words "*(x), (xi)* or *(xiii)*" which had earlier been inserted in s. 6(9) by s. 47 of the National Minimum Wage Act, 2000. (More exactly, the words "*(x), (xi)* or *(xiii)* of subsection (2)(*a*)" had earlier been substituted by s. 47 of the National Minimum Wage Act, 2000 for the original reference merely to the first two subparagraphs, this being done in order to take account of the insertion of s. 6(2)(a)(xiii) in the 1984 Act by s. 47 of the 2000 Act.) Most recently, the words "or (xxv)" substituted into s. 6(9) by Regulation 6 of the European Communities (Protection of Employees (Employers' Insolvency)) Regulations, 2005 were replaced with the words ", (xxv) or (xxvi)" by Paragraph 6(2) of Schedule 2 to the Employment Permits Act 2006 (as given effect to by s. 26(4) of that Act).

[73] Paragraph (aa) was inserted by s. 15 of the Redundancy Payments Act 2003, in consequence of the changes effected by that section of the 2003 Act to s. 6(2)(a) of this Act. Note that in Article 3(1) of the Redundancy Payments Act 2003 (Commencement) Order 2003 (S.I. No. 194 of 2003), the Minister for Enterprise, Trade and Employment appointed 25 May, 2003 to be the day on which s. 15 of the 2003 Act came into operation. Section 6(9)(aa) thus applies only to circumstances where the relevant date defined by s. 6(9) of the Protection of Employees (Employers' Insolvency) Act, 1984 occurs on or after 25 May, 2003. (See, confirming this latter point, Article 3(2) of S.I. No. 194 of 2003).

(ii) in any other case, the date on which such employer became insolvent;

"the relevant period" means in relation to a debt to which this section applies, the period of eighteen months immediately preceding the relevant date.

(10) No reference in *subsection (3)* of this section to an award shall be construed as including a reference to any amount allowed as regards costs.

Payment of unpaid contributions to occupational pension scheme.

7. —(1) If, on an application made to him in the prescribed form [74] by an employee or by the persons competent to act in respect of an occupational pension scheme or Personal Retirement Savings Account (within the meaning of the Pensions Act, 1990) [75], the Minister is satisfied that—

(*a*) an employer (being in case the application is made by a person otherwise than in his capacity as the person competent so to act the employer of the applicant) has become insolvent,

(*b*) the date on which for the purposes of this Act the employer became insolvent is a day not earlier than the 22nd day of October, 1983, and

(*c*) on that day there remained unpaid relevant contributions remaining to be paid by the employer to the scheme or Personal Retirement Savings Account (within the meaning of the Pensions Act, 1990) [76],

on the date on which the employer became insolvent, being a date not earlier than the said 22nd day of October the Minister shall, subject to this section, pay into the assets of the scheme or Personal Retirement Savings Account (within the meaning of

---

[74] See now the Protection of Employees (Employers' Insolvency) (Forms and Procedure) Regulations 2005 (S.I. No. 682 of 2005).

[75] The words "or Personal Retirement Savings Account (within the meaning of the Pensions Act, 1990)" were inserted here by s. 121(9) of the Pensions Act, 1990. Section 121(9) was inserted in the 1990 Act by s. 3 of the Pensions (Amendment) Act, 2002.

[76] The words "or Personal Retirement Savings Account (within the meaning of the Pensions Act, 1990)" were inserted here by s. 121(9) of the Pensions Act, 1990. Section 121(9) was inserted in the 1990 Act by s. 3 of the Pensions (Amendment) Act, 2002.

the Pensions Act, 1990) [77] out of the Social Insurance Fund [78] the sum which in his opinion is payable in respect of the unpaid relevant contributions.

(2) In this section "relevant contributions" means contributions falling to be paid by an employer in accordance with an occupational pension scheme or Personal Retirement Savings Account (within the meaning of the Pensions Act, 1990) [79], either on his own account or on behalf of an employee; provided that for the purposes of this section a contribution of any amount shall not be treated as falling to be paid on behalf of an employee unless a sum equal to that amount has been deducted from the pay of the employee by way of a contribution from him.

(3) The sum payable under this section in respect of unpaid contributions of an employer on his own account to an occupational pension scheme or Personal Retirement Savings Account (within the meaning of the Pensions Act, 1990) [80] shall be the lesser of the following amounts—

(*a*) the balance of relevant contributions remaining unpaid on the date on which he became insolvent and payable by the employer on his own account to the scheme or Personal Retirement Savings Account (within the meaning of the Pensions Act, 1990) [81] in

---

[77] The words "or Personal Retirement Savings Account (within the meaning of the Pensions Act, 1990)" were inserted here by s. 121(9) of the Pensions Act, 1990. Section 121(9) was inserted in the 1990 Act by s. 3 of the Pensions (Amendment) Act, 2002.

[78] The words "Social Insurance Fund" were substituted for the words 'Redundancy and Employers' Insolvency Fund' by s. 28 of the Social Welfare Act, 1990.

[79] The words "or Personal Retirement Savings Account (within the meaning of the Pensions Act, 1990)" were inserted here by s. 121(9) of the Pensions Act, 1990. Section 121(9) was inserted in the 1990 Act by s. 3 of the Pensions (Amendment) Act, 2002.

[80] The words "or Personal Retirement Savings Account (within the meaning of the Pensions Act, 1990)" were inserted here by s. 121(9) of the Pensions Act, 1990. Section. 121(9) was inserted in the 1990 Act by s. 3 of the Pensions (Amendment) Act, 2002.

[81] The words "or Personal Retirement Savings Account (within the meaning of the Pensions Act, 1990)" were inserted here by s. 121(9) of the Pensions Act,

respect of the period of twelve months ending on the day immediately preceding that date,

(*b*) the amount certified by an actuary (or, where the employer is an undertaking which is insolvent under the laws, regulations and administrative procedures of another Member State in accordance with Article 2(1) of Council Directive 80/987/EEC of 20 October 1980 as amended by Article 1(2) of Directive 2002/74/EC of the European Parliament and of the Council of 23 September 2002 and the employees concerned are employed or habitually employed in the State, an actuary or person performing a similar task) [82] to be necessary for the purpose of meeting the liability of the scheme or Personal Retirement Savings Account (within the meaning of the Pensions Act, 1990) [83] on dissolution to pay the benefits provided by the scheme or Personal Retirement Savings Account (within the meaning of the Pensions Act, 1990) [84] to or in respect of the employees of the employer.

(4) Any sum payable under this section in respect of unpaid contributions on behalf of an employee shall not exceed the amount deducted from the pay of the employee in respect of the employee's contributions to the occupational pension scheme or Personal Retirement Savings Account (within the

---

1990. Section 121(9) was inserted in the 1990 Act by s. 3 of the Pensions (Amendment) Act, 2002.

[82] The parenthesised words (and the parentheses themselves) immediately preceding the footnote marker in the text above were inserted by Regulation 7 of the European Communities (Protection of Employees (Employers' Insolvency)) Regulations 2005 (Statutory Instrument No. 630 of 2005).

[83] The words "or Personal Retirement Savings Account (within the meaning of the Pensions Act, 1990)" were inserted here by s. 121(9) of the Pensions Act, 1990. Section 121(9) was inserted in the 1990 Act by s. 3 of the Pensions (Amendment) Act, 2002.

[84] The words "or Personal Retirement Savings Account (within the meaning of the Pensions Act, 1990)" were inserted here by s. 121(9) of the Pensions Act, 1990. Section 121(9) was inserted in the 1990 Act by s. 3 of the Pensions (Amendment) Act, 2002.

meaning of the Pensions Act, 1990) [85] during the period of twelve months ending on the day immediately preceding the date on which the employer became insolvent.

(5) The provisions of *subsections (6), (7)* and *(8)* of this section shall apply in a case where a relevant officer is either appointed or required to be appointed.

(6) Subject to *subsection (8)* of this section, the Minister shall not in a case which is a case referred to in *subsection (5)* of this section make any payment under this section in respect of unpaid relevant contributions until he has received a statement in the prescribed form from the relevant officer of the amount of relevant contributions which appear to have been unpaid on the date on which the employer became insolvent and to remain unpaid; and the relevant officer shall, on request made by the Minister provide him, as soon as reasonably practicable, with such a statement.

(7) Subject to *subsection (8)* of this section, an amount shall be taken to be payable under *subsection (3)* or to have been deducted in the manner referred to in *subsection (4)* of this section, only if it is certified by the relevant officer as being so payable, or to have been so deducted.

(8) Where—

(*a*) a period of six months has elapsed since the application for a payment under this section was received by the Minister, but no such payment has been made,

(*b*) the Minister is satisfied that a payment under this section should be made, and

(*c*) it appears to the Minister that there is likely to be further delay before he receives a statement or certificate about the contributions in question,

then, the Minister may, if the applicant so requests or, if the Minister thinks fit, without such a request, make a payment

---

[85] The words "or Personal Retirement Savings Account (within the meaning of the Pensions Act, 1990)" were inserted here by s. 121(9) of the Pensions Act, 1990. Section 121(9) was inserted in the 1990 Act by s. 3 of the Pensions (Amendment) Act, 2002.

under this section, notwithstanding the fact that no statement or certificate referred to in *subsection (6)* or *(7)* of this section has been received.

Minister may require certain information and documents.

8. —(1) Where an application is made to the Minister under *section 6* or *7* of this Act in respect of a debt owed or unpaid contributions to an occupational pensions scheme, the Minister may require—

(*a*) the employer concerned, or, in case a relevant officer is or is required to be appointed, that officer, to provide him with such information as the Minister may reasonably require for the purpose of determining whether the application is well-founded, and

(*b*) any person having the custody or control of any relevant record kept and retained pursuant to section 10 of the Holidays (Employees) Act, 1973, or any register, card, wages sheet, record of wages or other document which an officer of the Minister may reasonably consider to be relevant to the application to produce to such officer such document for examination by him.

(2) A requirement under this section shall be made by notice in writing given to the person on whom the requirement is imposed and may be varied or revoked by a subsequent notice so given.

Complaints to Tribunal.

9. —(1) A person who has applied for a payment under *section 6* of this Act of a debt described in *subparagraph (i), (ii)* or *(iv)* of *subsection (2) (a)* of that section may within the period of six weeks beginning on the day on which the decision of the Minister on the application was communicated to him or, if that is not reasonably practicable, within such further period as the Tribunal considers reasonable, present a complaint to the Tribunal that—

(*a*) the Minister has failed to make any such payment;

or

(*b*) any such payment made by the Minister is less than the amount which should have been paid.

(2) Any person who has applied for a payment to be made under *section 7* of this Act into the resources of a pension scheme may, within the period of six weeks beginning on the day on which the decision of the Minister on that application was communicated to him, or, if that is not reasonably practicable, within such further period as the Tribunal considers reasonable, present a complaint to the Tribunal that—

(*a*) the Minister has failed to make any such payment;

or

(*b*) any such payment made by him is less than the amount which should have been paid.

(3) Where a claim for payment is made under *section 6* or *7* of this Act and it appears to the Minister that a doubt exists as to whether or not such claim is allowable, either in whole or in part, he may refer any matter arising in connection with the claim to the Tribunal for a decision by it as regards the matter.

(4) Where on the hearing of a complaint presented under this section the Tribunal finds that the Minister is liable to make a payment under *section 6* or *7* of this Act, it shall make a declaration to that effect and shall specify in the declaration the amount of such payment.

(5) Subsection (14) of section 39 of the Act of 1967 shall apply to a decision of the Tribunal on any matter referred to it under this section as it applies to a decision of the Tribunal on a question referred to it under that section.

Transfer to Minister of certain rights and remedies.

10. —(1) Where, in pursuancc of *section 6* of this Act, the Minister makes any payment to an employee in respect of any debt to which that section applies, any rights and remedies of the employee in respect of that debt (or, if the Minister has paid only part of it, in respect of that part) shall, on the making of the payment, become rights and remedies of the Minister.

(2) Without prejudice to the generality of *subsection (1)* of this section, where rights and remedies become, by virtue of *subsection (1)* of this section, rights and remedies of the Minister, there shall be included amongst them any right to be paid in priority to all other debts under—

(*a*) [section 81(1) of the Bankruptcy Act, 1988] [86]; or

(*b*) section 285, as amended by section 10 of the Companies (Amendment) Act, 1982, of the Companies Act, 1963 [87],

and the Minister shall be entitled to be so paid in priority to any other unsatisfied claim of the employee concerned being a claim which, but for this subsection, would be payable to the employee in such priority; and in computing for the purposes of any of the provisions of the said section [81(1)] or the said section 285, as so amended, any limit on the amount of sums to be paid, any sums paid to the Minister shall be treated as if they had been paid to the employee.

(2A) Where the Minister makes a payment to an employee under section 6(2)(*a*)(iii)(II) (inserted by section 15 of the Redundancy Payments Act 2003) of this Act, that payment shall be recoverable by the Minister as a debt to be paid in priority to all other debts under— [88]

(*a*) section 81 of the Bankruptcy Act 1988, or

(*b*) section 285 (as amended by section 10 of the Companies (Amendment) Act 1982 and section 134 of the Companies Act 1990) of the Companies Act 1963,

and any amount of that payment which would, but for the limit set by section 6(4)(*a*) (as may be varied by regulations under section 11(5)), be payable to an employee, shall be treated for all purposes as if it were a payment required to be paid by virtue of an award under section 12(1) of the Act of 1973.

---

[86] The text of the Act originally referred to s. 4 of the Preferential Payments in Bankruptcy (Ireland) Act, 1889. However, the Preferential Payments in Bankruptcy (Ireland) Act, 1889 was repealed by s. 6 of the Bankruptcy Act, 1988. Under s. 81(1) of the Bankruptcy Act, 1988, any reference to s. 4 of the 1889 Act of the kind which was to be found here is to be construed as a reference to s. 81(1) of the 1988 Act.

[87] Section 285 of the 1963 Act has also been amended by s. 134 of the Companies Act, 1990 but this later amendment has not been reflected in any change in the manner of reference here to s. 285 of the 1963 Act.

[88] The entirety of s. 10(2A) was inserted by s. 15 of the Industrial Relations (Miscellaneous Provisions) Act 2004.

(3) Where in pursuance of *section 7* of this Act the Minister makes any payment into the resources of an occupational pension scheme in respect of any contributions to the scheme, any rights and remedies in respect of those contributions belonging to the persons competent to act in respect of the scheme shall, on the making of the payment, become rights and remedies of the Minister.

(4) Any sum recovered by the Minister in exercising any right or pursuing any remedy which is his by virtue of this section shall be paid into the Social Insurance Fund.[89]

11. —(1) The Minister may from time to time by order amend *section 3* of this Act so as to— Power to amend Act.

(*a*) extend the application of this Act to employees who are of a class or description specified in the order,[90]

(*b*) exclude from such application employees who are of a class or description so specified.

(2) The Minister may from time to time by order amend *section 6* of this Act so as to effect either or both of the following—

(*a*) substitute for the number of weeks specified in all or any of the following subsections, namely, *subsection (2) (a) (i)*, *(2) (a) (ii)* or *(2) (a) (iv)* a different number of weeks,

(*b*) substitute for the number of months specified in the definition of "the relevant period" contained in *subsection (9)* thereof a different number of months.

(3) The Minister may from time to time by order amend section 4 (2), as amended by section 17 of the Redundancy

---

[89] The words "Social Insurance Fund" were substituted for the words "Redundancy and Employers' Insolvency Fund" by s. 28 of the Social Welfare Act, 1990.

[90] See now the Protection of Employees (Employers' Insolvency) Act, 1984 (Amendment Order) Order, 1988 (S.I. No. 48 of 1988), the substantive content of which has been re-enacted as primary legislation by virtue of the substitution of s. 3 in the 1984 Act by Article 4 of the European Communities (Protection of Employees (Employers' Insolvency) Regulations 2005 (S.I. No. 630 of 2005)

Payments Act, 1979, and by *section 12* of this Act, of the Act of 1967, so as to vary the number of hours specified therein.[90a]

(4) The Minister may from time to time by order amend—

(*a*) paragraph (a) of section 3 (1), as amended by *section 13* of this Act, of the Act of 1973,

(*b*) paragraph 8, as amended by the said *section 13*, of the First Schedule to the Act of 1973,

so as to vary the number of hours specified in that paragraph.

(5) The Minister may by regulation amend *section 6* of this Act so as to vary the limit specified in *subsection (4) (a)*.[91]

(6) The reference in section 2 (4) of the Act of 1977 to the First Schedule to the Act of 1973 shall be construed as being a reference—

(*a*) in case an order under this section amending that Schedule is for the time being in forcc, that Schedule as amended by section 20 of the Act of 1977, by *section 13* of this Act and by the order,

(*b*) in case no such order is so in force, that Schedule as amended both by the said section 20 and the said *section 13*.

(7) Where an order under this section is proposed to be made, the Minister shall cause a draft of the order to be laid before each House of the Oireachtas and the order shall not be made until a resolution approving of the draft has been passed by each such House.

Amendment of section 4 of Act of 1967.

12. *(Substitution of text in s. 4(2) of the Redundancy Payments Act, 1967)* [92]

[90a] This provision, although it has never been amended, has been superseded, since s. 4(2) of the 1967 Act, as substituted by s. 4 of the Redundancy Payments Act, 2003, no longer specifies any number of hours.

[91] See now the Protection of Employees (Employers' Insolvency) (Variation of Limit) Regulations 2004 (S.I. No. 696 of 2004), Article 3(1) of which specifies a limit of €600.

[92] This amendment has now been superseded, since s. 4 of the Redundancy Payments Act 2003 substituted s. 4(2) of the Redundancy Payments Act, 1967 in its entirety.

13. *(Substitution in s. 3(1)(a) of the Minimum Notice and Terms of Employment Act, 1973)* [93]

Amendment of section 3 of and First Schedule to Act of 1973.

(Substitution in para. 8 of the First Schedule to the Minimum Notice and Terms of Employment Act, 1973) [94]

14. —Proceedings for an offence under *section 15* of this Act shall not be instituted except by or with the consent of the Minister.

Institution of proceedings for offence.

15. —(1) If any person, in relation to an application under *section 6* or *7* of this Act, whether for himself or for some other person,

Offences.

(*a*) knowingly makes any false statement or false representation or knowingly conceals a material fact, or

(*b*) produces or furnishes, or causes or knowingly allows to be produced or furnished, any document or information which he knows to be false in a material particular,

he shall be guilty of an offence.

(2) If a person refuses or wilfully neglects to provide any information or produce any document which he has been required to provide or produce by a notice under *section 8* of this Act he shall be guilty of an offence.

(3) If a person, in purporting to comply with a requirement of a notice under *section 8* of this Act, knowingly or recklessly makes any false statement he shall be guilty of an offence.

---

[93] This amendment was deprived of much of its significance on the coming into force of the Worker Protection (Regular Part-Time Employees) Act, 1991, which extended the protection of much of Irish employment protection legislation to so-called regular part-time employees. The 1991 Act was subsequently repealed by s. 5 of the Protection of Employees (Part-Time Work) Act, 2001, but the effect of the coming into force of the 2001 Act itself, which provides for the application of employment protection legislation to a far wider category of part-time employees than did the 1991 Act, has been to render this amendment (and indeed the provision which it amended) entirely obsolete, even if neither the amendment nor the amended provision has ever been repealed.

[94] See previous footnote.

(4) A person who is guilty of an offence under this section shall be liable on summary conviction to a fine not exceeding [€634.87]. [95]

(5) [Subsections (7) and (8) of section 251 of the Social Welfare Consolidation Act 2005] [96] shall apply in relation to an offence under this section which is committed by a body corporate as they apply to offences under [Part 9 of the Social Welfare Consolidation Act 2005] [97] which are so committed.

---

[95] The amount specified in the Act is £500, the equivalent in punts of the above amount. Under Article 14 of Council Regulation (EC) No 974/98 of 3 May 1998 on the introduction of the euro (read in conjunction with Article 1 of the same instrument), references made in legislative and statutory provisions existing on 31 December 2001 to units of Irish currency as they existed before the start of the third stage of economic and monetary union are to be read as references to the euro unit according to the respective conversion rates (with the rounding rules laid down in Regulation (EC) No. 1103/97 of 17 June 1997 on certain provisions relating to the introduction of the euro applying).

[96] The text of s.15 (5) originally began with a reference to subsections (8) and (9) of section 266 of the Social Welfare (Consolidation) Act, 1981, but these provisions were repealed by s. 300 of the Social Welfare (Consolidation) Act, 1993 and replaced by s. 213(7) and s. 213(8) of the 1993 Act. Subsequently, these provisions in turn, *inter alia*, were repealed by s. 360 of the Social Welfare Consolidation Act 2005 with, again, equivalent new provisions being enacted in the form of s. 251(7) and 251(8) of the 2005 Act. The effect of s. 361(b) of the Social Welfare Consolidation Act 2005, however, appears to be that references to provisions of a repealed enactment such as those originally found in s. 15(5) of the 1984 Act are now to be read as references to the corresponding provisions of the 2005 Act. Even if this is not the effect of s. 361(b), the matter will in any case come within the more general provisions of s. 26 (2) of the Interpretation Act 2005, according to which, where an enactment is repealed and reenacted, with or without modification, by another enactment, a reference in any other enactment to the former enactment shall, with respect to a subsequent transaction, matter or thing, be read as a reference to the provisions of the new enactment relating to the same subject-matter as that of the former enactment. The appropriate references have therefore been substituted in the text above.

[97] The parenthesised words in the latter part of s. 15(5) originally referred to Part V of the Social Welfare (Consolidation) Act, 1981, the provisions of which were repealed by s. 300 of the Social Welfare (Consolidation) Act, 1993 and replaced by other provisions of the 1993 Act. Subsequently, these provisions in turn, *inter alia*, were repealed by s. 360 of the Social Welfare Consolidation Act 2005 with, again, equivalent new provisions being enacted, on this occasion in Part 9 of the 2005 Act. The effect of

(6) [Subsection (9) of section 251 of the Social Welfare Consolidation Act 2005] [98] shall be construed and have effect as if the reference therein to proceedings under [Part 9 of the Social Welfare Consolidation Act 2005] [99] contained a reference to proceedings under this section.

16. —(1) The Minister may make regulations for giving effect to this Act. Regulations.

---

s. 361(b) of the Social Welfare Consolidation Act 2005, however, appears to be that a reference to provisions of a repealed enactment such as that originally found in the latter part of s. 15(5) of the 1984 Act is now to be read as a reference to the corresponding provisions of the 2005 Act. Even if this is not the effect of s. 361(b), the matter will in any case come within the more general provisions of s. 26 (2) of the Interpretation Act 2005, according to which, where an enactment is repealed and reenacted, with or without modification, by another enactment, a reference in any other enactment to the former enactment shall, with respect to a subsequent transaction, matter or thing, be read as a reference to the provisions of the new enactment relating to the same subject-matter as that of the former enactment. The appropriate reference has therefore been substituted in the text above.

[98] The opening words of s. 15(6) originally referred to subsection (10) of section 266 of the Social Welfare (Consolidation) Act, 1981, but this provision was repealed by s. 300 of the Social Welfare (Consolidation) Act, 1993 and an equivalent provision adopted in the shape of s. 213(9) of the 1993 Act. Subsequently, these provisions in turn, *inter alia*, were repealed by s. 360 of the Social Welfare Consolidation Act 2005 with, again, an equivalent new provision being enacted, in the shape of s. 251(9) of the 2005 Act. The effect of s. 361(b) of the Social Welfare Consolidation Act 2005 appears to be that a reference to provisions of a repealed enactment such as that originally found in s. 15(6) of the 1984 Act is now to be read as a reference to the corresponding provisions of the 2005 Act. Even if this is not the effect of s. 361(b), the matter will in any case come within the more general provisions of s. 26 (2) of the Interpretation Act 2005, according to which, where an enactment is repealed and reenacted, with or without modification, by another enactment, a reference in any other enactment to the former enactment shall, with respect to a subsequent transaction, matter or thing, be read as a reference to the provisions of the new enactment relating to the same subject-matter as that of the former enactment. The appropriate reference has therefore been substituted in the text above.

[99] The parenthesised words in the latter part of s. 15(6) originally referred to Part V of the Social Welfare (Consolidation) Act, 1981, the provisions of which were repealed by s. 300 of the Social Welfare (Consolidation) Act, 1993 and replaced by other provisions of the 1993 Act. Subsequently, these provisions in turn, *inter alia*, were repealed by s. 360 of the Social

(2) Without prejudice to the generality of *subsection (1)* of this section, regulations under this section may make provision requiring an applicant under *section 6* or *7* of this Act to make the application within the prescribed time.

(3) The Minister may make regulations for prescribing any matter referred to in this Act as prescribed.[100]

(4) Regulations under this section may apply to applications under this Act generally or to such applications which are of a prescribed class or description.

(5) Every regulation made under this Act by the Minister shall be laid before both Houses of the Oireachtas as soon as may be after it is made and, if a resolution annulling the regulation is passed by either such House within the next twenty-one days on which that House has sat after the regulation is laid before it, the regulation shall be annulled accordingly but without prejudice to the validity of anything previously done thereunder.

Expenses, etc. **17.**—(1) The expenses incurred by the Minister in the administration of this Act shall, to such extent as may be sanctioned by the Minister for Finance, be paid out of moneys provided by the Oireachtas.[101]

Welfare Consolidation Act 2005 with, again, equivalent new provisions being enacted, on this occasion in Part 9 of the 2005 Act. The effect of s. 361(b) of the Social Welfare Consolidation Act 2005 appears to be that references to provisions of a repealed enactment such as that originally found in the latter part of s. 15(6) of the 1984 Act are now to be read as references to the corresponding provisions of the 2005 Act. Even if this is not the effect of s. 361(b), the matter will in any case come within the more general provisions of s. 26 (2) of the Interpretation Act 2005, according to which, where an enactment is repealed and reenacted, with or without modification, by another enactment, a reference in any other enactment to the former enactment shall, with respect to a subsequent transaction, matter or thing, be read as a reference to the provisions of the new enactment relating to the same subject-matter as that of the former enactment. The appropriate reference has therefore been substituted in the text above.

[100] See now the Protection of Employees (Employers' Insolvency) (Forms and Procedure) Regulations 2005 (S.I. No 682 of 2005).

[101] See now also in this regard, s. 5(6) of the Social Welfare Consolidation Act 2005. See regarding the financing of payments made out of the Social Insurance Fund under, *inter alia*, the Protection of Employees

(2) The Minister may pay out of the Social Insurance Fund [102] to a relevant officer or a person to whom an appointment under *section 5* of this Act relates, in respect of the functions performed by him under this Act, such fees as the Minister shall, with the concurrence of the Minister for Finance, determine.

18. —(1) This Act may be cited as the Protection of Employees (Employers' Insolvency) Act, 1984.[103]

Short title and collective citations.

(2) *Section 12* of this Act and the Redundancy Payments Acts, 1967 to 1979, may be cited together as the Redundancy Payments Acts, 1967 to 1984.[104]

(Employers' Insolvency) Acts, s. 6 of the Social Welfare Consolidation Act 2005 (replacing s. 6 of the Social Welfare (Consolidation) Act, 1993 which was repealed by s. 360 of the 2005 Act).

[102] The words "Social Insurance Fund" were substituted for the words 'Redundancy and Employers' Insolvency Fund' by s. 28 of the Social Welfare Act, 1990.

[103] Note that the Protection of Employees (Employers' Insolvency) Act, 1984,s. 28 of the Social Welfare Act, 1990, the Protection of Employees (Part-Time Work) Act, 2001 (insofar as it relates to the foregoing legislation), s. 15 of the Industrial Relations (Miscellaneous Provisions) Act 2004 (insofar as it relates to the foregoing legislation) and s. 17(3) of the same Act may be cited together as the Protection of Employees (Employers' Insolvency) Acts 1984 to 2004. (See s. 1(5) of the Social Welfare Act, 1990, s. 1(3) of the Protection of Employees (Part-Time Work) Act, 2001 and s. 17(3) of the Industrial Relations (Miscellaneous Provisions) Act 2004).

[104] Note that the Redundancy Payments Act, 1967, the Redundancy Payments Act, 1971, the Redundancy Payments Act, 1973, the Redundancy Payments Act, 1979, s. 12 of the Protection of Employees (Employers' Insolvency) Act, 1984, ss. 26, 27 and 29 of the Social Welfare Act, 1990, s. 39 (other than sub-s. (2)) of the Social Welfare Act, 1991 (although apparently by oversight no mention is made of s. 39 of the 1991 Act in any subsequent statute included in this list), the Protection of Employees (Part-Time Work) Act, 2001 (insofar as it relates to the foregoing legislation, apart from s. 39 of the 1991 Act) and the Redundancy Payments Act 2003 may be cited together as the Redundancy Payments Acts 1967 to 2003.

See in this regard, in addition to s. 18(2) of the Protection of Employees (Employers' Insolvency) Act, 1984, s. 20(2) of the Redundancy Payments Act, 1971, s. 2(2) of the Redundancy Payments Act, 1973, s. 21(2) of the Redundancy Payments Act, 1979, s. 1(4) of the Social Welfare Act, 1990, s. 1(3) of the Social Welfare Act, 1991, s. 1(4) of the Protection of

(3) *Section 13* of this Act and the Act of 1973 may be cited together as the Minimum Notice and Terms of Employment Acts, 1973 and 1984.[104a]

Employees (Part-Time Work) Act, 2001 and s. 17(3) of the Redundancy Payments Act 2003.

[104a] Note that the Minimum Notice and Terms of Employment Act, 1973, s. 13 of the Protection of Employees (Employers' Insolvency) Act, 1984, the Protection of Employees (Part-Time Work) Act, 2001 (insofar as it relates to the foregoing legislation) and Part 7 of the Civil Service Regulation (Amendment) Act 2005 may be cited together as the Minimum Notice and Terms of Employment Acts 1973 to 2005 and are required to be construed together as one. (See s. 18(3) of the Protection of Employees (Employers' Insolvency) Act, 1984, s. 1(2) of the Protection of Employees (Part-Time Work) Act, 2001, and s. 1(4) of the Civil Service Regulation (Amendment) Act 2005.)

COUNCIL DIRECTIVE 80/987/EEC

of 20 October 1980

on the protection of employees in the event of the insolvency of their employer [1]

(Official Journal of the European Communities 28.10.1980 L 283/23)

THE COUNCIL OF THE EUROPEAN COMMUNITIES,

Having regard to the Treaty establishing the European Economic Community, and in particular Article 100 thereof,

Having regard to the proposal from the Commission ([1]),

Having regard to the opinion of the European Parliament ([2]),

Having regard to the opinion of the Economic and Social Committee ([3]),

([1]) OJ No C 135, 9.6.1978, p. 2.
([2]) OJ No C 39, 12.2.1979, p. 26.
([3]) OJ No C 105, 26.4.1979, p. 15.

Whereas it is necessary to provide for the protection of employees in the event of the insolvency of their employer, in particular in order to guarantee payment of their outstanding claims, while taking account of the need for balanced economic and social development in the Community;

Whereas differences still remain between the Member States as regards the extent of the protection of employees in this respect; whereas efforts should be directed towards reducing these differences, which can have a direct effect on the functioning of the common market;

Whereas the approximation of laws in this field should, therefore, be promoted while the improvement within the meaning of Article 117 of the Treaty is maintained;

[1] The original title of this Directive was replaced with the present version by Article 1 (1) of Directive 2002/74/EC of the European Parliament and of the Council of 23 September 2002 amending Council Directive 80/987/EEC on the approximation of the laws of the Member States relating to the protection of employees in the event of the insolvency of their employer (O.J. 8.10.2002 L 270/10).

Whereas as a result of the geographical situation and the present job structures in that area, the labour market in Greenland is fundamentally different from that of the other areas of the Community;

Whereas to the extent that the Hellenic Republic is to become a member of the European Economic Community on 1 January 1981 in accordance with the Act concerning the Conditions of Accession of the Hellenic Republic and the Adjustments to the Treaties, it is appropriate to stipulate in the Annex to the Directive under the heading "Greece", those categories of employees whose claims may be excluded in accordance with Article 1 (2) of the Directive,

HAS ADOPTED THIS DIRECTIVE:

SECTION I [2]

Scope and definitions

Article 1

1. This Directive shall apply to employees' claims arising from contracts of employment or employment relationships and existing against employers who are in a state of insolvency within the meaning of Article 2(1).

2. Member States may, by way of exception, exclude claims by certain categories of employee from the scope of this Directive, by virtue of the existence of other forms of guarantee if it is established that these offer the persons concerned a degree of protection equivalent to that resulting from this Directive.

3. Where such provision already applies in their national legislation, Member States may continue to exclude from the scope of this Directive:

(a) domestic servants employed by a natural person;

(b) share-fishermen.

[2] As replaced in its entirety by Article 1(2) of Directive 2002/74/EC of the European Parliament and of the Council of 23 September 2002.

Article 2

1. For the purposes of this Directive, an employer shall be deemed to be in a state of insolvency where a request has been made for the opening of collective proceedings based on insolvency of the employer, as provided for under the laws, regulations and administrative provisions of a Member State, and involving the partial or total divestment of the employer's assets and the appointment of a liquidator or a person performing a similar task, and the authority which is competent pursuant to the said provisions has:

(a) either decided to open the proceedings, or

(b) established that the employer's undertaking or business has been definitively closed down and that the available assets are insufficient to warrant the opening of the proceedings.

2. This Directive is without prejudice to national law as regards the definition of the terms "employee", "employer", "pay", "right conferring immediate entitlement" and "right conferring prospective entitlement".

However, the Member States may not exclude from the scope of this Directive:

(a) part-time employees within the meaning of Directive 97/81/EC;

(b) workers with a fixed-term contract within the meaning of Directive 1999/70/EC;

(c) workers with a temporary employment relationship within the meaning of Article 1(2) of Directive 91/383/EEC.

3. Member States may not set a minimum duration for the contract of employment or the employment relationship in order for workers to qualify for claims under this Directive.

4. This Directive does not prevent Member States from extending workers' protection to other situations of insolvency, for example where payments have been de facto stopped on a permanent basis, established by proceedings different from those mentioned in paragraph 1 as provided for under national law.

Such procedures shall not however create a guarantee obligation for the institutions of the other Member States in the cases referred to in Section IIIa.

SECTION II

Provisions concerning guarantee institutions

Article 3 [3]

Member States shall take the measures necessary to ensure that guarantee institutions guarantee, subject to Article 4, payment of employees' outstanding claims resulting from contracts of employment or employment relationships, including, where provided for by national law, severance pay on termination of employment relationships.

The claims taken over by the guarantee institution shall be the outstanding pay claims relating to a period prior to and/or, as applicable, after a given date determined by the Member States.

Article 4 [4]

1. Member States shall have the option to limit thc liability of the guarantee institutions referred to in Article 3.

2. When Member States exercise the option referred to in paragraph 1, they shall specify the length of the period for which outstanding claims are to be met by the guarantee institution. However, this may not be shorter than a period covering the remuneration of the last three months of the employment relationship prior to and/or after the date referred to in Article 3. Member States may include this minimum period of three months in a reference period with a duration of not less than six months.

Member States having a reference period of not less than 18 months may limit the period for which outstanding claims are met by the guarantee institution to eight weeks. In this case, those periods which are most favourable to the employee are used for the calculation of the minimum period.

3. Furthermore, Member States may set ceilings on the payments made by the guarantee institution. These ceilings must not fall below a level which is socially compatible with the social objective of this Directive.

When Member States exercise this option, they shall inform the Commission of the methods used to set the ceiling.

---

[3] As replaced by Article 1(3) of Directive 2002/74/EC of the European Parliament and of the Council of 23 September 2002.

[4] As replaced by Article 1(3) of Directive 2002/74/EC of the European Parliament and of the Council of 23 September 2002.

Article 5

Member States shall lay down detailed rules for the organization, financing and operation of the guarantee institutions, complying with the following principles in particular:

(a) the assets of the institutions shall be independent of the employers' operating capital and be inaccessible to proceedings for insolvency;

(b) employers shall contribute to financing, unless it is fully covered by the public authorities;

(c) the institutions' liabilities shall not depend on whether or not obligations to contribute to financing have been fulfilled.

SECTION III

Provisions concerning social security

Article 6

Member States may stipulate that Articles 3, 4 and 5 shall not apply to contributions due under national statutory social security schemes or under supplementary company or inter-company pension schemes outside the national statutory social security schemes.

Article 7

Member States shall take the measures necessary to ensure that non-payment of compulsory contributions due from the employer, before the onset of his insolvency, to their insurance institutions under national statutory social security schemes does not adversely affect employees' benefit entitlement in respect of these insurance institutions inasmuch as the employees' contributions were deducted at source from the remuneration paid.

Article 8

Member States shall ensure that the necessary measures are taken to protect the interests of employees and of persons having already left the employer's undertaking or business at the date of the onset of the employer's insolvency in respect of rights conferring on them immediate or prospective entitlement to old-age benefits, including survivors' benefits, under supplementary company or inter-company pension schemes outside the national statutory social security schemes.

SECTION IIIa [5]

Provisions concerning transnational situations

Article 8a

1. When an undertaking with activities in the territories of at least two Member States is in a state of insolvency within the meaning of Article 2(l), the institution responsible for meeting employees' outstanding claims shall be that in the Member State in whose territory they work or habitually work.

2. The extent of employees' rights shall be determined by the law governing the competent guarantee institution.

3. Member States shall take the measures necessary to ensure that, in the cases referred to in paragraph 1, decisions taken in the context of insolvency proceedings referred to in Article 2(1), which have been requested in another Member State, are taken into account when determining the employer's state of insolvency within the meaning of this Directive.

Article 8b

1. For the purposes of implementing Article 8a, Member States shall make provision for the sharing of relevant information between their competent administrative authorities and/or the guarantee institutions mentioned in Article 3, making it possible in particular to inform the guarantee institution responsible for meeting the employees' outstanding claims.

2. Member States shall notify the Commission and the other Member States of the contact details of their competent administrative authorities and/or guarantee institutions. The Commission shall make these communications publicly accessible.

---

[5] As inserted in its entirety by Article 1(4) of Directive 2002/74/EC of the European Parliament and of the Council of 23 September 2002.

SECTION IV

General and final provisions

Article 9

This Directive shall not affect the option of Member States to apply or introduce laws, regulations or administrative provisions which are more favourable to employees.

Implementation of this Directive shall not under any circumstances be sufficient grounds for a regression in relation to the current situation in the Member States and in relation to the general level of protection of workers in the area covered by it.[6]

Article 10

This Directive shall not affect the option of Member States:

(a) to take the measures necessary to avoid abuses;

(b) to refuse or reduce the liability referred to in Article 3 or the guarantee obligation referred to in Article 7 if it appears that fulfilment of the obligation is unjustifiable because of the existence of special links between the employee and the employer and of common interests resulting in collusion between them.

(c) to refuse or reduce the liability referred to in Article 3 or the guarantee obligation referred to in Article 7 in cases where the employee, on his or her own or together with his or her close relatives, was the owner of an essential part of the employer's undertaking or business and had a considerable influence on its activities.[7]

Article 10a [8]

Member States shall notify the Commission and the other Member States of the types of national insolvency proceedings falling within the

---

[6] This paragraph as inserted in Article 9 by Article 1(5) of Directive 2002/74/EC of the European Parliament and of the Council of 23 September 2002.

[7] Point (c) was added to Article 10 by Article 1(6) of Directive 2002/74/EC of the European Parliament and of the Council of 23 September 2002.

[8] Inserted by Article 1(7) of Directive 2002/74/EC of the European Parliament and of the Council of 23 September 2002.

scope of this Directive, and of any amendments relating thereto. The Commission shall publish these communications in the *Official Journal of the European Communities*.

Article 11

1. Member States shall bring into force the laws, regulations and administrative provisions necessary to comply with this Directive within 36 months of its notification. They shall forthwith inform the Commission thereof.

2. Member States shall communicate to the Commission the texts of the laws, regulations and administrative provisions which they adopt in the field governed by this Directive.

Article 12

Within 18 months of the expiry of the period of 36 months laid down in Article 11 (1), Member States shall forward all relevant information to the Commission in order to enable it to draw up a report on the application of this Directive for submission to the Council.

Article 13

This Directive is addressed to the Member States.

Done at Luxembourg, 20 October 1980.

For the Council

The President

J. SANTER [9]

---

[9] Article 1(8) of Directive 2002/74/EC of the European Parliament and of the Council of 23 September 2002 deleted the Annex originally attached to the Directive listing various categories of employee whose claims could be excluded from its scope, in accordance with the original version of Article 1 (2).

UNFAIR DISMISSALS (AMENDMENT) ACT, 1993

Number 23 *of* 1993

ARRANGEMENT OF SECTIONS

Section

ACTS REFERRED TO

Courts Act, 1981	1981, No. 11
Employment Agency Act, 1971	1971, No. 27
Income Tax Acts	
Industrial Relations Acts, 1946 to 1990	
Minimum Notice and Terms of Employment Act, 1973	1973, No. 4
Redundancy Payments Act, 1967	1967, No. 21
Social Welfare Acts, 1981 to 1993	
Trade Union Act, 1941	1941, No. 22
Unfair Dismissals Act, 1977	1977, No. 10
Unfair Dismissals Acts, 1977 and 1991	
Vocational Education Act, 1930	1930, No. 29

Number 22 *of* 1993

UNFAIR DISMISSALS (AMENDMENT) ACT, 1993

AN ACT TO AMEND AND EXTEND THE UNFAIR DISMISSALS ACTS, 1977 AND 1991, AND TO PROVIDE FOR RELATED MATTERS. [14*th July*, 1993]

BE IT ENACTED BY THE OIREACHTAS AS FOLLOWS:

1. —(1) In this Act "the Principal Act" means the Unfair Dismissals Act, 1977. Interpretation.

(2) In this Act, a reference to any enactment shall, unless the context otherwise requires, be construed as a reference to that enactment as amended, adapted or extended by or under any subsequent enactment including this Act.

2. *(Substitution in s. 1 of the Unfair Dismissals Act, 1977)* Amendment of section 1 of Principal Act.

(Substitution in s. 1 of the Unfair Dismissals Act, 1977)

(Insertion of s. 1(2) and s. 1(3) of the Unfair Dismissals Act, 1977)

3. —*(Substitution of s. 2(1)(j) of the Unfair Dismissals Act, 1977)* Amendment of section 2 of Principal Act.

(Insertion in. 2(2) of the Unfair Dismissals Act, 1977)

(Insertion of s. 2(5) of the Unfair Dismissals Act, 1977)

4. —*(Substitution of s. 5(1), s. 5(2) and s. 5(3) of the Unfair Dismissals Act, 1977)* Amendment of section 5 of Principal Act.

5. —*(Substitution of s. 6(2)(e) of the Unfair Dismissals Act, 1977)* Amendment of section 6 of Principal Act.

(Insertion of s. 6(2)(ee) of the Unfair Dismissals Act, 1977)

(Insertion of s. 6(2)(eee) of the Unfair Dismissals Act, 1977)

(Substitution of s. 6(7) of the Unfair Dismissals Act, 1977)

Amendment of section 7 of Principal Act.

6.—*(Substitution of s.7(1)(c) of the Unfair Dismissals Act, 1977)*

(Deletion in s. 7(2)(c) of the Unfair Dismissals Act, 1977)

(Substitution of s. 7(1)(d) of the Unfair Dismissals Act, 1977)

(Insertion of s. 7(1)(e) and 7(1)(f) of the Unfair Dismissals Act, 1977)

(Insertion of s. 7(2A) of the Unfair Dismissals Act, 1977)

Amendment of section 8 of Principal Act.

7.—*(Insertion of s. 8(1A) in the Unfair Dismissals Act, 1977)*

(Substitution of s. 8(2), s. 8(3) and s. 8(4) of the Unfair Dismissals Act, 1977)

(Deletion in s. 8(5) of the Unfair Dismissals Act, 1977)

(Substitution of s. 8(5)(b) of the Unfair Dismissals Act, 1977)

(Insertion in s. 8(9) in the Unfair Dismissals Act, 1977)

(Substitution of s. 8(10) of the Unfair Dismissals Act, 1977)

(Insertion of s. 8(11) and s. 8(12) of the Unfair Dismissals Act, 1977)

Amendment of section 9 of Principal Act.

8. — *(Substitution in s. 9(2) of the Unfair Dismissals Act, 1977)*

9. — *(Substitution of s. 14(3) and s. 14(4) of the Unfair Dismissals Act, 1977)*

Amendment of section 14 of Principal Act.

10. — *(Substitution of s. 15(2) and s. 15(3) of the Unfair Dismissals Act, 1977)*

Amendment of section 15 of Principal Act.

Appeals from, and enforcement of determinations of, Tribunal.

11. —(1) A party concerned may appeal to the Circuit Court from a determination of the Tribunal in relation to a claim for redress under the Principal Act within 6 weeks from the date on which the determination is communicated to the parties.

(2) (*a*) Where, in proceedings under this section, the Circuit Court finds that an employee is entitled to redress under the Principal Act, it shall order the employer concerned to make to the employee the appropriate redress.

(*b*) If an employer fails to comply with an order of the Circuit Court under *paragraph (a)* of this subsection ("the former order"), the Circuit Court shall, on application to it in that behalf by—

(i) the employee concerned, or

(ii) if he considers it appropriate to make the application having regard to all the circumstances, the Minister,

make—

(I) such order for the enforcement of the former order as it considers appropriate having regard to all the circumstances, or

(II) if the former order directed the re-instatement or re-engagement of the employee concerned and that Court considers it appropriate to do so having regard to all the circumstances, in lieu of making an order under *subparagraph (I)*, make an order directing the employer, in lieu of reinstating or re-engaging the employee, to pay compensation to him under section 7 (1) (*c*) of the Principal Act and giving such directions for the enforcement of the latter order as it considers appropriate having regard to all the circumstances.

(3) (*a*) If an employer fails to carry out in accordance with its terms a determination of the Tribunal in relation to a claim for redress under the Principal Act within 6 weeks from the date on which the determination is communicated to the parties, the Circuit Court shall, on application to it in that behalf by—

(i) the employee concerned, or

(ii) if he considers it appropriate to make the application having regard to all the circumstances, the Minister,

without hearing the employer or any evidence (other than in relation to the matters aforesaid) make—

(I) an order directing the employer to carry out the determination in accordance with its terms, or

(II) if the determination directed the re-instatement or re-engagement of the employee concerned and that Court considers it appropriate to do so having regard to all the circumstances, in lieu of making an order under *subparagraph (I)*, make an order directing the employer, in lieu of reinstating or re-engaging the employee, to pay compensation to him under section 7 (1) (*c*) of the Principal Act and giving such directions for the enforcement of the latter order as it considers appropriate having regard to all the circumstances.

(*b*) In *paragraph (a)* of this subsection the reference to a determination of the Tribunal is a reference to such a determination in relation to which, at the expiration of the time for bringing an appeal against it, no such appeal has been brought, or if such an appeal has been brought it has been abandoned and the reference to the date on which the determination is communicated to the parties shall, in a case where such an appeal is abandoned, be construed as a reference to the date of such abandonment.

(4) The Circuit Court may, in an order under this section, if in all the circumstances it considers it appropriate to do so—

(*a*) in case the order relates to the payment of compensation, direct the employer concerned to pay to the employee concerned interest on the compensation at the rate referred to in section 22 of the Courts Act, 1981, in respect of the whole or any part of the period beginning 6 weeks after the date on which the determination of the Tribunal is communicated to the parties and ending on the date of the order, and

(*b*) in case the order relates to re-instatement or re-engagement, direct the employer to pay to the employee compensation of such amount as it considers reasonable in respect of the loss of wages suffered by the employee by reason of the failure of the employer to comply with the determination aforesaid.

(5) Proceedings under this section shall be heard in the county where the employer concerned ordinarily resides or carries on any profession, business or occupation.

Evidence of failure to attend before or give evidence or produce documents to Tribunal.

12. —A document purporting to be signed by the chairman or a vice-chairman of the Tribunal stating that—

(*a*) a person named in the document was, by a notice under paragraph (*c*) of section 39 (17) of the Redundancy Payments Act, 1967, required to attend before the Tribunal on a day and at a time and place specified in the document, to give evidence or produce a document,

(*b*) a sitting of the Tribunal was held on that day and at that time and place, and

(*c*) the person did not attend before the Tribunal in pursuance of the notice or, as the case may be, having so attended, refused to give evidence or refused or failed to produce the document, shall, in a prosecution of the person under paragraph (*e*) of the said section 39 (17), be evidence of the matters so stated without further proof.

Employment agencies.

13. —Where, whether before, on or after the commencement of this Act, an individual agrees with another person, who is carrying on the business of an employment agency within the meaning of the Employment Agency Act, 1971, and is acting in the course of that business, to do or perform personally any work or service for a third person (whether or not the third person is a party to the contract and whether or not the third person pays the wages or salary of the individual in respect of the work or service), then, for the purposes of the Principal Act, as respects a dismissal occurring after such commencement—

(*a*) the individual shall be deemed to be an employee employed by the third person under a contract of employment,

(*b*) if the contract was made before such commencement, it shall be deemed to have been made upon such commencement, and

(*c*) any redress under the Principal Act for unfair dismissal of the individual under the contract shall be awarded against the third person.

Dismissal of persons during apprenticeship, training, etc., or during first year of service, for trade union membership or activities.

14. —Sections 2 (1), 3 and 4 and subsections (1) and (6) of section 6 of the Principal Act shall not apply to a person referred to in paragraph (*a*) or (*b*) of the said section 2 (1) or the said section 3 or 4 who is dismissed if the dismissal results wholly or mainly from one or more of the matters referred to in subsection (2) (*a*) of the said section 6.

Amendment of First Schedule to Minimum Notice and Terms of Employment Act, 1973.

15. — *(Substitution of para. 7 of the First Schedule to the Minimum Notice and Terms of Employment Act, 1973)*

16. —Section 10 of the Principal Act is hereby repealed. Repeal.

17. —(1) This Act may be cited as the Unfair Dismissals (Amendment) Act, 1993. Short title, collective citation, construction, commencement and application.

(2) The Unfair Dismissals Acts, 1977 and 1991, and this Act may be cited together as the Unfair Dismissals Acts, 1977 to 1993.[1]

(3) The Unfair Dismissals Acts, 1977 and 1991, and this Act shall be construed together as one.[2]

(4) This Act shall come into operation on the 1st day of October, 1993.

(5) This Act shall have effect as respects dismissals occurring after the commencement of this Act.

---

[1] Under s. 1(6) of the Protection of Employees (Part-Time Work) Act, 2001, insofar as the 2001 Act relates to the Unfair Dismissals Acts, 1977 to 1993, those Acts and the 2001 Act may be cited together as the Unfair Dismissals Acts, 1977 to 2001. Under s. 1(3) of the Civil Service Regulation (Amendment) Act 2005, the Unfair Dismissals Acts, 1977 to 2001 and Part 6 of that Act may be cited together as the Unfair Dismissals Acts 1977 to 2005.

[2] Under s. 1(6) of the Protection of Employees (Part-Time Work) Act, 2001, insofar as the 2001 Act relates to the Unfair Dismissals Acts, 1977 to 1993, those Acts and the 2001 Act are required to be construed together as one. Under s. 1(3) of the Civil Service Regulation (Amendment) Act 2005, the Unfair Dismissals Acts, 1977 to 2001 and Part 6 of that Act are required to be construed together as one.

TERMS OF EMPLOYMENT (INFORMATION) ACT, 1994

Number 5 *of* 1994

ARRANGEMENT OF SECTIONS

ACTS REFERRED TO

Companies Act, 1963	1963, No. 33
Courts Act, 1981	1981, No. 11
Employment Agency Act, 1971	1971, No. 27
Local Government Act, 1941	1941, No. 23
Minimum Notice and Terms of Employment Act, 1973	1973, No. 4
Redundancy Payments Act, 1967	1967, No. 21
Unfair Dismissals Act, 1977	1977, No. 10

Number 5 *of* 1994

TERMS OF EMPLOYMENT (INFORMATION) ACT, 1994

AN ACT TO PROVIDE FOR THE IMPLEMENTATION OF DIRECTIVE NO. 91/533/EEC OF 14 OCTOBER, 1991 OF THE COUNCIL OF THE EUROPEAN COMMUNITIES ON AN EMPLOYER'S OBLIGATION TO INFORM EMPLOYEES OF THE CONDITIONS APPLICABLE TO THE CONTRACT OR EMPLOYMENT RELATIONSHIP, TO AMEND THE MINIMUM NOTICE AND TERMS OF EMPLOYMENT ACT, 1973, AND TO PROVIDE FOR RELATED MATTERS. [*5th April*, 1994]

BE IT ENACTED BY THE OIREACHTAS AS FOLLOWS:

1. —(1) In this Act— Interpretation.

"the Act of 1973" means the Minimum Notice and Terms of Employment Act, 1973;

"the Council Directive" means Council Directive No. 91/533/EEC of 14 October, 1991[1]

[1] O.J. No. L 288, 18.10.91, p. 32.

"contract of employment" means—

(*a*) a contract of service or apprenticeship, and

(*b*) any other contract whereby an individual agrees with another person, who is carrying on the business of an employment agency within the meaning of the Employment Agency Act, 1971, and is acting in the course of that business, to do or perform personally any work or service for a third person (whether or not the third person is a party to the contract),

whether the contract is express or implied and if express, whether it is oral or in writing;

"employee" means a person who has entered into or works under (or, where the employment has ceased, entered into or worked under) a contract of employment and references, in relation to an employer, to an employee shall be construed as references to an employee employed by that employer; and for the purposes of this Act, a person holding office under, or in the service of, the State (including a member of the Garda Síochána or the Defence Forces) or otherwise as a civil servant, within the meaning of the Civil Service Regulation Act, 1956, shall be deemed to be an employee employed by the State or Government, as the case may be, and an officer or servant of a local authority for the purposes of the Local Government Act, 1941, a harbour authority, a health board or a vocational education committee shall be deemed to be an employee employed by the authority, board or committee, as the case may be;

"employer", in relation to an employee, means the person with whom the employee has entered into or for whom the employee works under (or, where the employment has ceased, entered into or worked under) a contract of employment subject to the qualification that the person who under a contract of employment referred to in paragraph (b) of the definition of "contract of employment is liable to pay the wages of the individual concerned in respect of the work or service concerned shall be deemed to be the individual's employer;

"the Minister" [1] means the [Minister for Enterprise, Trade and Employment];

[1] The text of the Act originally referred to the Minister for Enterprise and Employment. However, under Article 4 of the Enterprise and Employment (Alteration of Name of Department and Title of Minister) Order, 1997 (S.I. No. 305 of 1997), references in any enactment to the Minister for Enterprise and Employment are to be construed as references to the Minister for Enterprise, Trade and Employment. It should be noted that the powers and duties which are conferred on the Minister for Enterprise, Trade and Employment by or under the Terms of Employment (Information) Acts have been delegated by statutory instrument to the present Minister of State at the Department of Enterprise, Trade and Employment. (See now the Enterprise, Trade and Employment (Delegation of Ministerial Functions) Order 2004 (S.I. No. 809 of 2004).)

"the Tribunal" means the Employment Appeals Tribunal.

(2) A word or expression that is used in this Act and is also used in the Council Directive has, unless the contrary intention appears, the meaning in this Act that it has in the Council Directive.

(3) In this Act—

(*a*) a reference to any enactment shall, unless the context otherwise requires, be construed as a reference to that enactment as amended, adapted or extended by or under any subsequent enactment including this Act,

(*b*) a reference to a section is a reference to a section of this Act unless it is indicated that reference to some other enactment is intended,

(*c*) a reference to a subsection, paragraph or subparagraph is a reference to the subsection, paragraph or subparagraph of the provision in which the reference occurs unless it is indicated that reference to some other provision is intended.

2.—(1) This Act shall not apply to— Exclusions.

(*a*) employment in which the employee is normally expected to work for the employer for less than 8 hours in a week, [2] or

[2] Note, however, that under s. 8 of the Protection of Employees (Part-Time Work) Act, 2001, the Terms of Employment (Information) Act, 1994 is to apply to a part-time employee (meaning, under s. 7(1) of the 2001 Act, an employee whose normal hours of work are less than the normal hours of work of an employee who is a comparable employee in relation to him or her) in the same manner (and subject to the like exceptions not inconsistent with s. 8) as it applies (other than by virtue of the 2001 Act) to an employee to whom the Terms of Employment (Information) Act, 1994 relates. (Note also the broad definition given to "employee" by s. 3(1) of the Protection of Employees (Part-Time Work) Act, 2001 and note finally that under s. 1(5) of the Protection of Employees (Part-Time Work) Act, 2001, insofar as the 2001 Act relates to the Terms of Employment (Information) Act, 1994, the two Acts are required to be construed together as one and may be cited together as the Terms of Employment (Information) Acts, 1994 and 2001).

(*b*) employment in which the employee has been in the continuous service of the employer for less than 1 month.

(2) Where the exclusion of a class or classes of employment from any provision of this Act is justified by objective considerations, the Minister may, after consultation with representatives of employers and of employees within that class or classes of employment, by order declare that provision shall not apply to that class or those classes of employment and this Act shall have effect in accordance with the provisions of any such order for the time being in force.

(3) The First Schedule to the Act of 1973 shall apply for the purpose of ascertaining for the purposes of this Act the period of service of an employee and whether that service has been continuous with the following modifications and with any other necessary modifications— [3]

(*a*) the reference to 21 hours shall be construed as a reference to 8 hours,

(*b*) the references to an employee shall be construed as references to an employee within the meaning of this Act.

(4) The Minister may by order amend or revoke an order under this section, including an order under this subsection.

Written statement of terms of employment.

3. —(1) An employer shall, not later than 2 months after the commencement of an employee's employment with the employer, give or cause to be given to the employee a statement in writing containing the following particulars of the terms of the employee's employment, that is to say—

(*a*) the full names of the employer and the employee,

(*b*) the address of the employer in the State or, where appropriate, the address of the principal place of the relevant business of the employer in the State or the registered office (within the meaning of the Companies Act, 1963),

[3] See however the previous footnote.

(*c*) the place of work or, where there is no fixed or main place of work, a statement specifying that the employee is required or permitted to work at various places,

(*d*) the title of the job or nature of the work for which the employee is employed,

(*e*) the date of commencement of the employee's contract of employment,

(*f*) in the case of a temporary contract of employment, the expected duration thereof or, if the contract of employment is for a fixed term, the date on which the contract expires,

(*g*) the rate or method of calculation of the employee's remuneration,

(*h*) the length of the intervals between the times at which remuneration is paid, whether a week, a month or any other interval,

(*i*) any terms or conditions relating to hours of work (including overtime),

(*j*) any terms or conditions relating to paid leave (other than paid sick leave),

(*k*) any terms or conditions relating to—

(i) incapacity for work due to sickness or injury and paid sick leave, and

(ii) pensions and pension schemes,

(*l*) the period of notice which the employee is required to give and entitled to receive (whether by or under statute or under the terms of the employee's contract of employment) to determine the employee's contract of employment or, where this cannot be indicated when the information is given, the method for determining such periods of notice,

(*m*) a reference to any collective agreements which directly affect the terms and conditions of the employee's employment including, where the employer is not a party to such agreements, particulars of the bodies or institutions by whom they were made.

(2) A statement shall be given to an employee under *subsection (1)* notwithstanding that the employee's employment ends before the end of the period within which the statement is required to be given.

(3) The particulars specified in *paragraphs* (*g*), (*h*), (*i*), (*j*), (*k*) and (*l*) of the said *subsection* (1), may be given to the employee in the form of a reference to provisions of statutes or instruments made under statute or of any other laws or of any administrative provisions or collective agreements, governing those particulars which the employee has reasonable opportunities of reading during the course of the employee's employment or which are reasonably accessible to the employee in some other way.

(4) A statement furnished by an employer under *subsection (1)* shall be signed and dated by or on behalf of the employer.

(5) A copy of the said statement shall be retained by the employer during the period of the employee's employment and for a period of 1 year thereafter.

(6) (*a*) The Minister may by order require employers to give or cause to be given to employees within a specified time a statement in writing containing such particulars of the terms of their employment (other than those referred to in *subsection (1)*) as may be specified in the order and employers shall comply with the provisions of such an order.[4]

(*b*) The Minister may by order amend or revoke an order under this subsection, including an order under this paragraph.

(7) This section (other than *subsection (6)*) shall not apply or have effect as respects contracts of employment entered into before the commencement of this Act.

---

[4] See now the Terms of Employment (Information) Act, 1994 (Section 3 (6)) Order, 1997 (S.I. No. 4 of 1997) and the Terms of Employment (Additional Information) Order, 1998 (S.I. No. 49 of 1998).

Employment outside State.

4. —(1) Where, after the commencement of this Act, an employee is required to work outside the State for a period of not less than 1 month, the employer concerned shall give or cause to be given to the employee, prior to the departure of the employee from the State, a statement under *section 3* and there shall be added to the statement the following particulars, that is to say—

(*a*) the period of employment outside the State,

(*b*) the currency in which the employee is to be remunerated in respect of that period,

(*c*) any benefits in cash or kind for the employee attendant on the employment outside the State,

(*d*) the terms and conditions, where appropriate, governing the employee's repatriation.

(2) The particulars referred to in *paragraphs (b)* and (*c*) of *subsection (1)* may be given in the form of a reference to provisions of statutes or instruments made under statute or of any other laws or of any administrative provisions or collective agreements, governing such particulars.

Notification of changes.

5. —(1) Subject to *subsection (2)*, whenever a change is made or occurs in any of the particulars of the statement furnished by an employer under *section 3*, *4* or *6*, the employer shall notify the employee in writing of the nature and date of the change as soon as may be thereafter, but not later than—

(*a*) 1 month after the change takes effect, or

(*b*) where the change is consequent on the employee being required to work outside the State for a period of more than 1 month, the time of the employee's departure.

(2) *Subsection (1)* does not apply in relation to a change occurring in provisions of statutes or instruments made under statute or of any other laws or of any administrative provisions or collective agreements referred to in the statement given under *section 3* or *4*.

Existing contracts of employment.

6. —(1) Where, before the commencement of this Act, an employee has entered into a contract of employment with an employer, then, the employer shall, if so requested by the employee, furnish to the employee a statement under *section 3* and, if so requested by the employee, there shall be added to the statement the particulars specified in *section 4*.

(2) An employer shall, within 2 months after the employer has been required to do so under *subsection (1)*, furnish to the employee concerned a written statement in accordance with that subsection.

Complaints by employees in relation to contraventions of Act by their employers.

7. —(1) An employee may present a complaint to a rights commissioner that his or her employer has contravened *section 3, 4, 5* or *6* in relation to him or her and, if he or she does so, the commissioner shall give the parties an opportunity to be heard by the commissioner and to present to the commissioner any evidence relevant to the complaint, shall give a recommendation in writing in relation to it and shall communicate the recommendation to the parties.

(2) A recommendation of a rights commissioner under *subsection (1)* shall do one or more of the following:

(*a*) declare that the complaint was or, as the case may be, was not well founded,

(*b*) (i) confirm all or any of the particulars contained or referred to in any statement furnished by the employer under *section 3, 4, 5* or *6*, or

(ii) alter or add to any such statement for the purpose of correcting any inaccuracy or omission in the statement and the statement as so altered or added to shall be deemed to have been given to the employee by the employer,

(*c*) require the employer to give or cause to be given to the employee concerned a written statement containing such particulars as may be specified by the commissioner,

(*d*) order the employer to pay to the employee compensation of such amount (if any) as is just and equitable having regard to all the circumstances, but not exceeding 4 weeks remuneration in respect of the employee's employment calculated in accordance with regulations under section 17 of the Unfair Dismissals Act, 1977,

and the references in the foregoing paragraphs to an employer shall be construed, in a case where ownership of the business of the employer changes after a contravention to which the complaint relates, as references to the person who, by virtue of the change, becomes entitled to such ownership.

(3) A rights commissioner shall not entertain a complaint under this section if it is presented to the commissioner after the period of 6 months beginning on the date of termination of the employment concerned.

(4) (*a*) A complaint shall be presented by giving notice thereof in writing to a rights commissioner and the notice shall contain such particulars and be in such form as may be specified from time to time by the Minister.

(*b*) A copy of a notice under *paragraph (a)* shall be given to the other party concerned by the rights commissioner concerned.[5]

(5) Proceedings under this section before a rights commissioner shall be conducted otherwise than in public.[6]

(6) A rights commissioner shall furnish the Tribunal with a copy of any recommendation given by the commissioner under *subsection (1)*.[7]

---

[5] Note that under Regulation 6(4) of the European Communities (Protection of Employment) Regulations, 2000 (S.I. No. 488 of 2000), s. 7(4) of the Terms of Employment (Information) Act, 1994 is to apply — with any necessary modifications — in relation to a complaint presented under Regulation 6 of the 2000 Regulations as it applies in relation to a complaint presented under s. 7(1) of the 1994 Act.

[6] Under Regulation 6(4) of the European Communities (Protection of Employment) Regulations, 2000 (S.I. No. 488 of 2000), s. 7(5) of the Terms of Employment (Information) Act, 1994 is to apply — with any necessary modifications — in relation to a complaint presented under Regulation 6 of the 2000 Regulations as it applies in relation to a complaint presented under s. 7(1) of the 1994 Act.

[7] Under Regulation 6(5) of the European Communities (Protection of Employment) Regulations, 2000 (S.I. No. 488 of 2000), s. 7(6) of the Terms of Employment (Information) Act, 1994 is to apply in relation to a

(7) The Minister may by regulations—

(*a*) provide for any matters relating to proceedings under this section that the Minister considers appropriate, [8] and

(*b*) amend *paragraph (d)* of *subsection (2)* so as to vary the maximum amount of the compensation provided for in that paragraph, and this section shall have effect in accordance with the provisions of any regulations under this paragraph for the time being in force.

Appeals from and enforcement of recommendations of rights commissioner.

8. —(1) A party concerned may appeal to the Tribunal from a recommendation of a rights commissioner under *section 7* and, if the party does so, the Tribunal shall give the parties an opportunity to be heard by it and to present to it any evidence relevant to the appeal, shall make a determination in writing in relation to the appeal affirming, varying or setting aside the recommendation and shall communicate the determination to the parties.[9]

(2) (*a*) An appeal under this section shall be initiated by the party concerned giving, within 6 weeks of the date on which the recommendation to which it relates was communicated to the party, a notice in writing to the Tribunal containing such particulars (if any) as may be specified in regulations under *subsection (3)* and stating the intention of the party concerned to appeal against the recommendation.

---

complaint presented under Regulation 6 of the 2000 Regulations as it applies in relation to a complaint presented under s. 7(1) of the 1994 Act, with the modification that in s. 7(6), a reference to a decision is substituted for a reference to a recommendation, and with "any other necessary modifications".

[8] Under Regulation 6(4) of the European Communities (Protection of Employment) Regulations, 2000 (S.I. No. 488 of 2000), s. 7(7)(a) of the Terms of Employment (Information) Act, 1994 is to apply — with any necessary modifications — in relation to a complaint presented under Regulation 6 of the 2000 Regulations as it applies in relation to a complaint presented under s. 7(1) of the 1994 Act.

[9] Under Regulation 6(4) of the European Communities (Protection of Employment) Regulations, 2000 (S.I. No. 488 of 2000), all of s. 8 of the Terms of Employment (Information) Act, 1994 is to apply for the purposes

(*b*) A copy of a notice under *paragraph (a)* shall be given by the Tribunal to the other party concerned as soon as may be after the receipt of the notice by the Tribunal.

(3) The Minister may by regulations provide for all or any of the following matters in relation to proceedings before the Tribunal and for anything consequential thereon or incidental or ancillary thereto:[10]

(*a*) the procedure in relation to all matters concerning the initiation and the hearing by the Tribunal of appeals under this section,

(*b*) the times and places of hearings of such appeals,

(*c*) the representation of the parties to such appeals,

(*d*) the publication and notification of determinations of the Tribunal,

(*e*) the particulars to be contained in a notice under *subsection (2)*,

(*f*) the award by the Tribunal of costs and expenses in relation to such appeals and the payment thereof,

(*g*) the extension by the Tribunal of the time for initiating such appeals.

(4) (*a*) The Minister may, at the request of the Tribunal, refer a question of law arising in proceedings before it to the High Court for determination by it and the determination of the High Court shall be final and conclusive.

(*b*) A party to proceedings before the Tribunal may appeal to the High Court from a determination of the Tribunal on a point of law and the determination of the High Court shall be final and conclusive.

---

of the 2000 Regulations as it applies for the purposes of the 1994 Act, but with the substitution in it of references to a decision for references to a recommendation, and with any other necessary modifications.

[10] See the Terms of Employment (Information) (Appeals and Complaints) Regulations, 1994 (S.I. No. 244 of 1994).

(5) Section 39 (17) of the Redundancy Payments Act, 1967, shall apply in relation to proceedings before the Tribunal under this Act as it applies to matters referred to it under that section with the substitution in paragraph (*e*) of the said section 39 (17) of "a fine not exceeding [€1269.74]" for "a fine not exceeding [€25.39]".[11]

(6) (*a*) Where a recommendation of a rights commissioner in relation to a complaint under this Act has not been carried out by the employer concerned in accordance with its terms, the time for bringing an appeal against the recommendation has expired and no such appeal has been brought, the employee concerned may bring the complaint before the Tribunal and the Tribunal shall, without hearing the employer concerned or any evidence (other than in relation to the matters aforesaid), make a determination to the like effect as the recommendation.

(*b*) The bringing of a complaint before the Tribunal by virtue of this subsection shall be effected by giving to

[11] The amounts actually stipulated in s. 8(5) are, respectively, '£1,000' and 'twenty pounds', rather than €1269.74 and €25.39, but under Article 14 of Council Regulation (EC) No 974/98 of 3 May 1998 on the introduction of the euro (read in conjunction with Article 1 of the same instrument), references made in legislative and statutory provisions existing on 31 December 2001 to units of Irish currency as they existed before the start of the third stage of economic and monetary union are to be read as references to the euro unit according to the respective conversion rates (with the rounding rules laid down in Regulation (EC) No 1103/97 of 17 June 1997 on certain provisions relating to the introduction of the euro applying).
Note further that the amount of €190.46 (rather than €25.39) is the amount now stipulated in s. 39(17)(e) of the Redundancy Payments Act, 1967. This is because the amount of £150 (the equivalent in punts of €190.46) was substituted by s. 17 of the Redundancy Payments Act, 1979 for the original amount of £20 (the equivalent of €25.39), and, as already noted, under Article 14 of Council Regulation (EC) No 974/98 of 3 May 1998 on the introduction of the euro (read in conjunction with Article 1 of the same instrument), references made in legislative and statutory provisions existing on 31 December 2001 to units of Irish currency as they existed before the start of the third stage of economic and monetary union are to be read as references to the euro unit according to the respective conversion rates (with the rounding rules laid down in Regulation (EC) No 1103/97 of 17 June 1997 on certain provisions relating to the introduction of the euro applying).

the Tribunal a notice in writing containing such particulars (if any) as may be specified in regulations made for the purposes of *subsection (3)*.

Enforcement of determinations of Tribunal.

9.—(1)(*a*) If an employer fails to carry out in accordance with its terms a determination of the Tribunal in relation to a complaint under *section 7* within 6 weeks from the date on which the determination is communicated to the parties, the District Court shall, on application to it in that behalf by—

(i) the employee concerned,

(ii) the employee's trade union, or

(iii) the Minister, if the Minister considers it appropriate to make the application having regard to all the circumstances,

without hearing the employer or any evidence (other than in relation to the matters aforesaid) make an order directing the employer to carry out the determination in accordance with its terms.[12]

(*b*) In *paragraph (a)* the reference to a determination of the Tribunal is a reference to such a determination in relation to which, at the expiration of the time for bringing an appeal against it, no such appeal has been brought, or if such an appeal has been brought it has been abandoned and the

---

[12] Note the relevance in this regard of the District Court (Terms of Employment Information) Rules, 2003 (S.I. No. 409 of 2003). Note also that under Regulation 6(4) of the European Communities (Protection of Employment) Regulations, 2000 (S.I. No. 488 of 2000), s. 9 of the Terms of Employment (Information) Act, 1994 is to apply for the purposes of the 2000 Regulations as it applies for the purposes of the 1994 Act, but
(i) with the substitution in s. 9 of references to a decision for references to a recommendation;
(ii) with the substitution in s. 9 of references to the Circuit Court for references to the District Court and with the substitution in s. 9 of the following subsection for subsection (3):
"(3) An application under this section to the Circuit Court shall be made to the judge of the Circuit Court for the circuit in which the employer concerned ordinarily resides or carries on any profession, trade or business.";
and (iii) with any other necessary modifications.

reference to the date on which the determination is communicated to the parties shall, in a case where such an appeal is abandoned, be construed as a reference to the date of such abandonment.

(2) The District Court may, in an order under this section, if in all the circumstances it considers it appropriate to do so, where the order relates to the payment of compensation, direct the employer concerned to pay to the employee concerned interest on the compensation at the rate referred to in section 22 of the Courts Act, 1981, in respect of the whole or any part of the period beginning 6 weeks after the date on which the determination of the Tribunal is communicated to the parties and ending on the date of the order.

(3) Proceedings under this section shall be heard by the judge assigned to the district court district in which the employer concerned ordinarily resides or carries on any profession, business or occupation.

Evidence of failure to attend before or give evidence or produce documents to Tribunal.

10.—A document purporting to be signed by the chairman or a vice-chairman of the Tribunal stating that—

(*a*) a person named in the document was, by a notice under paragraph (*c*) of section 39 (17) of the Redundancy Payments Act, 1967, required to attend before the Tribunal on a day and at a time and place specified in the document, to give evidence or produce a document,

(*b*) a sitting of the Tribunal was held on that day and at that time and place, and

(*c*) the person did not attend before the Tribunal in pursuance of the notice or, as the case may be, having so attended, refused to give evidence or refused or failed to produce the document,

shall, in a prosecution of the person under paragraph (*e*) of the said section 39 (17), be evidence of the matters so stated without further proof.[13]

---

[13] Under Regulation 6(4) of the European Communities (Protection of Employment) Regulations, 2000 (S.I. No. 488 of 2000), s. 10 of the Terms

11. —Every order or regulation made under this Act shall be laid before each House of the Oireachtas as soon as may be after it is made and, if a resolution annulling the order or regulation is passed by either such House within the next 21 days on which that House has sat after the order or regulation is laid before it, the order or regulation shall be annulled accordingly but without prejudice to the validity of anything previously done thereunder.

Laying of orders and regulations before Houses of Oireachtas.

12. —The expenses incurred by the Minister in the administration of this Act shall, to such extent as may be sanctioned by the Minister for Finance, be paid out of moneys provided by the Oireachtas.

Expenses of Minister.

13. —Sections 9 and 10 of the Act of 1973 are hereby repealed.

Repeals.

14. —(1) This Act may be cited as the Terms of Employment (Information) Act, 1994.[14]

Short title and commencement.

(2) This Act shall come into operation on such day as the Minister may appoint by order.[15]

---

of Employment (Information) Act, 1994 is to apply for the purposes of the 2000 Regulations as it applies for the purposes of the 1994 Act, but with the substitution in it of references to a decision for references to a recommendation, and with any other necessary modifications.

[14] Note that under s. 1(5) of the Protection of Employees (Part-Time Work) Act, 2001, in so far as the 2001 Act relates to the Terms of Employment (Information) Act, 1994, the 2001 Act and the 1994 Act are to be construed together as one and may be cited together as the Terms of Employment (Information) Acts, 1994 and 2001.

[15] In the Terms of Employment (Information) Act, 1994 (Commencement) Order, 1994 (S.I. No. 96 of 1994), the Minister for Enterprise and Employment appointed 16 May, 1994 to be the day on which this Act came into operation.

COUNCIL DIRECTIVE 91/533/EEC

of 14 October 1991

on an employer's obligation to inform employees of the conditions applicable to the contract or employment relationship

(Official Journal of the European Communities 18.10.1991
L 288/32)

THE COUNCIL OF THE EUROPEAN COMMUNITIES,

Having regard to the Treaty establishing the European Economic Community, and in particular Article 100 thereof,

Having regard to the proposal from the Commission ([1]),

Having regard to the opinion of the European Parliament ([2]),

Having regard to the opinion of the Economic and Social Committee ([3]),

([1]) OJ No C 24, 31.1.1991, p. 3.

([2]) OJ No C 240, 16.9.1991, p. 21.

([3]) OJ No C 159, 17.6.1991, p. 32.

Whereas the development, in the Member States, of new forms of work has led to an increase in the number of types of employment relationship;

Whereas, faced with this development, certain Member States have considered it necessary to subject employment relationships to formal requirements; whereas these provisions are designed to provide employees with improved protection against possible infringements of their rights and to create greater transparency on the labour market;

Whereas the relevant legislation of the Member States differs considerably on such fundamental points as the requirement to inform employees in writing of the main terms of the contract or employment relationship;

Whereas differences in the legislation of Member States may have a direct effect on the operation of the common market;

Whereas Article 117 of the Treaty provides for the Member States to agree upon the need to promote improved working conditions and an improved standard of living for workers, so as to make possible their harmonization while the improvement is being maintained;

Whereas point 9 of the Community Charter of Fundamental Social Rights for Workers, adopted at the Strasbourg European Council on 9 December 1989 by the Heads of State and Government of 11 Member States, states:

'The conditions of employment of every worker of the European Community shall be stipulated in laws, a collective agreement or a contract of employment, according to arrangements applying in each country.';

Whereas it is necessary to establish at Community level the general requirement that every employee must be provided with a document containing information on the essential elements of his contract or employment relationship;

Whereas, in view of the need to maintain a certain degree of flexibility in employment relationships, Member States should be able to exclude certain limited cases of employment relationship from this Directive's scope of application;

Whereas the obligation to provide information may be met by means of a written contract, a letter of appointment or one or more other documents or, if they are lacking, a written statement signed by the employer;

Whereas, in the case of expatriation of the employee, the latter must, in addition to the main terms of his contract or employment relationship, be supplied with relevant information connected with his secondment;

Whereas, in order to protect the interests of employees with regard to obtaining a document, any change in the main terms of the contract or employment relationship must be communicated to them in writing;

Whereas it is necessary for Member States to guarantee that employees can claim the rights conferred on them by this Directive;

Whereas Member States are to adopt the laws, regulations and legislative provisions necessary to comply with this Directive or are to ensure that both sides of industry set up the necessary provisions by agreement, with Member States being obliged to take the necessary steps enabling them at all times to guarantee the results imposed by this Directive,

HAS ADOPTED THIS DIRECTIVE:

Article 1

Scope

1. This Directive shall apply to every paid employee having a contract or employment relationship defined by the law in force in a Member State and/or governed by the law in force in a Member State.

2. Member States may provide that this Directive shall not apply to employees having a contract or employment relationship:

(a) — with a total duration not exceeding one month, and/or

— with a working week not exceeding eight hours; or

(b) of a casual and/or specific nature provided, in these cases, that its non-application is justified by objective considerations.

Article 2

Obligation to provide information

1. An employer shall be obliged to notify an employee to whom this Directive applies, hereinafter referred to as 'the employee', of the essential aspects of the contract or employment relationship.

2. The information referred to in paragraph 1 shall cover at least the following:

(a) the identities of the parties;

(b) the place of work; where there is no fixed or main place of work, the principle that the employee is employed at various places and the registered place of business or, where appropriate, the domicile of the employer;

(c) (i) the title, grade, nature or category of the work for which the employee is employed; or

(ii) a brief specification or description of the work;

(d) the date of commencement of the contract or employment relationship;

(e) in the case of a temporary contract or employment relationship, the expected duration thereof;

(f) the amount of paid leave to which the employee is entitled or, where this cannot be indicated when the information is given, the procedures for allocating and determining such leave;

(g) the length of the periods of notice to be observed by the employer and the employee should their contract or employment relationship be terminated or, where this cannot be indicated when the information is given, the method for determining such periods of notice;

(h) the initial basic amount, the other component elements and the frequency of payment of the remuneration to which the employee is entitled;

(i) the length of the employee's normal working day or week;

(j) where appropriate;

(i) the collective agreements governing the employee's conditions of work;

or

(ii) in the case of collective agreements concluded outside the business by special joint bodies or institutions, the name of the competent body or joint institution within which the agreements were concluded.

3. The information referred to in paragraph 2 (f), (g), (h) and (i) may, where appropriate, be given in the form of a reference to the laws, regulations and administrative or statutory provisions or collective agreements governing those particular points.

Article 3

Means of information

1. The information referred to in Article 2 (2) may be given to the employee, not later than two months after the commencement of employment, in the form of:

(a) a written contract of employment; and/or

(b) a letter of engagement; and/or

(c) one or more other written documents, where one of these documents contains at least all the information referred to in Article 2 (2) (a), (b), (c), (d), (h) and (i).

2. Where none of the documents referred to in paragraph 1 is handed over to the employee within the prescribed period, the employer shall be obliged to give the employee, not later than two months after the commencement of employment, a written declaration signed by the employer and containing at least the information referred to in Article 2 (2).

Where the document(s) referred to in paragraph 1 contain only part of the information required, the written declaration provided for in the first subparagraph of this paragraph shall cover the remaining information.

3. Where the contract or employment relationship comes to an end before expiry of a period of two months as from the date of the start of work, the information provided for in Article 2 and in this Article must be made available to the employee by the end of this period at the latest.

Article 4

Expatriate employees

1. Where an employee is required to work in a country or countries other than the Member State whose law and/or practice governs the contract or employment relationship, the document(s) referred to in Article 3 must be in his/her possession before his/her departure and must include at least the following additional information:

(a) the duration of the employment abroad;

(b) the currency to be used for the payment of remuneration;

(c) where appropriate, the benefits in cash or kind attendant on the employment abroad;

(d) where appropriate, the conditions governing the employee's repatriation.

2. The information referred to in paragraph 1 (b) and (c) may, where appropriate, be given in the form of a reference to the laws, regulations and administrative or statutory provisions or collective agreements governing those particular points.

3. Paragraphs 1 and 2 shall not apply if the duration of the employment outside the country whose law and/or practice governs the contract or employment relationship is one month or less.

Article 5

Modification of aspects of the contract or employment relationship

1. Any change in the details referred to in Articles 2 (2) and 4 (1) must be the subject of a written document to be given by the employer to the employee at the earliest opportunity and not later than one month after the date of entry into effect of the change in question.

2. The written document referred to in paragraph 1 shall not be compulsory in the event of a change in the laws, regulations and administrative or statutory provisions or collective agreements cited in the documents referred to in Article 3, supplemented, where appropriate, pursuant to Article 4 (1).

Article 6

Form and proof of the existence of a contract or employment relationship and procedural rules

This Directive shall be without prejudice to national law and practice concerning:

— the form of the contract or employment relationship,

— proof as regards the existence and content of a contract or employment relationship,

— the relevant procedural rules.

Article 7

More favourable provisions

This Directive shall not affect Member States' prerogative to apply or to introduce laws, regulations or administrative provisions which are more favourable to employees or to encourage or permit the application of agreements which are more favourable to employees.

Article 8

Defence of rights

1. Member States shall introduce into their national legal systems such measures as are necessary to enable all employees who consider themselves wronged by failure to comply with the obligations arising from this Directive to pursue their claims by judicial process after possible recourse to other competent authorities.

2. Member States may provide that access to the means of redress referred to in paragraph 1 are subject to the notification of the employer by the employee and the failure by the employer to reply within 15 days of notification.

However, the formality of prior notification may in no case be required in the cases referred to in Article 4, neither for workers with a temporary contract or employment relationship, nor for employees not covered by a collective agreement or by collective agreements relating to the employment relationship.

Article 9

Final provisions

1. Member States shall adopt the laws, regulations and administrative provisions necessary to comply with this Directive no later than 30 June 1993 or shall ensure by that date that the employers' and workers' representatives introduce the required provisions by way of agreement, the Member States being obliged to take the necessary steps enabling them at all times to guarantee the results imposed by this Directive.

They shall forthwith inform the Commission thereof.

2. Member States shall take the necessary measures to ensure that, in the case of employment relationships in existence upon entry into force of the provisions that they adopt, the employer gives the employee, on request, within two months of receiving that request; any of the documents referred to in Article 3, supplemented, where appropriate, pursuant to Article 4 (1).

3. When Member States adopt the measures referred to in paragraph 1, such measures shall contain a reference to this Directive or shall be

accompanied by such reference on the occasion of their official publication. The methods of making such a reference shall be laid down by the Member States.

4. Member States shall forthwith inform the Commission of the measures they take to implement this Directive.

Article 10

This Directive is addressed to the Member States.

Done at Luxembourg, 14 October 1991.

For the Council

The President

B. de VRIES

TRANSNATIONAL INFORMATION AND CONSULTATION OF EMPLOYEES ACT, 1996

Number 20 *of* 1996

ARRANGEMENT OF SECTIONS

PART I

PRELIMINARY AND GENERAL

Section

PART III

MISCELLANEOUS

Section

FIRST SCHEDULE

ELECTION OF EMPLOYEES' REPRESENTATIVES

SECOND SCHEDULE

Subsidiary Requirements: European Works Council

Acts Referred To

Arbitration Acts, 1954 and 1980	
Industrial Relations Act, 1946	1946, No. 26
Trade Union Acts, 1871 to 1990	
Trade Union Act, 1941	1941, No. 22
Payment of Wages Act, 1991	1991, No. 25
Protection of Employment Act, 1977	1977, No. 7

Number 20 *of* 1996

TRANSNATIONAL INFORMATION AND CONSULTATION OF EMPLOYEES ACT, 1996

AN ACT TO IMPLEMENT DIRECTIVE NO. 94/45 EC OF 22 SEPTEMBER, 1994 OF THE COUNCIL OF THE EUROPEAN UNION BY PROVIDING FOR THE ESTABLISHMENT OF TRANSNATIONAL ARRANGEMENTS FOR THE INFORMATION AND CONSULTATION OF EMPLOYEES IN COMMUNITY-SCALE UNDERTAKINGS AND COMMUNITY-SCALE GROUPS OF UNDERTAKINGS WHERE REQUESTED IN THE MANNER PROVIDED FOR IN THIS ACT, TO PROVIDE FOR THE ESTABLISHMENT OF EUROPEAN WORKS COUNCILS IN SUCH UNDERTAKINGS OR GROUPS OF UNDERTAKINGS UNLESS AGREEMENTS ENTERED INTO IN ACCORDANCE WITH THIS ACT PROVIDE OTHERWISE, AND TO PROVIDE FOR RELATED MATTERS. [10*th July*, 1996]

BE IT ENACTED BY THE OIREACHTAS AS FOLLOWS:

PART I

PRELIMINARY AND GENERAL

1. —This Act may be cited as the Transnational Information and Consultation of Employees Act, 1996. Short title.

2. —This Act shall come into operation on such day as the Minister may by order appoint.[1] Commencement.

---

[1] In the Transnational Information and Consultation of Employees Act, 1996 (Commencement) Order, 1996 (S.I. No. 276 of 1996), the Minister for Enterprise and Employment appointed 22 September, 1996 to be the day on which this Act came into operation.

Interpretation. **3.** — (1) In this Act, unless the context otherwise requires—

"appointed" means, in the absence of an election, appointed by employees, or appointed by management on a basis agreed with employees;

"central management" means—

(*a*) in the case of a Community-scale undertaking, the central management of the undertaking, and

(*b*) in the case of a Community-scale group of undertakings, the central management of the controlling undertaking,

or such other level of management determined by the central management or agreed between the central management and the employees of the undertaking or group of undertakings;

"Community-scale undertaking" means any undertaking with at least 1,000 employees within the Member States and at least 150 employees in each of at least two Member States;

"Community-scale group of undertakings" means a group of undertakings with—

(*a*) at least 1,000 employees within the Member States, and

(*b*) at least one group undertaking with at least 150 employees in one Member State and at least one other group undertaking with at least 150 employees in another Member State;

"Community" means—

(*a*) the European Community [2]; and

(*b*) Norway, Iceland and Liechtenstein;

"consultation" means the exchange of views and establishment of dialogue between employees' representatives and the central management;

---

[2] The words "excluding the United Kingdom" were deleted from para. (a) of the definition of "Community" by Article 2 of the European Communities (Transnational Information and Consultation of Employees Act, 1996) (Amendment) Regulations, 1999 (S.I. No. 386 of 1999).

"contract of employment" means a contract of service or of apprenticeship, whether express or implied, and if express, whether oral or in writing;

"controlled undertaking" and "controlling undertaking" have the meanings assigned to them, respectively, by *section 5 (1)*;

"the Directive" means Council Directive 94/45/EC of 22 September 1994[1], on the establishment of a European Works Council or a procedure in Community-scale undertakings and Community-scale groups of undertakings for the purposes of informing and consulting employees;

---

[1] O.J. No. L254 of 30.9.1994, p. 64.

"elected" means elected in accordance with the *First Schedule*;

"employee" means a person who has entered into or works under a contract of employment with an undertaking or group of undertakings, other than a person who is employed in a managerial capacity in the central management of the undertaking or group of undertakings;

"employees' representatives" means—

(*a*) in the case of a Special Negotiating Body, persons elected or appointed to that Body, who may include—

(i) employees, and

(ii) trade union officials and officials of an excepted body, whether or not they are employees,

and

(*b*) in the case of a European Works Council or European Employees' Forum, or in relation to any other arrangement for the information and consultation of employees to which this Act applies, employees elected or appointed to those bodies or for the purposes of those arrangements;

"establishment", in relation to an undertaking, means a division (however described) of the undertaking physically separated from other parts of the undertaking;

"European Employees' Forum" means a European Employees' Forum established in accordance with an agreement referred to in *section 11 (1)*;

"European Works Council" means a Council established in accordance with the *Second Schedule* for the purpose of informing and consulting employees;

"excepted body" has the meaning assigned to it by section 6 (3) of the Trade Union Act, 1941, as amended;

"expert" means a natural person, and may be the holder from time to time of a named office or position in a body corporate or other body or organisation,

"group of undertakings" means a controlling undertaking and its controlled undertakings, and "group undertaking" has a corresponding meaning;

"information and consultation procedure" means an information and consultation procedure established in accordance with an agreement referred to in *section 11 (1)*;

"Member State" means a Member State of the Community;

"the Minister" means the Minister for Enterprise, Trade and Employment; [3]

"Special Negotiating Body" means a Special Negotiating Body established in accordance with *section 10* to negotiate with the central management for an agreement for the establishment of arrangements for the information and consultation of employees;

---

[3] The text of the Act originally referred to the Minister for Enterprise and Employment. However, Article 4 of the Enterprise and Employment (Alteration of Name of Department and Title of Minister) Order, 1997 (S.I. No. 305 of 1997) has subsequently provided that references in any enactment to the Minister for Enterprise and Employment are to be construed as references to the Minister for Enterprise, Trade and Employment. It should further be noted that the powers and duties which are conferred on the Minister for Enterprise, Trade and Employment by or under the Transnational Information and Consultation of Employees Act, 1996 have been delegated by statutory instrument to the Minister of State at the Department of Enterprise, Trade and Employment. (See now the Enterprise, Trade and Employment (Delegation of Ministerial Functions) Order 2004 (S.I. No. 809 of 2004)).

"trade union official" means an official of a trade union licensed under the Trade Union Acts, 1871 to 1990, which is already recognised for collective bargaining or information and consultation purposes by the business units of the Community-scale undertaking or group of undertakings located in the State;

"undertaking" means any form of economic activity.

(2) A word or expression used in this Act that is also used in the Directive has, unless the context otherwise requires, the same meaning in this Act as it has in the Directive.

(3) In construing a provision of this Act, a court shall give it a construction that will give effect to the Directive, and for that purpose the court shall have regard to the provisions of the Directive, including its preamble.

(4) In this Act, including a Schedule to this Act—

(*a*) a reference to a section is a reference to a section of this Act, unless it is indicated that reference to some other enactment is intended,

(*b*) a reference to a subsection, paragraph or subparagraph is a reference to the subsection, paragraph or subparagraph of the provision in which the reference occurs, unless it is indicated that a reference to some other provision is intended, and

(*c*) a reference to a Schedule is a reference to a Schedule to this Act.

(5) A reference in this Act to the performance of functions includes a reference to the exercise of powers and the performance of duties.

Workforce thresholds.

4. —(1) In determining whether, for the purposes of the establishment of a Special Negotiating Body, an undertaking is a Community-scale undertaking or undertakings are a Community-scale group of undertakings, the number of employees employed in the undertaking or group of undertakings shall be taken to be the average number of employees, including part-time employees, employed in the undertaking or group of undertakings during the two years immediately preceding the request for the establishment of the Special Negotiating Body.[4]

(2) The central management shall, on being so requested by an employees' representative, give to that representative such information about the numbers and status of employees employed in an undertaking or undertakings as is reasonably necessary to enable the numbers referred to in *subsection (1)* to be assessed.

(3) For the purposes of this section—

"employees' representatives" includes those employees' representatives already recognised by the undertaking or group of undertakings for collective bargaining or information and consultation purposes;

"part-time employees", in relation to employment in the State, means employees—

(*a*) in the continuous service of an employer for not less than 13 weeks, and

(*b*) normally expected to work not less than eight hours each week for the employer.

Definition of controlling and controlled undertaking.

5.—(1) In this Act "controlling undertaking" means an undertaking which can exercise a dominant influence over another undertaking by virtue of ownership, financial participation or the rules which govern the controlled undertaking, and "controlled undertaking" means an undertaking over which that dominant influence can be exercised.

(2) The ability of an undertaking to exercise a dominant influence shall be presumed, unless the contrary is proved, when in relation to another undertaking it directly or indirectly—

---

[4] Note in this respect, s. 11 of the Protection of Employees (Fixed-Term Work) Act 2003. According to s. 11(1), fixed-term employees are required to be taken into account when calculating the threshold above which employees' representatives bodies may be constituted in an undertaking in accordance with section 4 of the Transnational Information and Consultation of Employees Act, 1996. According to s. 11(2) of the 2003 Act, as far as practicable, employers are required to consider providing information to employees' representatives about fixed-term work in the undertaking.

(*a*) holds a majority of that other undertaking's subscribed capital,

(*b*) controls a majority of the votes attached to that other undertaking's issued share capital, or

(*c*) can appoint more than half of the members of that other undertaking's administrative, management or supervisory body.

(3) Subject to *subsection (4)*, if more than one undertaking in the State meets the criteria in *subsection (2)*, the undertaking that meets the criterion in *subsection (2) (c)* shall be regarded as the controlling undertaking, or if no undertaking meets the criterion in *subsection (2) (c)*, then the undertaking that meets the criterion in *subsection (2) (b)* shall be regarded as the controlling undertaking in preference to one that meets the criterion in *subsection (2) (a)*.

(4) Where an undertaking (in this section referred to as a "joint venture"), wherever in the Community located, is carried on by two undertakings in the State neither of whom can exercise a dominant influence over the joint venture, it shall be regarded as a controlled undertaking of each of them unless they agree that it is a controlled undertaking of one only of them for the purposes of this Act, in which case, but subject to *subsection (5)*, that undertaking shall be regarded as the controlling undertaking of the joint venture.

(5) If being the controlled undertaking of one undertaking would result in employees of a joint venture being deprived of an entitlement to be informed and consulted under this Act they would have if the joint venture were a controlled undertaking of the other undertaking, that other undertaking shall be regarded as the controlling undertaking of the joint venture.

(6) For the purposes of *subsections (2)* and *(3)* but without prejudice to proof that another undertaking is able to exercise a dominant influence, a controlling undertaking's rights as regards voting and appointment referred to in *subsection (2) (b)* or *(c)* shall include—

(*a*) the rights of any other of its controlled undertakings, and (*b*) the rights of any person or body acting in the person's or body's own name but on behalf of the controlling undertaking (or any other of the controlling undertaking's controlled undertakings) as the controlling undertaking.

(7) Notwithstanding *subsections (1)*, *(2)*, *(3)*, *(4)* and *(5)*, an undertaking shall not be regarded as a controlling undertaking of another undertaking in which it has holdings where the first-mentioned undertaking is a company referred to in Article 3 (5) *(a)* and *(c)* of Council Regulation (EEC) No. 4064/89 of 21 December 1989 [2] , on the control of concentrations between undertakings.

[2] O.J. No. L395, 30.12.1989, p. 1.

(8) A dominant influence shall not be presumed to be exercised solely by virtue of the fact that an office holder is exercising functions, according to the law of a Member State, relating to liquidation, winding-up, insolvency, cessation of payments, compositions of creditors or analogous proceedings.

(9) The law applicable in order to determine whether an undertaking is a controlling undertaking shall be the law of the Member State which governs that undertaking. Where the law governing an undertaking is not that of a Member State, the law applicable shall be the law of the Member State within whose territory the representative of the undertaking or, in the absence of such a representative, the central management of the group undertaking which employs the highest number of employees in any one Member State, is situated.

(10) Where, in the case of a conflict of laws in the application of *subsection (2)* (except in its application in relation to *subsection (3)*, two or more undertakings from a group satisfy one or more of the criteria in *subsection (2)*, the undertaking which satisfies the criterion in *subsection (2) (c)* shall be regarded as the controlling undertaking unless it is proved that another undertaking is able to exercise a dominant influence.

Exemption.

6.—(1) Subject to *subsections (3)*, *(4)* and *(5)*, the obligations under this Act shall not apply to Community-scale undertakings or Community-scale groups of undertakings in which, on the commencement of this Act or the 22nd day of September, 1996, whichever is the earlier, there is or was in force within the same Community-scale undertaking or Community-scale group of undertakings an agreement covering the entire workforce providing for the transnational information and consultation of employees, and while that agreement remains in force.

(1A) Subject to *subsections (3)*, *(4)* and *(5)*, the obligations under this Act shall also not apply to Community-scale undertakings or Community-scale groups of undertakings in the United Kingdom which come within the scope of this Act by virtue of the application of Directive 97/74/EC of 15 December, 1997 of the Council of the European Union and in which there was in force within the same Community-scale undertaking or Community scale group of undertakings on 15 December, 1999 an agreement covering the entire workforce providing for the transnational information and consultation of employees, and while the agreement remains in force.[5]

(2) An agreement referred to in *subsection (1) or (1A)* may comprise multiple agreements within the same Community-scale undertaking or group of undertakings if, construed together, they satisfy the requirements of that subsection.[6]

(3) At any time before an agreement referred to in *subsection (1) or (1A)* expires or within the period of six months immediately after it expires, the parties to the agreement may jointly renew it for such further period as they think fit.[7]

(4) An agreement renewed under *subsection (3)* within the six months period referred to in that subsection shall be deemed to have remained in force from the date it would otherwise have expired.

---

[5] Section 6(1A) of the 1996 Act was inserted by Article 3 of the European Communities (Transnational Information and Consultation of Employees Act, 1996) (Amendment) Regulations, 1999 (S.I. No. 386 of 1999).

[6] The words "*subsection (1)* or *(1A)*" were substituted for the words "*subsection (1)*" in s. 6(2) of the 1996 Act by Article 3 of the European Communities (Transnational Information and Consultation of Employees Act, 1996) (Amendment) Regulations, 1999 (S.I. No. 386 of 1999).

[7] The words "*subsection (1)* or *(1A)*" were substituted for the words "*subsection (1)*" in s. 6(3) of the 1996 Act by Article 3 of the European Communities (Transnational Information and Consultation of Employees Act, 1996) (Amendment) Regulations, 1999 (S.I. No. 386 of 1999).

(5) Where an agreement is not renewed in pursuance of *subsection (3)* before its expiration or before the expiration of the six months period referred to in that subsection, this Act shall, on the expiration of that six months period, but not before, apply in full to and in relation to the Community-scale undertaking or group of undertakings to which the agreement applied.

(6) An agreement referred to in *subsection (1) or (1A)* shall be presumed to be valid unless proved to the contrary, and shall remain in force—[8]

(*a*) for such period, if any, as is specified in the agreement or the agreement as renewed; or

(*b*) in the case of an open ended agreement, until it is brought to an end in accordance with its terms.

(7) An agreement referred to in *subsection (1) or (1A)* shall not be valid unless it has been accepted by a majority of the workforce to which it applies.[9]

(8) In this section "agreement" includes an open ended agreement subject to review and alteration by the parties.

Regulations.

7. —(1) The Minister may make such regulations as are necessary for the purpose of giving effect to this Act and in particular in relation to—

(*a*) expenses to be borne by the central managements in relation to undertakings and groups of undertakings;

(*b*) the appointment of an arbitrator for the purposes of *section 20* and the terms and conditions to which such an appointment shall be subject;

---

[8] The words "*subsection (1)* or *(1A)*" were substituted for the words "*subsection (1)*" in s. 6(6) of the 1996 Act by Article 3 of the European Communities (Transnational Information and Consultation of Employees Act, 1996) (Amendment) Regulations, 1999 (S.I. No. 386 of 1999).

[9] The words "*subsection (1)* or *(1A)*" were substituted for the words "*subsection (1)*" in s. 6(7) of the 1996 Act by Article 3 of the European Communities (Transnational Information and Consultation of Employees Act, 1996) (Amendment) Regulations, 1999 (S.I. No. 386 of 1999).

(*c*) the powers and procedures of arbitrators, and the conduct of arbitration proceedings, under *sections 20* and *21*; and

(*d*) subject to the *Second Schedule* in relation to a European Works Council, the funding by central managements of the expenses of the operation of Special Negotiating Bodies, European Works Councils, European Employees' Fora or information and consultation procedures.

(2) Regulations under this Act may contain such incidental, supplementary and consequential provisions as appear to the Minister to be expedient for any purpose of this Act.

(3) Every regulation made by the Minister under this section shall be laid before each House of the Oireachtas as soon as practicable after it is made and, if a resolution annulling the regulation is passed by either such House within the next subsequent 21 days on which that House has sat after the regulation is laid before it, the regulation shall be annulled accordingly, but without prejudice to the validity of anything previously done under it.

General obligations.

8. —(1) In order to improve the right of employees in Community-scale undertakings and Community-scale groups of undertakings to be informed and consulted, a European Works Council or arrangements for the information and consultation of employees shall be established in every such undertaking and group of undertakings in the manner and under terms, and with the effects, laid down in this Act.

(2) Where a Community-scale group of undertakings consists of one or more undertakings or groups of undertakings which in themselves are Community-scale undertakings or Community-scale groups of undertakings and the employees or their representatives request the establishment of a European Works Council or arrangements for the information and consultation of employees, the European Works Council or, where those arrangements require its establishment, a European Employees' Forum shall be established at the level of the group, unless an agreement referred to in *section 11 (1)* provides otherwise.

(3) Unless a wider application is provided for in an agreement referred to in *section 11 (1)*, the powers and competence of or in relation to an arrangement for the information and consultation of employees (including a European Employees' Forum or an information and consultation procedure), or of a European Works Council established pursuant to this Act, shall—

(*a*) in the case of a Community-scale undertaking, cover all the establishments; and

(*b*) in the case of a Community-scale group of undertakings, cover all group undertakings,

located within the Member States.

PART II

Establishment Of An Employee Information And Consultation Procedure Or A European Employees' Forum Or A European Works Council

Responsibility of central management.

9. —(1) The central management shall be responsible for creating the conditions and means necessary for the setting up of an arrangement for the information and consultation of employees, as required by *section 8 (1)*, in a Community-scale undertaking and a Community-scale group of undertakings.

(2) Subject to *subsection (3)*, where the central management is not located in a Member State, the central management's representative agent in the State, which must be the management of an establishment or part-undertaking of the undertaking or group of undertakings and nominated in writing for that purpose by the central management if not otherwise appointed, shall assume the responsibility referred to in *subsection (1)*.

(3) In the absence of a representative referred to in *subsection (2)*, the management of the establishment or group undertaking in which the greatest number of employees are employed in any one Member State shall assume the responsibility referred to in *subsection (1)*.

(4) For the purposes of this Act, the representative or representatives or, in the absence of any such representative, the

management referred to in *subsection (3)*, shall be regarded as the central management.

10. —(1) In order to facilitate the information and consultation of employees in Community-scale undertakings and Community-scale groups of undertakings, the central management may on its own initiative, or shall at the written request of at least a total of 100 employees or their representatives spread over at least two undertakings or establishments one or more of which are in one Member State and the other or others of which are in at least one other Member State, establish a Special Negotiating Body to negotiate with the central management for the establishment of a European Employees' Forum or an information and consultation procedure.

Establishment of Special Negotiating Body.

(2) For the purposes of *subsection (1)*, "representatives" includes those employees' representatives already recognised by the undertaking or group of undertakings for collective bargaining or information and consultation purposes.

(3) (*a*) A request by employees for the establishment of a Special Negotiating Body shall be addressed to the central management but may be lodged with the local management where the identity or location of the central management is not readily discernible to the employees or their representatives making the request.

(*b*) Where the request is lodged with the local management, the local management shall ensure that the request is passed on to the central management within a period of 15 working days from its receipt.

(*c*) Any avoidable or unreasonable delay after that period in the transmission of the request to the central management shall not of itself extend the six month period referred to in *section 13 (1) (b)*.

(4) A Special Negotiating Body shall be established in accordance with the following:

(*a*) subject to *paragraphs (b)* and *(c)*, the Body shall have not less than three but not more than 18 members elected or appointed in accordance with this Act; [10]

(*b*) each Member State in which the Community-scale undertaking has one or more establishments, or in which the Community-scale group of undertakings has the controlling undertaking or one or more controlled undertakings, shall be represented by at least one member;

(*c*) there shall be the following additional members in proportion to the number of employees employed in the establishments, the controlling undertaking or the controlled undertakings:

(i) one additional member from a Member State where between 25 per cent. and 50 per cent. of the employees of the undertaking or group of undertakings are employed;

(ii) two additional members from a Member State where more than 50 per cent. but not more than 75 per cent. of the employees of the undertaking or group of undertakings are employed;

(iii) three additional members from a Member State where more than 75 per cent. of the employees of the undertaking or group of undertakings are employed;

(*d*) employees' representatives from countries that are not within the Community may be permitted to participate in the meetings and activities of the Body but shall not be entitled to a vote.

(5) The central management and local managements shall be informed by notice in writing of the composition of the Special Negotiating Body as soon as practicable after the election or appointment of its members.

---

[10] The words "18 members" were substituted for the words "17 members" in s. 10(4)(a) of the 1996 Act by Article 4 of the European Communities (Transnational Information and Consultation of Employees Act, 1996) (Amendment) Regulations, 1999 (S.I. No. 386 of 1999).

11. —(1) Subject to *subsection (4)* and *section 12 (8)*, the function of the Special Negotiating Body shall be to negotiate with the central management for a written agreement or agreements for the establishment of arrangements for the information and consultation of employees and determining the matters referred to in *section 12 (3)*, *(4)* or *(5)*.

Functions of Special Negotiating Body.

(2) With a view to the conclusion of an agreement referred to in *subsection (1)*, the central management shall convene a meeting with the Special Negotiating Body and shall inform local managements accordingly.

(3) The Special Negotiating Body may be assisted by experts of its choice.

(4) The Special Negotiating Body may decide, by at least two thirds of the votes of its members present and entitled to vote at the meeting, not to open negotiations referred to in *subsection (1)*, or to terminate negotiations already opened.

(5) A decision taken under *subsection (4)* shall cause the cessation of the procedure to conclude an agreement referred to in *subsection (1)* and when it has been taken the provisions in the *Second Schedule* shall not apply.

(6) A new request to convene a Special Negotiating Body shall not be made earlier than two years after a decision taken under *subsection (4)*, unless the parties concerned agree on a shorter period.

(7) The reasonable expenses relating to the negotiations referred to in *subsection (1)* shall be borne by the central management so as to enable the Special Negotiating Body to carry out its functions in an appropriate manner.

(8) For the purposes of *subsection (7)*, reasonable expenses shall include the cost of meetings of the Special Negotiating Body, whether with the central management or otherwise, including the cost of materials, the venue, translations, travel and accommodation, and the equivalent cost of one expert per meeting.

12.—(1) The central management and the Special Negotiating Body shall carry out the negotiations referred to in *section 11 (1)* in a spirit of co-operation with a view to reaching an agreement or agreements.

Content of agreement.

(2) An arrangement for the information and consultation of employees referred to in *section 11 (1)* may invoke the establishment of a European Employees' Forum but the parties may also agree to establish one or more information and consultation procedures instead of a European Employees' Forum.

(3) Without prejudice to the autonomy of the parties or the generality of *section 11 (1)*, an agreement making arrangements for the information and consultation of employees, whether it involves the establishment of a European Employees' Forum or an information and consultation procedure, shall determine—

(*a*) the undertakings of the Community-scale group of undertakings, or the establishments of the Community-scale undertaking, covered by the agreement,

(*b*) the duration of the agreement and, subject to *subsection (8)*, the procedure for its re-negotiation, and

(*c*) by what method the information conveyed to employees' representatives shall be conveyed to employees in the State and the opinion of employees given on the information so conveyed shall be recorded, irrespective of the Member State in which the central management is located.

(4) Where an agreement requires the establishment of a European Employees' Forum, it shall also determine—

(*a*) the composition of the Forum, the number of members, the allocation of seats and the term of office,

(*b*) the functions, and the procedure for information and consultation, of the Forum,

(*c*) the venue, frequency and duration of meetings of the Forum, and

(*d*) the financial and other resources to be allocated to the Forum.

(5) Where an agreement requires the establishment of an information and consultation procedure, it shall also determine—

(*a*) what that procedure shall be,

(*b*) the issues for information and consultation,

(*c*) the methods according to which the employees' representatives in the different Member States can meet for exchange of views regarding the information conveyed to them, and

(*d*) the financial and other resources to be allocated to ensure the operation of the procedure and the holding of the meetings referred to in *paragraph (c)*.

(6) Unless it otherwise provides, an agreement shall not be subject to the subsidiary requirements of the *Second Schedule.*

(7) For the purposes of concluding an agreement, the Special Negotiating Body shall act by a majority of its members present and entitled to vote at a meeting.

(8) An agreement which results in the establishment of a European Employees' Forum or an information and consultation procedure shall not provide for its re-negotiation by a Special Negotiating Body but may be re-negotiated with the central management by the European Employees' Forum (which shall be deemed to continue in existence as may be necessary for that purpose) or the employees' representatives to the information and consultation procedure, as the case may be.

(9) A Special Negotiating Body shall remain in existence for as long only as it continues to have the function of negotiating for an agreement referred to in *section 11 (1)* and shall automatically dissolve on its ceasing to have that function.

Subsidiary requirements.

13. —(1) The subsidiary requirements set out in the *Second Schedule* shall apply to an undertaking or group of undertakings, and a European Works Council shall be established—

(*a*) where the central management and the Special Negotiating Body so agree,

(*b*) where the central management refuses to commence negotiations within six months of a request referred to in *section 10 (1)*, or (*c*) where after the expiration of a period of three years from the date of the request, the parties are unable to conclude an agreement and the Special Negotiating Body has not taken the decision provided for in *section 11 (4)*.

(2) Where the subsidiary requirements apply to an undertaking or group of undertakings, the central management shall as soon as practicable, but in any case not later than six months after they first become applicable, comply with the requirements.

PART III

MISCELLANEOUS

Employees' representatives representing employees employed in the State.

14. —Employees' representatives who represent employees employed in the State on a Special Negotiating Body, European Works Council or European Employees' Forum, or in relation to an information and consultation procedure, shall be—

(*a*) elected by those employees,

(*b*) appointed by those employees as determined by them, or

(*c*) appointed by the central management on a basis agreed with those employees,

and on written notification to the central management of their election or appointment being given shall, unless the contrary is proved, be regarded as having been duly elected or appointed.

Confidential information.

15. —(1) Subject to subsection (2) and section 20, a person who is or at any time was—

(*a*) a member of—

(i) a Special Negotiating Body,

(ii) a European Employees' Forum, or

(iii) a European Works Council,

or

(*b*) an employees' representative to an information and consultation procedure, shall not reveal any information expressly provided in confidence to him or her or to the Body, Forum or Council.

(2) A person may, in accordance with his or her duties as a member, expert or employees' representative to the procedure, disclose such information—

(*a*) to the Body, Forum or Council of which he or she is or was then a member,

(*b*) to another employees' representative to the procedure, or

(*c*) to the member, body or person he or she is or was then employed to advise.

(3) The central management may withhold from a Special Negotiating Body, European Employees' Forum, European Works Council or in connection with an information and consultation procedure, information that it claims is commercially sensitive—

(*a*) where it can show that the disclosure would be likely to prejudice significantly and adversely the economic or financial position of an undertaking or group of undertakings or breach statutory or regulatory rules, or

(*b*) where the information is of a kind that meets objective standards for determining that it should be withheld agreed between the central management and the Special Negotiating Body, European Employees' Forum, European Works Council or the employees' representatives to an information and consultation procedure.

(4) In this section "member" and "employees' representative to an information and consultation procedure" includes a person who at any time, as an expert, assists or assisted such a member or person.

Operation of information and consultation arrangements and European Works Council.

16. —The central management and the employees' representatives, in the framework of an arrangement for the information and consultation of employees (being either a European Employees' Forum or an information and consultation procedure) or a European Works Council, shall work in a spirit of co-operation with due regard to their reciprocal rights and obligations.

Protection of employees' representatives.

17. —(1) Employees' representatives who are employees and who perform their functions in accordance with this Act shall not—

(*a*) be dismissed or suffer any unfavourable change in their conditions of employment or any unfair treatment, including selection for redundancy, or

(*b*) suffer any other action prejudicial to their employment,

because of their status or reasonable activities as employees' representatives.

(2) Employees' representatives shall be afforded such reasonable facilities, including time off, as will enable them to carry out their functions as employees' representatives promptly and efficiently.

(3) *Subsections (1)* and *(2)* shall apply in particular to attendance by employees' representatives at meetings of Special Negotiating Bodies, European Employees' Fora, European Works Councils or any other meetings within the framework of an agreement referred to in *section 11 (1)* or of the *Second Schedule.*

(4) Employees' representatives who are employed in a Community-scale undertaking or a Community-scale group of undertakings shall be paid their wages (within the meaning of the Payment of Wages Act, 1991) for any period of absence for the purposes of the performance of their functions under this Act.

Offences.

18. —(1) An undertaking or group of undertakings the central management of which refuses to provide information about the workforce numbers or status of employees for the purposes of *section 4* or unreasonably and wilfully obstructs or delays the provision of such information, shall be guilty of an offence.

(2) An undertaking or group of undertakings the central management of which does not comply with the requirements referred to in *section 13 (2)* applicable to it shall be guilty of an offence.

(3) A person to whom *section 15 (1)* applies who, except as permitted by *section 15*, reveals information expressly provided in confidence to him or her, the Body, Forum or Council of which he or she is a member, or the member or body he or she is employed to advise, shall be guilty of an offence.

(4) Where an offence under this Act which is committed by a body corporate is proved to have been committed with the consent or connivance of, or to be attributable to any neglect on the part of, any person who, when the offence was committed, was a director, manager, secretary or other similar officer of the body or a person who was purporting to act in such capacity, that person (as well as the body corporate) shall be guilty of an offence and liable to be proceeded against and punished as if guilty of the offence committed by the body corporate.

19.—(1) A person guilty of an offence under *section 18 (1)* or *(2)* shall be liable— Prosecution and penalties.

(*a*) on summary conviction, to a fine not exceeding £1,500 or, at the discretion of the court, to imprisonment for a term not exceeding six months or to both the fine and the imprisonment, or

(*b*) on conviction on indictment, to a fine not exceeding £10,000 or, at the discretion of the court, to imprisonment for a term not exceeding three years or to both the fine and the imprisonment.

(2) If the offence under *section 18 (1)* or *(2)* of which a person was convicted is continued after conviction, the person shall be guilty of a further offence on every day on which the act or omission constituting the offence continues, and for each such further offence the person shall be liable on summary conviction to a fine not exceeding £200 or on conviction on indictment to a fine not exceeding £1,000.

(3) A person guilty of an offence under *section 18 (3)* shall be liable—

(*a*) on summary conviction, to a fine not exceeding £1,500 or, at the discretion of the court, to imprisonment for a term not exceeding six months or to both the fine and the imprisonment, or

(*b*) on conviction on indictment, to a fine not exceeding £10,000 or, at the discretion of the court, to imprisonment for a term not exceeding three years or to both the fine and the imprisonment.

(4) Proceedings in relation to a summary offence under section 18 may be brought and prosecuted by the Minister for Enterprise and Employment.

Arbitration relating to confidentiality and withholding of sensitive information.

20. —(1) Disputes between the central management and employees (or their representatives) employed in the State concerning the withholding by the central management of commercially sensitive information or as to whether information disclosed by the central management in confidence to employees' representatives is of a kind that, pursuant to *section 15*, may not be revealed, may be referred by either the central management or employees' representatives to an independent arbitrator appointed by the Minister under regulations made for the purposes of this section.

(2) An arbitrator appointed under *subsection (1)* shall be paid, from moneys made available for that purpose by the Oireachtas, such fees as the Minister, with the consent of the Minister for Finance, may determine.

(3) The parties to an arbitration under this section shall each bear their own costs.

(4) The procedure adopted by the arbitrator shall, as far as practi- cable, protect the confidentiality of the information concerned.

(5) A party to an arbitration under this section may not appeal to a court against a determination of the arbitrator except on a point of law.

Arbitration relating to disputes concerning interpretation or operation of agreements.

21. —(1) Disputes between the central management and employees (or their representatives) concerning the interpretation or operation of an agreement referred to in *section 11 (1)* may be referred by either the central management or employees' representatives to an independent arbitrator appointed, on such terms as to remuneration or otherwise, as agreed between the parties.

(2) If the parties cannot reach agreement on the appointment or terms of appointment of an arbitrator, either of them may apply to the Labour Court established by section 10 of the Industrial Relations Act, 1946, which shall refer the dispute to the arbitration of one or more persons as it thinks fit.

(3) An arbitrator to whom under *subsection (2)* a dispute is referred shall be paid such fees as the Minister, with the consent of the Minister for Finance, may determine, which fees shall be paid by the parties or a party to the arbitration as directed by the arbitrator.

(4) An arbitrator to whom under *subsection (2)* a dispute is referred shall make his or her determination on the basis of the written submissions of the parties, but may conduct a hearing, at which both parties may be present, if he or she thinks the circumstances of the case require it.

(5) Subject to *subsection (3)*, the parties to an arbitration under this section shall bear their own costs.

(6) A party to an arbitration under this section may not appeal to a court against a determination of the arbitrator except on a point of law.

22.—This Act shall apply without prejudice to— Application.

(*a*) the Protection of Employment Act, 1977, as amended,

(*b*) [the European Communities (Protection of Employees on Transfer of Undertakings) Regulations 2003 (S.I. No. 131 of 2003)].[11]

---

[11] The original version of para. (b) of s. 22 referred to the European Communities (Safeguarding of Employees' Rights on Transfer of Undertakings) Regulations, 1980 (S.I. No. 306 of 1980). Under s. 26 (2) of the Interpretation Act 2005, however, where an enactment is repealed and reenacted, with or without modification, by another enactment, (with the concept of 'enactment' including, in this context, a statutory instrument and the concept of 'repeal' including revocation, (see s. 2(1) of the 2005 Act)) a reference in any other enactment to the former enactment shall, with respect to a subsequent transaction, matter or thing, be read as a reference to the provisions of the new enactment relating to the same subject-matter as that of the former enactment. The European

Arbitration Acts not to apply to arbitrations under *sections 20* and *21*.

23. —The Arbitration Acts, 1954 and 1980, shall not apply to or in relation to an arbitration under *section 20* or *21*.

FIRST SCHEDULE

Paragraph 2 (2) of *Second Schedule*.

Election of Employees' Representatives

1. An employee who is employed in the State by the relevant undertaking or group of undertakings (wherever located) on the day or days of the election for employees' representatives, shall be entitled to vote in such an election.

2. An employee who has been employed in the State by the undertaking or group of undertakings in a full-time or regular part-time capacity for a continuous period of not less than one year on the nomination day, or, in relation to a Special Negotiating Body, a trade union official or official of an excepted body, whether or not he or she is an employee, shall be eligible to stand as a candidate for election as an employees' representative provided that he or she is nominated—

(*a*) by a trade union or an excepted body which is already recognised by the business units of the undertaking or group of undertakings located in the State for collective bargaining or information and consultation purposes, or

(*b*) by at least two employees.

3. Where the number of candidates on the nomination day exceeds the number of employees' representatives to be elected to the Special Negotiating Body or a European Works Council,

---

Communities (Safeguarding of Employees' Rights on Transfer of Undertakings) Regulations, 1980 (S.I. No. 306 of 1980) (as well as the European Communities (Safeguarding of Employees' Rights on Transfer of Undertakings) (Amendment) Regulations, 2000 (S.I. No. 487 of 2000, which both amended and built upon the 1980 Regulations) were revoked by Regulation 15 of the European Communities (Protection of Employees on Transfer of Undertakings) Regulations 2003 (S.I. No. 131 of 2003). The 2003 Regulations reenacted the provisions of S.I. No. 306 of 1980 and S.I. No. 487 of 2000 with substantial modifications.

or in connection with an arrangement for the information and consultation of employees, a poll shall be taken by the returning officer and voting in the poll shall take place by secret ballot on a day or days to be decided by the returning officer and according to the principle of proportional representation.

4. The central management in consultation with existing employee representatives shall appoint a returning officer whose duties shall include the organisation and conduct of nominations and elections and that officer may authorise other persons to assist in the performance of the duties of returning officer.

5. The returning officer shall perform his or her duties in a fair and reasonable manner and in the interests of an orderly and proper conduct of nomination and election procedures.

6. The cost of the nomination and election procedure shall be borne by the central management.

SECOND SCHEDULE

Section 13 (1).

Subsidiary Requirements: European Works Council

Competence.

1. (1) The competence of the European Works Council (in this Schedule referred to as "the Council") shall be limited to information and consultation on matters which concern the Community-scale undertaking or Community-scale group of undertakings as a whole or at least two of its establishments or group undertakings situated in different Member States. This provision shall apply whether the central management is located within the Community or elsewhere.

(2) In the case of undertakings or groups of undertakings referred to in *section 9 (2)*, the competence of the Council shall be limited to those matters concerning all their establishments or group undertakings located within the Member States or concerning at least two of their establishments or group undertakings located in different Member States.

Composition.

2. (1) The Council shall be composed of employees' representatives who shall be employees of the Community-scale undertaking or Community-scale group of undertakings.

(2) The representatives of employees based in the State shall be elected in accordance with the *First Schedule*.

(3) In the absence of elections, the representatives shall be appointed.

(4) The Council shall have at least three but not more than 30 members but, where it considers that its size so warrants, it shall elect a select committee from among its members comprising not more than three members.

Procedure.

3. The Council shall adopt its own rules of procedure subject to the following:

(*a*) the arrangements for the meetings of the Council shall be agreed by the central management in consultation with employees or their representatives but the management may not unreasonably withhold consent to proposals made by employees or their representatives;

(*b*) the minutes of the Council meetings shall be approved by both management and employees' representatives to the Council;

(*c*) before any meeting with the central management, the Council or a select committee, where necessary enlarged in accordance with *paragraph 5 (5)*, shall be entitled to meet without the management concerned being present;

(*d*) without prejudice to *section 15*, the members of the Council shall inform the representatives of the employees employed in the establishments of, or employees of the undertakings of, a Community-scale group of undertakings, or in the absence of such representatives, the workforce as a whole, of the content and outcome of the information and consultation procedures carried out in accordance with this Schedule;

(*e*) the Council or the select committee may be assisted by such experts of its choice as are necessary for it to carry out its task.

4. (1) In the election or appointment of members of the Council, the central management shall, as far as it is able to, ensure— Election or appointment of members.

(*a*) that each Member State in which the Community-scale undertaking has one or more establishments or in which the Community-scale group of undertakings has the controlling undertaking or one or more controlled undertakings, is represented by one member, and

(*b*) that there are additional or supplementary members in proportion to the number of employees employed in the establishments, or by the controlling undertaking or the controlled undertakings, in accordance with the following:

(i) one additional member from a Member State where between 25 per cent. and 50 per cent. of the employees of the undertaking or group of undertakings are employed;

(ii) two additional members from a Member State where more than 50 per cent. but not more than 75 per cent. of the employees of the undertaking or group of undertakings are employed;

(iii) three additional members from a Member State where more than 75 per cent. of the employees of the undertaking or group of undertakings are employed.

(2) The central management, or such other level of management as the central management thinks more appropriate, shall be informed of the composition of the Council as soon as practicable after election or appointment of its members.

5. (1) The Council shall have the right to meet with the central management once a year, to be informed and consulted, on the basis of a report drawn up by the central management, on the progress of the business of the Community-scale undertaking or Community-scale group of undertakings and its prospects, and local managements shall be informed accordingly. Functions.

(2) The meeting shall relate in particular to the structure, economic and financial situation and probable trends in employment, investments, and substantial changes concerning the organisation, introduction of new working methods or production processes, transfer of production, mergers, cutbacks or closures of undertakings, establishments or important parts thereof, and collective redundancies.

(3) Where there are exceptional circumstances affecting the employees' interests to a considerable extent, particularly in the event of relocation, the closure of establishments or undertakings or collective redundancies, a select committee or, where no such committee exists, the Council, shall have the right to be informed and the right to meet, at its request, the central management or such other level of management as the central management thinks more appropriate and advises the Council, so as to be informed and consulted on measures significantly affecting employees' interests.

(4) For the purposes of *subparagraph (3)*, collective redundancies are those which concern a significant number of employees in relation to the size of the Community-scale undertaking, the establishment, the Community-scale group of undertakings or the undertaking which is a member or part of the Community-scale group of undertakings, in which the collective redundancy is taking place.

(5) Those members of the Council who have been elected or appointed from the establishments or undertakings which are directly concerned with the measures referred to in *subparagraph (3)* shall also have the right to participate in the meeting organised with the select committee.

(6) The information and consultation meeting referred to in *subparagraph (3)* shall take place as soon as possible after any request to meet the central management, on the basis of a report prepared by the central management, on which an opinion may be delivered at the end of the meeting or within a reasonable time.

(7) The meeting shall not affect the prerogatives of the central management.

6. (1) The operating expenses of the Council, including a select committee where one is established, shall be borne by the central management. Expenses.

(2) The central management concerned shall provide the members of the Council with such financial and other resources as are necessary to enable them to perform their duties in an appropriate manner.

(3) In particular, the cost of ongoing meetings and arranging for interpretation facilities and the accommodation and travelling expenses of members of the Council and its select committee shall be met by the central management unless otherwise agreed.

(4) The funding of experts by the central management shall be limited to funding the equivalent of one expert per meeting.

7. (1) Four years after the establishment of the Council it shall examine whether to open negotiations for the conclusion of an agreement referred to in *section 11 (1)* or to continue to apply the requirements adopted in accordance with this Schedule. Miscellaneous.

(2) *Sections 11* and *12*, with any necessary modifications, shall apply if a decision has been taken to negotiate an agreement referred to in *section 11 (1)*, in which case "Special Negotiating Body" in those sections shall be read as "European Works Council".

COUNCIL DIRECTIVE 94/45/EC

of 22 September 1994

on the establishment of a European Works Council or a procedure in Community-scale undertakings and Community-scale groups of undertakings for the purposes of informing and consulting employees

(Official Journal of the European Communities 30.9.1994 L 254/64)

THE COUNCIL OF THE EUROPEAN UNION,

Having regard to the Agreement on social policy annexed to Protocol 14 on social policy annexed to the Treaty establishing the European Community, and in particular Article 2 (2) thereof,

Having regard to the proposal from the Commission (1),

Having regard to the opinion of the Economic and Social Committee (2),

Acting in accordance with the procedure referred to in Article 189c of the Treaty (3),

---

(1) OJ No C 135, 18.5.1994, p. 8 and OJ No C 199, 21.7.1994, p. 10.

(2) Opinion delivered on 1 June 1994 (not yet published in the Official Journal).

(3) Opinion of the European Parliament of 4 May 1994 (OJ No C 205, 25.7.1994) and Council common position of 18 July 1994 (OJ No C 244, 31.8.1994, p. 37).

Whereas, on the basis of the Protocol on Social Policy annexed to the Treaty establishing the European Community, the Kingdom of Belgium, the Kingdom of Denmark, the Federal Republic of Germany, the Hellenic Republic, the Kingdom of Spain, the French Republic, Ireland, the Italian Republic, the Grand Duchy of Luxembourg, the Kingdom of the Netherlands and the Portuguese Republic (hereinafter referred to as 'the Member States'), desirous of implementing the Social Charter of 1989, have adopted an Agreement on Social Policy;

Whereas Article 2 (2) of the said Agreement authorizes the Council to adopt minimum requirements by means of directives;

Whereas, pursuant to Article 1 of the Agreement, one particular objective of the Community and the Member States is to promote dialogue between management and labour;

Whereas point 17 of the Community Charter of Fundamental Social Rights of Workers provides, inter alia, that information, consultation and participation for workers must be developed along appropriate lines, taking account of the practices in force in different Member States; whereas the Charter states that 'this shall apply especially in companies or groups of companies having establishments or companies in two or more Member States';

Whereas the Council, despite the existence of a broad consensus among the majority of Member States, was unable to act on the proposal for a Council Directive on the establishment of a European Works Council in Community-scale undertakings or groups of undertakings for the purposes of informing and consulting employees ([4]), as amended on 3 December 1991 ([5]);

([4]) OJ No C 39, 15.2.1991, p. 10.
([5]) OJ No C 336, 31.12.1991, p. 11.

Whereas the Commission, pursuant to Article 3 (2) of the Agreement on Social Policy, has consulted management and labour at Community level on the possible direction of Community action on the information and consultation of workers in Community-scale undertakings and Community-scale groups of undertakings;

Whereas the Commission, considering after this consultation that Community action was advisable, has again consulted management and labour on the content of the planned proposal, pursuant to Article 3 (3) of the said Agreement, and management and labour have presented their opinions to the Commission;

Whereas, following this second phase of consultation, management and labour have not informed the Commission of their wish to initiate the process which might lead to the conclusion of an agreement, as provided for in Article 4 of the Agreement;

Whereas the functioning of the internal market involves a process of concentrations of undertakings, cross-border mergers, take-overs, joint ventures and, consequently, a transnationalization of undertakings and groups of undertakings; whereas, if economic activities are to develop in a harmonious fashion, undertakings and groups of undertakings operating in two or more Member States must inform and consult the representatives of those of their employees that are affected by their decisions;

Whereas procedures for informing and consulting employees as embodied in legislation or practice in the Member States are often not geared to the transnational structure of the entity which takes the decisions affecting those employees; whereas this may lead to the unequal treatment of employees affected by decisions within one and the same undertaking or group of undertakings;

Whereas appropriate provisions must be adopted to ensure that the employees of Community-scale undertakings are properly informed and consulted when decisions which affect them are taken in a Member State other than that in which they are employed;

Whereas, in order to guarantee that the employees of undertakings or groups of undertakings operating in two or more Member States are properly informed and consulted, it is necessary to set up European Works Councils or to create other suitable procedures for the transnational information and consultation of employees;

Whereas it is accordingly necessary to have a definition of the concept of controlling undertaking relating solely to this Directive and not prejudging definitions of the concepts of group or control which might be adopted in texts to be drafted in the future;

Whereas the mechanisms for informing and consulting employees in such undertakings or groups must encompass all of the establishments or, as the case may be, the group's undertakings located within the Member States, regardless of whether the undertaking or the group's controlling undertaking has its central management inside or outside the territory of the Member States;

Whereas, in accordance with the principle of autonomy of the parties, it is for the representatives of employees and the management of the under- taking or the group's controlling undertaking to determine by agreement the nature, composition, the function, mode of operation, procedures and financial resources of European Works Councils or other information and consultation procedures so as to suit their own particular circumstances;

Whereas, in accordance with the principle of subsidiarity, it is for the Member States to determine who the employees' representatives are and in particular to provide, if they consider appropriate, for a balanced representation of different categories of employees;

Whereas, however, provision should be made for certain subsidiary requirements to apply should the parties so decide or in the event of the central management refusing to initiate negotiations or in the absence of agreement subsequent to such negotiations;

Whereas, moreover, employees' representatives may decide not to seek the setting-up of a European Works Council or the parties concerned may decide on other procedures for the transnational information and consultation of employees;

Whereas, without prejudice to the possibility of the parties deciding otherwise, the European Works Council set up in the absence of agreement between the parties must, in order to fulfil the objective of this Directive, be kept informed and consulted on the activities of the undertaking or group of undertakings so that it may assess the possible impact on employees' interests in at least two different Member States; whereas, to that end, the undertaking or controlling undertaking must be required to communicate to the employees' appointed representatives general information concerning the interests of employees and information relating more specifically to those aspects of the activities of the undertaking or group of undertakings which affect employees' interests; whereas the European Works Council must be able to deliver an opinion at the end of that meeting;

Whereas certain decisions having a significant effect on the interests of employees must be the subject of information and consultation of the employees' appointed representatives as soon as possible;

Whereas provision should be made for the employees' representatives acting within the framework of the Directive to enjoy, when exercising their functions, the same protection and guarantees similar to those provided to employees' representatives by the legislation and /or practice of the country of employment; whereas they must not be subject to any discrimination as a result of the lawful exercise of their activities and must enjoy adequate protection as regards dismissal and other sanctions;

Whereas the information and consultation provisions laid down in this Directive must be implemented in the case of an undertaking or a group's controlling undertaking which has its central management outside the territory of the Member States by its representative agent, to be designated if necessary, in one of the Member States or, in the absence of such an agent, by the establishment or controlled undertaking employing the greatest number of employees in the Member States;

Whereas special treatment should be accorded to Community-scale undertakings and groups of undertakings in which there exists, at the time when this Directive is brought into effect, an agreement, covering the entire workforce, providing for the transnational information and consultation of employees;

Whereas the Member States must take appropriate measures in the event of failure to comply with the obligations laid down in this Directive,

HAS ADOPTED THIS DIRECTIVE:

SECTION I
GENERAL

Article 1

Objective

1. The purpose of this Directive is to improve the right to information and to consultation of employees in Community-scale undertakings and Community-scale groups of undertakings.

2. To that end, a European Works Council or a procedure for informing and consulting employees shall be established in every Community-scale undertaking and every Community-scale group of undertakings, where requested in the manner laid down in Article 5 (1), with the purpose of informing and consulting employees under the terms, in the manner and with the effects laid down in this Directive.

3. Notwithstanding paragraph 2, where a Community-scale group of undertakings within the meaning of Article 2 (1) (c) comprises one or more undertakings or groups of undertakings which are Community-scale undertakings or Community-scale groups of undertakings within the meaning of Article 2 (1) (a) or (c), a European Works Council shall be established at the level of the group unless the agreements referred to in Article 6 provide otherwise.

4. Unless a wider scope is provided for in the agreements referred to in Article 6, the powers and competence of European Works Councils and the scope of information and consulation procedures established to achieve the purpose specified in paragraph 1 shall, in the case of a Community-scale undertaking, cover all the establishments located within the Member States and, in the case of a Community-scale group of undertakings, all group undertakings located within the Member States.

5. Member States may provide that this Directive shall not apply to merchant navy crews.

Article 2

Definitions

1. For the purposes of this Directive:

(a) 'Community-scale undertaking' means any undertaking with at least 1000 employees within the Member States and at least 150 employees in each of at least two Member States;

(b) 'group of undertakings' means a controlling undertaking and its controlled undertakings;

(c) 'Community-scale group of undertakings' means a group of undertakings with the following characteristics:

— at least 1000 employees within the Member States,

— at least two group undertakings in different Member States, and

— at least one group undertaking with at least 150 employees in one Member State and at least one other group undertaking with at least 150 employees in another Member State;

(d) 'employees' representatives' means the employees' representatives provided for by national law and/or practice;

(e) 'central management' means the central management of the Community-scale undertaking or, in the case of a Community-scale group of undertakings, of the controlling undertaking;

(f) 'consultation' means the exchange of views and establishment of dialogue between employees' representatives and central management or any more appropriate level of management;

(g) 'European Works Council' means the council established in accordance with Article 1 (2) or the provisions of the Annex, with the purpose of informing and consulting employees;

(h) 'special negotiating body' means the body established in accordance with Article 5 (2) to negotiate with the central management regarding the establishment of a European Works Council or a procedure for informing and consulting employees in accordance with Article 1 (2).

2. For the purposes of this Directive, the prescribed thresholds for the size of the workforce shall be based on the average number of employees, including part-time employees, employed during the previous two years calculated according to national legislation and/or practice.

Article 3

Definition of 'controlling undertaking'

1. For the purposes of this Directive, 'controlling undertaking' means an undertaking which can exercise a dominant influence over another undertaking ('the controlled undertaking') by virtue, for example, of ownership, financial participation or the rules which govern it.

2. The ability to exercise a dominant influence shall be presumed, without prejudice to proof to the contrary, when, in relation to another undertaking directly or indirectly:[1]

(a) holds a majority of that undertaking's subscribed capital; or

(b) controls a majority of the votes attached to that undertaking's issued share capital; or

(c) can appoint more than half of the members of that undertaking's administrative, management or supervisory body.

3. For the purposes of paragraph 2, a controlling undertaking's rights as regards voting and appointment shall include the rights of any other controlled undertaking and those of any person or body acting in his or its own name but on behalf of the controlling undertaking or of any other controlled undertaking.

4. Notwithstanding paragraphs 1 and 2, an undertaking shall not be deemed to be a 'controlling undertaking' with respect to another undertaking in which it has holdings where the former undertaking is a company referred to in Article 3 (5) (*a*) or (*c*) of Council Regulation (EEC) No 4064/89 of 21 December 1989 on the control of concentrations between undertakings ([6]).

([6]) OJ No L 395, 30.12.1989, p. 1.

5. A dominant influence shall not be presumed to be exercised solely by virtue of the fact that an office holder is exercising his functions, according to the law of a Member State relating to liquidation, winding up, insolvency, cessation of payments, compositions or analogous proceedings.

6. The law applicable in order to determine whether an undertaking is a 'controlling undertaking' shall be the law of the Member State which governs that undertaking.

[1] *Sic.*

Where the law governing that undertaking is not that of a Member State, the law applicable shall be the law of the Member State within whose territory the representative of the undertaking or, in the absence of such a representative, the central management of the group undertaking which employs the greatest number of employees is situated.

7. Where, in the case of a conflict of laws in the application of paragraph 2, two or more undertakings from a group satisfy one or more of the criteria laid down in that paragraph, the undertaking which satisfies the criterion laid down in point (*c*) thereof shall be regarded as the controlling under- taking, without prejudice to proof that another undertaking is able to exercise a dominant influence.

SECTION II

ESTABLISHMENT OF A EUROPEAN WORKS COUNCIL OR AN EMPLOYEE INFORMATION AND CONSULTATION PROCEDURE

Article 4

Responsibility for the establishment of a European Works Council or an employee information and consultation procedure

1. The central management shall be responsible for creating the conditions and means necessary for the setting up of a European Works Council or an information and consultation procedure, as provided for in Article 1 (2), in a Community-scale undertaking and a Communuty-scale group of undertakings.

2. Where the central management is not situated in a Member State, the central management's representative agent in a Member State, to be designated if necessary, shall take on the responsibility referred to in paragraph 1.

In the absence of such a representative, the management of the establishment or group undertaking employing the greatest number of employees in any one Member State shall take on the responsibility referred to in paragraph 1.

3. For the purposes of this Directive, the representative or representatives or, in the absence of any such representatives, the management referred to in the second subparagraph of paragraph 2, shall be regarded as the central management.

Article 5

Special negotiating body

1. In order to achieve the objective in Article 1 (1), the central management shall initiate negotiations for the establishment of a European Works Council or an information and consultation procedure on its own initiative or at the written request of at least 100 employees or their representatives in at least two undertakings or establishments in at least two different Member States.

2. For this purpose, a special negotiating body shall be established in accordance with the following guidelines:

(a) The Member States shall determine the method to be used for the election or appointment of the members of the special negotiating body who are to be elected or appointed in their territories.

Member States shall provide that employees in undertakings and/or establishments in which there are no employees' representatives through no fault of their own, have the right to elect or appoint members of the special negotiating body.

The second subparagraph shall be without prejudice to national legislation and/or practice laying down thresholds for the establishment of employee representation bodies.

(b) The special negotiating body shall have a minimum of three and a maximum of 18 members.[2]

(c) In these elections or appointments, it must be ensured:

— firstly, that each Member State in which the Community-scale undertaking has one or more establishments or in which the Community-scale group of undertakings has the controlling undertaking or one or more controlled undertakings is represented by one member,

— secondly, that there are supplementary members in proportion to the number of employees working in the establishments, the controlling undertaking or the controlled undertakings as laid

[2] The number 17 was replaced by the number 18 in Article 5(2)(b) by Article 2 of Council Directive 97/74/EC of 15 December 1997 extending, to the United Kingdom of Great Britain and Northern Ireland, Directive 94/45/EC on the establishment of a European Works Council or a procedure in Community-scale undertakings and Community-scale groups of undertakings for the purposes of informing and consulting employees.

down by the legislation of the Member State within the territory of which the central management is situated.

(d) The central management and local management shall be informed of the composition of the special negotiating body.

3. The special negotiating body shall have the task of determining, with the central management, by written agreement, the scope, composition, functions, and term of office of the European Works Council(s) or the arrangements for implementing a procedure for the information and consultation of employees.

4. With a view to the conclusion of an agreement in accordance with Article 6, the central management shall convene a meeting with the special negotiating body. It shall inform the local managements accordingly.

For the purpose of the negotiations, the special negotiating body may be assisted by experts of its choice.

5. The special negotiating body may decide, by at least two-thirds of the votes, not to open negotiations in accordance with paragraph 4, or to terminate the negotiations already opened.

Such a decision shall stop the procedure to conclude the agreement referred to in Article 6. Where such a decision has been taken, the provisions in the Annex shall not apply.

A new request to convene the special negotiating body may be made at the earliest two years after the abovementioned decision unless the parties concerned lay down a shorter period.

6. Any expenses relating to the negotiations referred to in paragraphs 3 and 4 shall be borne by the central management so as to enable the special negotiating body to carry out its task in an appropriate manner.

In compliance with this principle, Member States may lay down budgetary rules regarding the operation of the special negotiating body. They may in particular limit the funding to cover one expert only.

Article 6

Content of the agreement

1. The central management and the special negotiating body must negotiate in a spirit of cooperation with a view to reaching an agreement on the detailed arrangements for implementing the information and consultation of employees provided for in Article 1 (1).

2. Without prejudice to the autonomy of the parties, the agreement referred to in paragraph 1 between the central management and the special negotiating body shall determine:

(a) the undertakings of the Community-scale group of undertakings or the establishments of the Community-scale undertaking which are covered by the agreement;

(b) the composition of the European Works Council, the number of members, the allocation of seats and the term of office;

(c) the functions and the procedure for information and consultation of the European Works Council;

(d) the venue, frequency and duration of meetings of the European Works Council;

(e) the financial and material resources to be allocated to the European Works Council;

(f) the duration of the agreement and the procedure for its renegotiation.

3. The central management and the special negotiating body may decide, in writing, to establish one or more information and consultation procedures instead of a European Works Council.

The agreement must stipulate by what method the employees' representatives shall have the right to meet to discuss the information conveyed to them.

This information shall relate in particular to transnational questions which significantly affect workers' interests.

4. The agreements referred to in paragraphs 2 and 3 shall not, unless provision is made otherwise therein, be subject to the subsidiary requirements of the Annex.

5. For the purposes of concluding the agreements referred to in paragraphs 2 and 3, the special negotiating body shall act by a majority of its members.

Article 7

Subsidiary requirements

1. In order to achieve the objective in Article 1 (1), the subsidiary requirements laid down by the legislation of the Member State in which the central management is situated shall apply:

— where the central management and the special negotiating body so decide, or

— where the central management refuses to commence negotiations within six months of the request referred to in Article 5 (1), or

— where, after three years from the date of this request, they are unable to conclude an agreement as laid down in Article 6 and the special negotiating body has not taken the decision provided for in Article 5 (5).

2. The subsidiary requirements referred to in paragraph 1 as adopted in the legislation of the Member States must satisfy the provisions set out in the Annex.

SECTION III

MISCELLANEOUS PROVISIONS

Article 8

Confidential information

1. Member States shall provide that members of special negotiating bodies or of European Works Councils and any experts who assist them are not authorized to reveal any information which has expressly been provided to them in confidence.

The same shall apply to employees' representatives in the framework of an information and consultation procedure.

This obligation shall continue to apply, wherever the persons referred to in the first and second subparagraphs are, even after the expiry of their terms of office.

2. Each Member State shall provide, in specific cases and under the conditions and limits laid down by national legislation, that the central management situated in its territory is not obliged to transmit information when its nature is such that, according to objective criteria, it would seriously harm the functioning of the undertakings concerned or would be prejudicial to them.

A Member State may make such dispensation subject to prior administrative or judicial authorization.

3. Each Member State may lay down particular provisions for the central management of undertakings in its territory which pursue directly and essentially the aim of ideological guidance with respect to information and the expression of opinions, on condition that, at the date of adoption of this Directive such particular provisions already exist in the national legislation.

Article 9

Operation of European Works Council and information and consultation procedure for workers

The central management and the European Works Council shall work in a spirit of cooperation with due regard to their reciprocal rights and obligations.

The same shall apply to cooperation between the central management and employees' representatives in the framework of an information and consultation procedure for workers.

Article 10

Protection of employees' representatives

Members of special negotiating bodies, members of European Works Councils and employees' representatives exercising their functions under the procedure referred to in Article 6 (3) shall, in the exercise of their functions, enjoy the same protection and guarantees provided for employees' representatives by the national legislation and/or practice in force in their country of employment.

This shall apply in particular to attendance at meetings of special negotiating bodies or European Works Councils or any other meetings within the framework of the agreement referred to in Article 6 (3), and the payment of wages for members who are on the staff of the Community-scale undertaking or the Community-scale group of undertakings for the period of absence necessary for the performance of their duties.

Article 11

Compliance with this Directive

1. Each Member State shall ensure that the management of establishments of a Community-scale undertaking and the management of undertakings

which form part of a Community-scale group of undertakings which are situated within its territory and their employees' representatives or, as the case may be, employees abide by the obligations laid down by this Directive, regardless of whether or not the central management is situated within its territory.

2. Member States shall ensure that the information on the number of employees referred to in Article 2 (1) (a) and (c) is made available by undertakings at the request of the parties concerned by the application of this Directive.

3. Member States shall provide for appropriate measures in the event of failure to comply with this Directive; in particular, they shall ensure that adequate administrative or judicial procedures are available to enable the obligations deriving from this Directive to be enforced.

4. Where Member States apply Article 8, they shall make provision for administrative or judicial appeal procedures which the employees' representatives may initiate when the central management requires confidentiality or does not give information in accordance with that Article.

Such procedures may include procedures designed to protect the confidentiality of the information in question.

Article 12

Link between this Directive and other provisions

1. This Directive shall apply without prejudice to measures taken pursuant to Council Directive 75/129/EEC of 17 February 1975 on the approximation of the laws of the Member States relating to collective redundancies ([7]), and to Council Directive 77/187/EEC of 14 February 1977 on the approximation of the laws of the Member States relating to the safeguarding of employees' rights in the event of transfers of undertakings, businesses or parts of businesses ([8]).

([7]) OJ No L 48, 22.2.1975, p. 29. Regulation as last amended by Directive 92/56/EEC (OJ No L 245, 26.8.1992, p. 3).
([8]) OJ No L 61, 5.3.1977, p. 26.

2. This Directive shall be without prejudice to employees' existing rights to information and consultation under national law.

Article 13

Agreements in force

1. Without prejudice to paragraph 2, the obligations arising from this Directive shall not apply to Community-scale undertakings or Community-scale groups of undertakings in which, on the date laid down in Article 14 (1) for the implementation of this Directive or the date of its transposition in the Member State in question, where this is earlier than the abovementioned date, there is already an agreement, covering the entire workforce, providing for the transnational information and consultation of employees.

2. When the agreements referred to in paragraph 1 expire, the parties to those agreements may decide jointly to renew them.

Where this is not the case, the provisions of this Directive shall apply.

Article 14

Final provisions

1. Member States shall bring into force the laws, regulations and administrative provisions necessary to comply with this Directive no later than 22 September 1996 or shall ensure by that date at the latest that management and labour introduce the required provisions by way of agreement, the Member States being obliged to take all necessary steps enabling them at all times to guarantee the results imposed by this Directive. They shall forthwith inform the Commission thereof.

2. When Member States adopt these measures, they shall contain a reference to this Directive or shall be accompanied by such reference on the occasion of their official publication. The methods of making such reference shall be laid down by Member States.

Article 15

Review by the Commission

Not later than 22 September 1999, the Commission shall, in consultation with the Member States and with management and labour at European level, review its operation and, in particular examine whether the workforce size thresholds are appropriate with a view to proposing suitable amendments to the Council, where necessary.

Article 16

This Directive is addressed to the Member States.

Done at Brussels, 22 September 1994.

For the Council

The President

N. BLÜM

ANNEX

SUBSIDIARY REQUIREMENTS

referred to in Article 7 of the Directive

1. In order to achieve the objective in Article 1 (1) of the Directive and in the cases provided for in Article 7 (1) of the Directive, the establishment, composition and competence of a European Works Council shall be governed by the following rules:

(a) The competence of the European Works Council shall be limited to information and consultation on the matters which concern the Community-scale undertaking or Community-scale group of undertakings as a whole or at least two of its establishments or group undertakings situated in different Member States.

In the case of undertakings or groups of undertakings referred to in Article 4 (2), the competence of the European Works Council shall be limited to those matters concerning all their establishments or group undertakings situated within the Member States or concerning at least two of their establishments or group undertakings situated in different Member States.

(b) The European Works Council shall be composed of employees of the Community-scale undertaking or Community-scale group of undertakings elected or appointed from their number by the employees' representatives or, in the absence thereof, by the entire body of employees.

The election or appointment of members of the European Works Council shall be carried out in accordance with national legislation and/or practice.

(c) The European Works Council shall have a minimum of three members and a maximum of 30.

Where its size so warrants, it shall elect a select committee from among its members, comprising at most three members.

It shall adopt its own rules of procedure.

(d) In the election or appointment of members of the European Works Council, it must be ensured:

— firstly, that each Member State in which the Community-scale undertaking has one or more establishments or in which the Community-scale group of undertakings has the controlling undertaking or one or more controlled undertakings is represented by one member,

— secondly, that there are supplementary members in proportion to the number of employees working in the establishments, the controlling undertaking or the controlled undertakings as laid down by the legislation of the Member State within the territory of which the central management is situated.

(e) The central management and any other more appropriate level of management shall be informed of the composition of the European Works Council.

(f) Four years after the European Works Council is established it shall examine whether to open negotiations for the conclusion of the agreement referred to in Article 6 of the Directive or to continue to apply the subsidiary requirements adopted in accordance with this Annex.

Articles 6 and 7 of the Directive shall apply, *mutatis mutandis*, if a decision has been taken to negotiate an agreement according to Article 6 of the Directive, in which case 'special negotiating body' shall be replaced by 'European Works Council'.

2. The European Works Council shall have the right to meet with the central management once a year, to be informed and consulted, on the basis of a report drawn up by the central management, on the progress of the business of the Community-scale undertaking or Community-scale group of undertakings and its prospects. The local managements shall be informed accordingly.

The meeting shall relate in particular to the structure, economic and financial situation, the probable development of the business and of production and sales, the situation and probable trend of employment, investments, and substantial changes concerning organization, introduction of new working methods or production processes, transfers of production, mergers, cut-backs or closures of undertakings, establishments or important parts thereof, and collective redundancies.

3. Where there are exceptional circumstances affecting the employees' interests to a considerable extent, particularly in the event of relocations, the closure of establishments or undertakings or collective redundancies, the select committee or, where no such committee exists, the European Works Council shall have the right to be informed. It shall have the right to meet, at its request, the central management, or any other more appropriate level of management within the Community-scale undertaking or group of undertakings having its own powers of decision, so as to be informed and consulted on measures significantly affecting employees' interests.

Those members of the European Works Council who have been elected or appointed by the establishments and/or undertakings which are directly concerned by the measures in question shall also have the right to participate in the meeting organized with the select committee.

This information and consultation meeting shall take place as soon as possible on the basis of a report drawn up by the central management or any other appropriate level of management of the Community-scale undertaking or group of undertakings, on which an opinion may be delivered at the end of the meeting or within a reasonable time.

This meeting shall not affect the prerogatives of the central management.

4. The Member States may lay down rules on the chairing of information and consultation meetings.

Before any meeting with the central management, the European Works Council or the select committee, where necessary enlarged in accordance with the second paragraph of point 3, shall be entitled to meet without the management concerned being present.

5. Without prejudice to Article 8 of the Directive, the members of the European Works Council shall inform the representatives of the employees of the establishments or of the undertakings of a Community-scale group of undertakings or, in the absence of representatives, the workforce as a whole, of the content and outcome of the information and consultation procedure carried out in accordance with this Annex.

6. The European Works Council or the select committee may be assisted by experts of its choice, in so far as this is necessary for it to carry out its tasks.

7. The operating expenses of the European Works Council shall be borne by the central management.

The central management concerned shall provide the members of the European Works Council with such financial and material resources as enable them to perform their duties in an appropriate manner.

In particular, the cost of organizing meetings and arranging for interpretation facilities and the accomodation and travelling expenses of members of the European Works Council and its select committee shall be met by the central management unless otherwise agreed.

In compliance with these principles, the Member States may lay down budgetary rules regarding the operation of the European Works Council. They may in particular limit funding to cover one expert only.

S.I. No. 370 of 1996

PROTECTION OF EMPLOYMENT ORDER 1996 [1]

I, Eithne Fitzgerald, Minister of State at the Department of Enterprise and Employment, in exercise of the powers conferred on me by section 3 (2) of the Protection of Employment Act, 1977 (No. 7 of 1977), and the Enterprise and Employment (Delegation of Ministerial Functions) (No. 2) Order, 1995 (No. 43 of 1995) and for the purposes of implementing Council Directive No. 92/56/EEC of 24 June 1992 amending Directive No. 75/129/EEC on the approximation of the laws of the Member States relating to collective redundancies,[1a] hereby order as follows:

1. (1) This Order may be cited as the Protection of Employment Order, 1996.

(2) This Order shall come into effect on the 9th day of December, 1996

2. In this Order:

"the Act" means the Protection of Employment Act, 1977;

"the Minister" means the means the Minister for Enterprise and Employment.[2]

---

[1] Somewhat bizarrely, although Article 1(1) of this Order provides that it may be cited as the Protection of Employment Order, 1996, the title of the Order omits the comma.

[1a] Note that Directive 92/56/EEC of 24 June 1992 amending Directive 75/129/EEC on the approximation of the laws of the Member States relating to collective redundancies was repealed by Article 8 of Council Directive 98/59/EC of 20 July 1998 on the approximation of the laws of the Member States relating to collective redundancies. The 1998 Directive, which now sets out European Community law in this area, is reproduced in this volume.

[2] Article 4 of the Enterprise and Employment (Alteration of Name of Department and Title of Minister) Order, 1997 (S.I. No. 305 of 1997) has provided that references in any "enactment" to the Minister for Enterprise and Employment are to be construed as references to the Minister for Enterprise, Trade and Employment and that references in any "enactment" to the Department of Enterprise and Employment shall be construed as references to the Department of Enterprise, Trade and Employment. The word "enactment" is not, however, defined in the 1997 Order, and *quaere* whether it refers to statutory instruments (such as the Protection of Employment

3. The Act is hereby amended as provided in the subsequent Articles of this Order.

4. *(Substitutions in s. 2(1) of the Protection of Employment Act, 1977)*

(Insertion in s. 2(1) of the Protection of Employment Act, 1977)

(Deletion in s. 2(1) of the Protection of Employment Act, 1977)

5. *(Substitution of s. 6 of the Protection of Employment Act, 1977)*

6. Section 7 (2) (e) is deleted.

7. *(Deletion in s. 9(1) of the Protection of Employment Act, 1977)*

8. *(Substitution in s. 9(2)(a) of the Protection of Employment Act, 1977)*

9. *(Substitution of s. 10(2)(c) of the Protection of Employment Act, 1977)*

(Insertion of s. 10(2)(e) and s. 10(2)(f) of the Protection of Employment Act, 1977)

10. *(Insertion of s. 10A of the Protection of Employment Act, 1977)*

11. *(Insertion of s. 12(4) of the Protection of Employment Act, 1977)*

12. *(Insertion of s. 14(3) of the Protection of Employment Act, 1977)*

GIVEN under my hand, this 4th day of December 1996.

EITHNE FITZGERALD

Minister of State at the

Department of Enterprise

and Employment.

Order, 1996) in addition to Acts of the Oireachtas. Perhaps somewhat fortuitously, the matter seems to be academic in the context of S.I. No. 370 of 1996 as these Regulations provide only for substitutions, insertions and deletions in the text of the Protection of Employment Act, 1977, which certainly qualifies as an "enactment" for the purposes of S.I. No. 305 of 1997. Note that the powers and duties which are conferred on the Minister for Enterprise, Trade and Employment by or under the Redundancy Payments Acts have been delegated by statutory instrument to the present Minister of State at the Department of Enterprise, Trade and Employment. (See now the Enterprise, Trade and Employment (Delegation of Ministerial Functions) Order 2004 (S.I. No. 809 of 2004).)

EXPLANATORY NOTE

(This note is not part of the Instrument and does not purport to be a legal interpretation.)

The Protection of Employment Act, 1977, transposed into law Council Directive No. 75/129/EEC on the approximation of the laws of the Member States relating to collective redundancies. This Directive was subsequently amended by Council Directive 92/56/EEC and the purpose of this order is to give effect to those amendments in the 1977 Act.

S.I. No. 386 of 1999

EUROPEAN COMMUNITIES (TRANSNATIONAL INFORMATION AND CONSULTATION OF EMPLOYEES ACT, 1996) (AMENDMENT) REGULATIONS, 1999

I, MARY HARNEY, Minister for Enterprise, Trade and Employment, in exercise of the powers conferred on me by section 3 of the European Communities Act, 1972 (No. 27 of 1972), for the purpose of giving effect to Council Directive No. 97/74/EC of 15 December 1997([1]) hereby order as follows:

([1]) O.J. No. L010, 16.1.98, p. 22.

1. (1) These Regulations may be cited as the European Communities (Transnational Information and Consultation of Employees Act, 1996) (Amendment) Regulations, 1999.

(2) These Regulations shall come into operation on 15 December, 1999.

2. *(Deletion in s. 3(1) of the Transnational Information and Consultation of Employees Act, 1996)*

3. (Insertion of sub-s. (1A) in s. 6 of the Transnational Information and Consultation of Employees Act, 1996)

(Substitution in sub-ss. (2), (3), (6) and (7) of s. 6 of the Transnational Information and Consultation of Employees Act, 1996)

4. (Substitution in s. 10(4)(a) of the Transnational Information and Consultation of Employees Act, 1996)

GIVEN under my Official Seal, this 7th day of December, 1999.

(L.S.)

MARY HARNEY,

Tánaiste and Minister for Enterprise, Trade and Employment.

EXPLANATORY NOTE

(This note is not part of the Instrument and does not purport to be a legal interpretation.)

The effect of these Regulations is to transpose into Irish law Directive 97/74/EC of 15 December, 1997 extending to the United Kingdom of Great Britain and Northern Ireland, Directive 94/45/EC on the establishment of a European Works Council or a procedure in Community-scale undertakings or Community-scale groups of undertakings for the purposes of informing and consulting employees.

COUNCIL DIRECTIVE 97/74/EC

of 15 December 1997

extending, to the United Kingdom of Great Britain and Northern Ireland, Directive 94/45/EC on the establishment of a European Works Council or a procedure in Community-scale undertakings and Community-scale groups of undertakings for the purposes of informing and consulting employees

(Official Journal of the European Communities 16.1.1998 L 10/22)

THE COUNCIL OF THE EUROPEAN UNION,

Having regard to the Treaty establishing the European Community, and in particular Article 100 thereof,

Having regard to the proposal from the Commission ([1]),

Having regard to the opinion of the European Parliament ([2]),

Having regard to the opinion of the Economic and Social Committee ([3]),

Whereas the Council, acting in accordance with the Agreement on social policy annexed to Protocol 14 to the Treaty, and in particular Article 2(2) thereof, adopted Directive 94/45/EC ([4]); whereas, as a result, the said Directive does not apply to the United Kingdom of Great Britain and Northern Ireland;

([1]) OJ C 335, 6.11.1997.
([2]) OJ C 371, 8.12.1997.
([3]) OJ C 355, 21.11.1997.
([4]) OJ L 254, 30.9.1994, p. 64.

Whereas the Amsterdam European Council held on 16 and 17 June 1997 noted with approval the agreement of the Intergovernmental Conference to incorporate the Agreement on social policy in the Treaty and also noted that a means should be found to give legal effect to the wish of the United Kingdom of Great Britain and Northern Ireland to accept the Directives already adopted on the basis of that Agreement before the signature of the Amsterdam Treaty; whereas this Directive seeks to achieve this aim by extending Directive 94/45/EC to the United Kingdom;

Whereas the fact that Directive 94/45/EC is not applicable in the United Kingdom directly affects the functioning of the internal market; whereas implementation of the said Directive in all the Member States will improve the functioning of the internal market;

Whereas Directive 94/45/EC provides for a maximum of 17 members of the special negotiating body; whereas such a number corresponds to the 14 Member States which are party to the Agreement on social policy plus the three remaining Contracting Parties of the European Economic Area; whereas the adoption of this Directive will bring the total number of States covered by Directive 94/45/EC to 18; whereas, therefore, the abovementioned maximum should be increased to 18 so that each Member State in which the Community-scale undertaking has one or more establishments or in which the Community-scale group of undertakings has the controlling undertaking or one or more controlled undertakings is represented;

Whereas Directive 94/45/EC provides for special treatment to be accorded to Community-scale undertakings and groups of undertakings in which there is, at 22 September 1996, an agreement covering the entire workforce providing for the transnational information and consultation of employees; whereas, accordingly, Community-scale undertakings and groups of undertakings falling within the scope of that Directive solely as a result of its application to the United Kingdom should be granted similar treatment;

Whereas the adoption of this Directive will make Directive 94/45/EC applicable in all Member States including the United Kingdom; whereas, from the date on which this Directive enters into force, the term 'Member States' in Directive 94/45/EC should be construed as including, where appropriate, the United Kingdom;

Whereas Member States were required to bring into force the laws, regulations and administrative provisions to comply with Directive 94/45/EC no later than two years after its adoption; whereas a similar period should be granted to the United Kingdom, as well as to the other Member States, to bring into force the necessary measures to comply with this Directive,

HAS ADOPTED THIS DIRECTIVE:

Article 1

Without prejudice to Article 3, Directive 94/45/EC shall apply to the United Kingdom of Great Britain and Northern Ireland.

Article 2

(Substitution in Article 5(2)(b) of Directive 94/45/EC)

Article 3

1. The obligations resulting from this Directive shall not apply to Community-scale undertakings or Community-scale groups of undertakings, which, solely by virtue of Article 1, fall within the scope of this Directive, provided that, on the date laid down in Article 4(1) or the date of its transposition in the Member State in question, where this is earlier than the said date, there is already an agreement covering the entire workforce providing for the transnational information and consultation of employees.

2. When the agreements referred to in paragraph 1 expire, the parties to those agreements may decide jointly to renew them. Where this is not the case, Directive 94/45/EC, as extended by this Directive, shall apply.

Article 4

1. Member States shall bring into force the laws, regulations and administrative provisions necessary to comply with this Directive no later than 15 December 1999 or shall ensure, by that date at the latest, that management and labour introduce the required provisions by way of agreement, the Member States being obliged to take all necessary steps enabling them at all times to guarantee the results imposed by this Directive. They shall forthwith inform the Commission thereof.

2. When Member States adopt these measures, they shall contain a reference to this Directive or shall be accompanied by such reference on the occasion of their official publication. The methods of making such reference shall be laid down by the Member States.

Article 5

This Directive is addressed to the Member States.

Done at Brussels, 15 December 1997.

For the Council

The President

J.-C. JUNCKER

S.I. No. 488 of 2000

EUROPEAN COMMUNITIES (PROTECTION OF EMPLOYMENT) REGULATIONS, 2000

I, MARY HARNEY, Minister for Enterprise, Trade and Employment, in exercise of the powers conferred on me by section 3 of the European Communities Act, 1972 (No. 27 of 1972), and for the purpose of giving further effect to Council Directive No. 75/129/EEC of 17 February 1975 relating to collective redundancies[1], as amended by Council Directive No. 92/56/EEC of 24 June 1992[2], make the following Regulations:[1]

[1] OJ No. L 48, 22.2.75, p.29
[2] OJ No. L 245, 26.8.92, p.3

1. These Regulations may be cited as the European Communities (Protection of Employment) Regulations, 2000.

2. (1) In these Regulations—

"Act of 1977" means Protection of Employment Act, 1977 (No. 7 of 1977), as amended by the Protection of Employment Order, 1996 (S.I. No. 370 of 1996);

"Act of 1994" means Terms of Employment (Information) Act, 1994 (No. 5 of 1994).

3. *Substitution in s. 2(1) of the Protection of Employment Act, 1977*

Insertion in s. 2(1) of the Protection of Employment Act, 1977

4. *Substitution in s. 9(2)(a) of the Protection of Employment Act, 1977*

5. *Substitution in s. 11 of the Protection of Employment Act, 1977*

[1] Note that both Directive 75/129/EEC of 17 February 1975 on the approximation of the laws of the Member States relating to collective redundancies and Directive 92/56/EEC of 24 June 1992 amending Directive 75/129/EEC on the approximation of the laws of the Member States relating to collective redundancies have been repealed by Article 8 of Council Directive 98/59/EC of 20 July 1998 on the approximation of the laws of the Member States relating to collective redundancies. The 1998 Directive, which now consolidates European Community legislation concerning collective redundancies, is reproduced in this volume.

Substitution in s. 13 of the Protection of Employment Act, 1977

Substitution in s. 17(3) of the Protection of Employment Act, 1977

Substitution in s. 18(3) of the Protection of Employment Act, 1977

6. (1) An employee, or a trade union, staff association or excepted body on behalf of an employee, may present a complaint to a rights commissioner that an employer has contravened section 9 or 10 of the Act of 1977 and, if he, she or it does so, the commissioner shall give the parties an opportunity to be heard by him or her and to present to him or her any evidence relevant to the complaint, shall give a decision in writing in relation to it and shall communicate the decision to the parties.

(2) A decision of a rights commissioner under paragraph (1) of this Regulation shall do one or more of the following:

(*a*) declare that the complaint is or, as the case may be, is not well founded,

(*b*) require the employer to comply with the provision of the Act of 1977 concerned and, for that purpose, to take a specified course of action,

(*c*) require the employer to pay to the employee compensation of such amount (if any) as is just and equitable having regard to all of the circumstances, but not exceeding 4 weeks remuneration in respect of the employee's employment calculated in accordance with regulations under section 17 of the Unfair Dismissals Act, 1977 (No. 10 of 1977),

and the references in this paragraph to an employer shall be construed, in a case where ownership of the business or part of the business of the employer changes after the contravention to which the complaint relates occurred, as references to the person who, by virtue of the change, becomes entitled to such ownership.

(3) A rights commissioner shall not entertain a complaint under this Regulation unless it is presented to him or her within the period of 6 months beginning on the date of the alleged contravention to which the complaint relates or (in a case where the rights commissioner is satisfied that exceptional circumstances prevented the presentation of the complaint within the period aforesaid) such further period, not exceeding

6 months from the expiration of the first-mentioned period of 6 months, as the rights commissioner considers reasonable.

(4) For the purposes of this Regulation—

(*a*) subsections (4) to (6) and (7) (*a*) of section 7 of the Act of 1994 shall apply in relation to a complaint presented under this Regulation as they apply in relation to a complaint presented under subsection (1) of that section 7, with the modification that in that subsection (6) a reference to a decision is substituted for a reference to a recommendation, and any other necessary modifications, and

(*b*) sections 8 to 10 of the Act of 1994 shall apply as they apply for the purposes of that Act, with the following modifications, namely—

(i) the substitution in those provisions of references to a decision for references to a recommendation,

(ii) the substitution in section 9 of the Act of 1994 of—

(I) references to the Circuit Court for references to the District Court, and

(II) the following subsection for subsection (3):

"(3) An application under this section to the Circuit Court shall be made to the judge of the Circuit Court for the circuit in which the employer concerned ordinarily resides or carries on any profession, trade or business.",

and any other necessary modifications.

GIVEN under my Official Seal, this 21st day of December, 2000.

(L.S.)

MARY HARNEY, T.D.,

Minister for Enterprise, Trade and Employment.

EXPLANATORY NOTE

(This note is not part of the Instrument and does not purport to be a legal interpretation.)

These Regulations amend the Protection of Employment Act, 1977, to provide for representation of, and consultation with, employees in the absence of a trade union, staff association or excepted body; to provide for a right of complaint to a rights commissioner where an employer contravenes section 9 or 10 (information and consultation of employees) and to provide for increases in the levels of fines for offences.

COUNCIL DIRECTIVE 98/59/EC

of 20 July 1998

on the approximation of the laws of the Member States relating to collective redundancies

(Official Journal of the European Communities 12.8.98 L 225/16)

THE COUNCIL OF THE EUROPEAN UNION,

Having regard to the Treaty establishing the European Community, and in particular Article 100 thereof,

Having regard to the proposal from the Commission,

Having regard to the opinion of the European Parliament ([1]),

Having regard to the opinion of the Economic and Social Committee ([2]),

(1) Whereas for reasons of clarity and rationality Council Directive 75/129/EEC of 17 February 1975 on the approximation of the laws of the Member States relating to collective redundancies ([3]) should be consolidated;

(2) Whereas it is important that greater protection should be afforded to workers in the event of collective redundancies while taking into account the need for balanced economic and social development within the Community;

(3) Whereas, despite increasing convergence, differences still remain between the provisions in force in the Member States concerning the practical arrangements and procedures for such redundancies and the measures designed to alleviate the consequences of redundancy for workers;

(4) Whereas these differences can have a direct effect on the functioning of the internal market;

(5) Whereas the Council resolution of 21 January 1974 concerning a social action programme ([4]) made provision for a directive on the approximation of Member States' legislation on collective redundancies;

([1]) OJ C 210, 6. 7. 1998.

([2]) OJ C 158, 26. 5. 1997, p. 11.

([3]) OJ L 48, 22. 2. 1975, p. 29. Directive as amended by Directive 92/56/EEC (OJ L 245, 26. 8. 1992, p. 3).

([4]) OJ C 13, 12. 2. 1974, p. 1.

(6) Whereas the Community Charter of the fundamental social rights of workers, adopted at the European Council meeting held in Strasbourg on 9 December 1989 by the Heads of State or Government of 11 Member States, states, *inter alia*, in point 7, first paragraph, first sentence, and second paragraph; in point 17, first paragraph; and in point 18, third indent:

'7. The completion of the internal market must lead to an improvement in the living and working conditions of workers in the European Community (…).

The improvement must cover, where necessary, the development of certain aspects of employment regulations such as procedures for collective redundancies and those regarding bankruptcies.

(…)

17. Information, consultation and participation for workers must be developed along appropriate lines, taking account of the practices in force in the various Member States.

(…)

18. Such information, consultation and participation must be implemented in due time, particularly in the following cases:

(— …)

(— …)

— in cases of collective redundancy procedures;

(— …)';

(7) Whereas this approximation must therefore be promoted while the improvement is being maintained within the meaning of Article 117 of the Treaty;

(8) Whereas, in order to calculate the number of redundancies provided for in the definition of collective redundancies within the meaning of this Directive, other forms of termination of employment contracts on the initiative of the employer should be equated to redundancies, provided that there are at least five redundancies;

(9) Whereas it should be stipulated that this Directive applies in principle also to collective redundancies resulting where the establishment's activities are terminated as a result of a judicial decision;

(10) Whereas the Member States should be given the option of stipulating that workers' representatives may call on experts on grounds of the technical complexity of the matters which are likely to be the subject of the informing and consulting;

(11) Whereas it is necessary to ensure that employers' obligations as regards information, consultation and notification apply independently of whether the decision on collective redundancies emanates from the employer or from an undertaking which controls that employer;

(12) Whereas Member States should ensure that workers' representatives and/or workers have at their disposal administrative and/or judicial procedures in order to ensure that the obligations laid down in this Directive are fulfilled;

(13) Whereas this Directive must not affect the obligations of the Member States concerning the deadlines for transposition of the Directives set out in Annex I, Part B,

HAS ADOPTED THIS DIRECTIVE:

SECTION I

Definitions and scope

Article 1

1. For the purposes of this Directive:

(a) 'collective redundancies' means dismissals effected by an employer for one or more reasons not related to the individual workers concerned where, according to the choice of the Member States, the number of redundancies is:

(i) either, over a period of 30 days:

— at least 10 in establishments normally employing more than 20 and less than 100 workers,

— at least 10 % of the number of workers in establishments normally employing at least 100 but less than 300 workers,

— at least 30 in establishments normally employing 300 workers or more,

(ii) or, over a period of 90 days, at least 20, whatever the number of workers normally employed in the establishments in question;

(b) 'workers' representatives' means the workers' representatives provided for by the laws or practices of the Member States.

For the purpose of calculating the number of redundancies provided for in the first subparagraph of point (a), terminations of an employment contract which occur on the employer's initiative for one or more reasons not related to the individual workers concerned shall be assimilated to redundancies, provided that there are at least five redundancies.

2. This Directive shall not apply to:

(a) collective redundancies effected under contracts of employment concluded for limited periods of time or for specific tasks except where such redundancies take place prior to the date of expiry or the completion of such contracts;

(b) workers employed by public administrative bodies or by establishments governed by public law (or, in Member States where this concept is unknown, by equivalent bodies);

(c) the crews of seagoing vessels.

SECTION II

Information and consultation

Article 2

1. Where an employer is contemplating collective redundancies, he shall begin consultations with the workers' representatives in good time with a view to reaching an agreement.

2. These consultations shall, at least, cover ways and means of avoiding collective redundancies or reducing the number of workers affected, and of mitigating the consequences by recourse to accompanying social measures aimed, *inter alia*, at aid for redeploying or retraining workers made redundant.

Member States may provide that the workers' representatives may call on the services of experts in accordance with national legislation and/or practice.

3. To enable workers' representatives to make constructive proposals, the employers shall in good time during the course of the consultations:

(a) supply them with all relevant information and

(b) in any event notify them in writing of:

(i) the reasons for the projected redundancies;

(ii) the number of categories of workers to be made redundant;

(iii) the number and categories of workers normally employed;

(iv) the period over which the projected redundancies are to be effected;

(v) the criteria proposed for the selection of the workers to be made redundant in so far as national legislation and/or practice confers the power therefore upon the employer;

(vi) the method for calculating any redundancy payments other than those arising out of national legislation and/or practice.

The employer shall forward to the competent public authority a copy of, at least, the elements of the written communication which are provided for in the first subparagraph, point (b), subpoints (i) to (v).

4. The obligations laid down in paragraphs 1, 2 and 3 shall apply irrespective of whether the decision regarding collective redundancies is being taken by the employer or by an undertaking controlling the employer.

In considering alleged breaches of the information, consultation and notification requirements laid down by this Directive, account shall not be taken of any defence on the part of the employer on the ground that the necessary information has not been provided to the employer by the undertaking which took the decision leading to collective redundancies.

SECTION III

Procedure for collective redundancies

Article 3

1. Employers shall notify the competent public authority in writing of any projected collective redundancies.

However, Member States may provide that in the case of planned collective redundancies arising from termination of the establishment's activities as a result of a judicial decision, the employer shall be obliged to notify the competent public authority in writing only if the latter so requests.

This notification shall contain all relevant information concerning the projected collective redundancies and the consultations with workers' representatives provided for in Article 2, and particularly the reasons for the redundancies, the number of workers to be made redundant, the number of workers normally employed and the period over which the redundancies are to be effected.

2. Employers shall forward to the workers' representatives a copy of the notification provided for in paragraph 1.

The workers' representatives may send any comments they may have to the competent public authority.

Article 4

1. Projected collective redundancies notified to the competent public authority shall take effect not earlier than 30 days after the notification referred to in Article 3(1) without prejudice to any provisions governing individual rights with regard to notice of dismissal.

Member States may grant the competent public authority the power to reduce the period provided for in the preceding subparagraph.

2. The period provided for in paragraph 1 shall be used by the competent public authority to seek solutions to the problems raised by the projected collective redundancies.

3. Where the initial period provided for in paragraph 1 is shorter than 60 days, Member States may grant the competent public authority the power to extend the initial period to 60 days following notification where the problems raised by the projected collective redundancies are not likely to be solved within the initial period.

Member States may grant the competent public authority wider powers of extension.

The employer must be informed of the extension and the grounds for it before expiry of the initial period provided for in paragraph 1.

4. Member States need not apply this Article to collective redundancies arising from termination of the establishment's activities where this is the result of a judicial decision.

SECTION IV

Final provisions

Article 5

This Directive shall not affect the right of Member States to apply or to introduce laws, regulations or administrative provisions which are more favourable to workers or to promote or to allow the application of collective agreements more favourable to workers.

Article 6

Member States shall ensure that judicial and/or administrative procedures for the enforcement of obligations under this Directive are available to the workers' representatives and/or workers.

Article 7

Member States shall forward to the Commission the text of any fundamental provisions of national law already adopted or being adopted in the area governed by this Directive.

Article 8

1. The Directives listed in Annex I, Part A, are hereby repealed without prejudice to the obligations of the Member States concerning the deadlines for transposition of the said Directive set out in Annex I, Part B.

2. References to the repealed Directives shall be construed as references to this Directive and shall be read in accordance with the correlation table in Annex II.

Article 9

This Directive shall enter into force on the 20th day following its publication in the *Official Journal of the European Communities*.

Article 10

This Directive is addressed to the Member States.

Done at Brussels, 20 July 1998.

For the Council

The President

W. MOLTERER

ANNEX I

PART A

Repealed Directives

(referred to by Article 8)

Council Directive 75/129/EEC and its following amendment:

Council Directive 92/56/EEC.

PART B

Deadlines for transposition into national law

(referred to by Article 8)

Directive	Deadline for transposition
75/129/EEC (OJ L 48, 22.2.1975, p. 29)	19 February 1977
92/56/EEC (OJ L 245, 26.8.1992, p. 3)	24 June 1994

ANNEX II

CORRELATION TABLE

Directive 75/129/EEC	This Directive
Article 1(1), first subparagraph, point (a), first indent, point 1	Article 1(1), first subparagraph, point (a)(i), first indent
Article 1(1), first subparagraph, point (a), first indent, point 2	Article 1(1), first subparagraph, point (a)(i), second indent

Directive 75/129/EEC	This Directive
Article 1(1), first subparagraph, point (a), first indent, point 3	Article 1(1), first subparagraph, point (a)(i), third indent
Article 1(1), first subparagraph, point (a), second indent	Article 1(1), first subparagraph, point (a)(ii)
Article 1(1), first subparagraph, point (b)	Article 1(1), first subpararaph, point (b)
Article 1(1), second subparagraph	Article 1(1), second subparagraph
Article 1(2)	Article 1(2)
Article 2	Article 2
Article 3	Article 3
Article 4	Article 4
Article 5	Article 5
Article 5a	Article 6
Article 6(1)	—
Article 6(2)	Article 7
Article 7	—
—	Article 8
—	Article 9
—	Article 10
—	Annex I
—	Annex II

S.I. No. 131 of 2003

EUROPEAN COMMUNITIES (PROTECTION OF EMPLOYEES ON TRANSFER OF UNDERTAKINGS) REGULATIONS 2003

I, Mary Harney, Minister for Enterprise, Trade and Employment, in exercise of the powers conferred on me by section 3 of the European Communities Act 1972 (No. 27 of 1972) and for the purpose of giving further effect to Council Directive No. 2001/23/EC of 12 March 2001 [1], hereby make the following regulations:

---

[1] OJ No. L. 82 p 16 22.03.200

---

1. These Regulations may be cited as the European Communities (Protection of Employees on Transfer of Undertakings) Regulations 2003.

Definitions.

2. (1) In these Regulations—

"Act of 1963" means the Companies Act 1963 (No. 33 of 1963);

"Act of 1988" means the Bankruptcy Act 1988 (No. 27 of 1988);

"contract of employment" means—

(a) a contract of service or apprenticeship, and

(b) any other contract whereby an individual agrees with another person, who is carrying on the business of an employment agency within the meaning of the Employment Agency Act 1971 (No. 27 of 1971), and is acting in the course of that business, to do or perform personally any work or service for a third person (whether or not the third person is a party to the contract),

whether the contract is express or implied and, if express, whether it is oral or in writing;

"Council Directive" means Council Directive No. 2001/23/EC of 12 March 2001;

"employee" means a person of any age, who has entered into or works under (or, where the employment has ceased, entered into or worked under) a contract of employment and references, in relation to an employer, to an employee shall be construed as references to an employee employed by that employer; and for the purposes of these Regulations, a person holding office under, or in the service of, the State (including a civil servant within the meaning of the Civil Service Regulation Act 1956 (No. 46 of 1956)) shall be deemed to be an employee employed by the State or Government, as the case may be, and an officer or servant of a harbour authority, health board [1] or vocational education committee shall be deemed to be an employee employed by the authority, board or committee, as the case may be;

"employees' representatives" means:

(a) a trade union, staff association or excepted body with which it has been the practice of the employees' employer to conduct collective bargaining negotiations, or

(b) in the absence of such a trade union, staff association or excepted body, a person or persons chosen by such employees (under an arrangement put in place by the employer under Regulation 7(2) or 8(5)) from among their number to represent them in negotiations with the employer,

and cognate expressions shall be construed accordingly;

"employer" means in relation to an employee, the person with whom the employee has entered into or for whom the employee works under (or, where the employment has ceased, entered into or worked under) a contract of employment, subject to the qualification that the person who under a contract of employment referred to in paragraph (b) of the definition of "contract of employment" is liable to pay the wages of the individual concerned in respect of the work or service concerned shall be deemed to be the individual's employer;

---

[1] Note that under s. 58 of the Health Act 2004, health boards were dissolved. Note also that under s. 62(3) of the 2004 Act all rights and liabilities of health boards arising by virtue of any contract or commitment (express or implied) entered into by that body were transferred to the Health Service Executive and that under s. 63 of the 2004 Act, it was provided that every contract, agreement or arrangement made between a health board and any other person (*a*) continued in force, (*b*) was to be read and have effect as if the name of the Health Service Executive were substituted in the contract, agreement or arrangement for that of the health board, and (*c*) was enforceable by and against the Health Service Executive.

"enactment" includes an instrument made under an enactment;

"excepted body" has the meaning assigned to it by section 6(3) of the Trade Union Act 1941 (No. 22 of 1941);

"merger" has the meaning assigned to it by the European Communities (Mergers and Divisions of Companies) Regulations 1987 (S.I. No. 137 of 1987);

"Minister" means the Minister for Enterprise, Trade and Employment; [2]

"trade union" means a trade union which holds a negotiating licence under the Trade Union Act 1941;

"transfer" shall be construed in accordance with Regulation 3;

"transferee" means any natural or legal person who, by reason of a transfer within the meaning of these Regulations, becomes the employer in respect of the undertaking, business or part of the undertaking or business;

"transferor" means any natural or legal person who, by reason of a transfer within the meaning of these Regulations, ceases to be the employer in respect of the undertaking, business or part of the undertaking or business;

"Tribunal" means the Employment Appeals Tribunal.

(2) A word or expression that is used in these Regulations and which is also used in the Council Directive has, unless the context otherwise requires, the same meaning in these Regulations as it has in the Directive.

(3) A reference in these Regulations to a regulation is a reference to a regulation of these Regulations, unless it is indicated that some other regulation is intended and a reference in these Regulations to a paragraph or subparagraph is a reference to a paragraph or subparagraph of the provision in which it occurs.

Application.

3. (1) These Regulations shall apply to any transfer of an undertaking, business, or part of an undertaking or business from one employer to

---

[2] The powers and duties which are conferred on the Minister for Enterprise, Trade and Employment by or under the European Communities (Protection of Employees on Transfer of Undertakings) Regulations 2003 (S.I. No. 131 of 2003) have been delegated by statutory instrument to the present Minister of State at the Department of Enterprise, Trade and Employment. (See now the Enterprise, Trade and Employment (Delegation of Ministerial Functions) Order 2004 (S.I. No. 809 of 2004).)

another employer as a result of a legal transfer (including the assignment or forfeiture of a lease) or merger.

(2) Subject to this Regulation, in these Regulations—

"transfer" means the transfer of an economic entity which retains its identity;

"economic entity" means an organised grouping of resources which has the objective of pursuing an economic activity whether or not that activity is for profit or whether it is central or ancillary to another economic or administrative entity.

(3) These Regulations shall apply to public and private undertakings engaged in economic activities whether or not they are operating for gain.

(4) An administrative reorganisation of public administrative authorities or the transfer of administrative functions between public administrative authorities is not a transfer for the purposes of these Regulations.

(5) These Regulations shall not apply to sea-going vessels.

Rights and obligations.

4. (1) The transferor's rights and obligations arising from a contract of employment existing on the date of a transfer shall, by reason of such transfer, be transferred to the transferee.

(2) Following a transfer, the transferee shall continue to observe the terms and conditions agreed in any collective agreement on the same terms applicable to the transferor under that agreement until the date of termination or expiry of the collective agreement or the entry into force or application of another collective agreement.

(3) Subject to paragraph (4), this Regulation shall not apply in relation to employees' rights to old-age, invalidity or survivors' benefits under supplementary company or inter-company pension schemes that do not fall within the Social Welfare Acts.[3]

[3] Under s. 3(8) of the Social Welfare Consolidation Act 2005, references in any other "enactment" to the "Social Welfare Acts" are now to mean "this Act and every enactment which is to be read together with it as one." (Note that under s. 14(2) of the Social Welfare Act 2005 the Social Welfare Acts and the Social Welfare Act 2005 (other than section 13 thereof) are to be read together as one. Under s. 1(2) of Social Welfare Law Reform and Pensions Act 2006, the

(4) (*a*) The interests of employees and of persons no longer employed in the transferor's business at the time of the transfer in respect of rights conferring on them immediate or prospective entitlement to old-age benefits, including survivors' benefits, under a supplementary company pension scheme that is an occupational pension scheme within the meaning of the Pensions Acts 1990 to 2003 are protected under those Acts.

(*b*) The transferee shall ensure that the interests of employees and of persons no longer employed in the transferor's business at the time of the transfer in respect of rights conferring on them immediate or prospective entitlement to old-age benefits, including survivors' benefits, under a supplementary company pension scheme, other than a supplementary pension scheme that is an occupational pension scheme within the meaning of the Pensions Acts 1990 to 2003, are protected.

Dismissals and termination of employment.

5. (1) The transfer of an undertaking, business or part of an undertaking or business shall not in itself constitute grounds for dismissal by the transferor or the transferee and such a dismissal, the grounds for which are such a transfer, by a transferor or a transferee is prohibited.

(2) Nothing in this Regulation shall be construed as prohibiting dismissals for economic, technical or organisational reasons which entail changes in the workforce.

(3) If a contract of employment is terminated because the transfer involves a substantial change in working conditions to the detriment of the employee concerned, the employer concerned shall be regarded as having been responsible for the termination of the contract of employment.

(4) If a dismissal of an employee, in contravention of paragraph (1), constitutes a dismissal of the employee within the meaning of the Unfair Dismissals Acts 1977 to 2001,[4] relief may not be granted to the

---

Social Welfare Acts and sections 1 to 37 of that Act are also to be read together as one). *Quaere,* however, whether the European Communities (Protection of Employees on Transfer of Undertakings) Regulations 2003 can be regarded as constituting an "enactment" for the purposes of the 2005 Act.

[4] Note that under s. 5(4) of the Civil Service Regulation (Amendment) Act 2005, the Unfair Dismissals Acts, 1977 to 2001 and Part 6 of that Act may be

employee in respect of that dismissal both under these Regulations and under those Acts.

Bankruptcy or insolvency.

6. (1) Regulations 3 and 4 of these Regulations shall not apply to any transfer of an undertaking, business or part of an undertaking or business where the transferor is the subject of bankruptcy proceedings or insolvency proceedings.

(2) For the purposes of paragraph (1) bankruptcy proceedings or insolvency proceedings shall mean the following:

(a) proceedings whereby the transferor may be adjudicated bankrupt under section 14 or 15 of the Act of 1988;

(b) proceedings whereby the estate of a deceased transferor may be administered in bankruptcy under section 115 of the Act of 1988;

(c) where the transferor is a partnership, proceedings whereby all the members of the partnership may be adjudicated bankrupt under section 106 of the Act of 1988;

(d) proceedings whereby the transferor may become the subject of a protection order under section 87 of the Act of 1988 where all or part of the property of the transferor vests (under section 93 of that Act) in the Official Assignee for realisation and distribution;

(e) proceedings where the transferor may be wound up under section 213(e) of the Act of 1963;

(3) Notwithstanding paragraph (1), if the sole or main reason for the institution of bankruptcy or insolvency proceedings in respect of a transferor is the evasion of an employer's legal obligations under these Regulations, the Regulations shall apply to a transfer effected by that transferor.

Representation of employees.

7. (1) Where an undertaking, business or part of an undertaking or business the subject of a transfer, preserves its autonomy after the transfer, the

---

cited together as the Unfair Dismissals Acts 1977 to 2005 and are required to be construed together as one.

status and function of the representatives or of the representation of the employees affected by the transfer shall be preserved by the transferee concerned on the same terms and subject to the same conditions as existed before the date of the transfer as specified in any enactment, or in any agreement between the employer and the employees' representatives.

(2) Where an undertaking, business or part of an undertaking or business does not preserve its autonomy, the transferee shall arrange for the employees transferred who were represented before the transfer to choose a person or persons from among their number to represent them (including by means of an election), during the period necessary for the reappointment of the representatives of the employees' or the reconstitution of their representation.

(3) If the term of office of the representatives of the employees affected by the transfer expires as a result of the transfer, the former representatives of the employees shall continue to enjoy the protection provided by section 6(2)(a) of the Unfair Dismissals Act 1977 (No. 10 of 1977) and any other enactment.

Information and consultation.

8. (1) The transferor and transferee concerned in a transfer shall inform their respective employees' representatives affected by the transfer of—

(a) the date or proposed date of the transfer;

(b) the reasons for the transfer;

(c) the legal implications of the transfer for the employees and a summary of any relevant economic and social implications of the transfer for them

and

(d) any measures envisaged in relation to the employees.

(2) The transferor shall give the information in paragraph (1) to the employees' representatives, where reasonably practicable, not later than 30 days before the transfer is carried out and, in any event, in good time before the transfer is carried out.

(3) The transferee shall give the information in paragraph (1) to the employees' representatives, where reasonably practicable, not later than 30 days before the transfer is carried out and, in any event, in good time

before the employees are directly affected by the transfer as regards their conditions of work and employment.

(4) Where the transferor or the transferee envisages any measures in relation to employees, he or she shall consult the representatives of the employees, where reasonably practicable, not later than 30 days before the transfer is carried out and, in any event, in good time before the transfer is carried out, in relation to any such measures with a view to reaching an agreement.

(5) Where there are no employees' representatives in the undertaking or business of the transferor or, as the case may be, in the undertaking or business of the transferee, the transferor or the transferee, as may be appropriate, shall put in place a procedure whereby the employees may choose from among their number a person or persons to represent them (including by means of an election) for the purposes of this Regulation.

(6) Where, notwithstanding paragraph (5), there are still no representatives of the employees in an undertaking or business concerned (through no fault of the employees), each of the employees concerned must be informed in writing, where reasonably practicable, not later than 30 days before the transfer and, in any event, in good time before the transfer, of the following:

(a) the date or proposed date of the transfer;

(b) the reasons for the transfer;

(c) the legal implications of the transfer for the employee and a summary of any relevant economic and social implications for that employee;

and

(d) any measures envisaged in relation to the employees.

(7) The obligations specified in this Regulation shall apply irrespective of whether the decision resulting in the transfer is taken by the employer or an undertaking controlling the employer and the fact that the information concerned was not provided to the employer by the undertaking controlling the employer shall not release the employer from those obligations.

Agreements.

9. (1) A provision in any agreement shall be void in so far as it purports to exclude or limit the application of any provision of these Regulations or is inconsistent with any provision of these Regulations.

(2) A provision in any agreement which is or becomes less favourable in relation to an employee than a similar or corresponding entitlement conferred on the employee by these Regulations shall be deemed to be modified so as not to be less favourable.

(3) Nothing in these Regulations shall be construed as prohibiting the inclusion in an agreement of a provision more favourable to an employee than any provision of these Regulations.

Complaints.

10. (1) A complaint that an employer has contravened any of these Regulations (other than Regulations 4(4)(a) and 13) in relation to an employee may be presented to a rights commissioner by:

(a) the employee, or

(b) a trade union, staff association or excepted body on behalf and with the consent of the employee.

(2) A complaint under paragraph (1) shall be presented by giving notice of it in writing to a rights commissioner and the notice shall contain such particulars and be in such form as may be specified from time to time by the Minister.

(3) A copy of a notice under paragraph (2) shall be given to the other party or parties concerned, by the rights commissioner concerned.

(4) Where a complaint is presented to a rights commissioner under paragraph (1), the rights commissioner shall—

(a) give the parties an opportunity to be heard and to present any evidence relevant to the complaint;

(b) give a decision in writing in relation to the complaint; and

(c) communicate the decision to the parties.

(5) A decision of a rights commissioner under paragraph (4) shall do one or more of the following:

(*a*) declare that the complaint is or, as the case may be, is not well founded;

(*b*) require the employer to comply with these Regulations and, for that purpose, to take a specified course of action; or (*c*) require the employer to pay to the employee compensation of such amount (if any) as in the opinion of the rights commissioner, is just and equitable in the circumstances, but—

(i) in the case of a contravention of Regulation 8, not exceeding 4 weeks remuneration and,

(ii) in the case of a contravention of any other Regulation, not exceeding 2 years remuneration,

in respect of the employee's employment calculated in accordance with Regulations made under section 17 of the Unfair Dismissals Act 1977,

and a reference in this paragraph to an employer shall be construed, in a case where ownership of the relevant undertaking or business, or the part concerned of that undertaking or business, of the employer changes after the contravention to which the complaint relates occurred, as a reference to the person who, by virtue of the change, becomes entitled to such ownership.

(6) A rights commissioner shall not entertain a complaint under this Regulation unless it is presented to the commissioner within the period of 6 months beginning on the date of the alleged contravention to which the complaint relates, or where the rights commissioner is satisfied that exceptional circumstances prevented the presentation of the complaint within that period, such further period, not exceeding 6 months from the expiration of the first-mentioned period, as the rights commissioner considers reasonable.

(7) Proceedings under this Regulation before a rights commissioner shall be conducted otherwise than in public.

(8) A rights commissioner shall furnish the Tribunal with a copy of each decision given by the commissioner under paragraph (4).

(9) A rights commissioner shall maintain a register of all decisions made by him or her under this Regulation and shall make the register available for inspection by members of the public during normal office hours.

Appeals and enforcement.

11. (1) A party concerned may appeal to the Tribunal from a decision of a rights commissioner under Regulation 10, and if the party does so, the Tribunal shall—

(a) give the parties an opportunity to be heard by it and to present to it any evidence relevant to the appeal,

(b) make a determination in writing in relation to the appeal affirming, varying or setting aside the decision, and

(c) communicate the determination to the parties.

(2) An appeal under this Regulation shall be initiated by the party concerned by a notice in writing to the Tribunal containing such particulars as may have been determined under paragraph (4)(e) and stating the intention of the party concerned to appeal against the decision. Such a notice in writing shall be given within 6 weeks of the date on which the decision to which it relates was communicated to the party or such greater period as the Tribunal may, in accordance with paragraph 4(f), determine in the particular circumstances.

(3) A copy of a notice under paragraph (2) shall be given by the Tribunal to the other party or parties concerned as soon as may be after the receipt of the notice by the Tribunal.

(4) The following matters, or the procedures to be followed in relation to them shall be determined by the Tribunal namely—

(a) the procedure in relation to all matters concerning the initiation and the hearing by the Tribunal of appeals under this Regulation;

(b) the times and places of hearings of such appeals;

(c) the representation of the parties to such appeals;

(d) the publication and notification of determinations of the Tribunal;

(e) the particulars to be contained in a notice under paragraph (2);

(f) any matters consequential on, or incidental to, the foregoing matters.

12. (1) The Minister may, at the request of the Tribunal, refer a question of law arising in proceedings before it under Regulation 11 to the High Court for determination and the determination of the High Court shall be final and conclusive.

(2) A party to proceedings before the Tribunal under Regulation 11 may appeal to the High Court from a determination of the Tribunal on a point of law and the determination of the High Court shall be final and conclusive.

13. (1) The Tribunal shall, on the hearing of any matter referred to it under this Regulation, have power to take evidence on oath and for that purpose may cause to be administered oaths to persons attending as witnesses at such hearing.

(2) Any person who, upon examination on oath authorised by this Regulation, wilfully and corruptly makes any statement which is material for that purpose and which he or she knows to be false or does not believe to be true is guilty of an offence and on summary conviction shall be liable to a fine not exceeding €3000 or imprisonment for a term not exceeding 12 months or both.

(3) The Tribunal may, by giving notice in that behalf in writing to any person, require such person to attend at such time and place as is specified in the notice to give evidence in relation to any matter referred to the Tribunal under this Regulation or to produce any documents in his or her possession, custody or control which relate to any such matter.

(4) A notice under paragraph (3) may be given either by delivering it to the person to whom it relates or by sending it by post in a prepaid registered letter addressed to such person at the address at which he or she ordinarily resides.

(5) A person to whom a notice under paragraph (3) has been given and who refuses or wilfully neglects to attend in accordance with the notice or who, having so attended, refuses to give evidence or refuses or wilfully fails to produce any document to which the notice relates is guilty of an offence and is liable on summary conviction to a fine not exceeding €3,000.

14. (1) If an employer fails to carry out in accordance with its terms a decision of a rights commissioner or a determination of the Tribunal under Regulation 10 or 11 within 6 weeks from the date on which the decision or determination is communicated to the parties, the Circuit Court shall, on application to it in that behalf by—

(a) the employee concerned,

(b) with the consent of the employee, any trade union of which the employee is a member, or

(c) the Minister, if the Minister considers it appropriate to make the application having regard to all the circumstances,

without hearing the employer or any evidence (other than in relation to the matters aforesaid) make an order directing the employer to carry out the decision or the determination in accordance with its terms.

(2) The reference in paragraph (1) to a decision of a rights commissioner or to a determination of the Tribunal is a reference to such a decision or determination in relation to which, at the expiration of the time for bringing an appeal against it, no such appeal has been brought, or if such an appeal has been brought it has been abandoned and the references to the date on which the decision or the determination is communicated to the parties shall, in a case where such an appeal is abandoned, be construed as a reference to the date of such abandonment.

(3) The Circuit Court may, in an order under this Regulation, if in all the circumstances it considers it appropriate to do so, where the order relates to the payment of compensation, direct the employer concerned to pay to the employee concerned interest on the compensation at the rate referred to in section 22 of the Courts Act 1981 (No. 11 of 1981) in respect of the whole or any part of the period beginning 6 weeks after the date on which the decision of the rights commissioner or the determination of the Tribunal is communicated to the parties and ending on the date of the order.

(4) An application under this Regulation to the Circuit Court shall be made to the judge of the Circuit Court for the circuit in which the employer concerned ordinarily resides or carries on any profession, trade or business.

Revocations.

15. The following are revoked:

(*a*) the European Communities (Safeguarding of Employees' Rights on Transfer of Undertakings) Regulations 1980 (S.I. No. 306 of 1980); and

(*b*) the European Communities (Safeguarding of Employees' Rights on Transfer of Undertakings) (Amendment) Regulations 2000 (S.I. No. 487 of 2000).

(L.S.)

GIVEN under my Official Seal,

11th day of April 2003

MARY HARNEY T.D.,

Minister for Enterprise, Trade and Employment

EXPLANATORY NOTE

(This note is not part of the Instrument and does not purport to be a legal interpretation.)

These Regulations protect the rights of employees arising from an employment contract in the event of a transfer of a business or part of a business, in which they are employed, which entails a change of employer. Complaints that an employer has contravened these Regulations may, generally, be referred in the first instance to a rights commissioner and, on appeal, to the Employment Appeals Tribunal.

COUNCIL DIRECTIVE 2001/23/EC

of 12 March 2001

on the approximation of the laws of the Member States relating to the safeguarding of employees' rights in the event of transfers of undertakings, businesses or parts of undertakings or businesses

(Official Journal of the European Communities 22.3.2001 L 82/16)

THE COUNCIL OF THE EUROPEAN UNION,

Having regard to the Treaty establishing the European Community, and in particular Article 94 thereof,

Having regard to the proposal from the Commission,

Having regard to the opinion of the European Parliament ([1]),

Having regard to the opinion of the Economic and Social Committee ([2]),

Whereas:

(1) Council Directive 77/187/EEC of 14 February 1977 on the approximation of the laws of the Member States relating to the safeguarding of employees' rights in the event of transfers of undertakings, businesses or parts of undertakings or businesses ([3]) has been substantially amended ([4]). In the interests of clarity and rationality, it should therefore be codified.

(2) Economic trends are bringing in their wake, at both national and Community level, changes in the structure of undertakings, through transfers of undertakings, businesses or parts of undertakings or businesses to other employers as a result of legal transfers or mergers.

(3) It is necessary to provide for the protection of employees in the event of a change of employer, in particular, to ensure that their rights are safeguarded.

(4) Differences still remain in the Member States as regards the extent of the protection of employees in this respect and these differences should be reduced.

(5) The Community Charter of the Fundamental Social Rights of Workers adopted on 9 December 1989 ('Social Charter') states, in points 7, 17 and 18 in particular that: 'The completion of the internal market must lead to an improvement in the living and working conditions of

workers in the European Community. The improvement must cover, where necessary, the development of certain aspects of employment regulations such as procedures for collective redundancies and those regarding bankruptcies. Information, consultation and participation for workers must be developed along appropriate lines, taking account of the practice in force in the various Member States. Such information, consultation and participation must be implemented in due time, particularly in connection with restructuring operations in undertakings or in cases of mergers having an impact on the employment of workers'.

(6) In 1977 the Council adopted Directive 77/187/EEC to promote the harmonisation of the relevant national laws ensuring the safeguarding of the rights of employees and requiring transferors and transferees to inform and consult employees' representatives in good time.

(7) That Directive was subsequently amended in the light of the impact of the internal market, the legislative tendencies of the Member States with regard to the rescue of undertakings in economic difficulties, the case-law of the Court of Justice of the European Communities, Council Directive 75/129/EEC of 17 February 1975 on the approximation of the laws of the Member States relating to collective redundancies ([5]) and the legislation already in force in most Member States.

(8) Considerations of legal security and transparency required that the legal concept of transfer be clarified in the light of the case-law of the Court of Justice. Such clarification has not altered the scope of Directive 77/187/EEC as interpreted by the Court of Justice.

(9) The Social Charter recognises the importance of the fight against all forms of discrimination, especially based on sex, colour, race, opinion and creed.

(10) This Directive should be without prejudice to the time limits set out in Annex I Part B within which the Member States are to comply with Directive 77/187/EEC, and the act amending it,

---

([1]) Opinion delivered on 25 October 2000 (not yet published in the Official Journal).

([2]) OJ C 367, 20.12.2000, p. 21.

([3]) OJ L 61, 5.3.1977, p. 26.

([4]) See Annex I, Part A.

([5]) OJ L 48, 22.2.1975, p. 29. Directive replaced by Directive 98/ 59/EC (OJ L 225, 12.8.1998, p. 16).

HAS ADOPTED THIS DIRECTIVE:

CHAPTER I

Scope and definitions

Article 1

1. (a) This Directive shall apply to any transfer of an undertaking, business, or part of an undertaking or business to another employer as a result of a legal transfer or merger.

(b) Subject to subparagraph (a) and the following provisions of this Article, there is a transfer within the meaning of this Directive where there is a transfer of an economic entity which retains its identity, meaning an organised grouping of resources which has the objective of pursuing an economic activity, whether or not that activity is central or ancillary.

(c) This Directive shall apply to public and private undertakings engaged in economic activities whether or not they are operating for gain. An administrative reorganisation of public administrative authorities, or the transfer of administrative functions between public administrative authorities, is not a transfer within the meaning of this Directive.

2. This Directive shall apply where and in so far as the undertaking, business or part of the undertaking or business to be transferred is situated within the territorial scope of the Treaty.

3. This Directive shall not apply to seagoing vessels.

Article 2

1. For the purposes of this Directive:

(a) 'transferor' shall mean any natural or legal person who, by reason of a transfer within the meaning of Article 1(1), ceases to be the employer in respect of the undertaking, business or part of the undertaking or business;

(b) 'transferee' shall mean any natural or legal person who, by reason of a transfer within the meaning of Article 1(1), becomes the employer in respect of the undertaking, business or part of the undertaking or business;

(c) 'representatives of employees' and related expressions shall mean the representatives of the employees provided for by the laws or practices of the Member States;

(d) 'employee' shall mean any person who, in the Member State concerned, is protected as an employee under national employment law.

2. This Directive shall be without prejudice to national law as regards the definition of contract of employment or employment relationship.

However, Member States shall not exclude from the scope of this Directive contracts of employment or employment relationships solely because:

(a) of the number of working hours performed or to be performed,

(b) they are employment relationships governed by a fixed-duration contract of employment within the meaning of Article 1(1) of Council Directive 91/383/EEC of 25 June 1991 supplementing the measures to encourage improvements in the safety and health at work of workers with a fixed-duration employment relationship or a temporary employment relationship ([1]), or

([1]) OJ L 206, 29.7.1991, p. 19.

(c) they are temporary employment relationships within the meaning of Article 1(2) of Directive 91/383/EEC, and the undertaking, business or part of the undertaking or business transferred is, or is part of, the temporary employment business which is the employer.

CHAPTER II

Safeguarding of employees' rights

Article 3

1. The transferor's rights and obligations arising from a contract of employment or from an employment relationship existing on the date of a transfer shall, by reason of such transfer, be transferred to the transferee.

Member States may provide that, after the date of transfer, the transferor and the transferee shall be jointly and severally liable in respect of obligations which arose before the date of transfer from a contract of employment or an employment relationship existing on the date of the transfer.

2. Member States may adopt appropriate measures to ensure that the transferor notifies the transferee of all the rights and obligations which will

be transferred to the transferee under this Article, so far as those rights and obligations are or ought to have been known to the transferor at the time of the transfer. A failure by the transferor to notify the transferee of any such right or obligation shall not affect the transfer of that right or obligation and the rights of any employees against the transferee and/or transferor in respect of that right or obligation.

3. Following the transfer, the transferee shall continue to observe the terms and conditions agreed in any collective agreement on the same terms applicable to the transferor under that agreement, until the date of termination or expiry of the collective agreement or the entry into force or application of another collective agreement.

Member States may limit the period for observing such terms and conditions with the proviso that it shall not be less than one year.

4. (a) Unless Member States provide otherwise, paragraphs 1 and 3 shall not apply in relation to employees' rights to old-age, invalidity or survivors' benefits under supplementary company or intercompany pension schemes outside the statutory social security schemes in Member States.

(b) Even where they do not provide in accordance with subparagraph (a) that paragraphs 1 and 3 apply in relation to such rights, Member States shall adopt the measures necessary to protect the interests of employees and of persons no longer employed in the transferor's business at the time of the transfer in respect of rights conferring on them immediate or prospective entitlement to old age benefits, including survivors' benefits, under supplementary schemes referred to in subparagraph (a).

Article 4

1. The transfer of the undertaking, business or part of the undertaking or business shall not in itself constitute grounds for dismissal by the transferor or the transferee. This provision shall not stand in the way of dismissals that may take place for economic, technical or organisational reasons entailing changes in the workforce.

Member States may provide that the first subparagraph shall not apply to certain specific categories of employees who are not covered by the laws or practice of the Member States in respect of protection against dismissal.

2. If the contract of employment or the employment relationship is terminated because the transfer involves a substantial change in working

conditions to the detriment of the employee, the employer shall be regarded as having been responsible for termination of the contract of employment or of the employment relationship.

Article 5

1. Unless Member States provide otherwise, Articles 3 and 4 shall not apply to any transfer of an undertaking, business or part of an undertaking or business where the transferor is the subject of bankruptcy proceedings or any analogous insolvency proceedings which have been instituted with a view to the liquidation of the assets of the transferor and are under the supervision of a competent public authority (which may be an insolvency practitioner authorised by a competent public authority).

2. Where Articles 3 and 4 apply to a transfer during insolvency proceedings which have been opened in relation to a transferor (whether or not those proceedings have been instituted with a view to the liquidation of the assets of the transferor) and provided that such proceedings are under the supervision of a competent public authority (which may be an insolvency practitioner determined by national law) a Member State may provide that:

(*a*) notwithstanding Article 3(1), the transferor's debts arising from any contracts of employment or employment relationships and payable before the transfer or before the opening of the insolvency proceedings shall not be transferred to the transferee, provided that such proceedings give rise, under the law of that Member State, to protection at least equivalent to that provided for in situations covered by Council Directive 80/987/EEC of 20 October 1980 on the approximation of the laws of the Member States relating to the protection of employees in the event of the insolvency of their employer ([1]), and, or alternatively, that,

(*b*) the transferee, transferor or person or persons exercising the transferor's functions, on the one hand, and the representatives of the employees on the other hand may agree alterations, in so far as current law or practice permits, to the employees' terms and conditions of employment designed to safeguard employment opportunities by ensuring the survival of the undertaking, business or part of the undertaking or business.

([1]) OJ L 283, 20.10.1980, p. 23. Directive as last amended by the 1994 Act of Accession.

3. A Member State may apply paragraph 20(b)[1] to any transfers where the transferor is in a situation of serious economic crisis, as defined by national law, provided that the situation is declared by a competent public authority and open to judicial supervision, on condition that such provisions already existed in national law on 17 July 1998.

The Commission shall present a report on the effects of this provision before 17 July 2003 and shall submit any appropriate proposals to the Council.

4. Member States shall take appropriate measures with a view to preventing misuse of insolvency proceedings in such a way as to deprive employees of the rights provided for in this Directive.

Article 6

1. If the undertaking, business or part of an undertaking or business preserves its autonomy, the status and function of the representatives or of the representation of the employees affected by the transfer shall be preserved on the same terms and subject to the same conditions as existed before the date of the transfer by virtue of law, regulation, administrative provision or agreement, provided that the conditions necessary for the constitution of the employee's representation are fulfilled.

The first subparagraph shall not supply [2] if, under the laws, regulations, administrative provisions or practice in the Member States, or by agreement with the representatives of the employees, the conditions necessary for the reappointment of the representatives of the employees or for the reconstitution of the representation of the employees are fulfilled.

Where the transferor is the subject of bankruptcy proceedings or any analoguous insolvency proceedings which have been instituted with a view to the liquidation of the assets of the transferor and are under the supervision of a competent public authority (which may be an insolvency practitioner authorized by a competent public authority), Member States may take the necessary measures to ensure that the transferred employees are properly represented until the new election or designation of representatives of the employees.

If the undertaking, business or part of an undertaking or business does not preserve its autonomy, the Member States shall take the necessary measures to ensure that the employees transferred who were represented

---

[1] *Sic.* This should refer to paragraph 2(b), not paragraph 20(b).
[2] *Sic.*

before the transfer continue to be properly represented during the period necessary for the reconstitution or reappointment of the representation of employees in accordance with national law or practice.

2. If the term of office of the representatives of the employees affected by the transfer expires as a result of the transfer, the representatives shall continue to enjoy the protection provided by the laws, regulations, administrative provisions or practice of the Member States.

CHAPTER III

Information and consultation

Article 7

1. The transferor and transferee shall be required to inform the representatives of their respective employees affected by the transfer of the following:

— the date or proposed date of the transfer,

— the reasons for the transfer,

— the legal, economic and social implications of the transfer for the employees,

— any measures envisaged in relation to the employees.

The transferor must give such information to the representatives of his employees in good time, before the transfer is carried out.

The transferee must give such information to the representatives of his employees in good time, and in any event before his employees are directly affected by the transfer as regards their conditions of work and employment.

2. Where the transferor or the transferee envisages measures in relation to his employees, he shall consult the representatives of this [3] employees in good time on such measures with a view to reaching an agreement.

3. Member States whose laws, regulations or administrative provisions provide that representatives of the employees may have recourse to an arbitration board to obtain a decision on the measures to be taken in relation to employees may limit the obligations laid down in paragraphs 1 and 2 to cases where the transfer carried out gives rise to a change in the business likely to entail serious disadvantages for a considerable number of the employees.

The information and consultations shall cover at least the measures envisaged in relation to the employees.

---

[3] *Sic.*

The information must be provided and consultations take place in good time before the change in the business as referred to in the first subparagraph is effected.

4. The obligations laid down in this Article shall apply irrespective of whether the decision resulting in the transfer is taken by the employer or an undertaking controlling the employer.

In considering alleged breaches of the information and consultation requirements laid down by this Directive, the argument that such a breach occurred because the information was not provided by an undertaking controlling the employer shall not be accepted as an excuse.

5. Member States may limit the obligations laid down in paragraphs 1, 2 and 3 to undertakings or businesses which, in terms of the number of employees, meet the conditions for the election or nomination of a collegiate body representing the employees.

6. Member States shall provide that, where there are no representatives of the employees in an undertaking or business through no fault of their own, the employees concerned must be informed in advance of:

— the date or proposed date of the transfer,

— the reason for the transfer,

— the legal, economic and social implications of the transfer for the employees,

— any measures envisaged in relation to the employees.

CHAPTER IV

Final provisions

Article 8

This Directive shall not affect the right of Member States to apply or introduce laws, regulations or administrative provisions which are more favourable to employees or to promote or permit collective agreements or agreements between social partners more favourable to employees.

Article 9

Member States shall introduce into their national legal systems such measures as are necessary to enable all employees and representatives of employees who consider themselves wronged by failure to comply with the obligations arising from this Directive to pursue their claims by judicial process after possible recourse to other competent authorities.

Article 10

The Commission shall submit to the Council an analysis of the effect of the provisions of this Directive before 17 July 2006. It shall propose any amendment which may seem necessary.

Article 11

Member States shall communicate to the Commission the texts of the laws, regulations and administrative provisions which they adopt in the field covered by this Directive.

Article 12

Directive 77/187/EEC, as amended by the Directive referred to in Annex I, Part A, is repealed, without prejudice to the obligations of the Member States concerning the time limits for implementation set out in Annex I, Part B.

References to the repealed Directive shall be construed as references to this Directive and shall be read in accordance with the correlation table in Annex II.

Article 13

This Directive shall enter into force on the 20th day following its publication in the *Official Journal of the European Communities*.

Article 14

This Directive is addressed to the Member States.

Done at Brussels, 12 March 2001.

For the Council

The President

B. RINGHOLM

ANNEX I

PART A

Repealed Directive and its amending Directive

(referred to in Article 12)

Council Directive 77/187/EEC (OJ L 61, 5.3.1977, p. 26)

Council Directive 98/50/EC (OJ L 201, 17.7.1998, p. 88)

PART B

Deadlines for transposition into national law

(referred to in Article 12)

Directive	Deadline for transposition
77/187/EEC	16 February 1979
98/50/EC	17 July 2001

ANNEX II

CORRELATION TABLE

Directive 77/187/EEC	This Directive
Article 1	Article 1
Article 2	Article 2
Article 3	Article 3
Article 4	Article 4
Article 4a	Article 5
Article 5	Article 6
Article 6	Article 7
Article 7	Article 8
Article 7a	Article 9

Directive 77/187/EEC	This Directive
Article 7b	Article 10
Article 8	Article 11
—	Article 12
—	Article 13
—	Article 14
—	ANNEX I
—	ANNEX II

REDUNDANCY PAYMENTS ACT 2003

Number 14 *of* 2003

ARRANGEMENT OF SECTIONS

Section

ACTS REFERRED TO

Adoptive Leave Act 1995	1995, No. 2
Carer's Leave Act 2001	2001, No. 19
Civil Service Regulation Act 1956	1956, No. 46
Employment Agency Act 1971	1971, No. 27
Employment Equality Act 1998	1998, No. 21
Industrial Relations Act 1946	1946, No. 26
Local Government Act 2001	2001, No. 37
Maternity Protection Act 1994	1994, No. 34
National Minimum Wage Act 2000	2000, No. 5
Parental Leave Act 1998	1998, No. 30
Protection of Employees (Employers' Insolvency) Act 1984	1984, No. 21
Protection of Employees (Employers' Insolvency) Acts 1984 to 2001	
Redundancy Payments Act 1967	1967, No. 21
Redundancy Payments Act 1971	1971, No. 20
Redundancy Payments Act 1979	1979, No. 7
Redundancy Payments Acts 1967 to 2001	
Social Welfare (Consolidation) Act 1993	1993, No. 27

Number 14 *of* 2003

REDUNDANCY PAYMENTS ACT 2003

AN ACT TO AMEND AND EXTEND THE REDUNDANCY PAYMENTS ACT 1967, TO AMEND THE REDUNDANCY PAYMENTS ACT 1971, THE PROTECTION OF EMPLOYEES (EMPLOYERS' INSOLVENCY) ACT 1984, THE SOCIAL WELFARE (CONSOLIDATION) ACT 1993 AND THE EMPLOYMENT EQUALITY ACT 1998 AND TO PROVIDE FOR RELATED MATTERS. [15*th May*, 2003]

BE IT ENACTED BY THE OIREACHTAS AS FOLLOWS:

1.—(1) In this Act— [1] Interpretation.

"Minister" means the Minister for Enterprise, Trade and Employment; [2]

"Principal Act" means the Redundancy Payments Act 1967.

(2) In this Act—

(*a*) a reference to a section is to a section of this Act, unless it is indicated that reference to some other enactment is intended, and

(*b*) a reference to an enactment shall be construed as a reference to that enactment as amended, adapted or extended by or under any subsequent enactment including this Act.

---

[1] In Article 3(1) of the Redundancy Payments Act 2003 (Commencement) Order 2003 (S.I. No. 194 of 2003), the present Minister for Enterprise, Trade and Employment appointed 25 May, 2003 to be the day on which s. 1 of the 2003 Act came into operation.

[2] The powers and duties which are conferred on the Minister for Enterprise, Trade and Employment by or under the Redundancy Payments Acts have been delegated by statutory instrument to the present Minister of State at the Department of Enterprise, Trade and Employment. (See now the Enterprise, Trade and Employment (Delegation of Ministerial Functions) Order 2004 (S.I. No. 809 of 2004).)

Expenses.

2. *(Insertion of s. 5(6) of the Social Welfare (Consolidation) Act 1993)* [3]

Amendment of section 2 of Principal Act (Interpretation).

3. *(Insertions and substitution in s. 2(1) of the Redundancy Payments Act, 1967)* [4]

Amendment of section 4 of Principal Act (Classes of persons to which this Act applies).

4. *(Substitution of s. 4(2) of the Redundancy Payments Act, 1967)* [5]

Amendment of section 7 of Principal Act (General right to redundancy payment).

5. *(Insertion in s. 7(2) of the Redundancy Payments Act, 1967)* [6]

---

[3] This amendment (which inserted material relating to the payment from the Social Insurance Fund to the Minister of Enterprise, Trade and Employment of expenses incurred in carrying into effect, *inter alia,* the Redundancy Payments Acts) has since been superseded by virtue of the repeal by s. 360 of the Social Welfare Consolidation Act 2005 of the entirety of the Social Welfare (Consolidation) Act, 1993, and the enactment of an effectively identical provision to the repealed s. 5(6) of the 1993 Act in the shape of s. 5(6) of the Social Welfare Consolidation Act 2005.

[4] In Article 3(1) of the Redundancy Payments Act 2003 (Commencement) Order 2003 (S.I. No. 194 of 2003), the Minister for Enterprise, Trade and Employment appointed 25 May, 2003 to be the day on which s. 3 of the 2003 Act came into operation.

[5] In Article 3(1) of the Redundancy Payments Act 2003 (Commencement) Order 2003 (S.I. No. 194 of 2003), the Minister for Enterprise, Trade and Employment appointed 25 May, 2003 to be the day on which s. 4 of the 2003 Act came into operation.

[6] In Article 3(1) of the Redundancy Payments Act 2003 (Commencement) Order 2003 (S.I. No. 194 of 2003), the Minister for Enterprise, Trade and Employment appointed 25 May, 2003 to be the day on which s. 5 of the 2003 Act came into operation.

6. *(Substitution of s. 9(1)(b) of the Redundancy Payments Act, 1967)* [7]

Amendment of section 9 of Principal Act (Dismissal by employer).

7. *(Deletion in s. 17(1) of the Redundancy Payments Act, 1967)* [8]

(Substitution of s. 17(2)(b) and (c) of the Redundancy Payments Act, 1967 by a new s. 17(2)(b))

(Insertion of s. 17(2A) in the Redundancy Payments Act, 1967)

Amendment of section 17 of Principal Act (Notice of proposed dismissal for redundancy).

8. *(Substitution in s. 25(2) of the Redundancy Payments Act, 1967)* [9]

(Insertion of s. 25(2A) in the Redundancy Payments Act, 1967)

Amendment of section 25 of Principal Act (Employment wholly or partly abroad).

9. *(Insertion in s. 39(2)(b) of the Redundancy Payments Act, 1967)*

Amendment of section 39 of Principal Act (Redundancy Appeals Tribunal and appeals and references thereto).

[7] In Article 3(1) of the Redundancy Payments Act 2003 (Commencement) Order 2003 (S.I. No. 194 of 2003), the Minister for Enterprise, Trade and Employment appointed 25 May, 2003 to be the day on which s. 6 of the 2003 Act came into operation.

[8] In Article 3(1) of the Redundancy Payments Act 2003 (Commencement) Order 2005 (S.I. No. 77 of 2005), the Minister for Enterprise, Trade and Employment appointed 10 April, 2005 to be the day on which s. 7 of the 2003 Act came into operation. Section 7 applies to employees declared redundant on or after this date. (See, confirming this latter point, Article 3(2) of S.I. No. 77 of 2005).

[9] In Article 3(1) of the Redundancy Payments Act 2003 (Commencement) Order 2003 (S.I. No. 194 of 2003), the Minister for Enterprise, Trade and Employment appointed 25 May, 2003 to be the day on which s. 8 of the 2003 Act came into operation.

Transitional arrangements.

10. *(Substitutions in para. 1(a) and para. 1(b) of Schedule 3 to the Redundancy Payments Act, 1967)* [10]

Enhanced redundancy payments.

11. *(Substitution of paragraphs 1, 2 and 3 of Schedule 3 to the Redundancy Payments Act, 1967)* [11]

Amendment of Schedule 3 to Principal Act (Amount of lump sum).

12. *(Substitution of paragraph 5 of Schedule 3 to the Redundancy Payments Act, 1967)* [12]

(Substitution of paragraph 8 of Schedule 3 to the Redundancy Payments Act, 1967 and insertion of paragraph 8A)

(Substitution of paragraph 10 of Schedule 3 to the Redundancy Payments Act, 1967)

---

[10] In Article 3(1) of the Redundancy Payments Act 2003 (Commencement) Order 2003 (S.I. No. 194 of 2003), the Minister for Enterprise, Trade and Employment appointed 25 May, 2003 to be the day on which s. 10 of the 2003 Act came into operation. Section 10 applies to employees declared redundant on or after this date. (See, confirming this latter point, Article 3(2) of S.I. No. 194 of 2003). The amendments which were effected by s. 10 of the 2003 Act, which were always intended to be of a transitional nature only, were superseded on the coming into force of s. 11 of the 2003 Act. (S. 10(1) provided for alterations in the manner of calculation of redundancy lump sums. Under s. 10(2), s. 10 ceased to have effect on the commencement of s. 11.) Section 11 of the 2003 Act substituted a new method of calculation of redundancy lump sum payments into Schedule 3 of the Redundancy Payments Act, 1967. In Article 3(1) of the Redundancy Payments Act 2003 (Commencement) Order 2005 (S.I. No. 77 of 2005), the Minister for Enterprise, Trade and Employment appointed 10 April, 2005 to be the day on which s. 11 of the 2003 Act came into operation. Section 11 thus applies to employees declared redundant on or after this date. (See, confirming this latter point, Article 3(2) of S.I. No. 77 of 2005).

[11] As noted in the previous footnote, under Article 3(1) of the Redundancy Payments Act 2003 (Commencement) Order 2005 (S.I. No. 77 of 2005), s. 11 came into force on 10 April, 2005 and applies to employees declared redundant on or after this date.

[12] In Article 3(1) of the Redundancy Payments Act 2003 (Commencement) Order 2005 (S.I. No. 77 of 2005), the Minister for Enterprise, Trade and Employment appointed 10 April, 2005 to be the day on which s. 12 of the 2003 Act came into operation. Section 12 applies to employees declared redundant on or after this date. (See, confirming this latter point, Article 3(2) of S.I. No. 77 of 2005).

13. *(Substitution in s. 17(3) of the Redundancy Payments Act, 1967)* [13]

(Substitution in s. 18(4) of the Redundancy Payments Act, 1967)

(Substitution in s. 36(3) of the Redundancy Payments Act, 1967)

Increase in penalties for certain offences.

14. *(Insertion in s. 10 of the Redundancy Payments Act 1971)* [14]

Amendment of section 10 of Redundancy Payments Act 1971.

15. *(Substitution of s. 6(2)(a)(iii) of the Protection of Employees (Employers' Insolvency) Act 1984)* [15]

(Substitution in s. 6(9)(a) of the Protection of Employees (Employers' Insolvency) Act 1984)

(Insertion of s. 6(9)(aa) of the Protection of Employees (Employers' Insolvency) Act 1984)

Amendment of section 6 of Protection of Employees (Employers' Insolvency) Act 1984.

16. —Section 17(4) of the Employment Equality Act 1998 is repealed.[16]

Repeal of section 17(4) of Employment Equality Act 1998.

---

[13] In Article 3(1) of the Redundancy Payments Act 2003 (Commencement) Order 2003 (S.I. No. 194 of 2003), the Minister for Enterprise, Trade and Employment appointed 25 May, 2003 to be the day on which s. 13 of the 2003 Act came into operation.

[14] In Article 3(1) of the Redundancy Payments Act 2003 (Commencement) Order 2003 (S.I. No. 194 of 2003), the Minister for Enterprise, Trade and Employment appointed 25 May 2003 to be the day on which s. 14 of the 2003 Act came into operation.

[15] In Article 3(1) of the Redundancy Payments Act 2003 (Commencement) Order 2003 (S.I. No. 194 of 2003), the Minister for Enterprise, Trade and Employment appointed 25 May, 2003 to be the day on which s. 15 of the 2003 Act came into operation. Section 15 thus applies only to circumstances where the relevant date defined by s. 6(9) of the Protection of Employees (Employers' Insolvency) Act, 1984 occurs on or after 25 May, 2003. (See, confirming this latter point, Article 3(2) of S.I. No. 194 of 2003).

[16] In Article 3(1) of the Redundancy Payments Act 2003 (Commencement) Order 2003 (S.I. No. 194 of 2003), the Minister for Enterprise, Trade and Employment appointed 25 May, 2003 to be the day on which s. 16 of the 2003 Act came into operation.

Short title, commencement, collective citation and construction.

17. —(1) This Act may be cited as the Redundancy Payments Act 2003.[17]

(2) This Act shall come into operation on such day or days as the Minister may appoint by order or orders generally or with reference to any particular purpose or provision and different days may be appointed for different purposes or different provisions.[18]

(3) This Act and the Redundancy Payments Acts 1967 to 2001 may be cited together as the Redundancy Payments Acts 1967 to 2003 and shall be construed together as one.[19]

---

[17] In Article 3(1) of the Redundancy Payments Act 2003 (Commencement) Order 2003 (S.I. No. 194 of 2003), the Minister for Enterprise, Trade and Employment appointed 25 May, 2003 to be the day on which s. 17 of the 2003 Act came into operation.

[18] In Article 3(1) of the Redundancy Payments Act 2003 (Commencement) Order 2003 (S.I. No. 194 of 2003), the Minister for Enterprise, Trade and Employment appointed 25 May, 2003 to be the day on which ss. 1 to 6, 8, 10 and 13 to 17 of the 2003 Act came into operation. In Article 3(1) of the Redundancy Payments Act 2003 (Commencement) Order 2005 (S.I. No. 77 of 2005), the Minister for Enterprise, Trade and Employment appointed 10 April, 2005 to be the day on which ss. 7, 11 and 12 of the 2003 Act came into operation.

[19] Note that this means that the Redundancy Payments Act, 1967, the Redundancy Payments Act, 1971, the Redundancy Payments Act, 1973, the Redundancy Payments Act, 1979, s. 12 of the Protection of Employees (Employers' Insolvency) Act, 1984, ss. 26, 27 and 29 of the Social Welfare Act, 1990, s. 39 (other than sub-s. (2)) of the Social Welfare Act, 1991 (although apparently by oversight no mention is made of s. 39 of the 1991 Act in any subsequent statute included in this list), the Protection of Employees (Part-Time Work) Act, 2001 (insofar as it relates to the foregoing legislation, apart from s. 39 of the 1991 Act) and the Redundancy Payments Act 2003 may be cited together as the Redundancy Payments Acts 1967 to 2003.

See in this regard, in addition to s. 17(3) of the Redundancy Payments Act, 2003, s. 20(2) of the Redundancy Payments Act, 1971, s. 2(2) of the Redundancy Payments Act, 1973, s. 21(2) of the Redundancy Payments Act, 1979, s. 18(2) of the Protection of Employees (Employers' Insolvency) Act, 1984, s. 1(4) of the Social Welfare Act, 1990, s. 1(3) of the Social Welfare Act, 1991, and s. 1(4) of the Protection of Employees (Part-Time Work) Act, 2001.

S.I. No. 630 of 2005

EUROPEAN COMMUNITIES (PROTECTION OF EMPLOYEES (EMPLOYERS' INSOLVENCY)) REGULATIONS 2005

I, Micheál Martin, Minister for Enterprise, Trade and Employment, in exercise of the powers conferred on me by section 3 of the European Communities Act 1972 (No. 27 of 1972), for the purpose of giving effect to Directive 2002/74/EC of the European Parliament and of the Council of 23 September 2002 [1], hereby make the following regulations:

[1] OJ No. L270, 8.10.2002, p. 10

Citation, Commencement and Interpretation.

1. (1) These Regulations may be cited as the European Communities (Protection of Employees (Employers' Insolvency)) Regulations 2005.

(2) These Regulations come into operation on 8 October, 2005.

2. In these Regulations "Act of 1984" means the Protection of Employees (Employers' Insolvency) Act 1984 (No. 21 of 1984).

Amendment of Protection of Employees (Employers' Insolvency) Act 1984.

3. *(Insertions in s. 1(1) of the Protection of Employees (Employers' Insolvency) Act, 1984)*

(Substitutions in s. 1(3) of the Protection of Employees (Employers' Insolvency) Act, 1984)

(Insertion of s. 1(3)(e) of the Protection of Employees (Employers' Insolvency) Act, 1984)

4. *(Substitution of s. 3 of the Protection of Employees (Employers' Insolvency) Act, 1984)*

5. *(Deletion in s. 4(1)(e) of the Protection of Employees (Employers' Insolvency) Act, 1984)*

(Substitution in s. 4(1)(f) of the Protection of Employees (Employers' Insolvency) Act, 1984)

(Insertion of s. 4(1)(g) of the Protection of Employees (Employers' Insolvency) Act, 1984)

6. *(Substitution in s. 6(2)(a)(xiii) of the Protection of Employees (Employers' Insolvency) Act, 1984)*

(Insertion of s. 6(2)(a)(xiv) to s. 6(2)(a)(xxv) of the Protection of Employees (Employers' Insolvency) Act, 1984)

(Substitution in s. 6(2)(b) of the Protection of Employees (Employers' Insolvency) Act, 1984)

(Insertion of s. 6(2)(c) of the Protection of Employees (Employers' Insolvency) Act, 1984)

(Substitution in s. 6(9) of the Protection of Employees (Employers' Insolvency) Act, 1984)

7. *(Insertion in s. 7(3)(b) of the Protection of Employees (Employers' Insolvency) Act, 1984)*

(L.S.)

GIVEN under my Official Seal,

4th October, 2005.

MICHEÁL MARTIN

Minister for Enterprise,

Trade & Employment

EXPLANATORY NOTE

(This note is not part of the Instrument and does not purport to be a legal interpretation.)

These Regulations transpose into Irish law Directive 2002/74/EU [1] of 23 September 2002 amending Council Directive 80/987/EEC concerning the protection of employees in the event of insolvency of their employer.

---

[1] *Sic.*

The Regulations amend the Protection of Employees (Employers' Insolvency) Act 1984 by including a provision to cover employees who are employed in Ireland by an employer who has become insolvent under the laws, regulations and administrative procedures of another Member State. The Regulations also extend the coverage of the Act to include additional entitlements that may be owed to employees by an insolvent employer.

DIRECTIVE 2002/74/EC OF THE EUROPEAN PARLIAMENT AND OF THE COUNCIL

of 23 September 2002

amending Council Directive 80/987/EEC on the approximation of the laws of the Member States relating to the protection of employees in the event of the insolvency of their employer

(Text with EEA relevance)

(Official Journal of the European Communities 8.10.2002 L 270/10)

THE EUROPEAN PARLIAMENT AND THE COUNCIL OF THE EUROPEAN UNION,

Having regard to the Treaty establishing the European Community, and in particular Article 137(2) thereof,

Having regard to the proposal from the Commission ([1]),

Having regard to the opinion of the Economic and Social Committee ([2]),

Having consulted the Committee of the Regions,

Acting in accordance with the procedure laid down in Article 251 of the Treaty ([3]),

Whereas:

(1) The Community Charter of Fundamental Social Rights for Workers adopted on 9 December 1989 states, in point 7, that the completion of the internal market must lead to an improvement in the living and working conditions of workers in the European Community and that this improvement must cover, where necessary, the development of certain aspects of employment regulations such as procedures for collective redundancies and those regarding bankruptcies.

(2) Directive 80/987/EEC ([4]) aims to provide a minimum degree of protection for employees in the event of the insolvency of their employer. To this end, it obliges the Member States to establish a body which guarantees payment of the outstanding claims of the employees concerned.

(3) Changes in insolvency law in the Member States and the development of the internal market mean that certain provisions of that Directive must be adapted.

(4) Legal certainty and transparency also require clarification with regard to the scope and certain definitions of Directive 80/987/EEC. In particular the possible exclusions granted to the Member States should be indicated in the enacting provisions of the Directive and consequently the Annex thereto should be deleted.

(5) In order to ensure equitable protection for the employees concerned, the definition of the state of insolvency should be adapted to new legislative trends in the Member States and should also include within this concept insolvency proceedings other than liquidation. In this context, Member States should, in order to determine the liability of the guarantee institution, be able to lay down that where an insolvency situation results in several insolvency proceedings, the situation be treated as a single insolvency procedure.

(6) It should be ensured that the employees referred to in Directive 97/81/EC of 15 December 1997 concerning the Framework Agreement on part-time work concluded by UNICE, CEEP and the ETUC ([5]), Council Directive 1999/70/EC of 28 June 1999 concerning the framework agreement on fixed-term work concluded by the ETUC, UNICE and CEEP ([6]) and Council Directive 91/383/EEC of 25 June 1991 supplementing the measures to encourage improvements in the safety and health at work of workers with a fixed-duration employment relationship or a temporary employment relationship ([7]) are not excluded from the scope of this Directive.

([1]) OJ C 154 E, 29.5.2001, p. 109.

([2]) OJ C 221, 7.8.2001, p. 110.

([3]) Opinion of the European Parliament of 29 November 2001 (not yet published in the Official Journal), Council Common Position of 18 February 2002 (OJ C 119 E, 22.5.2002, p. 1) (not yet published in the Official Journal) and European Parliament Decision of 14 May 2002 (not yet published in the Official Journal). Council Decision of 27 June 2002.

([4]) OJ L 283, 28.10.1980, p. 23. Directive as last amended by the 1994 Act of Accession.

([5]) OJ L 14, 20.1.1998, p. 9. Directive as last amended by Directive 98/23/EC (OJ L 131, 5.5.1998, p. 10).

([6]) OJ L 175, 10.7.1999, p. 43.

([7]) OJ L 206, 29.7.1991, p. 19.

(7) In order to ensure legal certainty for employees in the event of insolvency of undertakings pursuing their activities in a number of Member States, and to strengthen workers' rights in line with the established case law of the Court of Justice, provisions should be introduced which expressly state which institution is responsible for meeting pay claims in these cases and establishes as the aim of cooperation between the competent administrative authorities of the Member States the early settlement of employees' outstanding claims. Furthermore it is necessary to ensure that the relevant arrangements are properly implemented by making provision for collaboration between the competent administrative authorities in the Member States.

(8) Member States may set limitations on the responsibility of the guarantee institutions which should be compatible with the social objective of the Directive and may take into account the different levels of claims.

(9) In order to make it easier to identify insolvency proceedings in particular in situations with a cross-border dimension, provision should be made for the Member States to notify the Commission and the other Member States about the types of insolvency proceedings which give rise to intervention by the guarantee institution.

(10) Directive 80/987/EEC should be amended accordingly.

(11) Since the objectives of the proposed action, namely the amendment of certain provisions of Directive 80/987/EEC to take account of changes in the activities of undertakings in the Community, cannot be sufficiently achieved by the Member States and can therefore be better achieved at Community level, the Community may adopt measures, in accordance with the principle of subsidiarity as set out in Article 5 of the Treaty. In accordance with the principle of proportionality, as set out in that Article, this Directive does not go beyond what is necessary in order to achieve that objective.

(12) The Commission should submit to the European Parliament and the Council a report on the implementation and application of this Directive in particular as regards the new forms of employment emerging in the Member States,

HAVE ADOPTED THIS DIRECTIVE:

Article 1

Directive 80/987/EEC is hereby amended as follows:

1. *(Replacement of original title of Council Directive 80/987/EEC of 20 October 1980)*

2. *(Replacement of Section I of Council Directive 80/987/EEC of 20 October 1980)*

3. *(Replacement of Articles 3 and 4 of Council Directive 80/987/EEC of 20 October 1980)*

4. *(Insertion of new Section IIIa in Council Directive 80/987/EEC of 20 October 1980)*

5. *(Addition of new paragraph to Article 9 of Council Directive 80/987/EEC of 20 October 1980)*

6. *(Addition of new point (c) in Article 10 of Council Directive 80/987/EEC of 20 October 1980)*

7. *(Insertion of new Article 10a in Council Directive 80/987/EEC of 20 October 1980)*

8. *(Deletion of Annex to Council Directive 80/987/EEC of 20 October 1980)*

Article 2

1. Member States shall bring into force the laws, regulations and administrative provisions necessary to comply with this Directive before 8 October 2005. They shall forthwith inform the Commission thereof.

They shall apply the provisions referred to in the first subparagraph to any state of insolvency of an employer occurring after the date of entry into force of those provisions.

When Member States adopt these measures, they shall contain a reference to this Directive or be accompanied by such reference on the occasion of their official publication. The methods of making such a reference shall be laid down by the Member States.

2. Member States shall communicate to the Commission the text of the provisions of national law which they adopt in the field covered by this Directive.

Article 3

This Directive shall enter into force on the day of its publication in the *Official Journal of the European Communities*.

Article 4

By 8 October 2010 at the latest, the Commission shall submit to the European Parliament and the Council a report on the implementation and application of this Directive in the Member States.

Article 5

This Directive is addressed to the Member States.

Done at Brussels, 23 September 2002.

For the European Parliament	*For the Council*
The President	*The President*
P. Cox	M. Fischer Boel

EMPLOYEES (PROVISION OF INFORMATION AND CONSULTATION) ACT 2006

Number 9 *of* 2006

ARRANGEMENT OF SECTIONS

Section

ACTS REFERRED TO

Courts Act 1981	1981, No. 11
Interpretation Act 2005	2005, No. 23
Payment of Wages Act 1991	1991, No. 25
Protection of Employment Act 1977	1977, No. 7
Trade Union Act 1941	1941, No. 22
Transnational Information and Consultation of Employees Act 1996	1996, No. 20
Unfair Dismissals Acts 1977 to 2005	

Number 9 *of* 2006

EMPLOYEES (PROVISION OF INFORMATION AND CONSULTATION) ACT 2006

AN ACT TO IMPLEMENT DIRECTIVE 2002/14/EC OF THE EUROPEAN PARLIAMENT [1] AND OF THE COUNCIL OF 11 MARCH 2002 BY PROVIDING FOR THE ESTABLISHMENT OF ARRANGEMENTS FOR INFORMING AND CONSULTING EMPLOYEES IN UNDERTAKINGS, TO IMPLEMENT ARTICLE 3(2) OF COUNCIL DIRECTIVE NO. 2001/23/EC OF 12 MARCH 2001 [2] ON THE APPROXIMATION OF THE LAWS OF THE MEMBER STATES RELATING TO THE SAFEGUARDING OF EMPLOYEES' RIGHTS IN THE EVENT OF TRANSFERS OF UNDERTAKINGS, BUSINESSES OR PARTS OF UNDERTAKINGS OR BUSINESSES AND TO PROVIDE FOR RELATED MATTERS. [*9th April,* 2006]

BE IT ENACTED BY THE OIREACHTAS AS FOLLOWS:

1.—(1) In this Act— Interpretation.

"appointed" means, in the absence of an election, appointed by the employees and the basis on which that appointment is made may, if the employees so determine, be such as is agreed by them with the employer;

"Commission" means the Labour Relations Commission;

"consultation" means the exchange of views and establishment of dialogue between either or both—

(*a*) one or more employees,

(*b*) the employees' representative or representatives,

and the employer;

[1] O.J. No. L080, 23/03/2002, p. 29

[2] O.J. No. L082, 22/03/2001, p. 16

"contract of employment" means a contract of service or of apprenticeship whether express or implied, and if express, whether oral or in writing;

"Court" means the Labour Court;

"Directive" means Directive 2002/14/EC of the European Parliament and of the Council of 11 March 2002 establishing a general framework for informing and consulting employees in the European Community;

"employee" means a person who has entered into or works under a contract of employment and references, in relation to an employer, to an employee shall be read as references to an employee employed by that employer;

"employee threshold" has the meaning assigned by *section 7*;

"employees' representative" has the meaning assigned by *section 6*;

"employer", in relation to an employee, means the person by whom the employee is employed under a contract of employment;

"excepted body" has the meaning assigned by section 6(3) of the Trade Union Act 1941, as amended;

"expert" means an individual, and may be the holder from time to time of a named office or position in a body corporate or other body or organisation;

"information" means transmission by the employer to one or more employees or their representatives (or both) of data in order to enable them to acquaint themselves with the subject matter and to examine it and cognate words shall be read accordingly;

"Information and Consultation Forum" means a Forum established in accordance with *Schedule 1* for the purpose of informing and consulting employees;

"Minister" means Minister for Enterprise, Trade and Employment;

"negotiated agreement" has the meaning assigned by *section 8*;

"pre-existing agreement" has the meaning assigned by *section 9*;

"prescribed" means prescribed by regulations made by the Minister;

"relevant workforce threshold" has the meaning assigned by *section 4*;

"trade union" means a trade union which holds a negotiation licence under Part II of the Trade Union Act 1941, as amended;

"undertaking" means a public or private undertaking carrying out an economic activity, whether or not operating for gain.

(2) A word or expression that is used in this Act and is also used in the Directive has the same meaning in this Act as it does in the Directive.

(3) For the avoidance of doubt, a reference in this Act—

(*a*) to the negotiation of an agreement establishing information and consultation arrangements or to such an agreement that has been negotiated, or

(*b*) to an Information and Consultation Forum,

includes a reference—

(i) to the negotiation of more than one such agreement or, as appropriate, to more than one such agreement that has been negotiated, or

(ii) to more than one such Forum.

(4) *Subsection (3)* is without prejudice to section 18(*a*) of the Interpretation Act 2005.

Regulations.

2. —(1) The Minister may make regulations prescribing any matter or thing referred to in this Act as prescribed or to be prescribed.[1]

(2) Regulations under this section may contain such incidental, supplementary and consequential provisions as appear to the Minister to be necessary or expedient for the purposes of the regulations or for giving full effect to this Act.

Right of employees to information and consultation.

3. —(1) Subject to the provisions of this Act, an employee employed in an undertaking employing 50 or more employees has a right to information and consultation.

---

[1] See now the Employees (Provision of Information and Consultation) Act 2006 (Prescribed Dates) Regulations 2006 (S.I. No. 383 of 2006).

(2) This Act is without prejudice to—

(*a*) the information and consultation procedures under the Protection of Employment Act 1977, as amended by the Protection of Employment Order 1996 (S.I. No. 370 of 1996), and the European Communities (Protection of Employment) Regulations 2000 (S.I. No. 488 of 2000),

(*b*) the information and consultation procedures under the European Communities (Protection of Employees on Transfer of Undertakings) Regulations 2003 (S.I. No. 131 of 2003),

(*c*) the information and consultation procedures under the Transnational Information and Consultation of Employees Act 1996 and the European Communities (Transnational Information and Consultation of Employees Act 1996) (Amendment) Regulations 1999 (S.I. No. 386 of 1999), and

(*d*) any right to information, consultation or participation conferred on employees by any other Act or instrument thereunder.

(3) For the avoidance of doubt, the according to employees of their rights through a European Employees' Forum, an Information and Consultation procedure or a European Works Council established under the Transnational Information and Consultation of Employees Act 1996 or by an agreement under section 6 of that Act, is not sufficient compliance by the employer with this Act.

Application — workforce thresholds.

4. —(1) This Act applies—

(*a*) from a date to be prescribed (being a date before 23 March 2007) to undertakings with at least 150 employees,[2]

(*b*) from 23 March 2007 to undertakings with at least 100 employees, and

[2] In Article 2 of the Employees (Provision of Information and Consultation) Act 2006 (Prescribed Dates) Regulations 2006, (S.I. No. 383 of 2006), the Minister for Enterprise, Trade and Employment prescribed 4 September, 2006 for the purposes of s. 4(1)(a).

(*c*) from 23 March 2008 to undertakings with at least 50 employees.

(2) The number of employees referred to in *subsection (1)* is referred to in this Act as a "relevant workforce threshold".

5. —(1) In determining whether employees are employed in an undertaking that meets a relevant workforce threshold, the number of employees in the undertaking shall be reckoned by calculating the average number of employees employed in the undertaking during the 2 years before the date that a request is— Calculating workforce thresholds.

(*a*) made under *subsection (2)*,

(*b*) received under *subsection (4)* by the Court or a nominee of the Court, or

(*c*) received under *section 7* by the employer, the Court or a nominee of the Court.

(2) Without prejudice to *subsection (4)*, following a request from one or more employees or employees' representatives (or both), the employer shall provide details of the number of employees in the undertaking during the period referred to in *subsection (1)* to those employees or employees' representatives (or both) not later than 4 weeks from the date of receipt of that request (but that period of 4 weeks may be extended by agreement between the parties).

(3) If the undertaking has been in existence for less than 2 years, the period of 2 years referred to in *subsection (1)* shall be replaced by the period the undertaking has been in existence.

(4) One or more employees may request the Court or a nominee of the Court to make the request referred to in *subsection (5)* of the employer and to do the other things mentioned therein.

(5) Where a request under *subsection (4)* is received by the Court or a nominee of the Court, the Court or the nominee shall—

(*a*) notify the employer as soon as is reasonably practicable that a request under that subsection has been made,

(*b*) request from the employer details of the numbers of employees in the undertaking during the period referred to in *subsection (1)*, and (*c*) issue a written notification to the employee or employees who made the request under *subsection (4)* confirming the number of employees in the undertaking during the period concerned.

(6) Where the Court or its nominee requests information from the employer under *subsection (5)(b)*, the employer shall provide the information requested not later than 4 weeks from the date of receipt of that request (but that period of 4 weeks may be extended by agreement between the employer and the Court or its nominee).

(7) If the number of employees for the time being in an undertaking falls below the relevant workforce threshold and remains below the threshold for 12 months, then, at the request of the employer or a majority of the employees, the Information and Consultation Forum established under *section 10* shall stand dissolved unless both parties agree to its continuation.

Employees' representative.

6. —(1) In this Act, "employees' representative" means an employee elected or appointed for the purposes of this Act.

(2) Subject to *subsections (3)* and *(4)*, the employer shall arrange for the election or appointment of one or more than one employees' representative under this section.

(3) Without prejudice to *section 11*, where it is the practice of the employer to conduct collective bargaining negotiations with a trade union or excepted body, employees who are members of a trade union or excepted body that represents 10 per cent or more of the employees in the undertaking shall be entitled to elect or appoint from amongst their members one or more than one employees' representative for the purposes of this Act.

(4) The number of employees' representatives (if any) elected or appointed under *subsection (3)* shall be determined on a pro rata basis by reference to the number of other employees' representatives (if any) elected or appointed under this section.

(5) Where a dispute arises under this section, it may be referred by the employer, trade union, excepted body or one or more than one employee to the Labour Court for determination in accordance with the procedures set out in *subsections (6), (7), (9)* and *(10)* of *section 15*.

Process for establishing information and consultation arrangements.

7.—(1) Subject to *subsection (2)* and *section 9*, the employer—

(*a*) may at his or her own initiative, or

(*b*) shall at the written request of at least 10 per cent of employees received either by him or her on the one hand, or by the Court or a nominee of the Court on the other hand,

enter into negotiations with employees or their representatives (or both) to establish information and consultation arrangements.

(2) The minimum requirement of 10 per cent of employees of the undertaking provided for in *subsection (1)(b)* shall be construed as meaning the lesser of—

(*a*) 10 per cent of the employees in the undertaking concerned (but not less, in any case, than 15 employees), or

(*b*) 100 employees,

(to be known and in this Act referred to as the "employee threshold").

(3) Where a request is received by the Court or a nominee of the Court under *subsection (1)(b)*, the Court or the nominee shall—

(*a*) notify the employer as soon as is reasonably practicable that the request has been made,

(*b*) request from the employer the information that it or its nominee requires to verify the number and names of the employees who have made the request, and

(*c*) issue a written notification to the employer and the employees who have made the request confirming how many employees have made the request and whether the employee threshold has been met on the basis of the information provided by the employees and the employer.

(4) Where the Court or its nominee requests information from the employer under *subsection (3)(b)*, the employer shall provide the information requested as soon as is reasonably practicable.

(5) Where a notification under *subsection (3)(c)* confirms that the request meets the employee threshold, the date of receipt of the notification by the employer shall be taken to be the date on which the employer received the request.

(6) Within 6 months from commencing negotiations, the parties shall agree to establish an information and consultation arrangement by means of—

(*a*) a negotiated agreement under *section 8*, or

(*b*) the Standard Rules under *section 10* (as set out in *Schedule 1*).

(7) The period of 6 months referred to in *subsection (6)* may be extended by agreement of the parties.

(8) If, at the time of making a request under *subsection (1)(b)*, the employee threshold is not met, the employees of the undertaking shall not make a further request for negotiations until 2 years have passed from the date on which the initial or previous request was received by the employer or the date of receipt of notification by the employer under *subsection (3)(c)*.

Negotiated agreements.

8.—(1) An agreement establishing one or more information and consultation arrangements may be negotiated by the employer and the employees or their representatives (or both) (to be known and in this Act referred to as a "negotiated agreement").

(2) A negotiated agreement shall be—

(*a*) in writing and dated,

(*b*) signed by the employer,

(*c*) approved by the employees,

(*d*) applicable to all employees to whom the agreement relates, and

(*e*) available for inspection by those persons and at the place agreed between the parties.

(3) For the purposes of *subsection (2)(c)*, the agreement shall be regarded as having been approved by the employees—

(*a*) where a majority of those employees employed in the undertaking who cast a preference do so in favour of the terms of the agreement,

(*b*) where a majority of employee representatives, elected or appointed for the purposes of negotiations under this Act, approve the agreement in writing, or (*c*) where the result of employing any other procedure agreed to by the parties for determining whether the agreement has been so approved discloses that it has been so approved.

(4) The employer shall ensure that the procedure for the casting of a preference referred to in *subsection (3)(a)* is confidential and capable of independent verification and of being used by all employees.

(5) A negotiated agreement shall include reference to the following matters:

(*a*) the duration of the agreement and the procedure, if any, for its renegotiation;

(*b*) the subjects for information and consultation;

(*c*) the method and timeframe by which information is to be provided, including as to whether it is to be provided directly to employees or through one or more employees' representatives;

(*d*) the method and timeframe by which consultation is to be conducted, including as to whether it is to be conducted directly with employees or through one or more employees' representatives; and

(*e*) the procedure for dealing with confidential information.

(6) At any time before a negotiated agreement expires or within 6 months after its expiry, the parties to the agreement may renew it for any further period they think fit.

(7) A negotiated agreement renewed under *subsection (6)* within the period of 6 months referred to in that subsection shall be deemed to have remained in force from the date it would otherwise have expired.

Pre-existing agreements.

9. —(1) Subject to the provisions of this section, where an agreement (to be known and in this Act referred to as a "pre-existing agreement") exists within—

(*a*) an undertaking referred to in *section 4(1)(a)*, on or before a date to be prescribed (being a date before 23 March 2007),[3]

(*b*) an undertaking referred to in *section 4(1)(b)*, on or before 23 March 2007, or

(*c*) an undertaking referred to in *section 4(1)(c)*, on or before 23 March 2008,

and that pre-existing agreement satisfies the requirements of this section, the employer is not obliged to comply with a request under *section 7*.

(2) A pre-existing agreement shall be—

(*a*) in writing and dated,

(*b*) signed by the employer,

(*c*) approved by the employees,

(*d*) applicable to all employees to whom the agreement relates, and

(*e*) available for inspection by those persons and at the location agreed by the parties.

(3) For the purposes of *subsection (2)(c)*, a pre-existing agreement shall be regarded as having been approved by the employees—

(*a*) where a majority of those employees employed in the undertaking who cast a preference do so in favour of the terms of the agreement, or

(*b*) where the result of employing any other procedure agreed to by the parties for determining whether the agreement has been so approved discloses that it has been so approved.

(4) The employer shall ensure that the procedure referred to in *subsection (3)(a)* is confidential and capable of independent verification and of being used by all employees.

---

[3] In Article 2 of the Employees (Provision of Information and Consultation) Act 2006 (Prescribed Dates) Regulations 2006 (S.I. No. 9 of 2006), the Minister for Enterprise, Trade and Employment prescribed 4 September, 2006 for the purposes of s. 9(1)(a).

(5) A pre-existing agreement shall be presumed to be valid unless proved to the contrary, and shall remain in force—

(*a*) for the period, if any, specified in the agreement or the agreement as renewed,

(*b*) in the case of an open ended agreement, until it is brought to an end in accordance with its terms, or

(*c*) until it is brought to an end by agreement of the parties.

(6) Where a pre-existing agreement is not in force for 6 months, *section 7* shall apply.

(7) A pre-existing agreement shall include reference to the following matters—

(*a*) the duration of the agreement and the procedure, if any, for its review,

(*b*) the subjects for information and consultation,

(*c*) the method by which information is to be provided, including as to whether it is to be provided directly to employees or through one or more employees' representatives, and

(*d*) the method by which consultation is to be conducted, including as to whether it is to be conducted directly with employees or through one or more employees' representatives.

Standard rules on information and consultation.

10. —(1) Where—

(*a*) the parties agree to adopt the Standard Rules set out in *Schedule 1* and the procedures for the election of employees' representatives set out in *Schedule 2*,

(*b*) the employer refuses to enter into negotiations within 3 months of receiving the written request from employees as provided for under *section 7(1)* or of the date of receipt of notification by the employer under *section 7(3)(c)*, or

(*c*) the parties to the negotiations cannot agree to the establishment of an information and consultation arrangement within the time limit specified in *section 7(6)* and *section 7(7)*, the Standard Rules shall apply to the undertaking and an Information and Consultation Forum shall be established.

(2) Subject to *section 14(4)* and *(5)*, where the Standard Rules apply to an undertaking, the employer shall as soon as practicable, but not later than 6 months after they first become applicable, comply with the requirements of the Standard Rules.

(3) After a minimum initial period of 2 years from the establishment of the Information and Consultation Forum and thereafter on a basis agreed by both parties, the application of the Standard Rules to an undertaking may be reviewed by the Information and Consultation Forum and the employer, and both parties may enter into negotiations for the purpose of changing the rules or procedures for that Forum and may change those rules or procedures accordingly.

(4) If the terms of a negotiated agreement are not approved in accordance with *section 8(3)*, the Standard Rules shall not apply until 2 years have passed.

(5) Where, during the period of 2 years referred to in *subsection (4)*, the parties seeking to approve a negotiated agreement re-enter negotiations and approve a negotiated agreement the Standard Rules shall not apply.

Direct involvement.

11. —(1) In relation to *sections 8* and *9*, an employee may exercise his or her right to information and consultation under *section 3* either directly or by means of his or her representatives elected or appointed for that purpose.

(2) Subject to *subsection (3)* and where a system of direct involvement is in operation for the whole or part only of the undertaking concerned, in order to be represented by his or her representatives at least 10 per cent of employees for whom the direct involvement system operates are required to make a written request to the employer, the Court or a nominee of the Court seeking to exercise the right to information and consultation through employees' representatives.

(3) The minimum requirement of 10 per cent of employees of the undertaking provided for in *subsection (2)* is subject to the approval of the majority of employees to whom the direct involvement system applies.

(4) For the purposes of *subsection (3)*, a request to change from a system of direct involvement to a system of representation through employees' representatives shall be regarded as having been approved by the employees for whom the direct involvement system operates where a majority of those employees who cast a preference are in favour of the change.

(5) The employer shall ensure that the procedure for the casting of a preference referred to in *subsection (4)* is confidential and capable of independent verification and of being used by all employees.

(6) On receipt of a request under *subsection (2)* which is approved under *subsection (3)*, an employer shall arrange for the election or appointment of representatives by the employees.

Co-operation.

12. —When defining or implementing practical arrangements for information and consultation under this Act, the employer and one or more employees or his or her representatives (or both) shall work in a spirit of co-operation, having due regard to their reciprocal rights and duties, and taking into account the interests both of the undertaking and of the employees.

Protection of employees' representatives.

13. —(1) An employer shall not penalise the employees' representative for performing his or her functions in accordance with this Act.

(2) For the purposes of this section, an employees' representative is penalised if he or she—

(*a*) is dismissed or suffers any unfavourable change to his or her conditions of employment or any unfair treatment (including selection for redundancy), or

(*b*) is the subject of any other action prejudicial to his or her employment.

(3) Subject to *subsection (5)*, the employees' representative shall be afforded any reasonable facilities, including time off, that will enable him or her to perform his or her functions as employees' representative promptly and efficiently.

(4) An employees' representative shall be paid his or her wages (within the meaning of the Payment of Wages Act

1991) for any period of absence afforded to him or her in accordance with *subsection (3)*.

(5) The granting of facilities under *subsection (3)* shall have regard to the needs, size and capabilities of the undertaking concerned and shall not impair the efficient operation of the undertaking.

(6) *Schedule 3* has effect in relation to an alleged contravention of *subsection (1)*.

(7) If a penalisation of an employees' representative, in contravention of *subsection (1)*, constitutes a dismissal of the representative within the meaning of the Unfair Dismissals Acts 1977 to 2005, relief may not be granted to the representative in respect of that penalisation both under *Schedule 3* and under those Acts.

Confidential information.

14.—(1) Subject to *subsections (4)* and *(5)* an individual who at any time is or was—

(*a*) a member of an Information and Consultation Forum,

(*b*) an employees' representative who is party to an information and consultation arrangement,

(*c*) an employee participant in an information and consultation arrangement, or

(*d*) an expert providing assistance,

shall not disclose to employees or to third parties any information which, in the legitimate interest of the undertaking, has been expressly provided to him or her by the undertaking in confidence.

(2) The duty of confidentiality imposed by *subsection (1)* shall continue to apply after the cessation of the employment of the individual concerned or the expiry of his or her term of office.

(3) Notwithstanding *subsection (1)*, the individual concerned may disclose information which has been expressly provided to him or her in confidence to employees and to third parties where those employees or third parties are subject to a duty of confidentiality under this Act.

(4) An employer may refuse to communicate information or undertake consultation where the nature of that information or consultation is such that, by reference to objective criteria, it would—

(*a*) seriously harm the functioning of the undertaking, or

(*b*) be prejudicial to the undertaking.

(5) An employer shall refuse to disclose information where disclosure of the information concerned is prohibited by any enactment.

(6) The Court or any member of the Court or the registrar or any officer or servant of the Court, including any person or persons appointed by the Court as an expert or mediator, shall not disclose any information obtained by it in confidence in the course of any proceedings before it under this Act.

Dispute resolution.

15. —(1) Disputes between an employer and one or more employees or his or her representatives (or both) concerning:

(*a*) negotiations under *section 8* or *10*,

(*b*) interpretation or operation of any agreement under *section 8* or *9*,

(*c*) interpretation or operation of the Standard Rules under *section 10* (as set out in *Schedule 1*) or the procedures for election of employees' representatives (as set out in *Schedule 2*), or

(*d*) interpretation or operation of a system of direct involvement under *section 11*,

may, subject to *subsection (2)*, be referred by the employer, one or more than one employee or his or her representatives (or both) to the Court for investigation.

(2) Such a dispute may be referred to the Court only after—

(*a*) recourse to the internal dispute resolution procedure (if any) in place in the employment concerned has failed to resolve the dispute, and

(*b*) the dispute has been referred to the Commission which, having made available such of its services as are appropriate for the purpose of resolving the dispute, furnishes a certificate to the Court stating that the Commission is satisfied that no further efforts on its part will advance the resolution of the dispute.

(3) Having investigated a dispute under *subsection (1)*, the Court may make a recommendation in writing giving its opinion in the matter.

(4) Where, in the opinion of the Court, a dispute that is the subject of a recommendation under *subsection (3)* has not been resolved, the Court may, at the request of—

(*a*) an employer, or

(*b*) one or more employees or their representatives (or both),

and, following a review of all relevant matters, make a determination in writing.

(5) Disputes between an employer and one or more than one employee or his or her representatives (or both) concerning—

(*a*) instances where the employer refuses to communicate information or undertake consultation under *section 14(4)* or *(5)*,

(*b*) instances where the employer discloses information to an individual to whom *section 14(1)* applies subject to the condition that the information is not to be disclosed to a third party due to its confidential nature, or

(*c*) instances where an individual to whom *section 14(1)* applies discloses information, which in the legitimate interest of the undertaking has been expressly provided to him or her in confidence, to employees or to third parties not subject to a duty of confidentiality,

may be referred by the employer, one or more employees or his or her representatives (or both) to the Court for determination.

(6) As regards a dispute referred to it under *subsection (1)* or *(5)*, the Court shall—

(*a*) give the parties an opportunity to be heard by it and to present any evidence relevant to the dispute,

(*b*) make a recommendation or, as the case may be, determination in writing in relation to the dispute, and

(*c*) communicate the recommendation or, as the case may be, determination to the parties.

(7) The following matters or procedures to be followed in relation to them, shall be determined by the Court, namely:

(*a*) the procedure in relation to all matters concerning the initiation and hearing by the Court of a dispute under this section;

(*b*) the times and places of hearings of such disputes;

(*c*) the publication and notification of recommendations and determinations of the Court;

(*d*) any matters consequential on, or incidental to, the matters referred to in *paragraphs (a)* to *(c)*.

(8) In deciding what constitutes confidential information, the Court may be assisted by a panel of experts.

(9) A party to a dispute under this section may appeal from a determination of the Court to the High Court on a point of law and the decision of the High Court shall be final and conclusive.

(10) The Court may refer a question of law arising in proceedings before it under this section to the High Court for determination and the decision of the High Court shall be final and conclusive.

Power of Court to administer oaths and compel witnesses.

16.—(1) The Court shall, on the hearing of a dispute referred to it for recommendation or determination under *section 6* or *section 15* or on the hearing of an appeal under *Schedule 3*, have power to take evidence on oath and for that purpose may cause to be administered oaths to persons attending as witnesses at that hearing.

(2) Any person who, upon examination on oath authorised by this section, wilfully makes any statement which is material for that purpose and which he or she knows to be false or does not believe to be true is guilty of an offence and is liable on summary conviction to a fine not exceeding €3,000 or imprisonment for a term not exceeding 6 months or both.

(3) The Court may, by giving notice in that behalf in writing to any person, require that person to attend at such time and place as is specified in the notice to give evidence in relation to a dispute referred to the Court for recommendation or determination under *section 6* or *section 15* or an appeal under *Schedule 3* or to produce any documents in his or her possession, custody or control which relate to any such matter.

(4) A notice under *subsection (3)* may be given either by delivering it to the person to whom it relates or by sending it by post in a prepaid registered letter addressed to that person at the address at which he or she ordinarily resides or, in the case of the employer, at the address at which the employer concerned ordinarily resides or carries on any profession, business or occupation.

(5) A person to whom a notice under *subsection (3)* has been given and who refuses or wilfully neglects to attend in accordance with the notice or who, having so attended, refuses to give evidence or refuses or wilfully fails to produce any document to which the notice relates is guilty of an offence and is liable on summary conviction to a fine not exceeding €3,000.

(6) A witness in a hearing of a dispute or appeal before the Court has the same privileges and immunities as a witness before the High Court.

Enforcement.

17.—(1) If—

(*a*) a party to a Court determination fails to carry out in accordance with its terms a determination of the Court in relation to a dispute under *section 6* or *15*, or

(*b*) a party to a complaint under *Schedule 3* fails to carry out in accordance with its terms a decision of a rights commissioner or a determination of the Court under that Schedule in relation to the complaint, within the period specified in the determination or decision or if no such period is so specified within 6 weeks from the date on which the determination or decision is communicated to the parties, the Circuit Court shall, on application to it in that behalf by one or more of the parties to the dispute or complaint, without hearing any evidence (other than in relation to the matters aforesaid) make an order directing the party concerned to carry out the determination or decision in accordance with its terms.

(2) The reference in *subsection (1)* to a determination of the Court or a decision of a rights commissioner is a reference to such a determination or decision in relation to which, at the end of the time for bringing an appeal against it, no such appeal has been brought or, if such an appeal has been brought it has been abandoned and the references to the date on which the determination or decision is communicated to the parties shall, in a case where such an appeal is abandoned, be read as references to the date of that abandonment.

(3) In an order under this section providing for the payment of compensation of the kind referred to in *paragraph 1(3)(c)* of *Schedule 3*, the Circuit Court may, if in all the circumstances it considers it appropriate to do so, direct the employer concerned to pay to the employee concerned interest on the compensation at the rate referred to in section 22 of the Courts Act 1981, in respect of the whole or any part of the period beginning 6 weeks after the date on which the determination of the Court or the decision of the rights commissioner is communicated to the parties and ending on the date of the order.

(4) An application under this section to the Circuit Court shall be made to the judge of the Circuit Court for the circuit in which the employer concerned ordinarily resides or carries on any profession, business or occupation.

18.—(1) In this section "inspector" means a person appointed *under subsection (2)*. Inspectors.

(2) The Minister may, in writing, appoint as many persons as the Minister thinks appropriate to be inspectors for the purposes of this Act.

(3) Subject to this section, an inspector may do all or any of the following things for the purposes of this Act—

(*a*) enter at all reasonable times any premises or place where the inspector believes on reasonable grounds that—

(i) an employee is employed in work, or

(ii) the work that an employee is employed to do is directed or controlled,

(*b*) make such examination or enquiry as may be necessary for ascertaining whether this Act is being complied with in respect of an employee employed in those premises or that place or an employee whose work is directed or controlled from the premises or place,

(*c*) require the employer of an employee, or the representative of the employer, to produce to the inspector any records the employer is required to keep under any other enactment that are relevant to the employer's obligations under this Act and inspect and take copies of entries in the records (including, in the case of information in a non-legible form, a copy of or an extract from that information in a more permanent legible form),

(*d*) require any person the inspector believes on reasonable grounds to be or to have been an employee or the employer of an employee to furnish such information to the inspector as the inspector may reasonably request,

(*e*) examine with regard to any matters under this Act any person the inspector has reasonable cause to believe to be or to have been an employer or employee and require the person to answer such questions (other than questions tending to incriminate the person) as the inspector may put relative to those matters and to sign a declaration of the truth of the answers.

(4) An inspector shall not, except with the consent of the occupier, enter a private dwelling (other than a part of the dwelling used as a place of work) unless he or she has obtained a warrant from the District Court under *subsection (7)* authorising the entry.

(5) Where an inspector in attempting to exercise his or her powers under this section is prevented from entering any premises, he or she may apply under *subsection (7)* for a warrant authorising the entry.

(6) An inspector, where he or she considers it necessary to be so accompanied, may be accompanied by a member of the Garda Síochána when exercising a power conferred on an inspector under this section.

(7) If a judge of the District Court is satisfied on the sworn information of an inspector that there are reasonable grounds for suspecting that information required by an inspector under this section is held on any premises or any part of the premises, the judge may issue a warrant authorising an inspector accompanied by other inspectors or a member of the Garda Síochána, at any time or times within one month from the date of issue of the warrant, on production, if so requested, of the warrant, to enter the premises (if need be by the use of reasonable force) and exercise all or any of the powers conferred on an inspector under *subsection (3)*.

(8) A person who—

(*a*) obstructs or impedes an inspector in the exercise of any of the powers conferred on an inspector under this section,

(*b*) refuses to produce a record which an inspector lawfully requires the person to produce,

(*c*) produces or causes to be produced, or knowingly allows to be produced, to an inspector a record which is false or misleading in a material respect, knowing it to be so false or misleading,

(*d*) gives to an inspector information which is false or misleading in a material respect knowing it to be so false or misleading, or

(*e*) fails or refuses to comply with a lawful requirement of an inspector under *subsection (3)*,

is guilty of an offence.

(9) Every inspector shall be furnished by the Minister with a certificate of his or her appointment and, on applying for admission to any premises or place for the purposes of this Act, shall, if requested by a person affected, produce the certificate or a copy of the certificate to that person.

Offences.

19.—(1) A person who fails to comply with *section 7, 8, 9, 10* or *13* is guilty of an offence.

(2) It is an offence for an employer to refuse to provide the information referred to in *section 5* or to unreasonably or wilfully obstruct or delay the provision of such information.

(3) It is an offence for an employer to fail to arrange for the election or appointment of one or more than one employees' representative under *section 6(2)*.

(4) It is an offence for an employer to fail to put in place a system of representation through employees' representatives where one has been requested and approved by employees under *section 11*.

(5) It is an offence for an individual to whom *section 14(1)* applies to disclose information to employees or third parties not subject to a duty of confidentiality under this Act where that information is expressly provided in confidence to the individual concerned.

Penalties.

20.—(1) A person guilty of an offence under *section 18* or *19* shall be liable—

(*a*) on summary conviction, to a fine not exceeding €3,000 or imprisonment for a term not exceeding 6 months or both, or

(*b*) on conviction on indictment, to a fine not exceeding €30,000 or imprisonment for a term not exceeding 3 years or both.

(2) If the offence under *section 18* or *19* of which a person was convicted is continued after conviction, that person shall be guilty of a further offence on every day on which the act or omission constituting the offence continues, and for each such further offence the person shall be liable on summary conviction to a fine not exceeding €500 or on conviction on indictment to a fine not exceeding €5,000.

(3) Proceedings for an offence under *section 18* or *19* may be brought and prosecuted by the Minister.

Notification obligations of transferor to transferee in the event of transfer of an undertaking.

21. —(1) For the purposes of this section—

"Council Directive" means Council Directive No. 2001/23/EC of 12 March 2001 on the approximation of the laws of the Member States relating to the safeguarding of employees' rights in the event of transfers of undertakings, businesses or parts of undertakings or businesses;

"Regulations" means the European Communities (Protection of Employees on Transfer of Undertakings) Regulations 2003 (S.I. No. 131 of 2003);

"transfer" means the transfer of an economic entity that retains its identity;

"transferee" means any natural or legal person who, by reason of a transfer within the meaning of the Regulations, becomes the employer in respect of the undertaking, business or part of the undertaking or business;

"transferor" means any natural or legal person who, by reason of a transfer within the meaning of the Regulations, ceases to be the employer in respect of the undertaking, business or part of the undertaking or business.

(2) A word or expression that is used in this section, and which is also used in the Council Directive or the Regulations, as appropriate, has the same meaning in this section as it has in the Council Directive or the Regulations, as appropriate.

(3) The transferor shall notify the transferee of all the rights and obligations, arising from a contract of employment existing on the date of a transfer, which will be transferred to the transferee, so far as those rights and obligations are, or ought to have been, known to the transferor at the time of transfer.

(4) A failure by the transferor to notify the transferee of any such right or obligation shall not affect the transfer of that right or obligation and the rights of any employees against the transferee or transferor in respect of that right or obligation.

(5) If—

(*a*) a failure of the foregoing kind consists of a failure to provide information or documents to the transferee the provision of which is necessary in order for the transferee to fulfil an obligation of the transferee owed to an employee,

(*b*) the transferee is, in proceedings finally determined under the Regulations, required by a decision of a rights commissioner or a determination of the Employment Appeals Tribunal to pay an amount of compensation to that employee in respect of a complaint that the transferee has not fulfilled that obligation, and

(*c*) the transferee has paid that amount of compensation to that employee,

then, subject to *subsection (6)*, the transferee has a right of action in any court of competent jurisdiction to recover from the transferor such proportion of that amount of compensation as the court determines to be attributable to the failure of the transferor to provide the information or documents concerned.

(6) An action under *subsection (5)* shall not lie unless it has been preceded by—

(*a*) service of a notice in writing on the transferor—

(i) indicating, in everyday language—

(I) the particular obligation the transferee considers he or she owes to one or more employees of the transferee, and

(II) the class of information or documents that the transferee believes may be in the possession or under the control of the transferor (and which is not also in the possession or under the control of any of the employees of the transferee), being information or documents of a class which the transferee considers an employer must possess in order to fulfil the obligation concerned,

and

(ii) requesting the transferor to provide to the transferee, within a specified period (not being less than 21 days beginning on the date of the service of the notice), information or documents falling within that class of information or documents,

and

(*b*) compliance by the transferee with any reasonable request in writing of the transferor for further details to be furnished to the transferor as to the particular items of information or documents that are being referred to in that notice (and any period which elapses before that request is complied with shall not be reckoned in calculating the period specified in that notice).

(7) An action under *subsection (5)* shall, for the purposes of this section and any other enactment, be regarded as an action founded on quasi-contract.

Short title and commencement.

22. —(1) This Act may be cited as the Employees (Provision of Information and Consultation) Act 2006.

(2) This Act shall come into operation on such day or days as the Minister may appoint by order or orders either generally or with reference to any particular purpose or provision and different days may be so appointed for different purposes or different provisions.[4]

[4] In Article 2 of the Employees (Provision of Information and Consultation) Act 2006 (Commencement) Order 2006 (S.I. No. 382 of 2006), the Minister for Enterprise, Trade and Employment appointed 24 July, 2006 as the day on which this Act came into operation.

Section 10.

SCHEDULE 1

STANDARD RULES ON INFORMATION AND CONSULTATION

Size and structure of Forum.

1. (1) The Information and Consultation Forum (in this Schedule referred to as the "Forum") shall be composed of employees' representatives who shall be employees of the undertaking.

(2) Employees' representatives shall be elected in accordance with *Schedule 2*. In the absence of elections, the representatives shall be appointed by the employees and the basis on which any such appointment is made may, if the employees so determine, be such as is agreed by them with the employer.

(3) The employer shall arrange for the election process referred to in *subparagraph (2)*.

(4) The Forum shall have at least 3 but not more than 30 members and may agree its own internal structures.

Rules of Procedure.

2. (1) The Forum shall adopt its own rules of procedure subject to the following:

(*a*) the arrangements for the meetings of the Forum shall be agreed by the employer in consultation with employees or their representatives but the employer may not unreasonably withhold consent to proposals made by employees or their representatives;

(*b*) the minutes of the Forum meetings with the employer shall be approved by both the employer and employees' representatives;

(*c*) before any meeting with the employer, the Forum shall be entitled to meet without the employer concerned being present;

(*d*) without prejudice to *section 14(1)*, *(2)* and *(3)*, the members of the Forum shall inform the employees of the content and outcome of the meetings of the Forum carried out in accordance with this Schedule;

(*e*) the Forum shall have the right to meet with the employer twice a year. Where there are exceptional circumstances, the Forum shall have the right to request a meeting with the employer and consent to this meeting shall not be unreasonably withheld.

Competence.

3. For the purposes of these Rules, "information and consultation" includes:

(*a*) information on the recent and probable development of the undertaking's activities and economic situation;

(*b*) information and consultation on the situation, structure and probable development of employment within the undertaking and on any anticipatory measures envisaged, in particular where there is a threat to employment;

(*c*) information and consultation on decisions likely to lead to substantial changes in work organisation or in contractual relations, including those covered by the European (Protection of Employees on Transfer of Undertakings) Regulations 2003 (S.I. No. 131 of 2003) and the Protection of Employment Act 1977 (as amended by the Protection of Employment Order 1996 (S.I. No. 370 of 1996) and the European Communities (Protection of Employment) Regulations 2000 (S.I. No. 488 of 2000)).

Practical arrangements for Information and Consultation.

4. (1) Information shall be given by the employer at the time, in the fashion and with the content appropriate to enable, in particular, the Forum to conduct an adequate study and, where necessary, prepare for consultation.

(2) Consultation shall take place:

(*a*) while ensuring that the method, content and timeframe thereof are appropriate;

(*b*) at the relevant level of management and representation, depending on the subject under discussion;

(*c*) on the basis of information supplied by the employer and of the opinion which the employees' representatives are entitled to formulate;

(*d*) in such a way as to enable the Forum to meet the employer and obtain a response, and the reasons for that response, to any opinion they might form;

(*e*) with a view to reaching an agreement on decisions referred to in *paragraph 3(c)* that are within the scope of the employer's powers.

Expenses.

5. (1) The expenses incurred in the operation of the Forum shall be borne by the employer.

(2) The employer shall provide the members of the Forum with any financial resources that are necessary and reasonable to enable them to perform their duties in an appropriate manner.

Section 10.

SCHEDULE 2

Election of Employees' Representatives

1. An employee who is employed in the State by the relevant undertaking on the day the date or dates for an election of members of the Information and Consultation Forum (in this Schedule referred to as the "Forum") is fixed and who is, on the election day or days, an employee of the undertaking, shall be entitled to vote in such an election.

2. An employee who is employed in the State by the undertaking for a continuous period of not less than one year on the nomination day shall be eligible to stand as a candidate for election as a member of the Forum, provided that he or she is nominated by—

(*a*) at least 2 employees, or

(*b*) a trade union or excepted body with whom it is the practice of the employer to conduct collective bargaining negotiations.

3. Where the number of candidates on the nomination day exceeds the number of members to be elected to the Forum, a poll shall be taken by the returning officer and voting in the poll shall take place by secret ballot on a day or days to be decided by the returning officer and according to the principle of proportional representation.

4. The employer in consultation with existing employees shall appoint a returning officer whose duties shall include the organisation and conduct of nominations and elections and that officer may authorise other persons to assist in the performance of the duties of returning officer.

5. The returning officer shall perform his or her duties in a fair and reasonable manner and in the interests of an orderly and proper conduct of nomination and election procedures.

6. The cost of the nomination and election procedure shall be borne by the employer.

SCHEDULE 3

Section 13.

Redress for Contravention of Section 13(1)

Complaints to rights commissioner.

1. (1) An employees' representative (the "employee") may present a complaint to a rights commissioner that his or her employer has contravened *section 13(1)* in relation to the employee.

(2) Where a complaint under *subparagraph (1)* is made, the rights commissioner shall—

(*a*) give the parties an opportunity to be heard by the commissioner and to present to the commissioner any evidence relevant to the complaint, (*b*) give a decision in writing in relation to it, and

(*c*) communicate the decision to the parties.

(3) A decision of a rights commissioner under *subparagraph (2)* shall do one or more of the following:

(*a*) declare that the complaint was or, as the case may be, was not well founded;

(*b*) require the employer to take a specified course of action;

(*c*) require the employer to pay to the employee compensation of such amount (if any) as is just and equitable having regard to all the circumstances but not exceeding 2 years remuneration in respect of the employee's employment;

and the references in the foregoing clauses to an employer shall be construed, in a case where ownership of the business of the employer changes after the contravention to which the complaint relates occurred, as references to the person who, by virtue of the change, becomes entitled to such ownership.

(4) A rights commissioner shall not entertain a complaint under this paragraph if it is presented to him or her after the expiration of the period of 6 months beginning on the date of the contravention to which the complaint relates.

(5) Notwithstanding *subparagraph (4)*, a rights commissioner may entertain a complaint under this paragraph presented to him or her after the expiration of the period referred to in *subparagraph (4)* (but not later than 6 months after such expiration) if he or she is satisfied that the failure to present the complaint within that period was due to reasonable cause.

(6) A complaint shall be presented by giving notice of it in writing to a rights commissioner.

(7) A copy of a notice under *subparagraph (6)* shall be given to the other party concerned by the rights commissioner concerned.

(8) Proceedings under this paragraph before a rights commissioner shall be conducted otherwise than in public.

Appeals from decisions of rights commissioner.

2. (1) A party concerned may appeal to the Court from a decision of a rights commissioner under *paragraph 1* and, if the party does so, the Court shall give the parties an opportunity to be heard by it and to present to it any evidence relevant to the appeal, shall make a determination in writing in relation to the appeal affirming, varying or setting aside the decision and shall communicate the determination to the parties.

(2) An appeal under this paragraph shall be initiated by the party concerned giving, within 6 weeks (or such greater period as the Court may determine in the particular circumstances) from the date on which the decision to which it relates was communicated to the party, a notice in writing to the Court containing such particulars as are determined by the Court under *subparagraph (4)* and stating the intention of the party concerned to appeal against the decision.

(3) A copy of a notice under *subparagraph (2)* shall be given by the Court to any other party concerned as soon as practicable after the receipt of the notice by the Court.

(4) The following matters, or the procedures to be followed in relation to them, shall be determined by the Court, namely—

(*a*) the procedure in relation to all matters concerning the initiation and the hearing by the Court of appeals under this paragraph,

(*b*) the times and places of hearings of such appeals,

(*c*) the representation of the parties to such appeals,

(*d*) the publication and notification of determinations of the Court,

(*e*) the particulars to be contained in a notice under *subparagraph (2)*, and

(*f*) any matters consequential on, or incidental to, the foregoing matters.

(5) The Court may refer a question of law arising in proceedings before it under this paragraph to the High Court for determination and the determination of the High Court shall be final and conclusive.

(6) A party to proceedings before the Court under this paragraph may appeal to the High Court from a determination of the Court on a point of law and the determination of the High Court shall be final and conclusive.

Paragraphs 1 and 2: supplemental provisions.

3. (1) A rights commissioner shall furnish the Court with a copy of each decision given by the commissioner under *paragraph 1(2)*.

(2) A rights commissioner shall maintain a register of all decisions given by him or her under *paragraph 1(2)* and shall make the register available for inspection by members of the public during normal office hours.

(3) The Court shall publish, in a manner it considers appropriate, particulars of any determination made by it under *subparagraph (4)(a)*, *(b)*, *(c)*, *(e)* and *(f)* of *paragraph 2* (not being a determination as respects a particular appeal under that paragraph).

DIRECTIVE 2002/14/EC OF THE EUROPEAN PARLIAMENT AND OF THE COUNCIL

of 11 March 2002

establishing a general framework for informing and consulting employees in the European Community

(Official Journal of the European Communities 23.3.2002 L 80/29)

THE EUROPEAN PARLIAMENT AND THE COUNCIL OF THE EUROPEAN UNION,

Having regard to the Treaty establishing the European Community, and in particular Article 137(2) thereof,

Having regard to the proposal from the Commission ([1]),

Having regard to the opinion of the Economic and Social Committee ([2]),

Having regard to the opinion of the Committee of the Regions ([3]),

Acting in accordance with the procedure referred to in Article 251 ([4]), and in the light of the joint text approved by the Conciliation Committee on 23 January 2002,

---

([1]) OJ C 2, 5.1.1999, p. 3

([2]) OJ C 258, 10.9.1999, p. 24

([3]) OJ C 144, 16.5.2001, p. 58

([4]) Opinion of the European Parliament of 14 April 1999 (OJ C 219, 30.7.1999, p. 223), confirmed on 16 September 1999 (OJ C 54, 25.2.2000, p. 55), Council Common Position of 27 July 2001 (OJ C 307, 31.10.2001, p. 16) and Decision of the European Parliament of 23 October 2001 (not yet published in the Official Journal). Decision of the European Parliament of 5 February 2002 and Decision of the Council of 18 February 2002.

Whereas:

(1) Pursuant to Article 136 of the Treaty, a particular objective of the Community and the Member States is to promote social dialogue between management and labour.

(2) Point 17 of the Community Charter of Fundamental Social Rights of Workers provides, inter alia, that information, consultation and participation

for workers must be developed along appropriate lines, taking account of the practices in force in different Member States.

(3) The Commission consulted management and labour at Community level on the possible direction of Community action on the information and consultation of employees in undertakings within the Community.

(4) Following this consultation, the Commission considered that Community action was advisable and again consulted management and labour on the contents of the planned proposal; management and labour have presented their opinions to the Commission.

(5) Having completed this second stage of consultation, management and labour have not informed the Commission of their wish to initiate the process potentially leading to the conclusion of an agreement.

(6) The existence of legal frameworks at national and Community level intended to ensure that employees are involved in the affairs of the undertaking employing them and in decisions which affect them has not always prevented serious decisions affecting employees from being taken and made public without adequate procedures having been implemented beforehand to inform and consult them.

(7) There is a need to strengthen dialogue and promote mutual trust within undertakings in order to improve risk anticipation, make work organisation more flexible and facilitate employee access to training within the undertaking while maintaining security, make employees aware of adaptation needs, increase employees' availability to undertake measures and activities to increase their employability, promote employee involvement in the operation and future of the undertaking and increase its competitiveness.

(8) There is a need, in particular, to promote and enhance information and consultation on the situation and likely development of employment within the undertaking and, where the employer's evaluation suggests that employment within the undertaking may be under threat, the possible anticipatory measures envisaged, in particular in terms of employee training and skill development, with a view to offsetting the negative developments or their consequences and increasing the employability and adaptability of the employees likely to be affected.

(9) Timely information and consultation is a prerequisite for the success of the restructuring and adaptation of undertakings to the new conditions

created by globalisation of the economy, particularly through the development of new forms of organisation of work.

(10) The Community has drawn up and implemented an employment strategy based on the concepts of "anticipation", "prevention" and "employability", which are to be incorporated as key elements into all public policies likely to benefit employment, including the policies of individual undertakings, by strengthening the social dialogue with a view to promoting change compatible with preserving the priority objective of employment.

(11) Further development of the internal market must be properly balanced, maintaining the essential values on which our societies are based and ensuring that all citizens benefit from economic development.

(12) Entry into the third stage of economic and monetary union has extended and accelerated the competitive pressures at European level. This means that more supportive measures are needed at national level.

(13) The existing legal frameworks for employee information and consultation at Community and national level tend to adopt an excessively a posteriori approach to the process of change, neglect the economic aspects of decisions taken and do not contribute either to genuine anticipation of employment developments within the undertaking or to risk prevention.

(14) All of these political, economic, social and legal developments call for changes to the existing legal framework providing for the legal and practical instruments enabling the right to be informed and consulted to be exercised.

(15) This Directive is without prejudice to national systems regarding the exercise of this right in practice where those entitled to exercise it are required to indicate their wishes collectively.

(16) This Directive is without prejudice to those systems which provide for the direct involvement of employees, as long as they are always free to exercise the right to be informed and consulted through their representatives.

(17) Since the objectives of the proposed action, as outlined above, cannot be adequately achieved by the Member States, in that the object is to establish a framework for employee information and consultation appropriate for the new European context described above, and can therefore, in view of the scale and impact of the proposed action, be better achieved at Community level, the Community may adopt measures in accordance

with the principle of subsidiarity as set out in Article 5 of the Treaty. In accordance with the principle of proportionality, as set out in that Article, this Directive does not go beyond what is necessary in order to achieve these objectives.

(18) The purpose of this general framework is to establish minimum requirements applicable throughout the Community while not preventing Member States from laying down provisions more favourable to employees.

(19) The purpose of this general framework is also to avoid any administrative, financial or legal constraints which would hinder the creation and development of small and medium-sized undertakings. To this end, the scope of this Directive should be restricted, according to the choice made by Member States, to undertakings with at least 50 employees or establishments employing at least 20 employees.

(20) This takes into account and is without prejudice to other national measures and practices aimed at fostering social dialogue within companies not covered by this Directive and within public administrations.

(21) However, on a transitional basis, Member States in which there is no established statutory system of information and consultation of employees or employee representation should have the possibility of further restricting the scope of the Directive as regards the numbers of employees.

(22) A Community framework for informing and consulting employees should keep to a minimum the burden on undertakings or establishments while ensuring the effective exercise of the rights granted.

(23) The objective of this Directive is to be achieved through the establishment of a general framework comprising the principles, definitions and arrangements for information and consultation, which it will be for the Member States to comply with and adapt to their own national situation, ensuring, where appropriate, that management and labour have a leading role by allowing them to define freely, by agreement, the arrangements for informing and consulting employees which they consider to be best suited to their needs and wishes.

(24) Care should be taken to avoid affecting some specific rules in the field of employee information and consultation existing in some national laws, addressed to undertakings or establishments which pursue

political, professional, organisational, religious, charitable, educational, scientific or artistic aims, as well as aims involving information and the expression of opinions.

(25) Undertakings and establishments should be protected against disclosure of certain particularly sensitive information.

(26) The employer should be allowed not to inform and consult where this would seriously damage the undertaking or the establishment or where he has to comply immediately with an order issued to him by a regulatory or supervisory body.

(27) Information and consultation imply both rights and obligations for management and labour at undertaking or establishment level.

(28) Administrative or judicial procedures, as well as sanctions that are effective, dissuasive and proportionate in relation to the seriousness of the offence, should be applicable in cases of infringement of the obligations based on this Directive.

(29) This Directive should not affect the provisions, where these are more specific, of Council Directive 98/59/EC of 20 July 1998 on the approximation of the laws of the Member States relating to collective redundancies ([1]) and of Council Directive 2001/23/EC of 12 March 2001 on the approximation of the laws of the Member States relating to the safeguarding of employees' rights in the event of transfers of undertakings, businesses or parts of undertakings or businesses ([2]).

(30) Other rights of information and consultation, including those arising from Council Directive 94/45/EEC of 22 September 1994 on the establishment of a European Works Council or a procedure in Community-scale undertakings and Community-scale groups of undertakings for the purposes of informing and consulting employees ([3]), should not be affected by this Directive.

(31) Implementation of this Directive should not be sufficient grounds for a reduction in the general level of protection of workers in the areas to which it applies,

---

([1]) OJ L 225, 12.8.1998, p. 16.

([2]) OJ L 82, 22.3.2001, p. 16.

([3]) OJ L 254, 30.9.1994, p. 64. Directive as amended by Directive 97/74/EC (OJ L 10, 16.1.1998, p. 22).

HAVE ADOPTED THIS DIRECTIVE:

Article 1

Object and principles

1. The purpose of this Directive is to establish a general framework setting out minimum requirements for the right to information and consultation of employees in undertakings or establishments within the Community.

2. The practical arrangements for information and consultation shall be defined and implemented in accordance with national law and industrial relations practices in individual Member States in such a way as to ensure their effectiveness.

3. When defining or implementing practical arrangements for information and consultation, the employer and the employees' representatives shall work in a spirit of cooperation and with due regard for their reciprocal rights and obligations, taking into account the interests both of the undertaking or establishment and of the employees.

Article 2

Definitions

For the purposes of this Directive:

(a) 'undertaking' means a public or private undertaking carrying out an economic activity, whether or not operating for gain, which is located within the territory of the Member States;

(b) 'establishment' means a unit of business defined in accordance with national law and practice, and located within the territory of a Member State, where an economic activity is carried out on an ongoing basis with human and material resources;

(c) 'employer' means the natural or legal person party to employment contracts or employment relationships with employees, in accordance with national law and practice;

(d) 'employee' means any person who, in the Member State concerned, is protected as an employee under national employment law and in accordance with national practice;

(e) 'employees' representatives' means the employees' representatives provided for by national laws and/or practices;

(f) 'information' means transmission by the employer to the employees' representatives of data in order to enable them to acquaint themselves with the subject matter and to examine it;

(g) 'consultation' means the exchange of views and establishment of dialogue between the employees' representatives and the employer.

Article 3

Scope

1. This Directive shall apply, according to the choice made by Member States, to:

(a) undertakings employing at least 50 employees in any one Member State, or

(b) establishments employing at least 20 employees in any one Member State.

Member States shall determine the method for calculating the thresholds of employees employed.

2. In conformity with the principles and objectives of this Directive, Member States may lay down particular provisions applicable to undertakings or establishments which pursue directly and essentially political, professional organisational, religious, charitable, educational, scientific or artistic aims, as well as aims involving information and the expression of opinions, on condition that, at the date of entry into force of this Directive, provisions of that nature already exist in national legislation.

3. Member States may derogate from this Directive through particular provisions applicable to the crews of vessels plying the high seas.

Article 4

Practical arrangements for information and consultation

1. In accordance with the principles set out in Article 1 and without prejudice to any provisions and/or practices in force more favourable to employees, the Member States shall determine the practical arrangements for exercising the right to information and consultation at the appropriate level in accordance with this Article.

2. Information and consultation shall cover:

(a) information on the recent and probable development of the undertaking's or the establishment's activities and economic situation;

(b) information and consultation on the situation, structure and probable development of employment within the undertaking or establishment and on any anticipatory measures envisaged, in particular where there is a threat to employment;

(c) information and consultation on decisions likely to lead to substantial changes in work organisation or in contractual relations, including those covered by the Community provisions referred to in Article 9(1).

3. Information shall be given at such time, in such fashion and with such content as are appropriate to enable, in particular, employees' representatives to conduct an adequate study and, where necessary, prepare for consultation.

4. Consultation shall take place:

(a) while ensuring that the timing, method and content thereof are appropriate;

(b) at the relevant level of management and representation, depending on the subject under discussion;

(c) on the basis of information supplied by the employer in accordance with Article 2(f) and of the opinion which the employees' representatives are entitled to formulate;

(d) in such a way as to enable employees' representatives to meet the employer and obtain a response, and the reasons for that response, to any opinion they might formulate;

(e) with a view to reaching an agreement on decisions within the scope of the employer's powers referred to in paragraph 2(c).

Article 5

Information and consultation deriving from an agreement

Member States may entrust management and labour at the appropriate level, including at undertaking or establishment level, with defining freely and at any time through negotiated agreement the practical arrangements for informing and consulting employees. These agreements, and agreements existing on the date laid down in Article 11, as well as any subsequent renewals of such agreements, may establish, while respecting the principles set out in Article 1 and subject to conditions and limitations laid down by the Member States, provisions which are different from those referred to in Article 4.

Article 6

Confidential information

1. Member States shall provide that, within the conditions and limits laid down by national legislation, the employees' representatives, and any experts who assist them, are not authorised to reveal to employees or to third parties, any information which, in the legitimate interest of the undertaking or establishment, has expressly been provided to them in confidence. This obligation shall continue to apply, wherever the said representatives or experts are, even after expiry of their terms of office. However, a Member State may authorise the employees' representatives and anyone assisting them to pass on confidential information to employees and to third parties bound by an obligation of confidentiality.

2. Member States shall provide, in specific cases and within the conditions and limits laid down by national legislation, that the employer is not obliged to communicate information or under- take consultation when the nature of that information or consultation is such that, according to objective criteria, it would seriously harm the functioning of the undertaking or establishment or would be prejudicial to it.

3. Without prejudice to existing national procedures, Member States shall provide for administrative or judicial review procedures for the case where the employer requires confidentiality or does not provide the information in accordance with paragraphs 1 and 2. They may also provide for procedures intended to safeguard the confidentiality of the information in question.

Article 7

Protection of employees' representatives

Member States shall ensure that employees' representatives, when carrying out their functions, enjoy adequate protection and guarantees to enable them to perform properly the duties which have been assigned to them.

Article 8

Protection of rights

1. Member States shall provide for appropriate measures in the event of non-compliance with this Directive by the employer or the employees' representatives. In particular, they shall ensure that adequate administrative or judicial procedures are available to enable the obligations deriving from this Directive to be enforced.

2. Member States shall provide for adequate sanctions to be applicable in the event of infringement of this Directive by the employer or the employees' representatives. These sanctions must be effective, proportionate and dissuasive.

Article 9

Link between this Directive and other Community and national provisions

1. This Directive shall be without prejudice to the specific information and consultation procedures set out in Article 2 of Directive 98/59/EC and Article 7 of Directive 2001/23/EC.

2. This Directive shall be without prejudice to provisions adopted in accordance with Directives 94/45/EC and 97/74/EC.

3. This Directive shall be without prejudice to other rights to information, consultation and participation under national law.

4. Implementation of this Directive shall not be sufficient grounds for any regression in relation to the situation which already prevails in each Member State and in relation to the general level of protection of workers in the areas to which it applies.

Article 10

Transitional provisions

Notwithstanding Article 3, a Member State in which there is, at the date of entry into force of this Directive, no general, permanent and statutory system of information and consultation of employees, nor a general, permanent and statutory system of employee representation at the workplace allowing employees to be represented for that purpose, may limit the application of the national provisions implementing this Directive to:

(*a*) undertakings employing at least 150 employees or establishments employing at least 100 employees until 23 March 2007, and

(*b*) undertakings employing at least 100 employees or establishments employing at least 50 employees during the year following the date in point (a).

Article 11

Transposition

1. Member States shall adopt the laws, regulations and administrative provisions necessary to comply with this Directive not later than 23 March 2005 or shall ensure that management and labour introduce by that date the required provisions by way of agreement, the Member States being obliged to take all necessary steps enabling them to guarantee the results imposed by this Directive at all times. They shall forthwith inform the Commission thereof.

2. Where Member States adopt these measures, they shall contain a reference to this Directive or shall be accompanied by such reference on the occasion of their official publication. The methods of making such reference shall be laid down by the Member States.

Article 12

Review by the Commission

Not later than 23 March 2007, the Commission shall, in consultation with the Member States and the social partners at Community level, review the application of this Directive with a view to proposing any necessary amendments.

Article 13

Entry into force

This Directive shall enter into force on the day of its publication in the *Official Journal of the European Communities.*

Article 14

Addresses

This Directive is addressed to the Member States.

Done at Brussels, 11 March 2002.

For the European Parliament	*For the Council*
The President	*The President*
P. Cox	J. Piqué i Camps

Statutory Instruments (Other Than Those Which Implement European Community Directives)

S.I. No. 5 of 1968

REDUNDANCY (REPAYMENT AND RECOVERY OF PAYMENTS) REGULATIONS, 1968

I, P. S. Ó h-IRIGHILE, Minister for Labour, in exercise of the power conferred on me by section 41 of the Redundancy Payments Act, 1967 (No. 21 of 1967), hereby make the following regulations:

1. These Regulations may be cited as the Redundancy (Repayment and Recovery of Payments) Regulations, 1968.

2. Where under section 41 of the Redundancy Payments Act, 1967 (No. 21 of 1967), —

(*a*) a decision of a deciding officer is revised so as to disallow or reduce redundancy payment paid or payable to a person, and

(*b*) the revised decision is given because the original decision had been given, or had continued in effect, by reason of any statement or representation (whether written or oral) which was to the knowledge of the person making it false or misleading in a material respect or by reason of the wilful concealment of any material fact,

any redundancy payment paid in pursuance of the original decision shall be repayable to the Redundancy Fund to the extent to which it would not have been payable if the revised decision had been given in the first instance and such person (and either any other person to whom the benefit was paid on behalf of such person or the personal representative of such person) shall be liable to pay to the Fund on demand by the Minister the sum so repayable.

3. Any benefit repayable in accordance with paragraph 2 may be recovered by deduction from any redundancy payment to which the person concerned (or any other person on the death of such person) then is or becomes entitled.

(L.S.)

GIVEN under my Official Seal,

this 3rd day of January, 1968.

P. S. Ó h-IRIGHILE,

Minister for Labour.

EXPLANATORY NOTE

(This note is not part of the Instrument and does not purport to be a legal interpretation.)

The purpose of these regulations is to provide for the recovery to the Redundancy Fund of payments (or overpayments) where a deciding officer's decision is revised because the original decision was based on information which was to the knowledge of the person giving it false or misleading.

S.I. No. 12 of 1968

REDUNDANCY (INSPECTION OF RECORDS) REGULATIONS, 1968

I, P. S. Ó h-IRIGHILE, Minister for Labour, in exercise of the powers conferred on me by sections 57 of the Redundancy Payments Act, 1967 (No. 21 of 1967), hereby make the following Regulations:

1. These Regulations may be cited as the Redundancy (Inspection of Records) Regulations, 1968.

2. In this Act—

"the Act" means the Redundancy Payments Act, 1967 (No. 21 of 1967);[1]

"eligible", in relation to an employee, means an employee to whom, by virtue of section 4 of the Act or an order thereunder, the Act applies;

"the Minister" means the Minister for [Enterprise, Trade and Employment];[2]

---

[1] Note that under s. 17(3) of the Redundancy Payments Act 2003, the Redundancy Payments Acts 1967 to 2003 are to be construed together as one.

[2] The text of the statutory instrument originally referred to the Minister for Labour. However, under Article 4(1) of the Labour (Transfer of Departmental Administration and Ministerial Functions) Order, 1993 (S.I. No. 18 of 1993), it was provided that the functions vested in the Minister for Labour by or under certain Acts (including the Redundancy Payments Act, 1967) be transferred to the Minister for Industry and Commerce. In Article 4(2) of the same Order, it was provided that references to the Minister for Labour contained in any such Act or instrument thereunder and relating to any functions transferred by Article 4 should, on and after the commencement of the Order, be construed as references to the Minister for Industry and Commerce. In Article 4 of the Industry and Commerce (Alteration of Name of Department and Title of Minister) Order, 1993 (S.I. No. 19 of 1993), which was adopted on the same day as S.I. No. 18 of 1993, it was provided that references in any enactment to the Minister for Industry and Commerce should be construed as references to the Minister for Enterprise and Employment. More recently, Article 4 of the Enterprise and Employment (Alteration of Name of Department and Title of Minister) Order, 1997 (S.I. No. 305 of 1997) has provided that references in any enactment to the Minister for Enterprise and Employment are to be construed as references to the Minister for Enterprise, Trade and Employment. Note further that under s. 19 of the Interpretation Act 2005, a word or expression used in a statutory instrument has the same meaning in the statutory

"officer" means an authorised officer of the Minister.

3. An officer may—

(*a*) enter any premises or place for the purpose of inspecting any documents or records liable to inspection under these Regulations,

(*b*) make such inspection of such documents or records as may be necessary for the purpose of ascertaining whether the Act (or any order thereunder) is being or has been complied with by the employer concerned,

(*c*) examine, either alone or in the presence of another person as the officer thinks fit, any person whom he finds in any premises or place entered by the officer under these Regulations with respect to any matter relating to the Act on which the officer may reasonably require information for the purpose of ensuring that the Act (or any order thereunder) is being effectively operated,

(*d*) require any person examined under subparagraph (*c*) to sign a declaration of the truth of any matter in respect of which that person has been so examined.

4. The occupier of any premises or place in which documents or records liable to inspection under these Regulations are deposited, and any person who is or has been employing a person who is or was an eligible employee, and the servants and agents of any such occupier or other person, and any such eligible employee, shall furnish to an officer all such information and shall produce to an officer for inspection all such registers, cards, wages sheets, records of wages and other documents as the officer may reasonably require for the purpose of ascertaining whether the Act (or any order thereunder) is being or has been complied with.

---

instrument as it has in the enactment under which the instrument is made. Finally, it should be noted that the powers and duties which are conferred on the Minister for Enterprise, Trade and Employment by or under the Redundancy Payments Acts have been delegated by statutory instrument to the present Minister of State at the Department of Enterprise, Trade and Employment. (See now the Enterprise, Trade and Employment (Delegation of Ministerial Functions) Order 2004 (S.I. No. 809 of 2004).)

5. Any person who— [3]

(*a*) wilfully delays or obstructs an officer in the exercise of any power under these Regulations,

(*b*) refuses or neglects to answer any question or to furnish any information or to produce any document when required so to do under these Regulations, or

(*c*) conceals or prevents or attempts to conceal or prevent any other person from appearing before or being examined by an officer,

shall be guilty of an offence and shall be liable on summary conviction thereof to a fine not exceeding [€63.49].[4]

6. An officer shall, while exercising powers under these Regulations, have in his possession a certificate of his appointment as such officer, and shall, on applying for admission to any premises or place under these Regulations, if so required, produce the certificate.

7. (1) An employer shall, on receipt by him from an officer of a notice in writing addressed to the employer at the address at which he resides or carries on business and incorporating or having annexed to it a form of declaration, furnish on the said form of declaration such information as is demanded in the notice in respect of any eligible employee who is or has been in his employment and shall sign and duly complete the declaration and deliver the same by hand or by registered post to the officer, within the time specified by the officer, not being less than six days from the date of the notice.

(2) Where a notice under subparagraph (1) is sent by post it shall be deemed to have been received by the person to whom it is addressed on the date on which it would be received in the ordinary course of post, unless the contrary is proved.

---

[3] The text of Regulation 5 was substituted by Regulation 2 of the Redundancy (Inspection of Records) Regulations, 1979 (S.I. No. 115 of 1979).

[4] The amount originally stipulated at the end of Regulation 5 was £50. However, under Article 14 of Council Regulation (EC) No. 974/98 of 3 May 1998 on the introduction of the euro (read in conjunction with Article 1 of the same instrument), references made in legislative and statutory provisions existing on 31 December, 2001 to units of Irish currency as they existed before the start of the third stage of economic and monetary union are to be read as references to the euro unit according to the respective conversion rates (with the rounding rules laid down in Regulation (EC) No. 1103/97 of 17 June 1997 on certain provisions relating to the introduction of the euro applying).

(L.S.)

GIVEN under my Official Seal,

this 9th day of January, 1968.

P. S. Ó h-IRIGHILE,

Minister for Labour.

EXPLANATORY NOTE

(This note is not part of the Instrument and does not purport to be a legal interpretation.)

The purpose of these Regulations is to specify the powers of authorised officers of the Minister for Labour in regard to the entry of premises, inspection of records and procurement of information for the purpose of ensuring the effective operation of the Redundancy Payments Act

The penalties for contraventions are specified in the Regulations.

S.I. No. 24 of 1968

REDUNDANCY (REDUNDANCY APPEALS TRIBUNAL) REGULATIONS, 1968

I, P. S. Ó h-IRIGHILE, Minister for Labour, in exercise of the powers conferred on me by section 39 (19) of the Redundancy Payments Act, 1967 (No. 21 of 1967), hereby make the following Regulations:

General.

1. These Regulations may be cited as the Redundancy (Redundancy Appeals Tribunal) Regulations, 1968.

2. In these Regulations—

"the Act" means the Redundancy Payments Act, 1967 (No. 21 of 1967); [1]

"the Minister" means the Minister for [Enterprise, Trade and Employment]; [2]

---

[1] Note that under s. 17(3) of the Redundancy Payments Act 2003, the Redundancy Payments Acts 1967 to 2003 are to be construed together as one.

[2] The text of Regulation 2 originally referred to the Minister for Labour. However, under Article 4(1) of the Labour (Transfer of Departmental Administration and Ministerial Functions) Order, 1993 (S.I. No. 18 of 1993), it was provided that the functions vested in the Minister for Labour by or under certain Acts (including the Redundancy Payments Act, 1967) be transferred to the Minister for Industry and Commerce. In Article 4(2) of the same Order, it was provided that references to the Minister for Labour contained in any such Act or instrument thereunder and relating to any functions transferred by Article 4 should, on and after the commencement of the Order, be construed as references to the Minister for Industry and Commerce. In Article 4 of the Industry and Commerce (Alteration of Name of Department and Title of Minister) Order, 1993 (S.I. No. 19 of 1993), which was adopted on the same day as S.I. No. 18 of 1993, it was provided that references in any enactment to the Minister for Industry and Commerce should be construed as references to the Minister for Enterprise and Employment. More recently, Article 4 of the Enterprise and Employment (Alteration of Name of Department and Title of Minister) Order, 1997 (S.I. No. 305 of 1997) has provided that references in any enactment to the Minister for Enterprise and Employment are to be construed as references to the Minister for Enterprise, Trade and Employment. Note further that under s. 19 of the Interpretation Act 2005, a word or expression used in a statutory instrument has the same

"notice of appeal" means the notice of appeal required by paragraph 3;

"the Tribunal" means the [Employment] Appeals Tribunal.[3]

Originating Application.

3. Where a person (in these Regulations referred to as the appellant) desires to appeal under section 39 (15) of the Act to the Tribunal he shall give written notice of appeal to the Secretary of the Tribunal.[4]

4. The notice of appeal shall be given on the form provided by the Minister for the purpose and shall be accompanied by a statement of the facts and contentions on which the appellant intends to rely.

Time Limit for and Withdrawal of Appeals.

5. No appeal shall be entertained by the Tribunal unless the appropriate notice of appeal has been submitted to the Tribunal within 21 days after the receipt by the appellant of the decision which constitutes the subject of the appeal; provided that notice of appeal given after that period may, with the consent of the Tribunal, be accepted.[5]

6. An appellant may withdraw an appeal to the Tribunal by sending notice of withdrawal to the Tribunal.[6]

---

meaning in the statutory instrument as it has in the enactment under which the instrument is made. Finally, it should be noted that the powers and duties which are conferred on the Minister for Enterprise, Trade and Employment by or under the Redundancy Payments Acts have been delegated by statutory instrument to the present Minister of State at the Department of Enterprise, Trade and Employment. (See now the Enterprise, Trade and Employment (Delegation of Ministerial Functions) Order 2004 (S.I. No. 809 of 2004).)

[3] Regulation 2 originally referred to the Redundancy Appeals Tribunal. However, s. 18 of the Unfair Dismissals Act, 1977 provided that this Tribunal should be known as the Employment Appeals Tribunal and that references in the Redundancy Payments Act, 1967 and any other Act of the Oireachtas and any instrument made under any Act of the Oireachtas to the Redundancy Appeals Tribunal should be construed as references to the Employment Appeals Tribunal.

[4] Regulation 3 was substituted by Regulation 2 of the Redundancy (Employment Appeals Tribunal) Regulations, 1979 (S.I. No. 114 of 1979).

[5] Regulation 5 was substituted by Regulation 2 of the Redundancy (Employment Appeals Tribunal) Regulations, 1979 (S.I. No. 114 of 1979).

[6] Regulation 6 was substituted by Regulation 2 of the Redundancy (Employment Appeals Tribunal) Regulations, 1979 (S.I. No. 114 of 1979).

Forwarding of Appeals.

7 (1) In the case of an appeal against a decision of a deciding officer and in the case of an employer who is appealing against a decision given by the Minister in relation to a rebate, the Secretary of the Tribunal shall forward to the Minister the notice of appeal together with a copy of the statement by the appellant required under paragraph 4, and the Minister shall, as soon as may be after receipt by him of such copy appeal and statement, cause to be furnished to the Secretary of the Tribunal a counter-statement given by or on behalf of the deciding officer or the Minister (as the case may be) showing to what extent the facts and contentions advanced by the appellant are admitted or disputed.[7]

(2) On receipt of the notice of appeal and the counter-statement, the Secretary of the Tribunal shall forward a copy of the counter-statement to the appellant.

8. In the case of an employee who is appealing against a decision given by an employer under the Redundancy Payments Acts, 1967 to 1979, the Secretary of the Tribunal shall on receipt of the notice of appeal forward to the employer concerned (in these Regulations referred to as "the respondent") a copy of the notice of appeal and of the statement by the appellant required under paragraph 4.[8]

Appearance by Respondent.

9. (1) A respondent shall within 14 days of receiving a copy of the appropriate notice of appeal enter an appearance to the proceedings by sending to the Secretary of the Tribunal a statement (on the form provided by the Minister for the purpose) indicating whether he intends to contest the appeal and, if so, to what extent the facts and contentions advanced by the appellant are admitted or disputed.

(2) Subject to subparagraph (3), a respondent who has not submitted a notice of appearance as required by subparagraph (1) shall not be entitled to take any part in the appeal proceedings or to be represented thereat.

---

[7] Paragraph 1 of Regulation 7 was substituted by Regulation 2 of the Redundancy (Employment Appeals Tribunal) Regulations, 1979 (S.I. No. 114 of 1979).

[8] Regulation 8 was substituted by Regulation 2 of the Redundancy (Employment Appeals Tribunal) Regulations, 1979 (S.I. No. 114 of 1979).

(3) A respondent may apply within the 14-day-period mentioned in subparagraph (1) for an extension of the time in which to enter an appearance.

(4) When the Secretary of the Tribunal receives a notice of appearance from the respondent, he shall forthwith send a copy thereof to the appellant.

Hearings by the Tribunal.

10. The chairman of the Tribunal shall from time to time fix dates, times and places for the hearing of appeals by the Tribunal and notice thereof shall be given by the Secretary to the Tribunal to all persons appearing to the chairman to be concerned.

11. The hearing of an appeal by the Tribunal shall take place in public unless the Tribunal decides at the request of either party to the appeal to hear the appeal in private.

12. Parties summoned to attend a hearing of the Tribunal may appear and be heard in person or may be represented by counsel or solicitor or by a representative of a trade union or of an employers' association or, with the leave of the Tribunal, by any other person.

Procedure at Hearings.

13. A party to an appeal heard by the Tribunal may—

(*a*) make an opening statement,

(*b*) call witnesses,

(*c*) cross-examine any witnesses called by any other party,

(*d*) give evidence on his own behalf, and

(*e*) address the Tribunal at the close of the evidence.

14. The Tribunal may postpone or adjourn the hearing of an appeal from time to time.

15. The Tribunal may admit any duly authenticated written statement as prima facie evidence of any fact whenever it thinks it just and proper so to do.

16. If, after notice of a hearing has been duly given, any of the parties fails to appear at the hearing, the Tribunal may determine the question under appeal or may adjourn the hearing to a later date: provided that before determining the question under appeal the Tribunal shall consider all the evidence before it at the time of the hearing.

17. (1) A decision of the Tribunal may be taken by a majority of the members thereof.

(2) A decision of the Tribunal shall be recorded in a document signed by the chairman and sealed with the seal of the Tribunal.

(3) A decision of the Tribunal shall be entered in a Register of Appeals and a copy of the decision shall be sent to the appellant and to any other person concerned.

(4) The Register of Appeals shall be open to inspection by any person without charge during normal business hours.

(5) The chairman of the Tribunal may by certificate under his hand correct any clerical mistake, error or omission in a decision of the Tribunal, and the correction shall be duly entered in the Register of Appeals and a copy of the corrected decision shall be sent to the appellant and to any other person concerned.

Notices.

18. (1) Any notice required by these Regulations shall be in writing, and all notices and documents required or authorised by these Regulations to be sent or given to any person may be deemed to be duly sent if sent by registered post and directed—

- (i) in the case of the Minister, to the head office of the Department of [Enterprise, Trade and Employment] [8a]
- (ii) in the case of the Secretary of the Appeals Tribunal, to the office of the Secretary,
- (iii) in the case of an appellant, to the address given by him in the notice of appeal,
- (iv) in the case of any other person, to his usual or last-known address or his place of business,
- (v) in the case of a body corporate, to its registered office.

[8a] The text of Regulation 18(1)(i) originally referred to the Department of Labour. However, the effect of Article 3(2) of the Labour (Transfer of Departmental Administration and Ministerial Functions) Order, 1993 (S.I. No. 18 of 1993) was that certain references to the Department of Labour (including references in the Redundancy Payments Acts and in instruments made thereunder) were required to be construed as references to the Department of Industry and Commerce. Subsequently, under Article 4 of the Industry and Commerce (Alteration of Name of Department and Title of

(2) A notice or document if sent or given to the authorised representative of a person shall be deemed to have been sent or given to that person.

(3) A party to an appeal may at any time by notice to the Tribunal and to any other party or parties concerned in the appeal change his address for service under these Regulations.

Costs and Expenses.

19. (1) Subject to subparagraph (2), the Tribunal shall not award costs against any party to an appeal.

(2) Where in the opinion of the Tribunal a party to the proceedings (and, if he is a respondent, whether or not he has entered an appearance) has acted frivolously or vexatiously, the Tribunal may make an order that that party shall pay to another party a specified amount in respect of travelling expenses and any other costs or expenses reasonably incurred by that other party in connection with the hearing.

(3) Notwithstanding subparagraph (2), costs shall not be awarded in respect of the costs or expenses in respect of the attendance of counsel, solicitors, officials of a trade union or of an employers' association appearing before the Tribunal in a representative capacity.

(4) Where the Tribunal has made an order under subparagraph (2), the amount referred to in the order shall be recoverable as a simple contract debt.

20. (1) The Tribunal may award to a person appearing before it a sum in respect of travelling expenses and subsistence allowances in accordance with such scale as the Minister, with the consent of the Minister for Finance, may from time to time determine.

Minister) Order, 1993 (S.I. No. 19 of 1993), which was adopted on the same day, references in any enactment to the Department of Industry and Commerce were required to be construed as references to the Department of Enterprise and Employment. Article 4 of the Enterprise and Employment (Alteration of Name of Department and Title of Minister) Order, 1997 (S.I. No. 305 of 1997) has since provided that references in any enactment to the Department of Enterprise and Employment are to be construed as references to the Department of Enterprise, Trade and Employment. Note further that under s. 19 of the Interpretation Act, 2005, a word or expression used in a statutory instrument has the same meaning in the statutory instrument as it has in the enactment under which the instrument is made.

(2) A sum awarded under subparagraph (1) shall be paid out of the Redundancy Fund.[9]

20A. (1) Subject to subparagraph (2), the Tribunal may, at its discretion, award to a person appearing before it and whose attendance is deemed essential by the Tribunal such sum in respect of expenses for loss of remunerative time as it considers reasonable.[10]

(2) The Tribunal shall not make an award under subparagraph (1) in respect of the attendance before the Tribunal of—

(*a*) appellant or respondents,

(*b*) any of the following persons appearing in a representative capacity—counsel, solicitors, officials of a trade union, officials of an employer's association.

(3) A sum awarded under subparagraph (1) shall be paid out of the Redundancy Fund.[11]

Miscellaneous.

21. (1) The Tribunal shall have an official seal which shall be judicially noticed.

(2) When affixed to any document the official seal of the Tribunal shall be authenticated by the signature of the chairman or vice-chairman of the Tribunal or by the secretary or such officer of the Tribunal as is authorised for that purpose by the chairman.

(3) Every document issued by the Tribunal and sealed with the official seal of the Tribunal shall be received in evidence without further proof.

---

[9] Since the coming into force of the Social Welfare Act, 1990, the role originally ascribed to the Redundancy Fund has been taken over by the Social Insurance Fund, however, and the definition in s. 1(1) of the Redundancy Payments Act, 1967 of "Redundancy Fund" has been substituted for one of the "Social Insurance Fund" by s. 28 of the Social Welfare Act, 1990. Regulation 20(2) has not been amended, however.

[10] Regulation 20A was inserted by Regulation 2 of the Redundancy (Employment Appeals Tribunal) Regulations, 1979 (S.I. No. 114 of 1979).

[11] Since the coming into force of the Social Welfare Act, 1990, the role originally ascribed to the Redundancy Fund has been taken over by the Social Insurance Fund, however, and the definition in s. 1(1) of the Redundancy Payments Act, 1967 of "Redundancy Fund" has been substituted for one of the "Social Insurance Fund" by s. 28 of the Social Welfare Act, 1990. Regulation 20(3) has not been amended, however.

22. (1) Where the Minister would not otherwise be a party to any proceedings before the Tribunal, he may request the Tribunal to treat him as a party to the proceedings and, where the Minister makes such a request, he shall be treated as such a party and be entitled to appear and be heard accordingly.

(2) Where under subparagraph (1) the Minister is treated as a party to proceedings, he may for the purposes of appearing or being heard before the Tribunal be represented by a person appointed by him.

23. The Tribunal may consider and decide any question duly referred to it for consideration and determination, notwithstanding the failure or neglect of any person to comply with any requirement of these Regulations.

23A. The Tribunal may consider and decide any appeal duly made to it notwithstanding the failure or neglect or any person to comply with any requirement of these Regulations.[12]

24. The Tribunal may require any party to an appeal to furnish in writing further particulars with regard to the facts and contentions contained in either the notice of appeal or the notice of appearance and when the required particulars have been received by the Secretary of the Tribunal he shall furnish the other party to the appeal with a copy of the particulars provided.

25. A reference by a deciding officer to the Tribunal under section 39 (16) of the Act shall be made on the form provided by the Minister for that purpose.

(L.S.)

GIVEN under my Official Seal,

this 29th day of January, 1968.

P. S. Ó h-IRIGHILE,

Minister for Labour.

---

[12] Regulation 23A was inserted by Regulation 2 of the Redundancy (Employment Appeals Tribunal) Regulations, 1979 (S.I. No. 114 of 1979).

EXPLANATORY NOTE

(This note is not part of the Instrument and does not purport to be a legal interpretation.)

These Regulations prescribe the procedure to be followed in relation to the submission and hearing of appeals against decisions given under the Redundancy Payments Act, 1967. They also provide for matters incidental to the hearing of appeals, including notifications of decisions, the keeping of a Register of Appeals, the use of an official seal and the awarding of costs and expenses.

S.I. No. 106 of 1968

REDUNDANCY PAYMENTS ACT (AUTHORISED OFFICERS) ORDER, 1968

I, P. S. Ó h-IRIGHILE, Minister for Labour, in exercise of the power conferred on me by section 55 of the Redundancy Payments Act, 1967 (No. 21 of 1967), hereby make the following order:

1. This Order may be cited as the Redundancy Payments Act (Authorised Officers) Order, 1968.

2. The Minister for [Enterprise, Trade and Employment] [1] may, with the consent of another Minister, designate an officer of that other Minister to be a duly authorised officer of the Minister for [Enterprise, Trade and Employment] for the purposes of the Redundancy Payments Act, 1967 (No. 21 of 1967).

---

[1] The text of the statutory instrument originally referred to the Minister for Labour in both of the parenthesised locations in Article 2. However, under Article 4(1) of the Labour (Transfer of Departmental Administration and Ministerial Functions) Order, 1993 (S.I. No. 18 of 1993), it was provided that the functions vested in the Minister for Labour by or under certain Acts (including the Redundancy Payments Act, 1967) be transferred to the Minister for Industry and Commerce. In Article 4(2) of the same Order, it was provided that references to the Minister for Labour contained in any such Act or instrument thereunder and relating to any functions transferred by Article 4 should, on and after the commencement of the Order, be construed as references to the Minister for Industry and Commerce. In Article 4 of the Industry and Commerce (Alteration of Name of Department and Title of Minister) Order, 1993 (S.I. No. 19 of 1993), which was adopted on the same day as S.I. No. 18 of 1993, it was provided that references in any enactment to the Minister for Industry and Commerce should be construed as references to the Minister for Enterprise and Employment. More recently, Article 4 of the Enterprise and Employment (Alteration of Name of Department and Title of Minister) Order, 1997 (S.I. No. 305 of 1997) has provided that references in any enactment to the Minister for Enterprise and Employment are to be construed as references to the Minister for Enterprise, Trade and Employment. Note further that under s. 19 of the Interpretation Act 2005, a word or expression used in a statutory instrument has the same meaning in the statutory instrument as it has in the enactment under which the instrument is made. Finally, it should be noted that the powers and duties which are conferred on the Minister for Enterprise,

(L.S.)

GIVEN under my Official Seal,

this 7th day of May, 1968.

P. S. Ó h-IRIGHILE,

Minister for Labour.

EXPLANATORY NOTE

(This note is not part of the Instrument and does not purport to be a legal interpretation.)

This Order empowers the Minister for Labour [2] to designate officers of other Ministers to be duly authorised officers of the Minister for Labour for the purposes of the Redundancy Payments Act.

Trade and Employment by or under the Redundancy Payments Acts have been delegated by statutory instrument to the present Minister of State at the Department of Enterprise, Trade and Employment. (See now the Enterprise, Trade and Employment (Delegation of Ministerial Functions) Order 2004 (S.I. No. 809 of 2004).)

[2] See previous footnote.

S.I. No. 243 of 1973

MINIMUM NOTICE AND TERMS OF EMPLOYMENT (REFERENCE OF DISPUTES) REGULATIONS, 1973

I, MICHAEL O'LEARY, Minister for Labour, in exercise of the powers conferred on me by section 39 (19) of the Redundancy Payments Act, 1967 (No. 21 of 1967), and sections 11 of the Minimum Notice and Terms of Employment Act, 1973 (No. 4 of 1973), hereby make the following regulations:

General.

1. (1) These Regulations may be cited as the Minimum Notice and Terms of Employment (Reference of Disputes) Regulations, 1973.

(2) These Regulations shall come into force on the 1st day of September, 1973.

2. In these Regulations—

"the Act" means the Minimum Notice and Terms of Employment Act, 1973 (No. 4 of 1973);

"appellant" has the meaning assigned to it by Regulation 3 of these Regulations;

"dispute", save where the context otherwise requires, means a dispute referred under section 11 of the Act to the Tribunal;

"the Minister" means the Minister for [Enterprise, Trade and Employment]; [1]

"respondent" has the meaning assigned to it by Regulation 6 of these Regulations.

---

[1] The text of Regulation 1(2) originally referred to the Minister for Labour. However, under Article 4(1) of the Labour (Transfer of Departmental Administration and Ministerial Functions) Order, 1993 (S.I. No. 18 of 1993), it was provided that the functions vested in the Minister for Labour by or under certain Acts (including the Minimum Notice and Terms of Employment Act, 1973) be transferred to the Minister for Industry and Commerce. In Article 4(2) of the same Order, it was provided that references to the Minister for Labour contained in any such Act or instrument thereunder and relating to any

Originating Application.

3. Where a person (in these Regulations referred to as the appellant) desires to have a dispute referred under section 11 of the Act to the Tribunal, he shall give written notice to the Secretary, [Employment] Appeals Tribunal, [2] Dublin.

4. The notice referred to in Regulation 3 of these Regulations shall be given on the form provided by the Minister for the purpose and shall be accompanied by a statement of the facts and contentions on which the appellant intends to reply.

Withdrawal of References.

5. An appellant may withdraw a reference of a dispute to the Tribunal by sending notice of withdrawal to the Secretary, [Employment] Appeals Tribunal, [3] Dublin.

---

functions transferred by Article 4 should, on and after the commencement of the Order, be construed as references to the Minister for Industry and Commerce. In Article 4 of the Industry and Commerce (Alteration of Name of Department and Title of Minister) Order, 1993 (S.I. No. 19 of 1993), which was adopted on the same day as S.I. No. 18 of 1993, it was provided that references in any enactment to the Minister for Industry and Commerce should be construed as references to the Minister for Enterprise and Employment. More recently, Article 4 of the Enterprise and Employment (Alteration of Name of Department and Title of Minister) Order, 1997 (S.I. No. 305 of 1997) has provided that references in any enactment to the Minister for Enterprise and Employment are to be construed as references to the Minister for Enterprise, Trade and Employment. Note further that under s. 19 of the Interpretation Act 2005, a word or expression used in a statutory instrument has the same meaning in the statutory instrument as it has in the enactment under which the instrument is made. Finally, it should be noted that the powers and duties which are conferred on the Minister for Enterprise, Trade and Employment by or under the Minimum Notice and Terms of Employment Acts have been delegated by statutory instrument to the present Minister of State at the Department of Enterprise, Trade and Employment. (See now the Enterprise, Trade and Employment (Delegation of Ministerial Functions) Order 2004 (S.I. No. 809 of 2004).)

[2] Regulation 3 originally referred to the Redundancy Appeals Tribunal. However, s. 18 of the Unfair Dismissals Act, 1977 provided that this Tribunal should be known as the Employment Appeals Tribunal and that references in the Redundancy Payments Act, 1967 and any other Act of the Oireachtas and any instrument made under any Act of the Oireachtas to the Redundancy Appeals Tribunal should be construed as references to the Employment Appeals Tribunal.

[3] Regulation 5 originally referred to the Redundancy Appeals Tribunal. However, s. 18 of the Unfair Dismissals Act, 1977 provided that this Tribunal

Forwarding of References.

6. On receipt of a notice referred to in Regulation 3 of these Regulations, the Secretary of the Tribunal shall forward to the employer concerned (in these Regulations referred to as the respondent) a copy of the statement received by him and required by Regulation 4 hereof.

Appearance by Respondent.

7. (1) A respondent shall within 14 days of receiving a copy of the appropriate notice enter an appearance to the proceedings by sending to the Secretary, [Employment] Appeals Tribunal, [4] Dublin, a statement indicating whether he intends to contest the reference and, if so, to what extent the facts and contentions advanced by the appellant are admitted or disputed.

(2) Subject to paragraph (3) of this regulation, a respondent who has not entered an appearance as required by paragraph (1) hereof shall not be entitled to take any part in the reference proceedings or to be represented thereat.

(3) A respondent may apply within the 14-day period mentioned in the said paragraph (1) for an extension of the time in which to enter an appearance.

(4) When the Secretary of the Tribunal receives a notice of appearance from a respondent, he shall forthwith send a copy thereof to the relevant appellant.

Register of References.

8. (1) A decision of the Tribunal on a dispute shall be entered in a Register of References and a copy of the decision shall be sent to the appellant and to any other person concerned.

---

should be known as the Employment Appeals Tribunal and that references in the Redundancy Payments Act, 1967 and any other Act of the Oireachtas and any instrument made under any Act of the Oireachtas to the Redundancy Appeals Tribunal should be construed as references to the Employment Appeals Tribunal.

[4] Regulation 7(1) originally referred to the Redundancy Appeals Tribunal. However, s. 18 of the Unfair Dismissals Act, 1977 provided that this Tribunal should be known as the Employment Appeals Tribunal and that references in the Redundancy Payments Act, 1967 and any other Act of the Oireachtas and

(2) The Register of References shall be open to inspection by any person without charge during normal business hours.

(3) In case the chairman of the Tribunal by certificate under his hand corrects a clerical mistake, error or omission in a decision of the Tribunal on a dispute, the correction shall be duly entered in the Register of References and a copy of the corrected decision shall be sent to the appellant and to any other person concerned.

Notices.

9. (1) Any notice required by these Regulations shall be in writing, and all notices and documents required or authorised by these Regulations to be sent or given to any person may be deemed to have been duly sent if sent by registered post and directed—

(i) in the case of the Secretary of the Tribunal, to the Secretary, [Employment] Appeals Tribunal, [5] Dublin.

(ii) in the case of an appellant, to the address specified in the notice given by him pursuant to Regulation 3 of these Regulations,

(iii) in the case of any other person, to his usual or last-known address or his place of business,

(iv) in the case of a body corporate, to its registered office.

(2) Any such notice or document if sent or given to the authorised representative of a person shall be deemed to have been sent or given to that person.

(3) A party to a dispute may at any time by notice to the Tribunal and to any other party or parties concerned in the dispute change his address for service under these Regulations.

---

any instrument made under any Act of the Oireachtas to the Redundancy Appeals Tribunal should be construed as references to the Employment Appeals Tribunal.

[5] Regulation 9 originally referred to the Redundancy Appeals Tribunal. However, s. 18 of the Unfair Dismissals Act, 1977 provided that this Tribunal should be known as the Employment Appeals Tribunal and that references in the Redundancy Payments Act, 1967 and any other Act of the Oireachtas and any instrument made under any Act of the Oireachtas to the Redundancy Appeals Tribunal should be construed as references to the Employment Appeals Tribunal.

Application and Non-Application of Certain Other Regulations.

10. (1) Regulations 10, 11, 13, 14, 16, 17 (1), 17(2), 19 and 24 of the Regulations of 1968 shall apply to a dispute as they apply to references to the Tribunal under section 39 of the Redundancy Payments Act, 1967 (No. 21 of 1967), and any reference to an appeal in the regulations hereinbefore specified shall be construed as including a reference to a dispute.

(2) Regulations 20(2) and 20A(3) (inserted by Regulation 2 of the Redundancy (Redundancy Appeals Tribunal) (Amendment) Regulations, 1969 (S.I. No. 26 of 1969)) of the Regulations of 1968 shall not apply to a dispute.

(3) In this Regulation "the Regulations of 1968" means the Redundancy (Redundancy Appeals Tribunal) Regulations, 1968 (S.I. No. 24 of 1968).

(L.S.)

GIVEN under my Official Seal,

this 17th day of August, 1973.

MICHAEL O'LEARY,

Minister for Labour.

EXPLANATORY NOTE

(This note is not part of the Instrument and does not purport to be a legal interpretation.)

These regulations prescribe the manner in which disputes under the Minimum Notice and Terms of Employment Act, 1973 shall be referred to the Redundancy Appeals Tribunal.

S.I. No. 140 of 1977

PROTECTION OF EMPLOYMENT ACT, 1977 (NOTIFICATION OF PROPOSED COLLECTIVE REDUNDANCIES) REGULATIONS, 1977

I, MICHAEL O'LEARY, Minister for Labour, in exercise of the power conferred on me by Section 12 of the Protection of Employment Act, 1977 (No. 7 of 1977), hereby make the following Regulations:

1. (1) These Regulations may be cited as the Protection of Employment Act, 1977 (Notification of Proposed Collective Redundancies) Regulations, 1977.

(2) These Regulations shall come into force on the 10th day of May, 1977.

2. The following particulars shall be specified by an employer in a notification under Section 12 of the Protection of Employment Act, 1977 (No. 7 of 1977) :—

(*a*) the name and address of the employer, indicating whether he is a sole trader, a partnership or a company;

(*b*) the address of the establishment where the collective redundancies are proposed;

(*c*) the total number of persons normally employed at that establishment;

(*d*) the number and descriptions or categories of employees whom it is proposed to make redundant;

(*e*) the period during which the collective redundancies are proposed to be effected, stating the dates on which the first and the final dismissals are expected to take effect;

(*f*) the reasons for the proposed collective redundancies;

(*g*) the names and addresses of the trade unions or staff associations representing employees affected by the proposed redundancies and with which it has been the practice of the employer to conduct collective bargaining negotiations;

(*h*) the date on which consultations with each such trade union or staff association commenced and the progress achieved in those consultations to the date of the notification.

(L.S.)

GIVEN under my Official Seal,

this 10th day of May, 1977.

MICHAEL O'LEARY,

Minister for Labour.

EXPLANATORY NOTE

(This note is not part of the Instrument and does not purport to be a legal interpretation.)

These Regulations prescribe the particulars to be specified by an employer in a notification under Section 12 of the Protection of Employment Act, 1977.

S.I. No. 286 of 1977

UNFAIR DISMISSALS (CLAIMS AND APPEALS) REGULATIONS, 1977

I, GENE FITZGERALD, Minister for Labour, in exercise of the powers conferred on me by section 17 of the Unfair Dismissals Act, 1977 (No. 10 of 1977), hereby make the following regulations:

1. (1) These Regulations may be cited as the Unfair Dismissals (Claims and Appeals) Regulations, 1977.

(2) These Regulations shall come into operation on the 14th day of September, 1977.

2. In these Regulations—

"the Act" means the Unfair Dismissals Act, 1977 (No. 10 of 1977);

"appeal" means an appeal under section 9 of the Act;

"claim" means a claim under section 8 (1) or section 8 (4) (a) of the Act;

"the Minister" means the Minister for [Enterprise, Trade and Employment]; [1]

---

[1] The text of Regulation 2 originally referred to the Minister for Labour. However, under Article 4(1) of the Labour (Transfer of Departmental Administration and Ministerial Functions) Order, 1993 (S.I. No. 18 of 1993), it was provided that the functions vested in the Minister for Labour by or under certain Acts (including the Unfair Dismissals Acts) be transferred to the Minister for Industry and Commerce. In Article 4(2) of the same Order, it was provided that references to the Minister for Labour contained in any such Act or instrument thereunder and relating to any functions transferred by Article 4 should, on and after the commencement of the Order, be construed as references to the Minister for Industry and Commerce. In Article 4 of the Industry and Commerce (Alteration of Name of Department and Title of Minister) Order, 1993 (S.I. No. 19 of 1993), which was adopted on the same day as S.I. No. 18 of 1993, it was provided that references in any enactment to the Minister for Industry and Commerce should be construed as references to the Minister for Enterprise and Employment. More recently, Article 4 of the Enterprise and Employment (Alteration of Name of Department and Title of Minister) Order, 1997 (S.I. No. 305 of 1997) has provided that references in any enactment to the Minister for Enterprise and Employment are to be

"the Tribunal" means the Employment Appeals Tribunal established by the Redundancy Payments Act, 1967.

3. A notice under subsection (2) of section 8 of the Act to the Tribunal or under subsection (4) of the said section 8 or section 9 (2) of the Act shall specify—

(*a*) the name and address of the person bringing the claim or appeal,

(*b*) the name and address of the employer or the employee, as the case may be, concerned,

(*c*) the date of the commencement of the employment to which the notice relates,

(*d*) the date of the dismissal to which the notice relates, and

(*e*) the amount claimed by the said person to be the weekly remuneration of the said person in respect of the said employment calculated in accordance with regulations under section 17 of the Act.

4. A claim or appeal may be withdrawn by sending a notification in writing signifying such withdrawal to the Tribunal.

5. (1) A party to a claim or appeal who receives notice thereof under section 8 or 9, as the case may be, of the Act and who intends to oppose the claim or appeal shall enter an appearance to the claim or appeal by giving to the Tribunal, within 14 days of the receipt by him of the said notice, a notice in writing stating that he intends to oppose the claim or appeal, as the case may be, and containing the facts and contentions on which he will ground such opposition.

(2) A party to a claim or appeal who does not enter an appearance to the claim or appeal in pursuance of this Regulation shall not be entitled to

---

construed as references to the Minister for Enterprise, Trade and Employment. Note further that under s. 19 of the Interpretation Act 2005, a word or expression used in a statutory instrument has the same meaning in the statutory instrument as it has in the enactment under which the instrument is made. Finally, it should be noted that the powers and duties which are conferred on the Minister for Enterprise, Trade and Employment by or under the Unfair Dismissals Acts have been delegated by statutory instrument to the Minister of State at the Department of Enterprise, Trade and Employment. (See now the Enterprise, Trade and Employment (Delegation of Ministerial Functions) Order 2004 (S.I. No. 809 of 2004).)

take part in or be present or represented at any proceedings before the Tribunal in relation to the claim or appeal.

(3) A party to a claim or appeal may, before the expiration of the period referred to in paragraph (1) of this Regulation, apply, by giving to the Tribunal a notice in writing containing the facts and contentions on which he grounds the application, for an extension of the said period and the Tribunal may make such order in relation to the application as it thinks just.

6. On receipt by the Tribunal of a notice referred to in Regulation 3 or 5 of these Regulations or a notification under Regulation 4 of these Regulations, the Tribunal shall cause a copy of the notice or notification, as the case may be, to be given to the other party concerned.

7. The chairman of the Tribunal may, by certificate under his hand, correct any mistake (including an omission) of a verbal or formal nature in a determination of the Tribunal.

8. (1) The Tribunal shall maintain a register, to be known as the Register of Unfair Dismissals Determinations (referred to subsequently in this Regulation as "the Register"), and shall cause to be entered in the Register particulars of every determination by the Tribunal under Section 8 or 9 of the Act.

(2) The Register may be inspected free of charge by any person during normal office hours.

(3) Where the chairman of the Tribunal makes a correction, pursuant to Regulation 7 of these Regulations, particulars thereof shall be entered in the Register.

(4) A copy of an entry in the Register shall be sent to the parties concerned.

9. (1) A notice required by subsection (2) or (4) of section 8 or section 9 (2) of the Act or by these Regulations to be given to the Tribunal may be sent by registered post addressed to the Secretary, Employment Appeals Tribunal, Dublin 4, [2] and a document required by these Regulations to

[2] Note that, although this provision has not been amended, the address of the Employment Appeals Tribunal is now Davitt House, 65a Adelaide Road, Dublin 2.

be given to a party to proceedings before the Tribunal may be sent by registered post addressed to the party—

(*a*) in case his address is specified in a notice referred to in Regulation 3 of these Regulations, at that address, and

(*b*) in the case of a body corporate (being a case to which paragraph (a) of this Regulation does not apply) at its registered office, and

(*c*) in any other case, at his known place of residence or at a place where he works or carries on business.

(2) Any such notice or notification as aforesaid that is sent or given to a person authorised to receive it by the person to whom it is required by these Regulations to be given shall be deemed to have been sent to the latter person.

10. Regulations 10 to 17 (2), 19, 20, 20A (inserted by the Redundancy (Redundancy Appeals Tribunal) (Amendment) Regulations, 1969 (S.I. No. 26 of 1969)), 23 and 24 of the Redundancy (Redundancy Appeals Tribunal) Regulations, 1968 (S.I. No. 24 of 1968), shall, with any necessary modifications, and in the case of the said Regulations 20 and 20A, with the modification that a sum awarded by the Tribunal under either such Regulation shall, in lieu of being paid out of the fund referred to therein, be paid by the Minister for [Enterprise, Trade and Employment] [3] with the consent of the Minister for Finance, apply in relation to a claim under Section 8 of the Act, an appeal under section 9 of the Act and proceedings in relation to such a claim or appeal as they

---

[3] The text of Regulation 10 originally referred to the Minister for Labour. However, under Article 4(1) of the Labour (Transfer of Departmental Administration and Ministerial Functions) Order, 1993 (S.I. No. 18 of 1993), it was provided that the functions vested in the Minister for Labour by or under certain Acts (including the Unfair Dismissals Acts) be transferred to the Minister for Industry and Commerce. In Article 4(2) of the same Order, it was provided that references to the Minister for Labour contained in any such Act or instrument thereunder and relating to any functions transferred by Article 4 should, on and after the commencement of the Order, be construed as references to the Minister for Industry and Commerce. In Article 4 of the Industry and Commerce (Alteration of Name of Department and Title of Minister) Order, 1993 (S.I. No. 19 of 1993), which was adopted on the same day as S.I. No. 18 of 1993, it was provided that references in any enactment to the Minister for Industry and Commerce should be construed as references to the Minister for Enterprise and Employment. More recently, Article 4 of the

apply in relation to appeals provided for by section 39 of the Redundancy Payments Act, 1967 (No. 21 of 1967).

(L.S.)

GIVEN under my Official Seal,

this 7th day of September, 1977.

GENE FITZGERALD,

Minister for Labour.

EXPLANATORY NOTE

(This note is not part of the Instrument and does not purport to be a legal interpretation.)

These regulations prescribe the procedure to be followed in relation to the submission and hearing of claims and appeals before the Employment Appeals Tribunal under the Unfair Dismissals Act, 1977.

Enterprise and Employment (Alteration of Name of Department and Title of Minister) Order, 1997 (S.I. No. 305 of 1997) has provided that references in any enactment to the Minister for Enterprise and Employment are to be construed as references to the Minister for Enterprise, Trade and Employment. Note further that under s. 19 of the Interpretation Act 2005, a word or expression used in a statutory instrument has the same meaning in the statutory instrument as it has in the enactment under which the instrument is made. Finally, it should be noted that the powers and duties which are conferred on the Minister for Enterprise, Trade and Employment by or under the Unfair Dismissals Acts have been delegated by statutory instrument to the present Minister of State at the Department of Enterprise, Trade and Employment. (See now the Enterprise, Trade and Employment (Delegation of Ministerial Functions) Order 2004 (S.I. No. 809 of 2004).)

S.I. No. 287 of 1977

UNFAIR DISMISSALS (CALCULATION OF WEEKLY REMUNERATION) REGULATIONS, 1977

I, GENE FITZGERALD, Minister for Labour, in exercise of the powers conferred on me by section 17 of the Unfair Dismissals Act, 1977 (No. 10 of 1977), hereby make the following Regulations:

1. (1) These Regulations may be cited as the Unfair Dismissals (Calculation of Weekly Remuneration) Regulations, 1977.

(2) These Regulations shall come into operation on the 14th day of September, 1977.

2. In these Regulations—

"the Act" means the Unfair Dismissals Act, 1977 (No. 10 of 1977);

"date of dismissal" has the meaning assigned to it by section 1 of the Act, and "date", in relation to a dismissal, shall be construed accordingly;

"relevant employment", in relation to an employee, means the employment in respect of which the weekly remuneration of the employee is calculated for the purposes of section 7 (1) (*c*) of the Act;

"week", in relation to an employee whose remuneration is calculated by reference to a week ending on a day other than a Saturday, means a week ending on that other day and, in relation to any other employee, means a week ending on a Saturday, and "weekly" shall be construed accordingly.

3. (*a*) A week's remuneration of an employee in respect of an employment shall be calculated for the purposes of section 7 (1) (*c*) of the Act in accordance with these Regulations.

(*b*) Where, at the date of his dismissal from an employment, an employee had less than 52 weeks' continuous service in the employment, a week's remuneration of the employee in respect of the employment shall be calculated, for the purposes of the said section 7 (1) (*c*), in the manner that in the opinion of the

Tribunal corresponds most closely with that specified in these Regulations.

4. In the case of an employee who is wholly remunerated in respect of the relevant employment at an hourly time rate or by a fixed wage or salary, and in the case of any other employee whose remuneration in respect of the relevant employment does not vary by reference to the amount of work done by him, his weekly remuneration in respect of the relevant employment shall be his earnings in respect of that employment (including any regular bonus or allowance which does not vary having regard to the amount of work done and any payment in kind) in the latest week before the date of the relevant dismissal in which he worked for the number of hours that was normal for the employment together with, if he was normally required to work overtime in the relevant employment, his average weekly overtime earnings in the relevant employment as determined in accordance with Regulation 5 of these Regulations.

5. For the purpose of Regulation 4 of these Regulations, the average weekly overtime earnings of an employee in the relevant employment shall be the amount obtained by dividing by 26 the total amount of his overtime earnings in that employment in the period of 26 weeks ending 13 weeks before the date of the dismissal of the employee.

6. For the purpose of Regulations 5 and 7 (*b*) of these Regulations, any week during which the employee concerned did not work shall be disregarded and the latest week before the period of 26 weeks mentioned in the said Regulation 5 or 7 (*b*), as the case may be, of these Regulations or before a week taken into account under this Regulation, as may be appropriate, shall be taken into account instead of a week during which the employee did not work as aforesaid.

7. (*a*) In the case of an employee who is paid remuneration in respect of the relevant employment wholly or partly at piece rates, or whose remuneration includes commissions (being piece rates or commissions related directly to his output at work) or bonuses, and in the case of any other employee whose remuneration in respect of the relevant employment varies in relation to the amount of work done by him, his weekly remuneration shall be the amount obtained by dividing the amount of the remuneration to be taken into account in accordance with paragraph (*b*) of this Regulation by the number of hours worked in the period of 26 weeks mentioned in the said paragraph (*b*) and multiplying the

resulting amount by the normal number of hours for which, at the date of the dismissal of the employee, an employee in the relevant employment was required to work in each week.

(*b*) The remuneration to be taken into account for the purposes of paragraph (*a*) of this Regulation shall be the total remuneration paid to the employee concerned in respect of the employment concerned for all the hours worked by the employee in the employment in the period of 26 weeks that ended 13 weeks before the date on which the employee was dismissed, adjusted in respect of any variations in the rates of pay which became operative during the period of 13 weeks ending on the date of dismissal of the employee.

(*c*) For the purposes of paragraph (*b*) of this Regulation, any week worked in another employment shall be taken into account if it would not have operated, for the purposes of the First Schedule to the Minimum Notice and Terms of Employment Act, 1973 (No. 4 of 1973), to break the continuity of service of the employee concerned in the employment from which he was dismissed.

8. (1) Where, under his contract of employment, an employee is required to work for more hours than the number of hours that is normal for the employment, the hours for which he is so required to work shall be taken, for the purposes of Regulations 4 and 7 *(b)* of these Regulations, to be, in the case of that employee, the number of hours that is normal for the employment.

(2) Where, under his contract of employment, an employee is entitled to additional remuneration for working for more than a specified number of hours per week—

(*a*) in case the employee is required under the said contract to work for more than the said specified number of hours per week, the number of hours per week for which he is so required to work shall, for the purposes of Regulations 4 and 7 (*b*) of these Regulations, be taken to be, in his case, the number of hours of work per week that is normal for the employment, and

(*b*) in any other case, the specified number of hours shall be taken, for the purposes of the said Regulations 4 and 7 (*b*), to be, in the case of that employee, the number of hours of work per week that is normal for the employment.

9. Where, in a particular week, an employee qualifies for a payment of a bonus, pay allowance or commission which relates to work the whole or part of which was not done in that particular week, the whole or the appropriate proportionate part of the payment as the case may be, shall, for the purposes of Regulations 4 and 7 (*b*) of these Regulations, be disregarded in relation to that particular week and shall for those purposes, be taken into account in relation to any week in which any of the work was done.

10. An employee who is normally employed on a shift cycle and whose remuneration in respect of the employment varies having regard to the particular shift on which he is employed, and an employee whose remuneration for working for the number of hours that is normal for the employment varies having regard to the days of the week or the times of the day on or at which he works, shall each be taken, for the purposes of these Regulations, to be an employee who is paid wholly or partly by piece rates.

11. Where, in respect of the relevant employment, there is no number of hours for which employees work in each week that is normal for the employment, the weekly remuneration of each such employee shall be taken, for the purposes of these Regulations, to be the average amount of the remuneration paid to each such employee in the 52 weeks in each of which he was working in the employment immediately before the date of the relevant dismissal.

12. Where under these Regulations account is to be taken of remuneration paid in a period which does not coincide with the periods for which the remuneration is calculated, the remuneration shall be apportioned in such manner as may be just.

13. For the purposes of Regulations 4 and 7 of these Regulations, account shall not be taken of any sums paid to an employee by way of recoupment of expenses incurred by him in the discharge of the duties of his employment.

(L.S.)

GIVEN under my Official Seal,

this 7th day of September, 1977.

GENE FITZGERALD,

Minister for Labour.

EXPLANATORY NOTE

(This note is not part of the Instrument and does not purport to be a legal interpretation.)

These regulations prescribe the method of calculating weekly remuneration for the purpose of redress in the form of compensation under the Unfair Dismissals Act, 1977.

S.I. No. 232 of 1985

PROTECTION OF EMPLOYEES (EMPLOYERS' INSOLVENCY) (SPECIFICATION OF DATE) REGULATIONS, 1985

I, RUAIRÍ QUINN, Minister for Labour, in exercise of the power conferred on me by section 4 (3) of the Protection of Employees (Employers' Insolvency) Act, 1984 (No. 21 of 1984), hereby make the following Regulations:

1. These Regulations may be cited as the Protection of Employees (Employers' Insolvency) (Specification of Date) Regulations, 1985.

2. In the case of an employer who is a company within the meaning of the Protection of Employees (Employers' Insolvency) Act, 1984, by virtue of being a body corporate under the Industrial and Provident Societies Act, 1893, and which, by virtue of section 1 (3) (*c*) of the said Protection of Employees (Employers' Insolvency) Act, 1984, has become insolvent as a result of the appointment of a receiver or manager of its undertaking by or on behalf of the holders of debentures secured by a floating charge, but not being a company within the meaning of section 2 of the Companies Act, 1963, the day on which the receiver or manager was appointed is hereby specified as the day on which that employer is to be regarded as having become insolvent for the purposes of the said Protection of Employees (Employers' Insolvency) Act, 1984.

(L.S.)

GIVEN under my Official Seal,

this 11th day of July, 1985.

RUAIRÍ QUINN,

Minister for Labour.

EXPLANATORY NOTE

(This note is not part of the Instrument and does not purport to be a legal interpretation.)

The purpose of these Regulations is to specify the day on which a body corporate under the Industrial and Provident Societies Act, 1893 is to be regarded as having become insolvent for the purposes of the Protection of Employees (Employers' Insolvency) Act, 1984, as being the day on which a receiver or manager was appointed.

S.I. No. 15 of 1986

THE RULES OF THE SUPERIOR COURTS

We, the Superior Courts Rules Committee, constituted pursuant to the provisions of the Courts of Justice Act, 1936, section 67, and reconstituted pursuant to the provisions of the Courts of Justice Act, 1953, section 15, by virtue of the powers conferred upon us by the Courts of Justice Act, 1924, section 36, and the Courts of Justice Act, 1936, section 68 (as applied by the Courts (Supplemental Provisions) Act, 1961, section 48), and the Courts (Supplemental Provisions) Act, 1961, section 14, and of all other powers enabling us in this behalf, do hereby make the annexed Rules of Court.

Dated this 19th day of December 1985.

Tomas A. Finlay	Harry Hill
Liam Hamilton	Frederick Morris
Brian Walsh	Mary Laffoy
Frank Griffin	W. B. Allen
Seán Gannon	D. R. Pigot
Mella Carroll	

I concur in the making of the annexed Rules of Court.

Dated this 17th day of January 1986.

MICHAEL NOONAN,

Aire Dlí agus Cirt.

THE RULES OF THE SUPERIOR COURTS

The following Rules (which may be cited as "The Rules of the Superior Courts" or, in the abbreviated form, "R.S.C.") shall come into operation on the 1st day of October, 1986, and shall on and after that date apply, where appropriate, to all proceedings in causes or matters whether then pending or commenced thereafter…

ORDER 105

APPEALS FROM THE EMPLOYMENT APPEALS TRIBUNAL

1. Every appeal to the Court under the Redundancy Payments Acts, 1967 and 1971,[1] or the Minimum Notice and Terms of Employment Act, 1973 [2] shall be brought by special summons.

2. The summons shall be entitled in the matter of the relevant Act, on the application of the person bringing the appeal, and shall state the decision of the [Employment] Appeals Tribunal, [3] (hereinafter referred to as the Tribunal), appealed against and the grounds of appeal.

3. The summons shall be served on the Minister for [Enterprise, Trade and Employment] [4] and on all parties to the decision of the Tribunal.

---

[1] Note that under s. 17(3) of the Redundancy Payments Act 2003, the Redundancy Payments Acts 1967 to 2003 are to be construed together as one.

[2] Note that the Minimum Notice and Terms of Employment Act, 1973, s. 13 of the Protection of Employees (Employers' Insolvency) Act, 1984, the Protection of Employees (Part-Time Work) Act, 2001 (insofar as it relates to the foregoing legislation) and Part 7 of the Civil Service Regulation (Amendment) Act 2005 may now be cited together as the Minimum Notice and Terms of Employment Acts 1973 to 2005 and are required to be construed together as one. (See in this regard s. 18(3) of the Protection of Employees (Employers' Insolvency) Act, 1984, s. 1(2) of the Protection of Employees (Part-Time Work) Act, 2001, and s. 1(4) of the Civil Service Regulation (Amendment) Act 2005.)

[3] The text of Order 105, Rule 2 originally referred to the Redundancy Appeals Tribunal. However, s. 18 of the Unfair Dismissals Act, 1977 provided that this Tribunal should be known as the Employment Appeals Tribunal and that references in the Redundancy Payments Act, 1967 and any other Act of the Oireachtas and any instrument made under any Act of the Oireachtas to the Redundancy Appeals Tribunal should be construed as references to the Employment Appeals Tribunal.

[4] The text of Order 105, Rule 3 originally referred to the Minister for Labour. However, under Article 4(1) of the Labour (Transfer of Departmental Administration and Ministerial Functions) Order, 1993 (S.I. No. 18 of 1993), it was provided that the functions vested in the Minister for Labour by or under certain Acts (including the Redundancy Payments Act, 1967 and the

4. The summons shall be issued within twenty-one days of the date on which notice of the decision of the Tribunal was given to the party appealing; provided that the time within which the summons may be issued may be extended on application ex parte at any time within six weeks from the date on which notice of the decision of the Tribunal was given to the party wishing to appeal.

5. Any question referred to the Court by the said Minister under either of the said Acts shall be brought by special summons, entitled in the matter of the relevant Act, on the application of the said Minister. The summons shall state concisely the question referred for the decision of the Court and shall be served on all parties to the application to the Tribunal.

6. No costs shall be allowed of any proceedings under this Order unless the Court shall by special order allow such costs.

Minimum Notice and Terms of Employment Acts) be transferred to the Minister for Industry and Commerce. In Article 4(2) of the same Order, it was provided that references to the Minister for Labour contained in any such Act or instrument thereunder and relating to any functions transferred by Article 4 should, on and after the commencement of the Order, be construed as references to the Minister for Industry and Commerce. In Article 4 of the Industry and Commerce (Alteration of Name of Department and Title of Minister) Order, 1993 (S.I. No. 19 of 1993), which was adopted on the same day as S.I. No. 18 of 1993, it was provided that references in any enactment to the Minister for Industry and Commerce should be construed as references to the Minister for Enterprise and Employment. More recently, Article 4 of the Enterprise and Employment (Alteration of Name of Department and Title of Minister) Order, 1997 (S.I. No. 305 of 1997) has provided that references in any enactment to the Minister for Enterprise and Employment are to be construed as references to the Minister for Enterprise, Trade and Employment. Note further that under s. 19 of the Interpretation Act 2005, a word or expression used in a statutory instrument has the same meaning in the statutory instrument as it has in the enactment under which the instrument is made. Finally, it should be noted that the powers and duties which are conferred on the Minister for Enterprise, Trade and Employment by or under both the Redundancy Payments Acts and the Minimum Notice and Terms of Employment Acts have been delegated by statutory instrument to the present Minister of State at the Department of Enterprise, Trade and Employment. (See now the Enterprise, Trade and Employment (Delegation of Ministerial Functions) Order 2004 (S.I. No. 809 of 2004).)

EXPLANATORY NOTE

(This note is not part of the Instrument and does not purport to be a legal interpretation.)

The effect of this Instrument is to make rules governing procedure in the Superior Courts set up by the Courts (Establishment and Constitution) Act, 1961.

S.I. No. 50 of 1986

PROTECTION OF EMPLOYEES (EMPLOYERS' INSOLVENCY) (SPECIFICATION OF DATE) REGULATIONS, 1986.

I, RUAIRI QUINN, Minister for Labour, in exercise of the power conferred on me by section 4(3) of the Protection of Employees (Employers' Insolvency) Act, 1984 (No. 21 of 1984), hereby make the following Regulations:

1. These Regulations may be cited as the Protection of Employees (Employers' Insolvency) (Specification of Date) Regulations, 1986.

2. In the case of an employer who is a company within the meaning of the Protection of Employees (Employers' Insolvency) Act, 1984, by virtue of being a body corporate under the Industrial and Provident Societies Acts, 1893 to 1978, and which, by virtue of section 1 (3)(c) of the said Protection of Employees (Employers' Insolvency) Act, 1984, has become insolvent as a result of the making of a winding up order or the passing of a resolution for voluntary winding up with respect to the said company, but not being a company within the meaning of section 2 of the Companies Act, 1963, the day on which the winding up order was made or the resolution for voluntary winding up was passed is hereby specified as the day on which that employer is to be regarded as having become insolvent for the purposes of the said Protection of Employees (Employers' Insolvency) Act, 1984.

(L.S.)

GIVEN under my Official Seal,

this 26th day of February, 1986.

RUAIRI QUINN,

Minister for Labour.

EXPLANATORY NOTE

(This note is not part of the Instrument and does not purport to be a legal interpretation.)

The purpose of these Regulations is to specify the day on which a winding up order was made or the resolution for voluntary winding up was passed as being the day on which a body corporate under the Industrial and Provident Societies Acts, 1893 to 1978 is to be regarded as having become insolvent for the purposes of the Protection of Employees (Employers' Insolvency) Act, 1984.

S.I. No. 48 of 1988

PROTECTION OF EMPLOYEES (EMPLOYERS' INSOLVENCY) ACT, 1984 (AMENDMENT ORDER) ORDER, 1988 [1]

I, BERTIE AHERN, Minister for Labour, in exercise of the powers conferred on me by Section 11 of the Protection of Employees (Employers' Insolvency) Act, 1984 (No. 21 of 1984), hereby order as follows:—

1. This Order may be cited as the Protection of Employees (Employers' Insolvency) Act, 1984, (Amendment Order) Order, 1988.

2. The application of the Protection of Employees (Employers' Insolvency) Act, 1984 is hereby extended to employees who have attained the age of 66 years and who are in employment which, but for the age of the employees, would be insurable for all benefits under the Social Welfare Acts, 1981 to 1987.

(L.S.)

Given under my Official Seal, this 25th day of March, 1988.

BERTIE AHERN,

Minister for Labour.

---

[1] The substantive content of this Order has been re-enacted in the form of primary legislation by virtue of the substitution of s. 3 of the Protection of Employees (Employers' Insolvency) Act, 1984 by Article 4 of the European Communities (Protection of Employees (Employers' Insolvency) Regulations 2005 (S.I. No. 630 of 2005)).

EXPLANATORY NOTE

(This note is not part of the Instrument and does not purport to be a legal interpretation.)

This Order extends the Protection of Employees (Employers' Insolvency) Act, 1984, to employees over the age of 66 years who are debarred from receiving payments from the Redundancy and Employers' Insolvency Fund because they are not fully insurable due to their age.

S.I. No. 122 of 1990

REDUNDANCY (REBATES) REGULATIONS, 1990

I, BERTIE AHERN, Minister for Labour, in exercise of the powers conferred on me by section 36 of the Redundancy Payments Act, 1967 (No. 21 of 1967), hereby make the following Regulations:

1. These Regulations may be cited as the Redundancy (Rebates) Regulations, 1990, and shall come into operation on the 23rd day of May, 1990.

2. In these Regulations

"the Acts" means the Redundancy Payments Acts, 1967 to 1990; [1]

"the Minister" means the Minister for [Enterprise, Trade and Employment]; [2]

---

[1] Note that under s. 17(3) of the Redundancy Payments Act 2003, the Redundancy Payments Acts 1967 to 2003 are to be construed together as one.

[2] The text of Regulation 2 originally referred to the Minister for Labour. However, under Article 4(1) of the Labour (Transfer of Departmental Administration and Ministerial Functions) Order, 1993 (S.I. No. 18 of 1993),it was provided that the functions vested in the Minister for Labour by or under certain Acts (including the Redundancy Payments Act, 1967) be transferred to the Minister for Industry and Commerce. In Article 4(2) of the same Order, it was provided that references to the Minister for Labour contained in any such Act or instrument thereunder and relating to any functions transferred by Article 4 should, on and after the commencement of the Order, be construed as references to the Minister for Industry and Commerce. In Article 4 of the Industry and Commerce (Alteration of Name of Department and Title of Minister) Order, 1993 (S.I. No. 19 of 1993), which was adopted on the same day as S.I. No. 18 of 1993, it was provided that references in any enactment to the Minister for Industry and Commerce should be construed as references to the Minister for Enterprise and Employment. More recently, Article 4 of the Enterprise and Employment (Alteration of Name of Department and Title of Minister) Order, 1997 (S.I. No. 305 of 1997) has provided that references in any enactment to the Minister for Enterprise and Employment are to be construed as references to the Minister for Enterprise, Trade and Employment. Note further that under s. 19 of the Interpretation Act 2005, a word or expression used in a statutory instrument has the same meaning in the statutory instrument as it has in the enactment under which the instrument is made. Finally, it should be noted that the powers and duties which are conferred on the Minister for Enterprise, Trade and Employment by or under the

"rebate" has the meaning assigned to it by section 29 of the Redundancy Payments Act, 1967 (No. 21 of 1967).

3. A claim for a rebate shall be made

(*a*) by the employer in the form set out in the Schedule to these Regulations (or a form substantially to the like effect) and shall contain the appropriate particulars referred to in that form,

(*b*) to the Minister for [Enterprise, Trade and Employment] [3] addressed to his office, in Dublin,

(*c*) before the expiration of six months from the date on which the employer made the relevant lump sum payment or, where a claimant proves that there was good cause for his failure to make

---

Redundancy Payments Acts have been delegated by statutory instrument to the present Minister of State at the Department of Enterprise, Trade and Employment. (See now the Enterprise, Trade and Employment (Delegation of Ministerial Functions) Order 2004 (S.I. No. 809 of 2004).)

[3] The text of Regulation 3(b) originally referred to the Minister for Labour. However, under Article 4(1) of the Labour (Transfer of Departmental Administration and Ministerial Functions) Order, 1993 (S.I. No. 18 of 1993), it was provided that the functions vested in the Minister for Labour by or under certain Acts (including the Redundancy Payments Act, 1967) be transferred to the Minister for Industry and Commerce. In Article 4(2) of the same Order, it was provided that references to the Minister for Labour contained in any such Act or instrument thereunder and relating to any functions transferred by Article 4 should, on and after the commencement of the Order, be construed as references to the Minister for Industry and Commerce. In Article 4 of the Industry and Commerce (Alteration of Name of Department and Title of Minister) Order, 1993 (S.I. No. 19 of 1993), which was adopted on the same day as S.I. No. 18 of 1993, it was provided that references in any enactment to the Minister for Industry and Commerce should be construed as references to the Minister for Enterprise and Employment. More recently, Article 4 of the Enterprise and Employment (Alteration of Name of Department and Title of Minister) Order, 1997 (S.I. No. 305 of 1997) has provided that references in any enactment to the Minister for Enterprise and Employment are to be construed as references to the Minister for Enterprise, Trade and Employment. Note further that under s. 19 of the Interpretation Act 2005, a word or expression used in a statutory instrument has the same meaning in the statutory instrument as it has in the enactment under which the instrument is made. Finally, it should be noted that the powers and duties which are conferred on the Minister for Enterprise, Trade and Employment by or under the Redundancy Payments Acts have been delegated by statutory instrument to the present Minister of State at the Department of Enterprise, Trade and Employment. (See now the Enterprise, Trade and Employment (Delegation of Ministerial Functions) Order 2004 (S.I. No. 809 of 2004).)

the claim before the expiration of that period, within such further period as the Minister may in any particular case or class of cases allow, and

(*d*) in writing and accompanied by the copy of the redundancy certificate on which the employee concerned has signed a receipt for the lump sum payment, except that where in a particular case a claimant proves to the satisfaction of the Minister that that copy cannot be produced the Minister may, at his discretion, accept in lieu of the certificate such other evidence as he thinks fit of the payment of the lump sum.

4. An employer who has made a claim for a rebate shall, if required to do so by the Minister, produce evidence of the following matters

(*a*) the period of continuous employment of the employee concerned, with the employer,

(*b*) the normal weekly remuneration of the employee concerned,

(*c*) the numbers of employees employed on material dates by the employer, and

(*d*) the receipt by the employee concerned of the lump sum in respect of which the rebate is claimed.

5. An employer who has made a claim for a rebate shall, if required to do so by the Minister, produce for examination on behalf of the Minister any or all such registers, cards, wages sheets, other records of wages and records of employment which may contain particulars of the employment of the employee or employees concerned with the employer and which are in the custody of the employer or under his control.

6. The Redundancy (Rebates) Regulations, 1984 (S.I. No. 222 of 1984) are hereby revoked.

SCHEDULE

Form RP3 *(text not reproduced here)* [4]

---

[4] This form is designed for the purposes of an employer's claim for a rebate from the Social Insurance Fund. Note that in recent times, however, the composite RP50 form (incorporating, *inter alia,* the RP3 form) has been made available for this purpose by the Department of Enterprise, Trade and

(L.S.)

GIVEN under my Official Seal

this 11th day of May, 1990.

BERTIE AHERN,

Minister for Labour.

EXPLANATORY NOTE

(This note is not part of the Instrument and does not purport to be a legal interpretation.)

The purpose of these Regulations is to set out the procedures which must be followed by employers when claiming rebates on lump-sum payments consequent on the amalgamation of the Redundancy and Employers' Insolvency Fund with the Social Insurance Fund. The place at which the claims must be made, the procedures and the time limit for the making of the claims are also prescribed. The Regulations also provide that claimants for rebates must, if required to do so by the Minister, produce evidence in support of the claims.

Employment. A copy of this is to be found online at http://www.entemp.ie/forms /formrp50.pdf

S.I. No. 347 of 1991

REDUNDANCY CERTIFICATE REGULATIONS, 1991

I, MICHAEL O' KENNEDY, T.D., Minister for Labour, in exercise of the powers conferred on me by sections 18 (as amended by the Redundancy Payments Act, 1971 (No. 20 of 1971)) and 58 (as amended by the Redundancy Payments Act, 1979 (No. 7 of 1979)) of the Redundancy Payments Act, 1967 (No. 21 of 1967), hereby make the following Regulations:

1. These Regulations may be cited as the Redundancy Certificate Regulations, 1991, and shall come into operation on the 30th day of December, 1991.

2. A redundancy certificate shall be in the form set out in the Schedule to these Regulations, or in a form substantially to like effect, and shall contain—

(*a*) the appropriate particulars referred to in that form,

(*b*) a declaration or declarations (as appropriate) by the employer concerned in the terms set out in that form, and

(*c*) a receipt, if appropriate, in the terms set out in that form, by the employee concerned for the lump sum payment referred to in that form.

3. An employer who fails to comply with these Regulations shall be guilty of an offence and shall be liable on summary conviction to a fine not exceeding [€63.49].[1]

[1] The amount originally stipulated in Regulation 3 was £50. However, under Article 14 of Council Regulation (EC) No 974/98 of 3 May 1998 on the introduction of the euro (read in conjunction with Article 1 of the same instrument), references made in legislative and statutory provisions existing on 31 December 2001 to units of Irish currency as they existed before the start of the third stage of economic and monetary union are to be read as references to the euro unit according to the respective conversion rates (with the rounding rules laid down in Regulation (EC) No 1103/97 of 17 June 1997 on certain provisions relating to the introduction of the euro applying).

4. The Redundancy Certificate Regulations, 1984 (S.I. No. 221 of 1984), are hereby revoked.

SCHEDULE

Form RP2 *(text not reproduced here)* [2]

(L.S.)

GIVEN under my Official Seal,

this 20th day of December, 1991.

MICHAEL O'KENNEDY,

Minister for Labour.

EXPLANATORY NOTE

(This note is not part of the Instrument and does not purport to be a legal interpretation.)

The purpose of these regulations is to require employers when giving a redundancy certificate under the Redundancy Payments Acts to use the amended form (RP2) provided by the Minister for this purpose and to furnish the appropriate declarations in the form. A penalty for failure to comply with the regulations is also specified.

---

[2] This form is designed for the purposes of the making of a redundancy certificate. Note that in recent times, however, the composite RP50 form (incorporating, *inter alia,* the RP2 form) has been made available for this purpose by the Department of Enterprise, Trade and Employment. A copy of this is to be found online at http://www.entemp.ie/forms/formrp50.pdf

S.I. No. 348 of 1991

REDUNDANCY (NOTICE OF DISMISSAL) REGULATIONS, 1991

I, MICHAEL O' KENNEDY, T.D., Minister for Labour, in exercise of the powers conferred on me by sections 17 (as amended by the Redundancy Payments Act, 1971 (No. 20 of 1971)) and 58 (as amended by the Redundancy Payments Act, 1979 (No. 7 of 1979)) of the Redundancy Payments Act, 1967 (No. 21 of 1967), hereby make the following Regulations:

1. These Regulations may be cited as the Redundancy (Notice of Dismissal) Regulations, 1991, and shall come into operation on the 30th day of December, 1991.

2. In these Regulations "the notice" means the notice required by section 17(1) of the Redundancy Payments Act, 1967 (No. 21 of 1967), as amended by the Redundancy Payments Act, 1971 (No. 20 of 1971).[1]

3. The notice shall be given in the form set out in the Schedule to these Regulations, or in a form substantially to like effect, and shall contain the appropriate particulars refered [1a] to in that form.

4. A copy of the notice shall, at the same time as it is given to the employee concerned, be sent by the employer concerned to the Minister for [Enterprise, Trade and Employment] [2] addressed to his office in Dublin.

---

[1] Note that since the adoption of these Regulations, s. 17(1) of the 1967 Act has been subsequently amended again by s. 7 of the Redundancy Payments Act, 2003, although the form of reference to s. 17(1) in Regulation 2 has not been altered.

[1a] *Sic.*

[2] The text of Regulation 4 originally referred to the Minister for Labour. However, under Article 4(1) of the Labour (Transfer of Departmental Administration and Ministerial Functions) Order, 1993 (S.I. No. 18 of 1993), it was provided that the functions vested in the Minister for Labour by or under certain Acts (including the Redundancy Payments Act, 1967) be transferred to the Minister for Industry and Commerce. In Article 4(2) of the same Order, it was provided that references to the Minister for Labour contained in any such Act or instrument thereunder and relating to any functions transferred by Article 4 should, on and after the commencement of the Order, be construed as references to the Minister for Industry and Commerce.

5. An employer who fails to comply with these Regulations shall be guilty of an offence and shall be liable on summary conviction to a fine not exceeding [€63.49].[3]

6. The Redundancy (Notice of Dismissal) Regulations, 1984 (S.I. No. 220 of 1984), are hereby revoked.

SCHEDULE

Form RP1 *(text not reproduced here)* [4]

In Article 4 of the Industry and Commerce (Alteration of Name of Department and Title of Minister) Order, 1993 (S.I. No. 19 of 1993), which was adopted on the same day as S.I. No. 18 of 1993, it was provided that references in any enactment to the Minister for Industry and Commerce should be construed as references to the Minister for Enterprise and Employment. More recently, Article 4 of the Enterprise and Employment (Alteration of Name of Department and Title of Minister) Order, 1997 (S.I. No. 305 of 1997) has provided that references in any enactment to the Minister for Enterprise and Employment are to be construed as references to the Minister for Enterprise, Trade and Employment. Note further that under s. 19 of the Interpretation Act 2005, a word or expression used in a statutory instrument has the same meaning in the statutory instrument as it has in the enactment under which the instrument is made. Finally, it should be noted that the powers and duties which are conferred on the Minister for Enterprise, Trade and Employment by or under the Redundancy Payments Acts have been delegated by statutory instrument to the present Minister of State at the Department of Enterprise, Trade and Employment. (See now the Enterprise, Trade and Employment (Delegation of Ministerial Functions) Order 2004 (S.I. No. 809 of 2004).)

[3] The amount originally stipulated in Regulation 5 was £50. However, under Article 14 of Council Regulation (EC) No 974/98 of 3 May 1998 on the introduction of the euro (read in conjunction with Article 1 of the same instrument), references made in legislative and statutory provisions existing on 31 December 2001 to units of Irish currency as they existed before the start of the third stage of economic and monetary union are to be read as references to the euro unit according to the respective conversion rates (with the rounding rules laid down in Regulation (EC) No 1103/97 of 17 June 1997 on certain provisions relating to the introduction of the euro applying).

[4] This form is designed for the purposes of giving notice of proposed dismissal for redundancy. Note that in recent times, however, the composite RP50 form (incorporating, *inter alia,* the RP1 form) has been made available for this purpose by the Department of Enterprise, Trade and Employment. A copy of this is to be found online at http://www.entemp.ie/forms/formrp50.pdf

(L.S.)

GIVEN under my Official Seal,

this 20th day of December, 1991.

MICHAEL O'KENNEDY,

Minister for Labour.

EXPLANATORY NOTE

(This note is not part of the instrument and does not purport to be a legal interpretation.)

The purpose of these regulations is to require employers when giving notice of dismissal under the Redundancy Payments Acts to use the amended form (RP 1) provided by the Minister for this purpose and to send a copy of the completed form to the Minister for Labour [4a] addressed to his office in Dublin. A penalty for failure to comply with the regulations is also specified.

[4a] See n. 2 above.

S.I. No. 244 of 1994

TERMS OF EMPLOYMENT (INFORMATION) (APPEALS AND COMPLAINTS) REGULATIONS, 1994

I, RUAIRÍ QUINN, Minister for Enterprise and Employment, in exercise of the powers conferred on me by section 8 of the Terms of Employment (Information) Act, 1994 (No. 5 of 1994), hereby make the following Regulations:

1. (1) These Regulations may be cited as the Terms of Employment (Information) (Appeals and Complaints) Regulations, 1994.

(2) These Regulations shall come into operation on the 2nd day of August, 1994.

2. In these Regulations—

"the Act" means the Terms of Employment (Information) Act, 1994 (No. 5 of 1994);

"appeal" means an appeal under section 8 (1) of the Act;

"complaint" means a complaint under section 8 (6) of the Act;

"the Minister" means the Minister for [Enterprise, Trade and Employment][1]

"the Tribunal" means the Employment Appeals Tribunal.

---

[1] The text of Regulation 2 originally referred to the Minister for Enterprise and Employment. However, Article 4 of the Enterprise and Employment (Alteration of Name of Department and Title of Minister) Order, 1997 (S.I. No. 305 of 1997) has provided that references in any enactment to the Minister for Enterprise and Employment are to be construed as references to the Minister for Enterprise, Trade and Employment. Note further that under s. 19 of the Interpretation Act 2005, a word or expression used in a statutory instrument has the same meaning in the statutory instrument as it has in the enactment under which the instrument is made. Finally, it should be noted that the powers and duties which are conferred on the Minister for Enterprise, Trade and Employment by or under the Terms of Employment (Information) Acts have been delegated by statutory instrument to the present Minister of State at the Department of Enterprise, Trade and Employment. (See now the Enterprise, Trade and Employment (Delegation of Ministerial Functions) Order 2004 (S.I. No. 809 of 2004).)

3. A notice under subsection (2) or (6) of section 8 of the Act shall contain—

(*a*) the names, addresses and descriptions of the parties to the proceedings to which the appeal or complaint relates,

(*b*) the date of the recommendation to which the appeal or complaint, as the case may be, relates and the name of the rights commissioner who made the recommendation, and

(*c*) a brief outline of the grounds of the appeal or complaint, as the case may be.

4. An appeal or complaint may be withdrawn by giving a notification in writing signifying such withdrawal to the Tribunal.

5. (1) A party to an appeal or complaint under subsection (2) or (6) of section 8 of the Act who receives a notice thereof shall—

(*a*) if he or she intends to contest the appeal or be heard by the Tribunal at the hearing of the appeal,

(*b*) if he or she intends to contest the complaint or be heard by the Tribunal in relation to the matters referred to in section 8 (6) (*a*) of the Act,

enter an appearance to the appeal or the complaint, as the case may be, by giving a notice of appearance to the Tribunal within 14 days (or such longer period as the Tribunal may fix under paragraph (3) of this Regulation) of receipt by him or her of the said notice.

(2) A notice of appearance under this Regulation shall contain a brief outline of the grounds on which the appeal or complaint concerned will be contested by the person entering the appearance.

(3) A party to an appeal or complaint may, before the expiration of the period referred to in paragraph (1) of this Regulation, apply to the Tribunal, by notice in writing given to the Tribunal and containing a brief outline of the grounds for the application, for an extension of that period for entering an appearance to the appeal or complaint, as the case may be, and the Tribunal may, if it is satisfied that there are reasonable grounds for doing so, extend the time aforesaid by such period as it considers appropriate.

6. On receipt by the Tribunal of a notification under Regulation 4 of these Regulations or of a notice of appearance under Regulation 5 of

these Regulations, the Tribunal shall cause a copy of the notice or notification, as the case may be, to be given to the other party concerned.

7. An error (including an omission) of a formal nature in a determination of the Tribunal may be corrected—

(*a*) in any case, by the chairman of the Tribunal, and

(*b*) in a case in which the determination concerned was made at a time when a vice-chairman was acting as chairman of the Tribunal, by the vice-chairman,

by a certificate signed by him or her.

8. (1) The Tribunal shall maintain a register, to be known as the Register of Terms of Employment (Information) Determinations (referred to subsequently in this Regulation as "the Register") and shall cause to be entered in the Register particulars of every determination of the Tribunal under section 8 of the Act.

(2) The Register may be inspected free of charge by any person during normal office hours.

(3) Particulars of any correction made under Regulation 7 of these Regulations shall be entered in the Register.

(4) A copy of an entry in the Register shall be sent to the parties concerned.

9. (1) A notice or notification under these Regulations or subsection (2) or (6) of section 8 of the Act may be given by sending it by registered post addressed to the Secretary, Employment Appeals Tribunal, Davitt House, 65A Adelaide Road, Dublin 2, and a notice or notification under these Regulations or a document under paragraph (b) of the said section 8(2) may be given to any other person by sending it by registered post addressed to the person—

(*a*) in case his or her address is specified correctly in a notice referred to in Regulation 5 of these Regulations, at that address, and

(*b*) in any other case—

(i) if the person is a company (within the meaning of the Companies Act, 1963), at its registered office,

(ii) if the person is not a company (within the meaning aforesaid) at a place where the person resides or carries on a profession, business or occupation.

(2) Any such notice or notification or document aforesaid that is given to a person authorised to receive it by the person to whom it is required

to be given by the Act or by these Regulations shall be deemed to have been given to the latter person.

10. Regulations 10 to 17 (2), 19, 20, 20A (inserted by the Redundancy (Employment Appeals Tribunal) Regulations, 1979 (S.I. No. 114 of 1979)), 23, 23A (inserted by the Redundancy (Employment Appeals Tribunal) Regulations, 1979) and 24 of the Redundancy (Redundancy Appeals Tribunal) Regulations, 1968 (S.I. No. 24 of 1968), shall, with any necessary modifications (and, in the case of the said Regulations 20 and 20A, with the modification that a sum awarded by the Tribunal under either of those Regulations shall, in lieu of being paid out of the Fund referred to therein, be paid by the Minister for [Enterprise, Trade and Employment] [2] with the consent of the Minister for Finance) apply in relation to appeals and complaints under section 8 of the Act and proceedings in relation to such appeals or complaints as they apply in relation to appeals provided for by section 39 of the Redundancy Payments Act, 1967 (No. 21 of 1967), and proceedings in relation to such appeals.

(L.S.)

GIVEN under my Official Seal,

this 29th day of July, 1994.

RUAIRÍ QUINN,

Minister for Enterprise and Employment.

---

[2] The text of Regulation 10 originally referred to the Minister for Enterprise and Employment. However, Article 4 of the Enterprise and Employment (Alteration of Name of Department and Title of Minister) Order, 1997 (S.I. No. 305 of 1997) has provided that references in any enactment to the Minister for Enterprise and Employment are to be construed as references to the Minister for Enterprise, Trade and Employment. Note further that under s. 19 of the Interpretation Act 2005, a word or expression used in a statutory instrument has the same meaning in the statutory instrument as it has in the enactment under which the instrument is made. Finally, it should be noted that the powers and duties which are conferred on the Minister for Enterprise, Trade and Employment by or under the Terms of Employment (Information) Acts have been delegated by statutory instrument to the present Minister of State at the Department of Enterprise, Trade and Employment. (See now the Enterprise, Trade and Employment (Delegation of Ministerial Functions) Order 2004 (S.I. No. 809 of 2004).)

EXPLANATORY NOTE

(This note is not part of the Instrument and does not purport to be a legal interpretation.)

These Regulations prescribe the procedures to be followed in relation to the submission and hearing of appeals and complaints before the Employment Appeals Tribunal under the Terms of Employment (Information) Act, 1994.

S.I. No. 4 of 1997

TERMS OF EMPLOYMENT (INFORMATION) ACT, 1994 (SECTION 3 (6)) ORDER, 1997

I, EITHNE FITZGERALD, Minister of State at the Department of Enterprise and Employment, in exercise of the powers conferred on me by section 3 (6) (*a*) of the Terms of Employment (Information) Act, 1994 (No. 5 of 1994) and the Enterprise and Employment (Delegation of Ministerial Functions) (No. 2) Order, 1995 (S.I. No. 43 of 1995), hereby order as follows:

1. This Order may be cited as the Terms of Employment (Information) Act, 1994 (Section 3 (6)) Order, 1997.

2. An employer who employs a child or young person (within the meaning of the Protection of Young Persons (Employment) Act, 1996 (No. 16 of 1996)), to work for him or her shall, not later than one month after the commencement of the employee's employment, give or cause to be given to the employee a copy of the abstract of the Protection of Young Persons (Employment) Act, 1996, prescribed for the purpose of section 12 of that Act.

(L.S.)

GIVEN under my hand,

this 2nd day of January, 1997.

EITHNE FITZGERALD, T.D.

Minister of State at the Department of Enterprise and Employment.

EXPLANATORY NOTE

(This note is not part of the Instrument and does not purport to be a legal interpretation.)

This Order provides that employees under 18 be given a copy of the abstract of the Protection of Young Persons (Employment) Act, 1996 not less than one month after employment commences.

S.I. No. 49 of 1998

TERMS OF EMPLOYMENT (ADDITIONAL INFORMATION) ORDER, 1998

I, TOM KITT, Minister of State at the Department of Enterprise, Trade and Employment, in exercise of the power conferred on me by section 3 (6) of the Terms of Employment (Information) Act, 1994 (No. 5 of 1994), as adapted by the Enterprise and Employment (Alteration of Name of Department and Title of Minister) Order, 1997 (S.I. No. 305 of 1997), and the Enterprise, Trade and Employment (Delegation of Ministerial Functions) (No. 2) Order, 1997 (S.I. No. 330 of 1997), hereby order as follows:

1. This Order may be cited as the Terms of Employment (Additional Information) Order, 1998, and shall come into operation on the 1st day of March, 1998.

2. In this Order "the Act" means the Organisation of Working Time Act, 1997 (No. 20 of 1997).

3. (1) In relation to an employee who enters into a contract of employment after the commencement of this Order, the employee's employer shall, within two months after the employee's commencement of employment with the employer, give or cause to be given to the employee a statement in writing containing particulars of the times and duration of the rest periods and breaks referred to in sections 11, 12 and 13 of the Act that are being allowed to the employee and of any other terms and conditions relating to those periods and breaks.

(2) In relation to an employee who has entered into a contract of employment before the commencement of this Order, the employee's employer shall, if requested by the employee to do so, give or cause to be given to the employee, within 2 months of the request being made, a statement in writing containing particulars of the times and duration of the rest periods and breaks referred to in sections 11, 12 and 13 of the Act that are being allowed to the employee and of any other terms and conditions relating to those periods and breaks.

GIVEN under my hand,

this 25th day of February, 1998.

TOM KITT, T.D.,

Minister for Labour, Trade and Consumer Affairs.

EXPLANATORY NOTE

(This note is not part of the Instrument and does not purport to be a legal interpretation.)

This Order provides that where, under the Terms of Employment (Information) Act, 1994, an employer is required to provide an employee with a written statement of certain particulars of his or her terms of employment, such statement shall, after 1st March, 1998, include details of the times and duration of (and any other terms and conditions relating to) the rest periods and breaks referred to in sections 11 of the Organisation of Working Time Act, 1997 that are being allowed to the employee.

S.I. No. 510 of 2001

CIRCUIT COURT RULES, 2001

We, the Circuit Court Rules Committee, constituted pursuant to the provisions of section 69 of the Courts of Justice Act, 1936, and section 12 of the Courts of Justice Act, 1947, by virtue of the powers conferred on us by section 66 of the Courts of Justice Act, 1924, and section 70 of the Courts of Justice Act, 1936, (as applied by section 48 of the Courts (Supplemental Provisions) Act, 1961) and section 27 of the Courts (Supplemental Provisions) Act, 1961, and of all other powers enabling us in this behalf, do hereby, with the concurrence of the Minister for Justice, make the annexed Rules of Court.

Dated this 26th day of October, 2001.

Esmond Smyth
(Chairman of the Circuit Court Rules Committee)

Kieran O'Connor

Carroll Moran

Anne Dunne

Fergal Foley

Joe Deane

Gerard Doherty

Susan Ryan (Secretary)

I concur in the making of the above Rules of Court.

Dated this 15th day of November, 2001.

JOHN O'DONOGHUE,

Minister for Justice, Equality and Law Reform.

RULES

THE CIRCUIT COURT RULES, 2001

...

ORDER 57 EMPLOYMENT

Rule 1 — Unfair Dismissals Acts, 1977-1993 (No. 10 of 1977, No. 5 of 1991 and No. 22 of 1993)

1. In this Order, "the Acts" mean the Unfair Dismissals Acts, 1977–1993, (No. 10 of 1977, No. 5 of 1991 and No. 22 of 1993),[1] "The Tribunal" means the Employment Appeals Tribunal, and "The Minister" means the Minister for Enterprise, Trade and Employment.

2. All applications under Section 10 of the 1977 Act or under Section 11 of the 1993 Act whether by way of claim for redress by the Minister or by way of claim for enforcement or by way of appeal from the Tribunal shall be made by way of Motion on Notice which shall set out the grounds upon which the plaintiff is relying for the reliefs sought. Such applications shall be in accordance with Form 36A of the Schedule of Forms annexed hereto.

3. Applications shall be brought in the County where the employer concerned ordinarily resides or carries on any profession, business or occupation.

4. All applications shall be served no later than 10 days prior to the return date set out in the Motion either in accordance with the provisions as to service of Civil Bills and other documents contained in Order 11 of these Rules or by being delivered to or served upon the Solicitor who is on record before the Tribunal as acting for the person named as the defendant before the Court; and service of an application or any other

---

[1] Note that under s. 1(6) of the Protection of Employees (Part-Time Work) Act, 2001, insofar as the 2001 Act relates to the Unfair Dismissals Acts, 1977 to 1993, those Acts and the 2001 Act are required to be construed together as one and may be cited together as the Unfair Dismissals Acts, 1977 to 2001, and that under s. 1(3) of the Civil Service Regulation (Amendment) Act 2005, the Unfair Dismissals Acts, 1977 to 2001 and Part 6 of that Act may be cited together as the Unfair Dismissals Acts 1977 to 2005 and are required to be construed together as one.

document upon such Solicitor, or delivery of the same at his office, or sending the same to him by prepaid post to such office shall be deemed to be good service upon the party for whom such Solicitor acts upon the day when the same is so delivered or served, or upon which in the ordinary course of postage it would be delivered. The Motion shall be listed for mention only on the return date set out therein at which time a date for hearing shall be fixed by the Court.

5. Notice of every application shall be given to the Tribunal. Such notice shall be effected before the filing of the application by the delivery of a copy of the application at, or by sending same by prepaid registered post to, the Office of the Secretary of the Tribunal.

6. The following documents shall be filed with the application:-

(*a*) a copy of the original Notice to Appeal to the Tribunal;

(*b*) a copy of the Notice of Appearance;

(*c*) a copy of the determination of the Tribunal;

(*d*) the original letter from the Tribunal notifying the making of communication of the said determination;

(*e*) a copy of any particulars provided by either party to the Tribunal.

7. Every application made by way of an appeal from a determination of the Tribunal shall contain a statement of the grounds upon which the applicant intends to rely. If the plaintiff wishes to appeal against part only of a determination of the Tribunal, the application shall clearly identify that part against which it is intended to appeal.

8. All applications shall be dated, and bear the name, address and description of the plaintiff and shall be signed by his Solicitor, if any, or, if none, by himself.

9. Upon the application on notice of any party the Judge may order any other party to deliver full and better particulars of any matters stated in the application, or to deliver copies of any documents referred to therein.

10. Save by special leave of the Court or save as otherwise provided for by the Acts, all applications under the Acts shall be heard upon oral evidence.

11. The Court may make such Order as to costs as may be appropriate, having regard to the provisions of Section 10 of the 1977 Act, including an Order measuring the costs.

12. The Secretary of the Tribunal shall have the right of access to all the information contained on the file kept in the Office of the County Registrar in respect of each application and shall be entitled upon request to receive a copy of any written Judgment delivered by the Judge relating thereto.

...

EXPLANATORY NOTE

(This note is not part of the Instrument and does not purport to be a legal interpretation.)

These Rules, which come into operation on the 3rd day of December, 2001, replace in revised and consolidated form the Rules listed in Schedule A hereto. They prescribe the practice and procedures to be followed and the forms to be used in the Circuit Court proceedings to which they relate on and from the operative date, save for proceedings pending in the Court on that date, which proceedings shall be continued and completed as if these Rules had not been made.

S.I. No. 409 of 2003

DISTRICT COURT (TERMS OF EMPLOYMENT INFORMATION) RULES, 2003

The District Court Rules Committee, in exercise of the powers conferred on them by section 91 of the Courts of Justice Act, 1924, section 72 of the Courts of Justice Act, 1936, section 17 of the Interpretation Act, 1937 [as applied by section 48 of the Courts (Supplemental Provisions) Act, 1961][1] and section 34 of the Courts (Supplemental Provisions) Act, 1961, do hereby, with the concurrence of the Minister for Justice, Equality and Law Reform, make the following rules of court:-

1. These rules may be cited as the District Court (Terms of Employment Information) Rules, 2003.

2. These rules shall come into operation on the 9th day of October, 2003 and shall be read together with all other District Court rules for the time being in force.

3. Order 99B of the District Court Rules, 1997 (S.I. No. 93 of 1997) shall be amended by the insertion immediately following Order 99B, rule 4 of the following:

> *5. "An application to the Court for an order pursuant to Section 9 of the Terms of Employment (Information) Act, 1994 may be made to any sitting of the Court for the court district in which the respondent employer carries on any trade, profession, business or occupation.*[2]
>
> *6. Such application shall be by notice of application in the Form 99B.3, Schedule C and shall be served on the respondent by prepaid registered post not later than seven days before the date of the sitting for which the application is returnable. An order made pursuant to section 9 of the said Act of 1994 on such application shall be in the Form 99B.4, Schedule C."*

---

[1] The square parentheses are in the original text of the Rules.

[2] The placing of the quotation mark after, rather than before, the number "5." appears to have been done in error.

4. The Forms numbered 99B.3 and 99B.4 in Schedule 1 hereof shall be added to the Forms in Schedule C of the District Court Rules, 1997 (S.I. No. 93 of 1997).

Form 99B.3 *(text not reproduced here)*

Form 99B.4 *(text not reproduced here)*

Given this 24th day of March, 2003

Peter Smithwick Chairman

John Garavan

Uinsin Mac Gruairc

John P Brophy

Mary C Devins

Sean McMullin

Hugh O'Neill Secretary

I concur in the making of the foregoing rules

Dated this 9th day of September, 2003

Michael McDowell

Minister for Justice, Equality and Law Reform

EXPLANATORY NOTE

(This note is not part of the Instrument and does not purport to be a legal interpretation.)

These Rules amend Order 99B of the District Court Rules, 1997 (S.I. No. 93 of 1997) to allow applications to be made pursuant to section 9 of the Terms of Employment (Information) Act, 1994 to any sitting of the Court for the court district in which the respondent employer carries on any trade, profession, business or occupation. Such application shall be by notice of application in the Form 99B.3, Schedule C and shall be served on the respondent by prepaid registered post not later than seven days before the date of the sitting for which the application is returnable. An order made pursuant to section 9 of the said Act of 1994 on such application shall be in the Form 99B.4, Schedule C.

S.I. No 682 of 2005

PROTECTION OF EMPLOYEES (EMPLOYERS' INSOLVENCY) (FORMS AND PROCEDURE) REGULATIONS 2005

I, Tony Killeen, Minister of State at the Department of Enterprise, Trade and Employment, in exercise of the powers conferred on me by sections 6, 7 and 16 of the Protection of Employees (Employers' Insolvency) Act 1984 (No. 21 of 1984) and the Labour (Transfer of Departmental Administration and Ministerial Functions) Order 1993 (S.I. No. 18 of 1993) (as adapted by the Enterprise and Employment (Alteration of Name of Department and Title of Minister) Order 1997 (S.I. No. 305 of 1997)) and the Enterprise, Trade and Employment (Delegation of Ministerial Functions) Order 2004 (S.I. No. 809 of 2004), hereby make the following regulations:

1. These Regulations may be cited as the Protection of Employees (Employers' Insolvency) (Forms and Procedure) Regulations 2005.

2. (1) In these Regulations—

"Act" means the Protection of Employees (Employers' Insolvency) Act 1984 (No. 21 of 1984) as amended or extended;

"Department" means the Department of Enterprise, Trade and Employment;

"PRSA" means a Personal Retirement Savings Account within the meaning of the Pensions Act 1990 (No. 25 of 1990).

(2) In these Regulations, unless otherwise indicated—

(a) a reference to any enactment shall be construed as a reference to that enactment as amended by any other enactment,

(b) a reference to a section is to a section of the Act, and

(c) a reference to a Regulation or Schedule is to a Regulation of, or Schedule to, these Regulations.

3. The following forms are prescribed as the forms to be used in respect of applications under the Act:

(a) in the case of an application for payment under section 6 in respect of unpaid normal weekly remuneration, entitlements under a sick pay scheme, holiday pay, payment in respect of the relevant statutory period of minimum notice specified under section 4 of the Minimum Notice and Terms of Employment Act 1973 (No. 4 of 1973) or an award by the Employment Appeals Tribunal under section 12 of that Act, Form EIP1 as set out in Part 1 of the Schedule;

(b) in the case of an application for payment in respect of any other debt to which section 6 applies, Form EIP4 as set out in Part 2 of the Schedule;

(c) in the case of a statement from a relevant officer under section 6 (6), Form EIP3 as set out in Part 3 of the Schedule;

(d) in the case of an application for payment in respect of section 7, Form EIP6 as set out in Part 4 of the Schedule;

(e) in the case of a certificate given by an actuary for the purposes of section 7(3), Form EIP 7 as set out in Part 5 of the Schedule.

4. (1) An application under section 6 or 7 of the Act shall be made to a relevant officer or person appointed under section 5 who shall examine it and, as soon as may be, forward it, together with Form EIP3 or Form EIP7, as appropriate, to the Insolvency Payments Section of the Department.

(2) Where there is not for the time being in relation to such employer a relevant officer, an application may be sent to the Secretary General of the Department.

(3) Payments in respect of applications under sections 6 and 7 shall be made to the relevant officer or person appointed under section 5 unless there are particular reasons which require that payment be made directly to the applicant.

(4) Where a payment has been made on foot of an application under secion 6 or 7 to a relevant officer or person appointed under section 5, such relevant officer or person shall make the appropriate payment to the applicant and, as soon as may be, shall confirm the payment in writing to the Insolvency Payments Section of the Department.

5. A person shall be deemed to have complied with any requirements under these Regulations to make an application or to prepare a statement in a form prescribed by these Regulations where the application or

statement, as the case may be, is made in a form to like effect to the prescribed form concerned.

6. The Protection of Employees (Employers' Insolvency) (Forms and Procedure) Regulations 1984 (S.I. No. 356 of 1984) and the Protection of Employees (Employers' Insolvency) (Occupational Pension Scheme) (Forms and Procedure) Regulations 1990 (S.I. No. 121 of 1990) are revoked.

SCHEDULE

Part 1

Form EIP1 (*text not reproduced here*) [1]

SCHEDULE

Part 2

Form EIP3 (*text not reproduced here*) [2]

SCHEDULE

Part 3

Form EIP4 (*text not reproduced here*) [3]

---

[1] Form EIP1 is used for an application by an employee in respect of arrears of wages, holiday pay, minimum notice and/or sick pay. A copy of Form EIP1 is downloadable online at http://www.entemp.ie/publications/employment/2005/eip1.doc

[2] Form EIP3 is used for an application by a relevant officer for funds in respect of employee claims. A copy of Form EIP3 is downloadable online at http://www.entemp.ie/publications/employment/2006/eip3.doc

[3] Form EIP4 is used for an application by an employee for payment under the insolvency payments scheme for entitlements due under the Unfair Dismissals Acts, under the common law in respect of wrongful dismissal, under the Employment Equality Act, 1998, the National Minimum Wage Act, 2000, the Maternity Protection Act, 1994, the Adoptive Leave Act, 1995, the Parental Leave Act, 1998, the Payment of Wages Act, 1991, the Terms of Employment (Information) Acts, 1994 and 2001, the Protection of Young Persons

SCHEDULE

Part 4

Form EIP6 (*text not reproduced here*) [4]

SCHEDULE

Part 5

Form EIP7 (*text not reproduced here*) [5]

L.S.

GIVEN under my hand,

2nd November, 2005,

Tony Killeen

Minister of State at the Department of Enterprise, Trade and Employment

---

(Employment) Act, 1996, the Organisation of Working Time Act, 1997, the Protections for Persons Reporting Child Abuse Act, 1998, the European Communities (Protection of Employment) Regulations, 2000, the Protection of Employees (Part-Time Work) Act, 2001, the Competition Act, 2002, the Protection of Employees (Fixed-Time Work) Act 2003, the European Communities (Protection of Employees on Transfer of Undertakings) Regulations 2003, the Industrial Relations Acts, 1946, 1969 and 1990 (regarding registered employment agreements or employment regulation orders) and the Industrial Relations (Miscellaneous Provisions) Act 2004 (concerning victimisation awards). A copy of Form EIP4 is downloadable online at http://www.entemp.ie/publications/employment/2006/eip4.doc

4 Form EIP6 is used for an application for the payment of unpaid contributions to an occupational pension scheme or personal savings retirement account (PRSA). A copy of Form EIP6 is downloadable online at http://www.entemp.ie/publications/employment/2006/eip6.doc

5 Form EIP7 is used for an occupational pension scheme actuarial certificate, required to accompany Form EIP6 when a claim in respect of unpaid pension scheme or PRSA contributions payable on an employer's own account is being made under the Insolvency Payments Scheme. A copy of Form EIP7 is downloadable online at http://www.entemp.ie/publications/employment/2006/eip7.doc

EXPLANATORY NOTE

(This note is not part of the Instrument and does not purport to be a legal interpretation.)

The purpose of these Regulations is to prescribe revised forms and certificates to be used in relation to claims under Section 6 and Section 7 of the Protection of Employees (Employers' Insolvency) Act 1984.

INDEX